Courtship and constraint

MANCHESTER
UNIVERSITY PRESS

Politics, culture and society in early modern Britain

General editors

PROFESSOR ANN HUGHES
DR ANTHONY MILTON
PROFESSOR PETER LAKE

This important series publishes monographs that take a fresh and challenging look at the interactions between politics, culture and society in Britain between 1500 and the mid-eighteenth century. It counteracts the fragmentation of current historiography through encouraging a variety of approaches which attempt to redefine the political, social and cultural worlds, and to explore their interconnection in a flexible and creative fashion. All the volumes in the series question and transcend traditional interdisciplinary boundaries, such as those between political history and literary studies, social history and divinity, urban history and anthropology. They thus contribute to a broader understanding of crucial developments in early modern Britain.

Already published in the series

Courtship and constraint

Rethinking the making of marriage in Tudor England

DIANA O'HARA

Manchester
University Press
Manchester and New York

distributed exclusively in the USA by Palgrave

Published by Manchester University Press
Oxford Road, Manchester M13 9NR, UK
and Room 400, 175 Fifth Avenue, New York, NY 10010, USA
http://www.manchesteruniversitypress.co.uk

Distributed exclusively in the USA by
Palgrave, 175 Fifth Avenue, New York, NY 10010, USA

Distributed exclusively in Canada by
UBC Press, University of British Columbia, 2029 West Mall,
Vancouver, BC, Canada V6T 1Z2

British Library Cataloguing-in-Publication Data
A catalogue record for this book is available from the British Library

Library of Congress Cataloging-in-Publication Data applied for

ISBN 0 7190 5074 x *hardback*
ISBN 0 7190 6251 9 *paperback*

First published 2000
First published in paperback 2002

06 05 04 03 02 01 00   10 9 8 7 6 5 4 3 2 1

Typeset in Scala with Pastonchi display
by Koinonia Ltd, Manchester

Printed in Great Britain
by Bookcraft (Bath) Ltd, Midsomer Norton

FOR MY PARENTS
IN TOKEN OF MY GRATITUDE

Contents

Figures

Maps

Tables

Acknowledgements

Mixed feelings are commonly experienced when a book is finished. One task that is particularly enjoyable, however, is to take this opportunity to thank all those who have helped and sustained me over the years.

First, I must thank the CVCP for their grant of an Overseas Research Scholarship and especially my parents, for their constant generosity and belief in me. I remain grateful to the archivists and staff at Canterbury and Maidstone for their assistance, and to the Cambridge Group for allowing me the use of their facilities in the summer of 1994. It has been a real pleasure working in those environments.

I owe much to the support and interests of my fellow graduates at Kent University whose friendship and comments have been invaluable to me. Seminar audiences at Cambridge, London, Sheffield and Hull, have also been encouraging and stimulating.

Others I have to thank individually: my supervisor Andrew Butcher for all his inspirational guidance; Patrick Collinson for his interest and enthusiasm; David Palliser for providing me with the population figures for my introduction; and Richard Wall, Charles Donahue, Lloyd Bonfield, Ralph Houlbrooke and Brian Outhwaite for their extremely helpful advice. I am much indebted to them. Also my examiners, Keith Wrightson and Ken Fincham, gave me the confidence and encouragement which I needed to publish my thesis. I owe Keith Wrightson a further debt, for his work on Terling was a real inspiration to me when I was an undergraduate.

I must thank, of course, Ann Hughes, the editor of this series, for her thoughtful and precise criticisms, and the team at Manchester University Press for their assistance in the publication of this book. I very much enjoyed working with them and it is an honour to be in this series.

Last, but not least, it is to my husband Jeremy Boulton that I owe the greatest thanks. Without him, this may never have been completed.

Abbreviations

All bibliographical references are given first in full, then in abbreviated form. For convenience the following archives are represented thus:

C.C.A.L.   Canterbury Cathedral Archives and Library
C.K.S.   Centre for Kentish Studies, Maidstone (formerly Kent Archives Office)

Explanatory notes

Place names are given their modern spelling. No attempt has been made to standardise the contemporary spelling of personal names or to modernise the spelling used in court cases. Words extended in quotations are italicised.

Introduction

Courtship, the means by which marriage partners were chosen, was a vitally important process in early modern England. It was a period of private and public negotiation, and of exploration fraught with anxiety, as hitherto ordinary relationships became transformed and vested with heightened significance. Courtship bridged the divide between the single and married state and was imbued with a host of expectations. Its final outcome, when successfully conducted, carried with it the promise of respectability, the privileges of marriage and adulthood, and a union perceived to be stable and socially, economically and emotionally compatible. Getting married was supposed to mark the end of youth, a change of status and the formation of a new productive partnership, sexually legitimised, economically viable and fundamental to social harmony.[1] As a 'rite of passage' marriage had crucial significance for the couple concerned, for the household, family, kin, community, and for social order itself.[2] That courtship and marriage were of central concern in the early modern period explains the volume of contemporary comment on the subject. From the advice offered in conduct books, to the sermons delivered on marriage and choice of partner, to the legislation restricting early marriages and to parochial interference in marriage plans, contemporaries proved themselves well aware of the pitfalls of unsuitable matches. With the path to marriage aimed at financially stable unions, correct choice of partners was vital in ensuring that communities would not be overburdened with paupers, the inevitable result of the setting up of 'over hastie' marriages.[3] Courtship was part of the essential negotiations that accompanied property transfers via dowry, portion or other settlements made on marriage. For both the wealthy and the humble it entailed the redistribution and accumulation of financial resources. The social status of partners, and the extent (or otherwise) to which individuals married their social equals, partly determined the degree of social mobility in a society obsessed by order, hierarchy and rank.[4] Courtship and marriage, therefore, mediated and determined the reproduction of the social and political order. The age at which couples began married life and the frequency with which individuals were able or willing to enter the married state, as demographers have long told us, determined the rate of population growth.[5] To examine the courtship strategies and expectations of early modern English society should reveal much about the normative influences that underlay bare demographic statistics.

At almost every point marriage practices are revealing of society and its attitudes. This is because marriage is a social act: it involves more than two people; it is hedged by law and custom: it is subject to often intense feelings of approval and disapproval; it profoundly alters the status of the parties, especially women and any children they might bear; and it is nearly always accompanied by transfers of legal rights and, frequently, of property.[6]

The process of getting married was thus potentially an extremely serious business in early modern England, more so perhaps than even recent interpretations would suggest. That scholars have long appreciated the importance of studying marriage is shown both by the extensive work done and by the different approaches scholars have taken.[7] Nevertheless, despite the vast quantity of research done in the area, no scholar has yet focused specifically on the question of courtship *per se*, or has given it the detailed holistic treatment it needs. Equally neglected is the specific context of the sixteenth century. Carlson's recent comment that still 'we know little about what courtship meant to the less exalted inhabitants in sixteenth-century villages and towns', is particularly apt. The courtship models presented by historians so far have not concentrated enough on behaviour in the sixteenth century, but instead they tend to read 'back from much later material, producing serious distortions of early modern practice'.[8]

This book seeks to rescue sixteenth-century courtship from this relative neglect, and offers thereby new interpretations on the process of marriage formation. In attempting to recapture the courtship strategies, and the behaviour and voices of the less wealthy and articulate, it relies primarily, although by no means exclusively, on the records of the ecclesiastical courts, whose burgeoning material in the sixteenth century makes it the first period that can be studied in sufficient depth and detail.[9] Most importantly, because it does not depend upon a study of the propertied elite, the book concentrates on the attitudes and concerns of those who are supposed to have been, at least *theoretically*, less constrained by wealth and status, and more free to love and marry whom they chose. The notion, commonly expressed, that individual freedom of choice of marriage partners most likely increased as social status and means diminished, has become a virtual textbook assertion.[10] This book seeks in part to challenge that conclusion. After all, one can question the logic of that supposition, since material possessions may arguably have meant *more* to those with less, rather than the reverse. One of the main themes of this work is that few individuals married without close regard for questions of property and their financial well-being post-marriage. As an examination of wills demonstrates, even the most humble cottagers sought to provide dowries for their daughters, and the size of those dowries was crucial in most courtship negotiations. In a period with only very rudimentary welfare systems very few couples married solely for 'romantic love', and it is surely no surprise that this should have been so. Indeed, it is argued that decisions regarding marriage and the courtship strategies employed, cannot really be understood properly without some appreciation of the *full range* of constraints and considerations that might affect even the humblest. Those might include the prevailing economic climate, the constraints of geography and distance, available meeting-places and opportunities, preconceived notions of proper age, size of dowry or estate, pressure from family and 'friends', as well as legal frameworks and individual feelings and emotions. This book looks at how family, kin and neighbourhood were involved in what was often a long-drawn-out process, a period of intense negotiation, structured by rituals and mediated by a host of intermediaries. Every stage of that process might be an occasion of gift-giving, of seeking advice or resisting pressure from a range of interested parties. Perhaps because courtship in the sixteenth century was taken more seriously by the participants than many historians have supposed, it also possessed far more structure and coherence than has been realised. Exploring the constant underlying pressures, the plethora of relations, and the ritual structure which helped set the parameters of marriage choice, this book offers a structural analysis of those courtship processes which might have preceded the final solemnisation of unions in church. Marriage decisions were conducted against a backdrop of constraints and expectations which did much to determine and shape individual choice. The final choice of partner, while it may indeed often have incorporated personal liking or love, was linked indissolubly to questions of family credit, economic worth and the successful handling of both courtship ritual and the sensitive negotiations that accompanied them.

By focusing on the social and cultural phenomena represented by English courtship in a period which has not received sufficient attention, by approaching topics which have hitherto been overlooked by most historians and by questioning some of the now established orthodoxy, this book essentially seeks to revive the importance of the subject and achieve a study of courtship 'in the round'. That there is still room to revitalise tired areas of debate may at first seem surprising, given the volume of high-quality work already done. Arguably, however, much of the best research has been informed, and perhaps skewed, by the reaction against Lawrence Stone's pioneering *Family, Sex and Marriage in England*. That ambitious and monumental interpretation of English family history provoked over a decade of controversy and stimulated extensive enquiry into the emotional and behavioural aspects of the family. In particular, scholars focused on the characteristics of courtship, selection of marriage partners and marital relations.[11] Stone's evolutionary schema of progressive family models sought to chart the growth of 'affective individualism' and the eventual emergence of the modern 'closed domesticated nuclear family'. The sixteenth century was portrayed as a period wherein the 'open lineage family', which was dominant in the early Tudor era, began to give way to the 'restricted patriarchal nuclear family' after the Reformation. It was thus a time when impersonal family relations, lack of individual freedom, and the wider collective interests of kin, community and lordship overlapped with the increasing enhancement of the nuclear core, and the strengthening of patriarchalism. According to Stone, the new-found emphasis upon somewhat warmer domestic and patriarchal values, still ensured parental control over marriage selection, the internalisation of filial duty and the 'pragmatic calculation of family interest' rather than personal choice as the accepted viewpoint. However, during the course of the late sixteenth and early seventeenth centuries Stone identified changes in the affective relations and familial functions of the English propertied classes. These included an uneasy transition in the pattern of marriage between values based on kin interest and arranged marriage, to those which allowed children a limited right of veto.[12]

In his characterisation of English family types, Stone may be criticised generally for being over-schematic and for overemphasising structural change which create problems in his chronology. He used largely unqualified and exclusive definitions of the family and of romantic love, and in particular, he based his interpretation upon the familial behaviour and sentiments of the upper classes alone.[13] By his own admission, 'any generalization on those complex and obscure subjects inevitably runs into the objection that any behavioural model of change over time imposes an artificial schematisation on a chaotic and ambiguous reality'.[14] Furthermore, he acknowledged his ignorance where the lower social levels were concerned, suggesting that, 'because the key to the system of controlled marriage was the exchange of property, it theoretically follows that children lower down the economic scale would enjoy greater freedom of choice. Whether this is so is not at present known for certain.'[15] This latter comment opened up a major avenue of further enquiry regarding the scope for personal choice when selecting marriage partners. The actual role and meaning of sentiment in matrimonial decisions compared to other kinds of criteria, also required elaboration. After all, 'love is a very inexact term and without careful definition its use must be more of a handicap than a help. People can be chosen for very different qualities, and attempting to discern and categorise the bases of such choices must be one of the priorities for future research.'[16]

Other historians of the family professed some uncertainty in discerning the pattern and basis of partner selection among more ordinary folk. Ingram claimed that 'it is uncertain how far attitudes varied at different social levels', and 'nor is it clear how much depended on the age of the individuals contemplating matrimony'. As far as the external influences of family, relations and friends are concerned, both 'the precise dimensions of these interest groups are somewhat unclear', and 'the precise standing and role of individuals referred to as "friends" ... is uncertain'.[17] Nevertheless, some speculation premised on the simple demographic features of parental mortality, geographical mobility, and the opportunities afforded by service and apprenticeship, as well as the lesser economic leverage attributed to parents among the lower orders, seemed to indicate greater fluidity, informality and a relative lack of supervision over courtship. In the English village of Terling, marriage choices 'based upon personal compatibility, even upon romantic love', were considered most likely.[18]

It is, however, probable that few historians would now accept the extreme theoretical position adopted by Alan Macfarlane, whose theme of intense individualism in English society even in the medieval period, described a pattern of family formation in stark contrast to Stone's characterisation.[19] Examining marriage as the critical institution in the development of English capitalism, he argued for the early existence of a Malthusian marriage system, dependent upon assumptions of largely individual choice, very limited constraint, and the calculated costs of marriage and procreation. Individual initiative and the strong emphasis on freedom, familiarity, and emotional and sexual compatibility, were the highlighted features of English courtship. The essentially love-based system Macfarlane described, the long, permissive, courtship pattern, the basically private and contractual nature of the wedding, and the exclusivity of married life, effectively polarises the individual and the family. By constructing 'a timeless model', however, the cultural, social and moral contexts within which individuals manoeuvred, and the complexities of pressures, conventions and controls brought to bear on marriage decisions and behaviour, tended to be ignored in his work.[20]

Between the polarised models presented by Stone and Macfarlane can be found the new consensus, namely the work of those historians who steer a cautious, middle-of-the-road, approach. Looking at courtship behaviour among different social groups, Wrightson argued 'that interpretations based upon the conventional dichotomies of arranged as against free matches, and parental choice against self-determination by the child do less than justice to the complexities of reality', for, 'there was no single "English" norm ... but rather a persisting variety of coexisting practices, a range of experience broad enough to call into question the validity of any single evolutionary schema'.[21] In a similar vein, Houlbrooke maintained that 'in practice, matches ranged across a wide spectrum which ran from the arranged at one end to the completely free at the other'.[22] Ingram, too, concluded that attitudes to marriage formation exhibited 'complexity and flexibility. Instead of any clear-cut pattern of "arranged" or "free" marriages, a more subtle system prevailed in which love had a part to play in combination with prudential considerations, the pressures of community values and (at middling and upper-class levels) the interests of parents and sometimes other family members.'[23]

This latter consensus would seem to suggest *continuity* in marital norms and courtship practice between the fifteenth and seventeenth centuries rather than any significant transition.[24] In seeking to qualify the extent of parental authority in marriage formation, it was said that

> while the patriarchal ideal certainly influenced the nature of marriage in this period, it was much modified in practice by the strength of personal choice in marriage formation and by flexibility and reciprocity in husband/wife relationships within marriage. Among the mass of the population this flexible pattern appears to have persisted unchanged at least through the later sixteenth and seventeenth centuries, and had probably existed since the later middle ages.[25]

Whether in prescriptive or actual behaviour, in the nature of relationships, or the criteria of marriage choice (especially lower down the social scale but even among the elite), what was also stressed was 'flexibility', 'ambivalence', 'complexity', 'variation' and 'lack of uniformity'.[26]

Nevertheless, within this *variable* framework, the freedom and initiative in courtship taken by young people appeared to characterise the pattern of matchmaking among the middling and, particularly, the ordinary ranks. Such initiative did not, of course, imply absolute freedom of choice, since the degree of freedom and the significance of external pressures, sanctions and advice, depended upon wealth, sex, birth order, and economic, social and personal circumstances. It was recognised that the actual realisation of individual marriage plans and romantic inclinations was subject to financial prospects, filial obligation, conventional requirements, practical considerations, and the influence of parents, kin, friends, peers, masters, neighbours and even of parish authorities.[27] But although that freedom was tempered and 'variable', the established conclusion would appear to be 'that in the final analysis agreement to marry was very much a matter for the couple themselves, for the match had little direct bearing on anyone else ... It seems reasonable to conclude that among the greater part of the common people marriage partners were freely chosen.'[28]

If such was the predominant position taken concerning the selection of partners, of the various criteria informing marriage choice, the role of love and affection has also been affirmed strongly.[29] While material considerations in the promotion of individuals and their family were considered important, and the ideals of parity in wealth, rank and age, together with personal reputation and religion, were conventionally held to judge the suitability of a match, the existence of love and mutual attraction were regarded as *essential*. It has been said that 'there were variations in the relative weight placed upon particular factors' and that 'it would be unwise ... to argue too rigid a distinction between material, social and emotional factors in matchmaking'. Such elements were 'in practice hopelessly intermingled' and the various criteria were not necessarily incompatible.[30] Despite this cautionary ambivalence, however, the contrasts in courtship behaviour and relationships between different social classes, and the increasing significance of love and romantic expectations as one descended the social scale, have been emphasised. The decisiveness of such sentiments in marriage choice and its widely held expression through the exchange of gifts and tokens have been asserted. Church court cases, it has been argued, reveal 'that passionate attachment was a common experience further down the social scale and suggest that the ideal of romantic love was deeply rooted in popular culture'.[31]

Subsequent to these latter findings, Rushton's brief but important study of matrimonial cases before the Durham consistory courts in the late sixteenth and early seventeenth centuries has sought to redress the reactionary emphasis upon romantic love and freedom in courtship. He attempted to 'estimate the limits to freedom', and examined the much neglected topics of power relationships, the fragility of marriage formation and the coercive processes at work from family, household and 'friends'.[32] Intimating at the 'social process' leading to marriage, and focusing primarily upon the negative exercise of power, Rushton maintained that 'while consent was the formal doctrine, matrimonial cases reveal both direct manipulation of marriage and the collective organization of kin and friends'. In identifying forms of constraint and power, he concluded that 'the cumulative effect of these different relationships and the unequal distribution of power combined to set limits to individual freedom'. Hence, 'significant areas of personal life were heavily circumscribed', and crucially, 'marriage and all personal affairs were still too important to others to be left entirely to the individual couple'.[33]

The historiography of courtship in early modern England briefly outlined above exposes areas of research which have been undervalued, neglected or perhaps misinterpreted. It is time, then, to take a fresh look at the subject. To achieve such a reappraisal, this book develops new techniques of analysis and takes new perspectives on aspects of marriage formation to further our understanding of that 'complex and important business'.[34] More traditional approaches to the subject are, consequently, of less concern here. This book is not concerned directly with any impact that political or religious change may have had on sixteenth-century courtship nor is any attempt made to locate particular cases in the context of a detailed community study. The perspective taken here, too, does not interest itself unduly with matters of marriage law, numbers and types of cases heard or sentences ultimately passed. Nor does it include demographic statistics of marriage behaviour as revealed through parish registers. Instead, this book's prime concern is to concentrate on the social, economic and cultural aspects of English courtship in the sixteenth century. Its focus is on those strategies, circumstances and influences which potentially informed the making of marriage.

To attempt what is in essence a 'holistic' study of courtship requires a sensitive blend of both qualitative and quantitative approaches, applied to a wide range of sometimes intractable source material. The ritual structures or 'stages' of courtship, the parts played by kin and 'friends', the symbolic use of gifts and tokens in negotiating marriage, the role and identification of intermediaries and courtship arenas, are all best studied using close and detailed textual analysis of church court records.

As previously indicated, several historians have used church court material to study aspects of courtship, marriage and sexual reputation in early modern England. Such studies have centred particularly on dioceses in the north and west of England, London, East Anglia and Essex. To date, however, no one has attempted an in-depth analysis of sixteenth-century courtship from the exceptionally rich material which survives for the diocese of Canterbury.[35] Nor have most of the studies so far really examined the subject of courtship comprehensively. Using the Kent records, this book offers, therefore, a distinctive regional comparison as well as a more concentrated treatment of the subject. At the same time, moreover, it makes some use of depositions taken from a wider range of litigation than matrimonial causes alone. Statements of witnesses in 'divorce', defamation and testamentary cases have all been consulted, in the belief that the information they contain provides extra, if sometimes oblique, insights into the complex web of relationships, expectations and matters of personal reputation within which marriages were made.[36]

Matrimonial suits arising within the Canterbury diocese came under the jurisdiction of the archbishop's Consistory Court.[37] Consistory court depositions, therefore, form the bulk of the material used here. Despite its apparent jurisdictional irrelevance, however, depositions from the lower Archdeaconry Court occasionally yielded information relevant to marriage. Throughout the book some use is made of miscellaneous court papers touching upon other aspects of legal procedure, and chapter 4 is based partly on an analysis of all surviving Consistory Court Act Books. However, most of the ecclesiastical court records used in this book come from those testimonies given in marriage contract disputes. These sources themselves are copious, but it should be remembered that such material forms only part of the total documentation generated by the complex legal processes of the church courts.[38] The first half of this book deploys these church court records to examine the structural aspects of courtship. In so doing, it borrows from long-standing anthropological thinking on family, reputation, ritual and exchange, and occasionally illustrates arguments with literary evidence.[39]

While the methodology used here often relies on close textual analysis of the depositions, this is combined with a quantitative approach where the sources allow. Courtship, of course, was often governed by the constraints on individual choice imposed by distance and customary expectations, and the transfer of property. Distance imposed a very real limitation on courtship and choice of partner in the past, especially in areas of low population densities. The vital mechanics of the courtship process depended on where couples met and courted, and the opportunities to meet provided by the local availability of suitable partners, information flows about possible partners and their geographical proximity. The geographical location and selection of partners might be influenced by the mobility of the unmarried population as well as by locally shared cultural and occupational expectations. Age as well as distance might act as a determinant of courtship. A study of courtship must seek to understand how the relatively late marriage age identified by demographers was both produced and sustained. It must also seek to uncover the views of courting couples on the ages of prospective partners. It is quite possible that a relatively late age at marriage was bolstered by adherence to customary and traditional notions of appropriate marriage age. Just as contemporaries wrestled with the psychological barriers represented by geographical distance or by parochial allegiances, weighed up carefully the ages or financial prospects of prospective partners, or reckoned the nature and value of gifts given or received, so must any serious study of courtship.

Only with some sort of quantification can we appreciate some of these more concrete determinants of courtship behaviour and make comparisons over time and across space. In particular, the analysis of the Act books and wills undertaken in the second half of the book can yield statistics which throw important new light on the environmental, customary and economic determinants underlying marriage choice. Both of these latter sources are different from those normally used by historians to study courtship and marriage horizons and ages at marriage. Unlike the parish registers used by demographers to study such subjects, moreover, they provide vital information dating here from the late fifteenth century. A quantitative analysis of Act books and wills allows innovatory approaches to topics such as the mobility experience of potential partners, perceptions of the timing of property transfer and marriage, and the significance of dowry provision in marriage formation. In looking at dowry sizes and expected ages of partners some possible variations have been addressed by using quantitative material taken from parishes with different social and economic structures. The very large number of wills used, drawn from five different Kent parishes, avoids the idiosyncrasies and possible atypicality of a single community study. In addition to possessing unusually early parish registers and exceptionally good extant probate material, the five parishes chosen were intended to express something of the regional and social variety that existed in sixteenth-century Kent.

It is through these approaches, that we may begin to move towards a better appreciation of what courtship actually meant to contemporaries. Certainly, the official, legal definition of marriage, with its implicit emphasis on free choice and the paramount defining event of a mutual verbal contract, is a poor guide to what popular courtship actually entailed in the sixteenth century. This book focuses on those features of courtship and marriage which may have carried little weight in establishing the *legal* validity of a union, but which represented more closely the true popular perception and social practice of marriage formation. The exchange of gifts and tokens, the external influences of family and friends, the formalities and procedures of courtship, the constraints of location and distance, conventional assumptions about appropriate timing and the importance of successful dowry negotiations were, it is argued here, the real essence of courtship in Tudor England.

Most of the matrimonial business handled by the church courts in the sixteenth century dealt with the formation of marriage. In most of these matrimonial cases the major concern was to prove the existence of an alleged contract. Adjudicating on whether or not a man and woman were legally bound in marriage to each other was, however, in practice, less straightforward than canon law supposed. In particular, 'clandestine', unsolemnised marriages were especially vulnerable and disposed to contention, in part due to the survival of traditional, secular practices and to the 'difficulties of proof and interpretation'. These marriage contract suits experienced a long-term decline between the fourteenth and seventeenth centuries. One interpretation for this reduction is that the laity were coming to accept the need for marriages to be solemnised in church, and were thus less ready to enter into formal, binding, contracts.[40] Just how widespread the rituals of handfasting and the contract ceremonies of whatever degree of formality were, however, has yet to be established satisfactorily.[41]

Gratian's *Decretum c.* 1140, and Lombard's *Libris IV Sententiarum,* had a profound influence on the formulation of marriage law, and the theory of marital consent adapted by Pope Alexander III (1159–81) became the definitive doctrine in England. Unlike the situation on the European continent, the marriage law as formulated in the twelfth century remained virtually intact in England, resisting attempts at any major reform in the sixteenth century. It survived in this form until 1753.[42]

By the law of marriage,[43] the mutual consent of a couple, as expressed by words of contract spoken in the present tense (*per verba de praesenti*), constituted an indissoluble marriage bond. Words of future consent (*verba de futuro*) and *conditional* contracts did not instantly create valid unions, but became absolute once sexual intercourse occurred and any specified conditions were fulfilled. Canonists debated the various safeguards, procedures and ceremonies which were seen as necessary for publicity and decorum. Local customs such as the use of gifts and rings, and other formalities which involved familial agreement and betrothal before witnesses, were called for but were not in fact essential for legal validity. Even the publication of banns and the formal solemnisation of marriage *in facie ecclesie*, which were required to make a marriage properly licit, were ultimately not essential for a binding act of marriage. That was the crucial paradox. Although the church sought to provide safeguards and prescribed procedural rules, so long as there were no existing impediments, it was the sole mutual consent of a couple which defined a legally valid marriage and which was sufficient to make an indissoluble union. In recognising the act of consent alone as valid, the church effectively marginalised any kind of public solemnity.[44]

Historians have identified that central anomaly in the concept of marriage adopted by the medieval church, and the scope for confusion generated at the popular, practical level of understanding and implementation. It seems that lovers were not only unsure of the types of contract discussed, they were imprecise in their wording and probably impulsive in their speech and actions.[45] By the sixteenth century, popular knowledge of the law may have become more widespread,[46] but uncertainty regarding the making and proving of a legally valid marriage remained. While some suitors might affirm 'that [they] cold make many proofes',[47] others who were less confident about matrimonial matters depending in law, sought legal opinion. The plaintiff William Turvye, for example, alleged that he was precontracted to one Nethersole's late widow who subsequently married William Harrison. He informed the public notary of Canterbury, 'that he had no wytnesses of his contract to the woman nor other proof but hyr owne confession', and was warned that then 'he should spend his mony in vayne to go to lawe for hyr'.[48]

The Romano-canonic system of witness proof, adopted in modified form by English church courts in the thirteenth century, constituted the main tradition of legal proof,[49] but proof by other means – such as public and private instruments like letters,[50] or circumstantial evidence touching on reputation, rumours, confession and status – were valid forms of proof which, some considered, should favour a cause even if but half-a-proof.[51] In the English medieval courts it would appear that there were no hard and fast rules of evidence, the matter being heavily dependent on the discerning power of the judge.[52] Furthermore, it seems that the kinds of testimony evaluated by the church courts became increasingly profuse, and were carefully scrutinised in the sixteenth century.[53]

The problem of creating an adequate system of proof as regards legal marriage[54] was inherent in the concepts and contradictions of canon law, and in the essential vulnerability of the contract. If, by canon law, simply the mutual feeling of 'marital affection' was what constituted the essence of matrimony, proving its existence and evaluating the external expression of that mutual consent was more complicated.

Arguably the theory of consent provided scope for regarding marriage as essentially a personal matter which was the private, contractual affair of individuals. Canon law theory contained within it, then, the potential for a more individualistic interpretation of marriage, reflected in the contemporary phrase that particular persons contracted of their 'own freewill and motion'.[55] However, the evidence generated by contract cases focuses our attention on the more complex family, social, cultural and economic realities which lay behind the making of marriage choices.

In addressing some of the general problems presented by the evidence, it should be emphasised just how voluminous the source material is. Not only is this book based on very extensive series of ecclesiastical court records, it also uses over two thousand probate records pertaining specifically to five parishes chosen from the Canterbury diocese.[56] While the problems inherent in the use of probate evidence are well known, and are discussed briefly in chapter 5, the difficulties of interpretation posed by the Canterbury church court records require some attention here.

The testimonies given by deponents in matrimonial cases derived from the Instance business of the ecclesiastical courts. Unlike the disciplinary, 'ex officio' cases which dealt with matters of correction arising upon presentment following visitations or from general 'ill fame', Instance cases were brought on private initiative. In the suits of marriage heard by the courts, plantiffs typically sought to have an alleged marriage contract enforced, although there were other types of marriage causes which were instigated by one or more parties. Some persons, for example, complained about the false boasting of a contract (*jactitation of matrimony*) and in other suits, two people alleged a matrimonial contract with the same individual (*marriage and divorce*, or *spousals and nullity*).[57] Marriage litigation involved often complex issues heard over a prolonged period. The production of witnesses was one stage in a legal process which usually began with the plaintiff's request for a citation, and ended, if it proceeded to its formal conclusion, with the hearing of 'definitive sentence'.

The introduction of the *libel* which contained the plaintiff's allegations, and which might be detailed in *positions*, required that the defendant be present to give answer. Usually the defendant negated the claim, or confessed the facts but posed a particular 'exception'. Following this 'contestation of suit', three probatory terms were allotted for the admission of witnesses. Thereupon the witnesses were produced to prove any points of contention. The sworn statement of at least two such witnesses of suitable credibility was required.[58] In theory they were examined individually and in private, without the presence of the parties or their proctors. Their testimonies were recorded by the scribes and were drawn up into the books of *depositions* kept separately from the rest of the cause papers and from the Act books. Witnesses were usually examined using the statements or *articles* and the *interrogatories* prepared by the parties and their proctors. The credibility of particular witnesses was questioned by 'exceptions' and the defendant's own witnesses provided proof for any counter allegation. Documentary proof and *additional positions* could also be admitted during the proceedings. A term was then assigned for 'propounding all acts' and for concluding the case, after which the judge gave a date for hearing sentence.[59]

The depositions formed the basis for the judge's final decision. For historians, they are an extremely rich source of information for the light they throw upon the circumstances and conventions surrounding courtship, and for their vividness of social detail. The quantity and quality of the evidence reflect the efficiency of the ecclesiastical court. In particular, changes in administrative practice probably made for better documentation and fuller, more graphic narratives. In the sixteenth century, the testimonies were frequently recorded in English and on paper, rather than being written in Latin and on parchment.[60] Nonetheless, accounts of individual cases still vary significantly, ranging from one single piece of fragmentary evidence to the massively well-documented hearing which involved over 70 deponents.[61]

Capitalising on the strength of these records is, however, less than straightforward. A study of disputed cases is itself problematic. Being ostensibly records of the essential failure of marriage communications, they may be considered somewhat exceptional, representing only a small proportion of actual marriages, whether 'informal' or duly solemnised and completed. It is difficult to assess with certainty the typicality of the relationships or of the marriage behaviour displayed. The meaning and relevance of the attitudes and customs revealed in church court cases are, moreover, open to a number of different interpretations and to presuppose that the issues discussed in the depositions somehow reflect ordinary life is inevitably debatable.[62] Nevertheless, the real value of the material should not be underestimated, and it is preferable to argue from the evidence available rather than from silence. One cannot know, for example, whether, in the majority of marriages, the ideal of 'multilateral consent' was really practised to the satisfaction of all parties and interest groups.[63] Elsewhere it has been said that these litigations do not represent marriages which were 'unusually formed'. All that was unusual was only the interruption in the marriage process as a consequence of altered circumstances and of personal and social dilemmas. Indeed it can be argued that the responses evoked and the pressures expressed in the court cases were believed to have been normal. As for the social representativeness of the litigants in matrimonial court cases, the general conclusion concerning their status profile would suggest that 'most ranks of society were represented ... except for the very rich and the desperately poor', although different social groups were probably disproportionately represented.[64]

Basic methodological problems are posed by positivist approaches in the treatment of depositions and by source-mining for qualitative evidence. The deposition should ideally be regarded as a particular type of discourse. At one level disputed cases can be interpreted as dramatic conflicts seeking resolution; the events, language and emotions are structured by legal argument and by the call upon dramatic climax and foci which seem to create a theatrical representation of issues. As an historical dramatic text, and as a legal document, the deposition is loaded with a language which reflects legal principles, literary influences and traditional ideologically derived images and speech. In defamation cases, it has been shown that witnesses manipulated recognisable images, metaphors and stories from a range of popular sources, to construct their own deposition narratives.[65] Themes which were familiar, cultured and gendered stereotypes, known plots and customary judgements informed the testimonies of litigants and their witnesses who sought to tell their explanatory tale in a good and plausible fashion. In providing evidence for the court to evaluate, they transformed key events which they had themselves interpreted, selected and remembered into a narrative related through their personal perspective and participation. Their own framing of the facts combined with the mediation of proctors and scribes to produce a 'legally comprehensible' testimony.[66] Moreover, the testimonies were bound by the plaintiff's libel and structured by the interrogatories which delimited the nature of the evidence, prompting particular responses and making it a difficult task to discriminate between social and legal interpretation, fact and fiction.[67] While the surviving depositions are, on the one hand, richly suggestive, authentic and represent partly verbatim accounts, they are at the same time frustratingly incomplete and formulaic, leaving much that is still untold. As 'the product of several competing and overlapping voices', they are 'both individual and typical, innovative and repetitive'.[68]

As well as needing to appreciate the complexities in the construction and in the meaning of the deposition text, the historical value of such evidence also needs to be understood within its administrative and judicial framework, as well as within its wider social and community context.[69] As previously indicated, the taking of testimonies did not constitute the entire procedural process, and a more complete study of matrimonial causes would incorporate the other kinds of court records relevant to the case.[70] In Canterbury's diocesan courts, the full proceedings of litigation are seldom easily identifiable among the confusingly arranged court records.[71] The often indeterminable nature of the disputes, and the associated problem of having disrupted accounts, can lead to a misrepresentation of the facts and circumstances of individual cases.[72] Where sentences survive, they have been said to be generally uninformative.[73]

Alternative actions help explain the apparently inconclusive state of cases in the archives. Some parties may have sought compensation later on by common law action for breach of promise, or through unofficial compositions, arbitration or agreement.[74] In the case of *Stokes* v. *Swanton*, an attempt to have the dispute 'put to arbitrament by her friends' seems to have occurred, although Mark Swanton may earlier have sought other means of resolving his predicament besides that of legal action. In a letter dated 14 May 1596 addressed to Thomas Cullen (a rival suitor), Swanton claimed that he was already contracted to Cecily Stokes and that he 'kold write diveres thinges which ar tokens that shee is my wiffe'. Cullen, he wrote, was thereby committing 'adultry', and if Cullen should marry with her, he (Swanton) would 'devorse' them again. Further professing to prove his claim, Swanton challenged him to meet secretly at an appointed place and time with a rapier and dagger to end the strife.[75]

Such incitement to a duel may have occurred during court proceedings, but it would probably have been an exceptional option in out-of-court settlements.[76] It was more likely that cases would be terminated by other means. It would appear, however, that the abandonment of contract suits became increasingly common practice, corresponding with a decline in confirmatory sentences passed, between the late fourteenth and seventeenth centuries.[77] Perhaps this partly represents the dilemma of judges evaluating cases. Certainly the lack of definitive sentences would frustrate any expectation of recovering complete records.[78]

Such interruptions in proceedings create obvious difficulties of interpretation, which are complicated further by other kinds of partiality existing in the records. Some witnesses in court either could not or would not remember the facts.[79] Their 'own strategic and unconscious reshapings' meant that 'remembered stories are already changed'.[80] What is more, in the constant telling and retelling of stories, there was the potential for tales to become inflated, distorted and misconstrued, resembling 'an enormous game of Chinese whispers'.[81] As for the credibility of witnesses, some were described as 'friends' or 'enemies' of the parties, favouring a cause and telling lies, or being 'not of sharp wit', perhaps 'beguiled'. They testified in the cause, they said, because they were either legally constrained, morally obliged, requested to do so, or bound 'to declare a troth'. The motives underlying their testimonies were entangled with a diversity of other circumstances, such as indebtedness, suggesting perhaps that the function of the courts touched upon a wider range of issues tangential to the apparent concerns of formal regulation. It would have been difficult enough for the judge to assess the reliability of the evidence, without having to distinguish the truth from perjured testimonies.[82] Some collusion inevitably occurred, with gifts offered to witnesses as bribes.[83] Discriminating between a gift and a bribe as morally separable 'sets of reciprocities' is, also, often difficult. Interpreting when gifts are tolerable and acceptable, or when they are legitimate rewards, can be as problematic as evaluating the testimonies themselves.[84]

Figure 1 Total number of cases styled 'causa matrimonialis', 'sive sponsalia' and 'et divorcii'

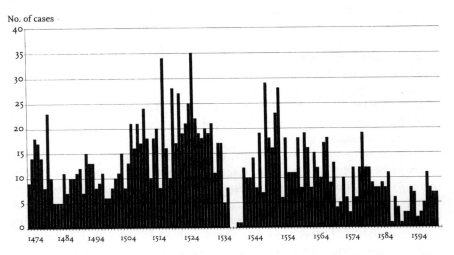

The use of depositions as historical records is thus a difficult task, given the complex nature of the source. The diversity of motives and circumstances, the partial, often perjured giving of testimonies and the fragmentary, inconclusive disputes, add to the elusiveness of the truth. Without the broader social, community and legal contexts, our understanding of the events described, themselves far from straightforward, is inevitably flawed. In deploying the evidence in this book, because of the necessarily conflicting accounts, and the variety of narratives and interpretation, the same cases can easily recur in different chapters, according to their different capacities, contexts and discussions. The representation of contradictory elements within cases is inevitable given the nature of the disputed testimonies, and should be regarded as a genuine attempt to explore the limits of plausibility and the ambiguity of interpretation.

While the deposition material is difficult to quantify, the series of ecclesiastical court Act books used in chapter 4 lends itself more easily to such enquiry. Act books in general record the procedural acts taken in all cases which were tried by the church courts, although the amount of information they contained and the quality of the writing declined over the fifteenth century.[85] At Canterbury, the Act books which are examined from the mid-fifteenth century to the end of the sixteenth century are massive in number, but the arrangement of the records is often inconsistent and chronologically confused.[86] Various kinds of marriage causes were heard by the court, although most of the Instance actions were indeed brought for the enforcement of marriage contracts, and might include suits involving a third party.[87]

Figure 1 illustrates the changing distribution of contract suits introduced into the consistory court. It is based on those types of marriage litigation recorded in the Act books which most likely dealt with allegations of spousals. The objective here is not to approach the data with a view to identifying legal trends to marriage. As chapter 4 will demonstrate, analysis of these Act books will be restricted to a specific examination of courtship horizons within the diocese made possible by the systematic recording of the parish of the litigants concerned.

The actual reaches of the diocese of Canterbury, as shown in the Appendix, covered the eastern side of the county of Kent. It embraced a variety of landscapes and a patchwork of parishes of diverse size, population density, and economic and administrative bases. That there was, clearly, no such thing as the 'typical' English parish has been reiterated by Carlson in his study of sixteenth-century marriage. He suggested that the degree of intervention in his Cambridgeshire villages by ecclesiastical courts, and their role in regulating interpersonal affairs, depended partly on local demographic regimes and on the nature of local governments as well as on their physical and practical cohesiveness.[88] Perhaps in the diocese of Canterbury, likewise, the peculiarities of particular places might have partly determined the extent of church court litigation. If the character of individual parishes was, in some measure, fashioned by the physical environment, the contrasting features of the Kent landscape offered much diversity.

From the salt marshland region of mixed farming on Kent's northern coast, and the area of marsh and ploughland on the Isle of Thanet, the diocese encompassed the fertile loams of northern Kent, and the variegated soils of the North Downland belt, with their emphasis on arable husbandry and generally larger wheat and barley farms.[89] With the main exception of Blean Forest, woodland in this region was scarce, and some unenclosed arable land could be found in the eastern district. By contrast, the southern half of the Canterbury diocese, which extended from the Wealden Vales and High Weald to the grazing lands of Romney Marsh, covered areas whose agriculture was principally pastoral. The southern coastal marshes provided additional resources in fish and fowl, and although there was also some arable for fodder crops and corn grown for domestic consumption, the land was devoted largely to the fattening of mutton and beef, Romney Marsh being the prime sheep-grazing region of Kent county. In the Wealden Vales, where common meadows and pasture were extensive, and where the soils enabled agriculture to be more mixed than in the cattle-rearing High Weald, the farming of both livestock and corn were practised, although the economy was still predominantly pastoral-based. Typical of the Wealden landscape and agriculture were woodlands, enclosed farms, an abundance of small estates, and small holders

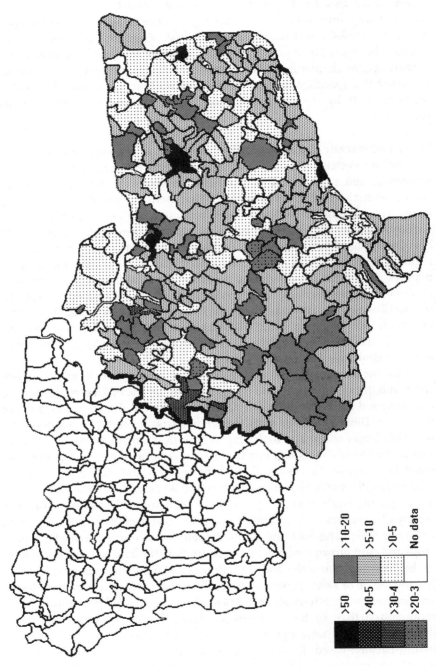

Map 1 Population density of Canterbury diocese, 1563

>50	**>10-20**
>40-5	**>5-10**
>30-4	**>0-5**
>20-3	**No data**

who grew wheat and oats, carried out some domestic dairying, kept some sheep, but focused on cattle farming. This was an area particularly character-ised by the kind of gavelkind tenure theoretically prevalent in Kent and by weak manorial control. The Weald also possessed essential raw materials which encouraged its growing proto-industrialisation in the sixteenth century. In particular, this meant the existence of a substantial rural-textile industry and also, to a lesser extent, iron and leather industries.[90]

The diocese then contained within its boundaries identifiably different physical sub-regions. It also incorporated a heterogeneity of parish sizes and population densities. Map 1, based on the household figures derived from the Canterbury diocesan survey of communicants in 1563, illustrates the degree of variation.[91] As is to be expected, the important city of Canterbury along with the traditional provincial centres of Hythe, Dover, Sandwich and Faversham were the most densely populated. To some extent, the urban hierarchy, market towns and centres of rural manufacturing, as opposed to predominantly rural parishes, are also depicted.[92] The Kent Weald was that region where parishes were generally large, while still recording relatively high population densities. Although it is usually regarded as a particularly populous area on account of its marked rural industry, even there the demographic experience differed. In the central Wealden cloth-making parishes, population density was high. Its population, which probably began to grow from the end of the fifteenth century, increased rapidly in the second half of the sixteenth century to reach saturation point. In the eastern Weald, however, outside such rural manufact-uring centres, agrarian-based parishes (including marshland areas) generally possessed below average population densities and, rather than population growth, experienced 'demographic stagnation' in the sixteenth century.[93]

The parish of Tenterden, one of the five sample parishes chosen for specific studies in chapters 5 and 6, lay within that east Wealden district identified by Zell. Its demographic experience illustrates the absence of any discernible population growth in the sixteenth century,[94] although it was an unusually populous and prosperous place compared to its neighbours. With an esti-mated population of over 1300 in the 1560s,[95] the parish extended over 8300 acres to include several hamlets and Tenterden borough, of privileged status as a limb of the Cinque Ports. While farming remained the most common occupation there, with the wealthiest among those inventoried engaged in livestock rearing and fattening, semi-urban Tenterden also functioned as a commercial and agricultural market centre, with trading links, and a diversity of goods, trades and services to offer. As the inventories suggest, the wood-working, textile, building, food and drink, and leather trades were all represented, along with the services of smiths and shopkeepers.[96] Likewise, the occupational status of testators revealed the predominance of yeomen and husbandmen, but included several clothiers, tanners and shipwrights, as well as the individual carpenter, mason, cooper, woodsetter, whitesmith, shoe-maker, glover, mercer and professional.[97] Among the grooms who married by licence in the late sixteenth and early seventeenth centuries, and their bonds-men, a further variety of crafts and services was manifested, with a range of textile workers, building workers, butcher, baker, grocer, carrier, barber, chandler, plumber and gardener.[98]

Of the other four sample parishes selected, that of Wye most closely approximated to Tenterden's size, stretching over roughly 7300 acres on the downland region; but, with only about 800 inhabitants in the 1560s, it was far less densely populated.[99] Its parish register suggests that the number of recorded baptisms suffered a modest slump in the late 1550s and 1570s which, together with the mortality crises of 1545 and 1559, may have inhibited any real increase in its overall population after the middle of the century.[100] Although Wye was clearly a market town in the sixteenth century, it ranked lower in the urban hierarchy than even Tenterden, and the evidence culled from probate material and marriage licence data indicates that the parish, in the sixteenth and early seventeenth centuries, was based upon an agricultural economy, while maintaining a small leather industry represented by tanners, shoe-makers and glovers, and some involvement in a clothing industry. Otherwise, a range of craftsmen served the needs of an agricultural community such as the blacksmith, carpenter, tilemaker, joiner, fletcher and cooper, with a number of others in the food and drink trade, notably butchers, bakers, a cook, vintner and maltman. The ruling elite of knight, esquire and gentleman, along with professional men, was further represented.[101]

Sturry parish on the outskirts of Canterbury, and the nearby parish of Chislet, were also selected to represent more of Kentish diversity. The former, being the smallest of the five parishes (*c.* 3100 acres), was less than half the size of Chislet (*c.* 6800 acres), but was nonetheless more densely populated. The 1563 returns list 42 households for Sturry and 60 for Chislet, indicating populations of about 200 and 285 persons respectively. In the course of the sixteenth century the population may have increased in Sturry, but the extent and timing of that increase is problematic.[102] The registered baptisms in Chislet, on the other hand, display a definitive population increase, despite slumps which checked expansion.[103] In the agricultural marshlands of Chislet, bequests of livestock to sons were commonly found, and so too in Sturry where testators left sheep and cattle to their beneficiaries with unusual frequency. While farming was the economic backbone of both parishes, Sturry did not apparently possess the same exclusive predominance of yeomen and husbandmen. Its topographical convenience, proximity to roads and its river crossing, its location close to the diocesan city of Canterbury and its partly wooded character may all have contributed to its more varied economic basis, as the parish also evidently accommodated tanners, shoemakers, glovers, tailors, a clothworker, weaver, blacksmith, carpenter, glazier, ropemaker and butcher.[104]

Another type of community was Whitstable on the northern Kent coast. The parish possessed a mixed economy in the sixteenth century of corn-growing, pastoral farming and grazing, dairying, baking and brewing for local consumption, and basic small crafts and provisioning. In particular, however, its inhabitants were involved in fishing and copperas-making, and followed maritime occupations. Together with the farming community, mariners, sailors and shipwrights were to be found among the probated population, and bequests include mention of weirs, boats, nets and other such occupational artefacts as well as livestock, reflecting the broad-based economy of the community. Whitstable would appear to have shared in the mortality crisis of 1558, and recorded 71 deaths in the plague of 1564, suffering relatively high mortality, too, in the period 1589–94. Although the 4100-acre parish was quite populous, with at least 70 households, and possibly as many as 630 inhabitants in the early 1560s, its parish register suggests a stagnant population.[105]

The experience of all five Kent parishes illustrates something of the diversity which is to be found among individual parishes in the sixteenth century, in their demographic trends, their economies and physical charac-teristics. Together they represent some of that local and regional variation within the ecclesiastical jurisdiction of Canterbury's church courts, and provide some of the economic and social context in which courtship and the making of marriage took place.

NOTES

1   M. Ingram, *Church Courts, Sex and Marriage in England, 1570–1640* (Cambridge, 1987), pp. 125–31; E. J. Carlson, 'Courtship in Tudor England', *History Today* 43 (August, 1993), 23–9 (p. 29); J. R. Gillis, *For Better, For Worse: British Marriages, 1600 to the Present* (Oxford and New York, 1985), pp. 11–17.

2   A. Van Gennep, *The Rites of Passage* (London, 1977); M. Gluckman, 'Les rites of passage', in M. Gluckman ed., *Essays on the Ritual of Social Relations* (Manchester, 1975), pp. 1–52.

3   K. M. Davies, 'Continuity and change in literary advice on marriage', in R. B. Outhwaite ed., *Marriage and Society: Studies in the Social History of Marriage* (London, 1981), pp. 58–80; Ingram, *Church Courts*, p. 131; R. A. Houlbrooke, *The English Family, 1450–1700* (London and New York, 1984), pp. 67–8.

4   K. Wrightson, *English Society, 1580–1680* (London, 1982), pp. 17–38. On marriage and social mobility, see, V. Brodsky Elliott, 'Single women in the London marriage market: age, status and mobility, 1598–1619', in Outhwaite ed., *Marriage and Society*, pp. 81–100; V. B. Elliott, 'Mobility and marriage in pre-industrial England: a demographic and social structural analysis of geographical and social mobility and aspects of marriage,

1570–1690, with particular reference to London and general reference to Middlesex, Kent, Essex and Hertfordshire' (Ph.D. thesis, University of Cambridge, 1979).

5 E. A. Wrigley and R. S. Schofield, *The Population History of England, 1541–1871: A Reconstruction* (London, 1981, ppbk edn, 1989), pp. 255–65, 423–4; E. A. Wrigley and R. S. Schofield, 'English population history from family reconstitution: summary results, 1600–1799', *Population Studies* 37 (1983), 157–84 (p. 161); R. Schofield, 'English marriage patterns revisited', *Journal of Family History* 10:1 (Spring 1985), 2–20; E. A. Wrigley, 'Age at marriage in early modern England', *Family History* 12 (1982), 219–34.

6 R. B. Outhwaite, 'Introduction', in Outhwaite ed., *Marriage and Society*, pp. 1–16 (p. 11).

7 *Ibid.*, 'Introduction'; Houlbrooke, *The English Family*, pp. 1–16; M. Anderson, *Approaches to the History of the Western Family, 1500–1914* (London and Basingstoke, 1980).

8 E. J. Carlson, *Marriage and the English Reformation* (Oxford, 1994), p. 105. For Carlson's own model of marriage formation in the diocese of Ely, see, *ibid.*, pp. 105–41.

9 Houlbrooke, *The English Family*, p. 3. See above, pp. 12–16, for a discussion of sources.

10 See above, pp. 4–7.

11 L. Stone, *The Family, Sex and Marriage in England, 1500–1800* (New York, 1977, abridged ppbk edn, Harmondsworth, 1979), pp. 69–299.

12 *Ibid.*, pp. 127–36.

13 See, e.g., for reviews of Stone's book, M. MacDonald, *Sixteenth-Century Journal* 10:2 (1979), 122–3; R. T. Vann, *Journal of Family History* 4:3 (1979), 308–15.

14 Cited in Houlbrooke, *The English Family*, p. 15.

15 Stone, *Family, Sex and Marriage*, p. 134.

16 Outhwaite, 'Introduction', p. 16.

17 M. Ingram, 'Spousals litigation in the English ecclesiastical courts, c. 1350–1640', in Outhwaite ed., *Marriage and Society*, pp. 35–57 (pp. 48–9); Wrightson, *English Society*, p. 77.

18 K. Wrightson and D. Levine, *Poverty and Piety in an English Village: Terling, 1525–1700* (New York and London, 1979), p. 131. See also, Wrightson, *English Society*, p. 74. Those preconditions for greater freedom in courtship are also mentioned in later works, see, e.g.: M. Ingram, 'The reform of popular culture? Sex and marriage in early modern England', in B. Reay ed., *Popular Culture in Seventeenth-Century England* (London, 1985), pp. 129–65 (pp. 133–4); Houlbrooke, *The English Family*, p. 72; R. A. Houlbrooke, 'The making of marriage in mid-Tudor England: evidence from the records of matrimonial contract litigation', *Journal of Family History* 10 (1985), 339–52.

19 A. Macfarlane, *Marriage and Love in England: Modes of Reproduction, 1300–1840* (Oxford, 1986); A. Macfarlane, *The Origins of English Individualism: the Family, Property and Social Transition* (Oxford, 1978); A. Macfarlane, 'The myth of the peasantry: family and economy in a northern parish', in R. M. Smith ed., *Land, Kinship and Life-Cycle*, pp. 333–49. For critiques of this notion of individualism, see the discussion by S. D. White and R. T. Vann, 'The invention of English individualism: Alan Macfarlane and the modernization of pre-modern England', *Social History* 8 (1983), 345–63; D. Herlihy, 'Origins of English individualism', *Journal of Family History* 5 (1980), 235–6; and K. Tribe, 'Origins of English individualism', *Social History* 4 (1979), 520–2. Also, L. Stone, 'Illusions of a changeless family', *The Times Literary Supplement* (16 May 1986).

20 For further thoughts along these lines, see, D. O'Hara, 'Review of A. Macfarlane, *Marriage and Love in England*', *Economic History Review*, 2nd ser. 40:1 (1987), 113–14.

21 Wrightson, *English Society*, pp. 78–9.

22 Houlbrooke, *The English Family*, p. 69.

23 Ingram, *Church Courts*, p. 142. Contemporary literature, too, explored the spectrum of perspectives, conflicts and possibilities, and the role of love. See A. J. Cook, *Making a Match: Courtship in Shakespeare and His Society* (Princeton, 1991), pp. 69–103.

24 Wrightson, *English Society*, pp. 71, 74, 79; Ingram, *Church Courts*, p. 138.

25 Ingram, 'The reform of popular culture?', p. 137.

26 See, e.g., Wrightson, *English Society*, pp. 72–4.

27 *Ibid.*, pp. 74–9; Ingram, 'Spousals litigation', pp. 49–50; Ingram, 'The reform of popular culture?', pp. 134–5; Ingram, *Church Courts*, pp. 139–40; Houlbrooke, *The English Family*, pp. 69–72; Houlbrooke, 'The making of marriage', *passim*.

28 Wrightson, *English Society*, pp. 77–8.

29 For the criteria of choice, see *ibid.*, pp. 79–86; Houlbrooke, *The English Family*, pp. 73–8; Ingram, *Church Courts*, pp. 140–1.

30 Wrightson, *English Society*, pp. 86–7; Houlbrooke, *The English Family*, p. 88.

31 Houlbrooke, *The English Family*, pp. 72–3, 78.

32 P. Rushton, 'Property, power and family networks: the problem of disputed marriages in early modern England', *Journal of Family History* 11 (1986), 205–19.

33 *Ibid.*, pp. 208, 216.

34 Carlson, 'Courtship in Tudor England', p. 29.

35 In addition to the works previously cited, see also, P. Rushton, 'The testament of gifts: marriage tokens and disputed contracts in north-east England, 1560–1630', *Folk Life* 24 (1985–6), 25–31; M. Ingram, 'Ecclesiastical justice in Wiltshire, 1600–1640, with special reference to cases concerning sex and marriage' (D. Phil. thesis, University of Oxford, 1976); R. A. Houlbrooke, *Church Courts and the People During the English Reformation, 1520–1570* (Oxford, 1979); G. R. Quaife, *Wanton Wenches and Wayward Wives: Peasants and Illicit Sex in Early Seventeenth-Century England* (London, 1979); J. A. Sharpe, 'Defamation and sexual slander in early modern England: the church courts at York', *Borthwick Papers* 58 (1980), 1–36; J. A. Sharpe, 'Litigation and human relations in early modern England: ecclesiastical defamation suits at York', Past & Present conference (1980), pp. 6–17; L. Gowing, 'Gender and the language of insult in early modern London', *History Workshop Journal* 35 (1993), 1–21; L. Gowing, *Domestic Dangers: Women, Words and Sex in Early Modern London* (Oxford, 1996); L. R. Poos, 'Sex, lies, and the church courts of pre-Reformation England', *Journal of Interdisciplinary History* 25:4 (Spring 1995), 585–607; S. Hindle, 'The shaming of Margaret Knowsley: gossip, gender and the experience of authority in early modern England', *Continuity and Change* 9:3 (1994), 391–419; C. A. Haigh, 'Slander and the church courts in the sixteenth century', *Transactions of the Lancashire and Cheshire Antiquarian Society* 78 (1975), 1–13; F. G. Emmison, *Elizabethan Life: Morals and the Church Courts* (Chelmsford, 1973); J. Addy, *Sin and Society in the Seventeenth Century* (London and New York, 1989). For the use of church court material in the study of medieval marriage practices, see, e.g., R. H. Helmholz, *Marriage Litigation in Medieval England*

(Cambridge, 1974); P. J. P. Goldberg, 'Marriage, migration, servanthood and life-cycle in Yorkshire towns of the later Middle Ages: some York cause paper evidence', *Continuity and Change* I (1986), 141–69. Further citations can be found in the bibliography.

36 I have consulted *all* such cases in the deposition volumes to gain the fullest possible sense of the contemporary context of sixteenth-century society. Most of the actual evidence cited in this book, however, is drawn from the matrimonial cases only.

37 The separate jurisdiction exercised by the consistory and archdeaconry courts can be found in B. L. Woodcock, *Medieval Ecclesiastical Courts in the Diocese of Canterbury* (London and Oxford, 1952), esp. pp. 25–8, 82–3.

38 Further discussion of the sources will follow below. See also, for a detailed listing, D. O'Hara, 'Sixteenth-century courtship in the diocese of Canterbury' (Ph.D. thesis, University of Kent, 1995), pp. 282–4.

39 On the advantages and disadvantages of combining the two disciplines see, e.g., K. Thomas, 'History and anthropology', *Past and Present* 24 (1963), 3–24. For a more critical treatment of method, see E. P. Thompson 'Anthropology and the discipline of historical context', *Midland History* 3 (1972), 41–55. The contribution which each subject makes to the other is summarised by D. I. Kertzer, 'Anthropology and family history', *Journal of Family History* 9 (1984), 201–16.

40 Helmholz, *Marriage Litigation*, pp. 25–6, 29–34, 166–8; Houlbrooke, *Church Courts*, pp. 55–7, 66; Houlbrooke, 'The making of marriage', pp. 339–40, 351; Houlbrooke, *The English Family*, pp. 78–80; Ingram, *Church Courts*, pp. 189, 192–6, 206. The early sixteenth century may, however, have been exceptional. Matrimonial suits tended to increase again after 1500 in the diocese of Canterbury, see Woodcock, *Medieval Ecclesiastical Courts*, pp. 82–5, 109–10.

41 Rushton stresses that informal need not mean haphazard, 'Property, power and family networks', p. 206, and 'The testament of gifts', pp. 27–8. Ingram, 'Ecclesiastical justice in Wiltshire', ch. on matrimonial causes, points out that formal contracts were not universal. He questions just how common handfastings were and how they were regarded in, 'The reform of popular culture?', pp. 141–3. Similarly, see, Ingram, 'Spousals litigation', pp. 54–5. Gowing, *Domestic Dangers*, p. 142, states that, despite the fall in the number of contract suits in London, espousals continued to play their part in the 'culture of courtship'. See also, pp. 177–8.

42 Helmholz, *Marriage Litigation*, pp. 25–73, esp. pp. 26–31; R. B. Outhwaite, *Clandestine Marriage in England, 1500–1850* (London and Rio Grande, 1995), esp. pp. 1–17. Carlson, *Marriage and the English Reformation*, argues that the successful integration of popular practice and marriage law in England explains its survival.

43 The most complete digest of types of contract is found in, H. Swinburne, *Treatise of Spousals or Matrimonial Contracts* (London, 1686, repr. New York and London, 1978). For further discussions of marriage law, see, M. M. Sheehan, 'Choice of marriage partner in the middle ages: the development and mode of application of a theory of practice', *Studies in Medieval and Renaissance History* n.s. 1 (1978), 3–33; M. M. Sheehan, 'The formation and stability of marriage in fourteenth-century England: evidence from an Ely register', *Medieval Studies* 33 (1971), 228-63 (esp. pp. 229–30, 253, 263); M. M. Sheehan, 'Marriage theory and practice in the conciliar legislation and diocesan statutes of medieval England', *Medieval Studies* 40 (1978), 408–60; M. M. Sheehan, 'The European family and canon law', *Continuity and Change* 6:3 (1991), 347–60 (esp. pp. 355–6); J. T. Noonan Jr, 'Power to choose', *Viator: Medieval and Renaissance Studies* 4 (1973),

419–34; C. Donahue Jr, 'The policy of Alexander the Third's consent theory of marriage', in S. Kuttner ed., *Proceedings of the Fourth International Congress of Medieval Canon Law* (Rome, 1976), pp. 251–6; C. Donahue Jr, 'The canon law on the formation of marriage and social practice in the later middle ages', *Journal of Family History* 8 (1983), 144–58 (pp. 144–7, 155–7); J. A. Brundage, 'Concubinage and marriage in medieval canon law', *Journal of Medieval History* I (1975), 1–17; B. Gottlieb, 'The meaning of clandestine marriage', in R. Wheaton and T. K. Hareven eds, *Family and Sexuality in French History* (Philadelphia, 1980), pp. 49–83. On specific matters of legal proofs, legal proxy and legal ages, see above, p. II and pp. 62–3, 103, 159.

44 See also, Ingram, *Church Courts*, pp. 131–6, 145–6, 189–90; Ingram, 'Spousals litigation', pp. 37–42.

45 Donahue, 'Policy of Alexander III', pp. 252–3, cites F. W. Maitland's remark that lovers were the least likely to distinguish between past and future tenses.

46 Carlson, *Marriage and the English Reformation*, pp. 126–7.

47 C.C.A.L., MS. X/11/4, fos 144–5v., *Boycot* v. *Fleet* (1602).

48 C.C.A.L., MS. X/11/3, fos 71v.–2, *Turvye* v. *Nethersole and Harrison* (1598).

49 C. Donahue Jr, 'Proof by witnesses in the church courts of medieval England: an imperfect reception of the learned law', in M. S. Arnold, T. A. Green, S. A. Scully and S. D. White eds, *On the Laws and Customs of England* (North Carolina, 1981), pp. 127–58; H. Conset, *The Practice of the Spiritual or Ecclesiastical Courts* (1st edn 1681; 3rd edn, London, 1708), pp. 140, 268. For procedural modifications regarding standards of proof in the thirteenth century, see, J. A. Brundage, 'Proof in canonical criminal law', *Continuity and Change* 11:3 (1996), 329–39.

50 Conset, *Practice of the Ecclesiastical Courts*, pp. 140, 146–51, 268.

51 R. Burn, *The Ecclesiastical Law* (London, 1824, 8th edn), ii, 487.

52 Helmholz, *Marriage Litigation*, pp. 131–3.

53 Houlbrooke, *Church Courts*, p. 61. His own conclusion is that circumstantial details probably did not affect the verdict, but he admits the impossibility of demonstrating the matter either way with any certainty.

54 Brundage, 'Concubinage and marriage', *passim*.

55 See, e.g., C.C.A.L., MS. X/10/11, fos 180v.–iv., *Wattle* v. *Dunnye and Kennet* (1570).

56 For the sources used, and their coverage, see the manuscript bibliography.

57 Ingram, *Church Courts*, pp. 190–1; see above, p. 16.

58 For the two-witness rule, see above, p. II.

59 The court records, the legal procedure and the role of witnesses are discussed in Helmholz, *Marriage Litigation*, pp. 6–22, 112–40, 154–9; Woodcock, *Medieval Ecclesiastical Courts*, pp. 50–62; Gowing, *Domestic Dangers*, pp. 30–41; Houlbrooke, *Church Courts*, pp. 38–54; Ingram, *Church Courts*, pp. 48–9; Conset, *Practice of the Ecclesiastical Courts*, pp. 140–6.

60 Helmholz, *Marriage Litigation*, pp. 130–1, 181–2; Houlbrooke, 'The making of marriage', p. 340.

61 It was theoretically considered desirable to limit the use of umpteen witnesses, and this was usually implemented in practice: Helmholz, *Marriage Litigation*, p. 128. Although

most matrimony cases involved a small number of witnesses, the case calling upon more than 70 witnesses was an extreme example of the complex ramifications of what was, apparently, a typical contract suit. The matrimonial cause of *Coppyn* v. *Richards* escalated into a tortuous investigation into the reputation, and thus the credibility, of the witness and midwife Agnes Butterwick, who died during the course of the proceedings. See, C.C.A.L., MSS. X/10/7–X/10/8, *passim*; X/10/9, fos 3–4; A. F. Butcher, 'The honest and the lewd in sixteenth-century Canterbury: the case of Mrs. Butterwick', unpublished paper delivered at the graduate research seminar, dept. of history, University of Kent (19 October 1983). The prominence of midwives in English communities, and the respectability of their practice, as opposed to the stereotype of the midwife-witch, is discussed in D. Harley, 'Historians as demonologists: the myth of the midwife-witch', *Social History of Medicine* 3 (1990), 1–26. See also, D. Cressy, *Birth, Marriage and Death: Ritual, Religion and the Life-Cycle in Tudor and Stuart England* (Oxford, 1997), pp. 59–63, for the midwives' social and ritual significance.

62 On the more general question of the typicality of records, see e.g., M. Chaytor, 'Household and kinship: Ryton in the late sixteenth and early seventeenth centuries', *History Workshop Journal* 10 (1980), 25–60 (pp. 50–1); Houlbrooke, 'The making of marriage', p. 350; Rushton, 'The testament of gifts', p. 29; Rushton, 'Property, power and family networks', pp. 206–7, 215–16; Gottlieb, 'Clandestine marriage', p. 54; Donahue, 'Policy of Alexander III', p. 267; Sheehan, 'Formation and stability', p. 231. Macfarlane warns that surviving records, in general, exaggerate tensions. See, *Marriage and Love*, p. 137.

63 Ingram emphasises the abnormality of conflict, and claims that the dominant social ideal was 'multilateral consent'. See, 'The reform of popular culture?', pp. 135–6, *Church Courts*, p. 136, and 'Ecclesiastical justice in Wiltshire', ch. on matrimonial causes.

64 For evidence of the social status of those involved in ecclesiastical court suits, see Ingram, 'Spousals litigation', pp. 44–5; Ingram, *Church Courts*, pp. 194–5; Rushton, 'Property, power and family networks', pp. 215–16; Helmholz, *Marriage Litigation*, pp. 160–1; Woodcock, *Medieval Ecclesiastical Courts*, pp. 104–6; Sheehan, 'Formation and stability', p. 234; Houlbrooke, *Church Courts*, p. 75; Houlbrooke, 'The making of marriage', pp. 341–2; Sharpe, 'Defamation and sexual slander', p. 17.

65 Gowing, 'Gender and the language of insult', pp. 1–21. On the popularity and accessibility of ballad literature, see, E. Foyster, 'A laughing matter? Marital discord and gender control in seventeenth-century England', *Rural History* 4:1 (1993), 5–21.

66 See, Gowing, *Domestic Dangers*, pp. 41–58, 232–9, for a fuller discussion of deposition texts and narratives of litigation.

67 Ingram, *Church Courts*, p. 20.

68 Gowing, *Domestic Dangers*, p. 58.

69 Woodcock, *Medieval Ecclesiastical Courts*, p. 4.

70 See above, pp. 12–13.

71 Woodcock, *Medieval Ecclesiastical Courts*, pp. 4, 139–40.

72 Ingram, 'Spousals litigation', p. 36; Donahue, 'Policy of Alexander III', p. 261.

73 Ingram, 'Spousals litigation', pp. 40–2; Helmholz, *Marriage Litigation*, pp. 20–2; Gowing, *Domestic Dangers*, pp. 39–40.

74 Helmholz, *Marriage Litigation*, pp. 135–8; Houlbrooke, *Church Courts*, p. 67; Ingram, 'Spousals litigation', p. 51; Ingram, *Church Courts*, pp. 207–8.

75 C.C.A.L., MSS. Y/3/15, f. 270v.; X/11/5, f. 186; J/J2 139.

76 Duelling was generally infrequent and informal in sixteenth-century English society, although statistical evidence from Kent suggests that the decades 1570–1620 experienced a peak in the incidence of sword-fights compared to any time thereafter. The evidence also suggests that the more sophisticated bladed weapons were used by the upper classes and by foreigners. See, J. S. Cockburn, 'Patterns of violence in English society: homicide in Kent, 1560–1985', *Past and Present* 130 (1991), 70–106 (esp. pp. 83–4).

77 Houlbrooke, 'The making of marriage', pp. 348–9; Houlbrooke, *Church Courts*, pp. 83–4; Ingram, 'Spousals litigation', p. 52; Ingram, *Church Courts*, pp. 208–9; Woodcock, *Medieval Ecclesiastical Courts*, pp. 59–60.

78 Donahue, 'Policy of Alexander III', p. 261, considers the problem of historical interpretation where the records are incomplete, assuming a possible disparity between legal principles and social conditions. Helmholz, *Marriage Litigation*, pp. 128–9, concluded, however, that court procedure was such that the medieval judge was probably no more enlightened than the modern historian.

79 See also, Ingram, *Church Courts*, p. 183.

80 Gowing, *Domestic Dangers*, pp. 54–5.

81 Hindle, 'The shaming of Margaret Knowsley', esp. pp. 399–403.

82 Helmholz, *Marriage Litigation*, pp. 154–9.

83 *Ibid.*, p. 162.

84 The question of when a gift is a bribe is discussed by J. T. Noonan Jr, *Bribes* (New York, 1984), *passim*. He isolates the importance of intention, form, the context of reciprocity, and the 'relational aspects', in identifying the moral differences.

85 Helmholz, *Marriage Litigation*, pp. 7–11.

86 O'Hara, 'Sixteenth-century courtship', pp. 259–61.

87 For the different types of matrimonial cases as styled in the Canterbury Act books, see, O'Hara, 'Sixteenth-century courtship', pp. 262–6. Any effort to examine the incidence of types of marriage litigation would require some qualification since the terms used should not necessarily be regarded as definitive or informative and might in fact, at times, obscure the complex nature of individual actions. For a comprehensive discussion of the types of marriage suits see Helmholz, *Marriage Litigation*, pp. 57–111, and esp. pp. 57–9, 107–8, for multi-party causes.

88 Carlson, *Marriage and the English Reformation*, pp. 156–80.

89 The paragraph which follows is based on the indentification of farming regions and Kentish agriculture and industry given by J. Thirsk, 'The farming regions of England', in J. Thirsk ed., *The Agrarian History of England and Wales, 1500–1640*, IV (Cambridge, 1967), pp. 1–112 (pp. 2–15, 55–64); A. Everitt, 'The community of Kent in 1640', in A. Everitt, *The Community of Kent and the Great Rebellion, 1640–60* (Leicester, 1966, 1973 edn), pp. 20–55; P. Clark, *English Provincial Society from the Reformation to the Revolution: Religion, Politics and Society in Kent, 1500–1640* (Hassocks, 1977), ch. 1 and esp. p. 5; C. W. Chalklin, *Seventeenth-Century Kent: a Social and Economic History* (London, 1965), esp. pp. 7–26, 45–109; *Victoria County History of Kent*, III; F. W. Jessup, *Kent History Illustrated* (Maidstone, 1973 edn). For a study of an East Kent area, see, E. J. Andrewes, 'Land, family and community in Wingham and its environs: an economic

and social history of rural society in east Kent from *c.* 1450–1640', (Ph.D. thesis, University of Kent, 1991).

90 For a detailed study of the Kent Weald, see, M. Zell, *Industry in the Countryside: Wealden Society in the Sixteenth Century* (Cambridge, 1994), esp. pp. 1–9, 88–112. The general influence of partible inheritance is also mentioned in Thirsk, 'Farming regions', pp. 11, 59; Chalklin, *Seventeenth-Century Kent*, pp. 55–6; Everitt, 'Community of Kent', pp. 46–7; Andrewes, 'Wingham and its environs', pp. 124–8.

91 I am very grateful to Professor David Palliser for providing me with a copy of his transcript of these returns, British Library, Harl. MS. 594, fos 63–84. To estimate the population size from the 1563 returns it has been assumed that the average household size was 4.75, following P. Laslett, 'Mean household size in England since the sixteenth century', in P. Laslett and R. Wall eds, *Household and Family in Past Time* (Cambridge, 1972), pp. 125–58. For calculations of population density, the parish acreages are those given in the *Census Returns of 1851*. The 1563 returns used here may understate the size of populations to a significant degree, but the census does still allow us to make consistent comparisons of parish size and density. For an extended discussion of the 1563 Kent returns, see, O'Hara, 'Sixteenth-century courtship', p. 19, n. 65.

92 For the population sizes of specific towns or parishes see below, ch. 4. The late sixteenth- and early seventeenth-century rise in population has been observed for the Wingham area, and for Dover, see Andrewes, 'Wingham and its environs', p. 241; M. Dixon, 'Economy and society in Dover, 1509–1640' (Ph.D. thesis, University of Kent, 1992), pp. 359–75. Seventeenth-century population figures are given in Chalklin, *Seventeenth-Century Kent*, pp. 27–41. Estimates of the county population from the mid-sixteenth century can be found in, Cockburn, 'Patterns of violence', p. 78, and M. Zell, 'Suicide in pre-industrial England', *Social History* 11:3 (1986), 303–17 (p. 309).

93 Zell, *Industry in the Countryside*, pp. 32, 52–87, esp. pp. 58–65. The only serious mortality crises in the Weald were the influenza outbreaks of 1557–59. Higher mortality was also recorded in some parts of the Weald in 1565–67, and in the early 1590s. Other crisis years in the second half of the sixteenth century in Kent generally, whether on account of harvest failures, disease, economic distress and popular disturbance, or increasing poverty, are cited in T. J. Tronrud, 'Dispelling the gloom: the extent of poverty in Tudor and early Stuart towns: some Kentish evidence', *Canadian Journal of History* 20 (1985), 1–21; T. J. Tronrud, 'The response to poverty in three English towns, 1560–1640: a comparative approach', *Histoire Sociale* 18:35 (1985), 9–27; P. Clark, 'Popular protest and disturbance in Kent, 1558–1640', *Economic History Review*, 2nd ser. 29:3 (1976), 365–82.

94 See O'Hara, 'Sixteenth-century courtship', pp. 20–1.

95 This figure is derived from an average of 47 baptisms per year between 1561 and 1565, assuming a crude birth rate of 35 per thousand. Cf. Zell's figure of 1200 persons, *Industry in the Countryside*, p. 86. The 1563 returns enumerate only 200 households.

96 For the demographic experience of Tenterden, and its occupational structure and wealth, see, Zell, *Industry in the Countryside*, pp. 57–9, 61–2, 116–21, 148–50, 154. For commercial links with Romney, see, A. F. Butcher, 'The origins of Romney freemen, 1433–1523', *Economic History Review*, 2nd ser. 27 (1974), 16–27. For the established heretical tradition in Tenterden and other parts of the Kentish Weald, see, P. Collinson, 'Cranbrook and the Fletchers: popular and unpopular religion in the Kentish Weald', in P. N. Brooks ed., *Reformation Principle and Practice: Essays in Honour of A. G. Dickens*

(London, 1980), pp. 171–202 (p. 176).

97 See O'Hara, 'Sixteenth-century courtship', pp. 285–328, for wills and inventories used in this brief survey.

98 J. M. Cowper ed., *Canterbury Marriage Licences, 1568–1618, passim.*

99 The 1563 returns, however, list only 72 households, and thus an estimated population of just 342 persons.

100 Wye parish formed part of the Cambridge Group's original sixteenth-century sample, see, Wrigley and Schofield, *Population History*, p. 487. The annual figures of registered baptisms supplied by them, however, are significantly different from my own aggregation from the parish register, see O'Hara, 'Sixteenth-century courtship', p. 22.

101 *V.C.H. Kent*, III, indicates brickmaking at Wye. For the parish's involvement in popular disturbances in the 1590s, see, Clark, 'Popular protest and disturbance', pp. 368, 382.

102 See C.C.A.L., U3/48/1/i (parish register of Sturry). Calculations based on the average number of baptisms between 1561 and 1565 would give a population of 554 in Sturry and 446 in Chislet. The Sturry parish register is a copied register of dubious accuracy, with a great deal of muddle and some gaps.

103 O'Hara, 'Sixteenth-century courtship', p. 24.

104 See also, K. H. McIntosh ed., *Sturry: The Changing Scene* (Ramsgate, 1972).

105 The 1563 returns would thus indicate a population only half the size of that calculated from the parish register, O'Hara, 'Sixteenth-century courtship', pp. 25–6.

Chapter 1

The structures of courtship
and the role of family,
kin and community[1]

The study of courtship and marriage must inevitably concern itself with the demarcation of the social and moral community and the location of the individual within them. This chapter shall begin by examining the role of family and 'friends', and that of the wider collective context which provided the framework for the structuring and restructuring of relationships, the negotiations of courtship, and the making and breaking of marriage decisions. As a life crisis, marriage is surrounded by values, conventions and rituals which encode and symbolically demonstrate a multi-level involvement in the marriage process.[2] This chapter seeks to explore how decision-making within that process was channelled by a wide range of constraining factors, from the internalised expectations of courting couples to the external pressures exercised by family, kin and community.

It is a central argument of this book that the so-called freedoms which individuals experienced in marriage choice could be rather superficial and transient in the face of contemporary realities. The marriages of very few individuals, no matter how humble, could escape some or all of the compromises and impediments put in place. That this was so is partly due to the nature of marriage itself. The kinds of restructuring which a marriage entailed affected not only the couple, but a range of people in varying degrees. As a result marriage formation was also influenced by collective values and was an activity which implicated various, sometimes conflicting, interests. Family, friends, neighbours and the wider community of parish or town had vital interests in local marriages. The union of two individuals united and restructured two kin groups and often involved the import of a newcomer into a community, with all the restructuring of local social relations that that might imply. Even the lowliest of marriages involved the exchange of some property between families, again potentially disrupting or disturbing local social structures and their concomitant power relations. Interests that individuals had in the marriage plans of others might extend, too, to questions of reputation, honour and morality, for, in addition to the social parity of partners, moral parity was conventionally expected. The reputation of partners or courting couples and their correct deportment during the courtship process, was important to family, friends and neighbours who made up what might be termed the 'moral community' and might even include the more stringent puritan-minded sort.

In probing the extent to which individuals found their marriage plans facilitated, inhibited or entirely prevented by their families, by their neighbours and by wider corporate structures like the parish or township, this chapter also seeks to explain how it was that such intervention could take place at all. In so doing it lays bare another less tangible constraint, namely, that courtship and marriage possessed more structure and ritual coherence than has been imagined. The intervention of family, friends and neighbours was made possible because of the conventional stages that structured courtship. These stages required the participation of outsiders at many different points, each with their own agendas and points of view about the suitability or otherwise of the intended match. Individuals hoping to marry were expected to undergo an increasingly public series of examinations and meetings. Many of these sometimes ritualised and formal gatherings drew on kin and neighbours to perform particular functions. The participation of particular persons at various stages of the marriage process, and the nature of that participation, has to be understood not simply as a means to publication, but interpreted as an expression of kin and community control, and of marriage as a central activity within family and social relations. This chapter will explore the behaviour and role of witnesses and the various gatherings that structured courtship from private betrothals and less formal feastings to the more public occasions. Individual freedom then was constrained not only because so many different sets of people possessed an interest in their union, but also because courtship possessed expected, traditional and formal rituals and structures which facilitated the intervention of outsiders, and without which few marriages were concluded.

The exercising of parental control, and the complex way in which it functioned to modify individual action, is crucial to an understanding of the various constraints upon marriage choice. The very concept of 'goodwill' which is expressed frequently and the implicit need for sanction should be understood in the contexts of that restructuring of relationships within the kin system and that of conflict and reconciliation which marriage engendered.[3] It is, of course, to be expected that the degree of parental control found within a society is linked to certain structural features such as social rank, inheritance systems, mobility, age of marriage and mortality.[4] The economic dependence of children may have been one critical factor. As testamentary evidence reveals, parental strategies might order the distribution of property to ensure that children complied with their wishes. It was not just parents who made conditional bequests governing the marriages of young people. The will of William a Bere of Ripple, for example, specified legacies of £3 6s 8d to each of the three daughters of John Pettit, 'upon condicion that they be rewelled and maried by the gode cowncell of myn exectour and of ther father and mother and ther gode frendes'.[5] One Kentish deposition indicated that Agnes Filcott, at Thornham, made her promise of marriage to Henry Mundell conditional upon the goodwill of her father, mother and friends. 'Wherapon Mundell answered that he did not passe for the goodwill of her friends but only for the goodwill of [her], then [she] answered hym agayn and said that if he obteyned not the goodwill of her freendes she shuld not enioye at their handes the benefite of her fathers bequeithe in his last will and testament.'[6] The place of financial transactions within the making of a marriage (discussed in chapter 6) and the way in which marriage was presumably limited by a set of social and economic expectations and necessities, argue for the leverage which parents might have in matters of choice of partners and in the timing of marriages (see chapter 5). But at the same time, as this case seems to demonstrate, this aspect of control by parents was itself incorporated within a wider framework of influences and pressures.

Whether marriages were arranged by parents, or were the romantic concern of individuals, imposes an artificial polarity on what was, in reality, a much more complex matter. The constraining pressures of family and kin may be seen to operate, both in terms of particular actions, and in the indirect form implied in the rhetoric and in the attitudes expressed. Arranged marriages need not be identical to the mode of arrangement found, for example, in classical peasant societies. One institutional feature of arranged marriages in such societies is the ritualised position of the go-between, but while the formally recognised, professional stereotype may not have been typical of sixteenth-century English marriage, there is a distinct suggestion of this to be found in the activities of various intermediaries, whose forms and functions are considered in chapter 3 below. Although, as we shall see, their position was often ill defined and informal, their actions may imply a measure of ritualised and structured activity. Clearly, love, choice and individual experience would have existed in the sixteenth century, but it is the bounds within which they existed that need to be understood. The process of marriage formation in this period was one which accommodated both individual expression and family constraint. 'I must be ruled by my freends', said Elizabeth Fletcher of Canterbury, 'as well as by myself.'[7]

The words of Alice Morling's father, of Benenden, are telling, because they can be interpreted as expressing with negative implication the potential power within family hands. Upon discovering that she had betrothed herself, her father said that 'he wold be a freend unto them, but he would be ne marriage maker ne marriage breaker'.[8] Clearly individuals were entering into secret and unsupervised liaisons. The resolve to keep to promises is couched, at times, in language that is dramatic and defiant. Rebecca Baker declared in respect of her betrothal at Lenham that 'she wouid stand to her promise though she shuld be torn with wild horses'.[9] Such promises could occasion much physical reproof. As one Alice Jenkyne reported, she was both beaten and driven out of her house for having bestowed herself on John Rolfe.[10]

It can be seen that individuals asserted their own emotional and sexual preferences in face of opposition. Nevertheless, the evidence suggests that this was not without significant personal cost and repercussions. In the case of *Turner* v. *Hubbard*, a servant, Marian Hubbard, was questioned about the promise she had made to a fellow servant, Richard Turner. She answered, 'In deede, I cannot denye, but I have made [him] a promis, the which I meane faythefullye to performe, thoughe all my freendes be ageynste yt, and though manye troobles followed the same.'[11] With the ill will of 'freends' incurred, the alternative for Isabelle Ladd of Chartham was to 'doo as well as I can and trust to godd that I shall lyve',[12] a prospect perhaps made easier because the man to whom she was contracted already had a good occupation to live by. No amount of pleading would move some kinsmen. The widow Christine Marsh fell down on her knees before her brother George Coppyn, desiring him to be a good brother unto her and a friend also, for he had rebuked and threatened her for the promise she had made to George Gaunt.[13]

Any argument for individualism needs to confront the manifest evidence for constraint and pressure, even if it is only psychological. Under extreme circumstances, individualism in attitude and thought might be translated into action. The deposition of Thomas Marshall highlights the point, for not only did Marion Rogers demonstrate her individuality but, it seems, she did so when forced under real psychological pressure. It was said that she had been sick, that she was not allowed to go out of William Hoball's house in Tenterden, and that she had been 'charged by hyr parents not to come in the company of William Austen nor to talke with him'. She did, nevertheless, meet with him in the garden and made him a promise but, before plighting, paused and said, 'I shall lease my frends goodwills in so doing, but yet notwithstanding I will marry for myself and not for my frends, for I know that they care not if I were dead so that they might have my goods for they have kept me in, (saying that I am madde) so longe, and wold not lett me go abroode to speake with him that I love so that it had almost cost me my lyffe.'[14]

There is always a danger of sentimentalising this kind of evidence, and it is difficult to know which of the conflicting accounts in the depositions to believe. In the end, though, the actual truth and whether or not we believe one deponent rather than another is not crucial. What is more relevant is not the facts of an individual experience, but the structure within which it is incorporated. How are we to interpret the 'sickness' and 'madness' of Marion Rogers? Were they matters of personal psychology and emotional expression or were they rather responses to external pressure?

In the Canterbury case of *Coppyn* v. *Richards*, Katherine Richards was offered a pair of gloves by Richard Dennys on behalf of one Edmund Coppyn. She refused them and, 'at the refusall therof [Dennys] declared unto her that she and Edmond should be suer together. And then she lamentted very sore howbeyt she wolde not declare any other cause of her lamentings saving that she said to [him] I pray you speake not for him for I will nev*er* have him nor I CANNOT love him.'[15] The emphasis is my own, but the rhetoric and Katherine's distraught condition suggest a tension arising from some prohibition other than personal inclination. Perhaps then, it is to this area of ambiguous meaning that attention needs to be drawn, in order for us to understand the problems which individuals had in internalising family and social norms, and the way in which personal desire was suppressed or constrained. The justification which respondents gave for the breakdown in their marriage promises should not be taken at face value. Rather we should look for more subtle approaches to interpret their position, and to such emotions as 'lamentation' which hint at less articulated considerations and feelings.

Katherine Richards's position as servant may have made her more susceptible to Edmund and, away from her immediate family context, sexual attraction might have been more easily translated into a love contract. If so, then her position would not have been an unusual one. The institution of service (as elaborated in chapter 4) provided opportunities for individuals to meet and enter into sexual relations, and for sexual harassment and exploitation to occur.[16] James Haffynden and Constance Austen were both servants in the household of Mr Robert Wyse of Woodchurch. According to her account, she was constantly under pressure from him because he was persistent, indeed, 'tedious' in his suit for marriage. Unable to attend to her duties she was forced to leave her master's service. The case is interesting because it indicates the possibilities of this kind of claustrophobic pressure. At the same time, further depositions allow another interpretation of the events. Constance was found by one Richard Wylls to be very sorrowful and weeping. It appeared that James Haffynden had made the rule that she should obtain the goodwill of her 'friends', namely her three uncles. Their refusal to grant their goodwill may well have hindered the marriage and it was possibly by their action that she was in fact recalled from service. That the couple talked of 'love and familiarities', and that James feared the influence and counsel of her 'friends' was testified by Alice Bett, who also claimed to have seen them lying together in 'naked bed', and to have heard them discussing the need for elopement if goodwill could not be had.[17]

Being carried away in secret can be seen as one form of individual action, but it was also used by family and kin for their own arrangements. In some of those cases where two persons claimed to be lawfully contracted to one party, and where one of those marriages had been formally solemnised, it may be possible to distinguish the love contracts and broken liaisons from the marriages which were properly completed and perhaps predominantly socially and economically determined. Conceivably, romantic and sexual inclinations and the expectations of marriage led to hasty promises, and these were broken under circumstances in which it was found that the individual was unsuitable, and where the reality of family, social and economic pressures forced different decisions to be taken. The case of *Tusten* v. *Allen* helps to illustrate such a distinction. It appears that Godlen Allen, a widow, received several marriage tokens from Richard Tusten. Their behaviour was seen to be 'very loving', and they had in fact obtained the goodwill of Godlen's 'cosyn', Thomas Sprott. Relations had proceeded in an orthodox way and included the necessary financial negotiations, but it would seem that the situation changed after 'certaine unkynde woords that [Richard Tusten] should speake against the wife of John Sprott brother of Thomas'. The ill will which it incurred probably made it impossible for the marriage to proceed any further. Godlen is alleged to have said that she would have married Richard if her cousin Sprott had not been against it, and that out of fear of her cousin, she dared not have the banns asked at Wye in Richard's absence. Instead she wanted them to be asked at Otham where he dwelled to see if he was clear from marriage with another.[18]

The case is complicated by reference to this other possible party, but it does nevertheless illustrate the breaking of one liaison in favour of alternative arrangements. The ensuing marriage between Godlen Allen and Simon Ansell was most likely an abuse of solemnisation.[19] It seems that the marriage occurred after the apparitor had already declared to Thomas Sprott that he had a citation from Richard Tusten containing an inhibition. On the day that the citation was declared, Godlen Allen was in hiding in her chamber, and afterwards suddenly went away with her 'cosyn' Simon Rolfe. Meeting up with Simon Ansell, they rode away that night, and the writings made by Thomas Sprott between Ansell and Allen were made after the citation was delivered, and before the marriage was solemnised. The deposition of one William Collyns is perhaps most revealing. In it he says that Godlen declared to him,

> weping, that she colde not tell what to do for that hyr cosyn Thomas Sprott had so earnistelye moved and perswaded her to assure hirselfe to Ansell owte of hand, in so muche that she was afraid (as she said) that he wolde have done hyr some evell, for that she wolde not graunt to contracte herself with Ansell the day before, and therefore wished that Richard Tusten were comde home at that tyme from London. And also afterwards [William Collyns] dyd hear that Ansell and Allen were maried together.

The marriage between Godlen Allen and Simon Ansell can be seen in this light as the consequence of kin constraints, which acted against the personal wishes and inclinations of Godlen herself. The determination of the kin to make these arrangements at a time of crisis demonstrates their control of widow Godlen, and her consent to such a marriage should be interpreted within this context. Apparently subject to external pressures, her position as widow makes the argument for the influence of kinsmen all the more potent. While it may be argued that the greater economic independence of widows and their increased maturity might allow them more personal freedom of action, it is equally possible to argue that through previous marriages, their actions and decisions involved a wider family and social network in which greater numbers of people had personal interests in a new marriage.[20]

Rayner v. *Chamber* is a case in point. It is of interest for the kinds of arrangement implied, for the social detail and information about those involved, and particularly for the focus placed on individual experience and collective pressures. It is clear that there had been several occasions in which communications concerning a marriage between the widow Elizabeth Chamber of Charing and the widower Matthew Rayner of Boughton-under-the-Blean had been made. Such talk had occurred at both her house and his, and at the house of her father Henry Adye. Discussions had centred on financial matters and had involved the active participation of a range of kin, in the negotiations and in the hospitality bestowed. The emphasis, however, was on the meeting at Matthew Rayner's house, where matters were to be concluded, and where Elizabeth Chamber was welcomed and 'frendly chere' provided for her entertainment. The company of 'kin', 'frends' and many other 'neighbours', in all up to 16 or 17 persons, dined together. Noticeably, though, within this grouping, a select few were singled out who were more directly involved in the marriage communications. They included those who had participated in the earlier stages – goodman Adye who was the widow's father, Cyriak Petit who was Matthew Rayner's master, Thomas Hawkins (of kin, as he said, because Rayner's first wife was his sister's daughter) and Christopher Southonsand (also of kin, because Rayner's first wife was within the third or fourth degree of him). Also present was Robert Castelyn (kin to Rayner but to what degree he did not know), one Bunce (brother to Rayner) and Bernard Bonar, a lodger in the house. Financial negotiations being concluded, Matthew Rayner named as his sureties his brother Bunce and his brother Andrew Rayner. That there was a sub-group within the company of persons present is indicated also in a physical separation. The select core moved to a separate chamber to finalise matters, because it appeared that Elizabeth Chamber was unwilling to contract herself in the presence of so many. Certain 'friends', therefore, were called forth.[21]

Perhaps Elizabeth Chamber was intimidated both by the group and by her father. The negotiations and finalising of the marriage would appear to have been largely determined by kin. One account reads that Cyriak Petit said to her, 'You have herd what you father hath doon for the preferment and advancement of yor marriage to whome you have put and did in tymes past your trust.' It seems that her father had 'married her twise afore', and that he trusted that 'she [would be] ruled by [him] as she hath been afore tymes'. Her silence when asked whether she was content with what her father and 'friends' had done is revealing, and so too is the private communication which her father had with her away from the rest of the company. In her own deposition, Elizabeth Chamber claimed, 'that they would have had her to have made [Rayner] promise with solemn contract and saith she hath twise been married and there was never contract desired of her so ernestly as at that tyme'. Furthermore she added, that 'she never consented in her heart to her father's sayings', although she allowed herself to be measured for wedding garments 'for fear of her father and mother's displeasure', indicating thereby her individual attitude but constrained action.

What the evidence suggests is the arrangement of a third marriage advanced by kinsmen, particularly the widow's father, with social and economic advantage in mind, as in previous times. Thomas Hawkins's opinion on the desirability of the match may support such a view. He said to her, at her house, 'that thone of them did know eche other well and their parents and bringing up. Wherfore [he] thought it shuld be a good match that they be marryed.' If, as it seems, Elizabeth Chamber was unwilling to proceed with the marriage, it helps to explain her desire that Matthew Rayner defer the date of solemnisation. The reasons stated are, however, in themselves of interest – one reason being that her previous husband had died lately, and the second, that she could not consent to the time appointed 'for that she did marry her husbands alwaies about that tyme and did not long enioye them after but died'. Some of the essential features of marriage practice are illustrated in this case with the participation of various representatives of kin and community in the witnessing process, and with the importance of ritual. A consideration of these aspects in the marriage process adds a further and crucial dimension to an understanding of the operation of the system of social constraint, and of the place of the individual within the community.

The fact that individuals entered into secret and sexual relations does not undermine the argument that family and community constraints nevertheless operated. It is clear that individuals made secret promises one to another, but with betrothal and publication through formal representative groups, such actions moved immediately from within the interpersonal to the institutional sphere. It is argued that the private promise must be seen as an aspect of a whole complex of processes involving kin and community. In arguing for various stages in the marriage process,[22] one might speculate that there is a structure that moves outwards from the interpersonal to the small groupings, and then to the community at large, where there is acceptance at the community level after a marriage has been secularised and popularised. Perhaps there is a danger here of seeing the process as too systematic, but the essential point is that witnessing and the broadcasting of intention was an important stage in marriage practice. When Agnes Butterwick warned Edmund Coppyn and Katherine Richards to 'take hede what they did, for ther was nothing doon in secrete, but it wold come to light', she was expressing the fact that a betrothal had to be made public and had to have the social ritual.[23] In cases where there was an intimate exchange of promises and yet no attempt to publicise them, then questions of deceit, and of secrecy out of fear, might be suspected.

In the case cited above, what is suggested is not only the need for a marriage to be publicised in order to give it status, but also the moral implications which attached to 'privy' as opposed to formalised, structured, lawfully contracted and open marriages, performed according to social conventions. In purely clandestine unions the element of dishonesty and secrecy implied in such conduct exposed the parties to criticism, and by implication extended to compromise the honesty of those involved. The honesty of the individual may be seen to be tied to the honesty of the transaction. When questioning the reputation of Mrs Butterwick, the issue was whether or not she was of the honest and godly sort and therefore suitable as a witness to the betrothal of Edmund Coppyn and Katherine Richard. It seems, therefore, that alongside the need to broadcast a marriage through a witnessing ceremony, was the need to have a contract publicised formally and among significant individuals – family, kin, or honest neighbours. In observing their participation, it has to be asked how those who were involved at the various stages of the marriage process and in matters of marriage ceremonial were affected by the marriage, and how their participation at the symbolic level of ritual demonstrates the importance of marriage as a personal, family and social event.

A detailed knowledge of who the witnesses were cannot be obtained without close local study. The problem of a vague, inconsistent and limited terminology classifying a range of kin and social relations, makes it difficult to identify precisely what the relationships were.[24] It seems, however, that those who participated in marriage processes and acted as witnesses in a passive or active capacity included members of the nuclear family and such persons as friends, kinsmen, kinswomen, cousins, uncles and aunts, in-laws, neighbours, 'fellows' (associates), bed-fellows, gossips, the godmother of a kinsman, masters and mistresses. Connections appear to derive therefore from family and the surrogate family of masters,[25] mistresses and fellow servants, from biological kin, affines, and a range of what may loosely be termed fictive kin.[26] In the case of *Handfeeld* v. *Franckwell*, the company, gathered together at Canterbury, comprised Richard Handfeeld's father and mother, his uncles, aunt and two or three of his kinsfolk. On Anne Franckwell's side, her mother was present and the goodwill of her 'friend' Mr Collens also had to be obtained.[27] To what degree members of kin were involved cannot be ascertained here, but the case of *Rayner v. Chamber*, cited earlier, gives some indication of how extended biological kin ties might be. How far marriages occurred between individuals who were already related in some way is also unknown, but a glimpse of it is seen in the contract made between Thomas Kennet and Bennet Dunnye in his father's parish of Mersham. Those present included Bennet Kennet (Thomas Kennet's mother) and Richard (Thomas's brother) as well as his natural aunt Elizabeth Davye and her husband William. It was also made clear that Elizabeth Davye was once the wife of Roger Luckas, natural uncle of Bennet Dunnye and therefore Dunnye's aunt by marriage.[28]

The evidence suggests, then, that those who were drawn upon for this formal occasion and its rituals were not restricted to the immediate family, but might include various categories of kin, even if there was no precisely definable range of kin present.[29] Further research on sixteenth-century terminology and an analysis of residence patterns might reveal the extent of kin connections and the geographical range from which witnesses were drawn. It may be that the importance of biological kin at a symbolic level might be translated into areas of practical and more mundane significance. In terms of marriage ritual, they had a vital role to play, and formed an essential and dominant element within the generally small and select groupings which crystallised at betrothal ceremonies.[30] That their participation was an essential feature of marriage practice does not, of course, preclude the importance of other kinds of social relations. Apart from the influence and role of biological kin, serious account has to be taken of a wider variety of influences and social groups. Those groups which congregated at such betrothal ceremonies, and which were by implication an integral part of the social system, were composed predominantly of biological and 'fictive' kin. Where larger groupings manifested themselves an identifiable sub-group might nevertheless form. When Joanne Harewood from Mersham married into Folkestone, it was reported that she arrived at Thomas Lambard's house with 'divers [of] her friends' and was met by 'divers of the towne ... And some said that knew her not, whiche is she shalbe our neighbour ... Wherapon they drancke to her.' The concern which she, in turn, voiced, was that of '[being] entertayned there as a neighbour among them'.[31] Here, the bonds of such fictive kinship were formally recognised by the community in an act of ritual acceptance.

Given that there were particular categories of persons involved as witnesses, the problem becomes one of trying to comprehend their various motivations. If marriage and its rituals are an institutionalised expression of the need for an adaptation and adjustment of particular ties and associations, then the involvement of various categories of persons as witnesses indicates the degree of investment in, and control of, marriage by family, kin and community.[32] The performance of particular rituals answers the needs of different interest groups, and repeated performances may at times be observed with the stages of contracting, confession, acknowledgement and recognition.[33] The repetition of vows which clearly occurred in certain cases before new witnesses, and which were ideally accompanied by particular ritualised behaviour, suggests that the ceremony itself was not sufficient without particular witnesses. It suggests also that the performance of ritual acts such as stepping across the threshold, 'trothplighting' or 'handfasting', kissing, drinking and the giving of tokens may have required the presence of those specific witnesses. In giving a token to Maria Wright, John Davye gave it in the presence of Edward Aucher of Eastchurch, saying 'here I do give her a pece of gold bycause you shall beare witness'.[34] Similarly, the witnesses too demonstrated that their participation was closely tied to ritual processes. In the case of *Edmonds* v. *Witherden*, a witness, John Trott of Canterbury, kissing Silvestra Witherden, said that 'in witnes therof I will kisse you also'.[35]

In view of the significance which a marriage would have had for the structural reorganisation of the community, it is not surprising that it should have been experienced on both a personal and a collective level. Nor is it surprising that the circles most involved in the marriage process should have been composed of close members of family, kin and community. The rituals which occurred may be seen as an institutionalised means of entering into a marriage, controlled by the codes of kin and community, and, more specifically, by those directly concerned with a particular marriage. They may best be understood as a way of facilitating harmony and the mutual protection of interests. That there was potential for conflict and tension and a polarising of issues is summarised neatly in the case of *Rolf* v. *Whiter*. Problems over financial matters caused William Rolf to say to Joanne Whiter's 'cosyn', 'You are ever agaynste me and my heyvie friend. Than said the wydowe, thers that be my friends by yor fowes ever.'[36] When interpreted within a context of conflict and changing loyalties, commensality rituals (the feasting which occurred before and after the contract, and the ritual of drinking) express symbolically the need for social unity, especially in circumstances when negotiations might be protracted, when harmony broke down and when individuals and groups were forced to readjust. Such rituals were not simply an integral part of the marriage process. They are known to have been performed in several other contexts of social and domestic tension where reconciliation was needed,[37] and on other life-crisis occasions.[38]

If attention is focused on formal drinkings, what is observed is the means by which that ritual marked the process of forming alliances. Noticeably, in the case below, it was concerned with the formation of kin ties. John and Thomas Austen, with their cousin Mark, were at Christine Burrett's house in

Canterbury. Having 'desired to drink a quarte of wine with her', John Austen said, 'Cousen, I will drink unto you upon condition that you will tell me whether I shall have a cousen of you or no, meanyng a marriage between her and [his] cousin.'[39] Such a ritual, although only one of a series of rituals performed, expresses the contractual nature of that kind of activity. The aspect of recognition, of witnessing and acceptance, the parallel with religious symbolism and the notion of a pledge are also expressed. This example synthesises those aspects found in other rituals too, and demonstrates the levels of participation in social constraint through ritual. Distinct phases may be identified in the case of *Lambard* v. *Harewood.* At Thomas Lambard's house in Folkestone, the vicar, Richard Sherington, took the cup and drank to the parties. Thomas, also taking the cup, drank to the woman, and then the whole company drank to their neighbour.[40] Similar phases can be seen in the contract made between Joan Parker and William Munday. Taking place in her father's brew house in Sandwich and gathered round the furnace hole, the parties contracted themselves. 'Then Munday desyred them that were present to bere witness and said further fecche a pot of bere let Joan and me drinke together, and [John Toose] fecched bere and then Munday dranke to Joan and then she dranke and after them all that were present.'[41] The ceremony of drinking recognised the wider implications of a marriage for family, kin, and community. As a pledge, it was immediately of significance because it implicated the reputation of those involved, and by extension perhaps, the reputation generally of family and kin. It may be argued that the practice of pledging and the plighting of troths, as acts of honour, even when restricted in performance to the couple alone, nevertheless immediately had associations for family and kin.

The repercussions which a marriage might have for the social standing and reputation of a family may help us to understand the nature of family and kin participation in matters of marriage choice. There is much evidence of sensitivity to defamation felt by family members, of the fear of gossip and the wish to avoid 'all rumours and evill speches that might ensue'.[42] Family and kindred at times demonstrated their unity in shows of protective or threatening actions.[43] What is clear is that communal sanctions and principles determined and were implicit in social relations. The reputation and name of an individual were considered important because, as part of a collective, he or she was subject to collective sanctions and public opinion. In societies where individuals interacted everyday in a plurality of ways and in a variety of contexts, the relevance of one's reputation was arguably much intensified. The 'public voice and fame' of a parish was an important reality to be contended with in sixteenth-century England.[44] The force with which communal sanctions operated may be observed in the repercussions which they had on personal health and individual psychology, in the sphere of economic and social relations, on marriage prospects, and within domestic and marital life. Deponents frequently expressed that they were 'much greved', 'worse thought of', and 'misused', 'shamed for ever', given the 'hinderance and injury' to their name which resulted in their 'discredit' and their 'utter undoing'. With her name 'impaired', Elizabeth Hogdekin found herself separated from honest society, socially isolated, and no longer part of the network of reciprocal visits and social exchange, as 'many honest neighbours refraineth to resort to her house or to kepe her company as they accustumablie have done'.[45] For one Stamner, the economic consequences were no less apparent. Men would 'shuve and avoyde to have do with him in buying or selling', and thus losing their estimation, 'his lyving [was] hindered therby'.[46] On the domestic and psychological front, it was said that Bouche's wife, slandered by the words of one William Cadman, 'taketh yt heavelyve and verrye sick', that 'the verrye words ar odious and therefore her name must a little be diminished'. It was further deposed that the 'words were said to slander her because otherwise [she] would not have taken such a greef that she would be sick, and also because yt hath caused strif between her and her husband'.[47] In these cases of defamation, the power of language as a coercive force, the very 'potency of words themselves', the psychological awareness of reputation and the ruinous consequences of a 'diminished' name are demonstrated.[48]

At every level the pressures and controls of society and the values and concepts of community confronted the individual. If individual decisions and behaviour are seen as representing an internalisation of social norms and having social resonance, then it becomes impossible to interpret behaviour without some sense of community, or indeed to regard it as unconstrained. Fear of communal censure, then, might be a very real constraint over both the conduct of courtship and the individual choice of marriage partner.

For both the secular and religious community, marriage was a vital 'matter of family and community concern'.[49] Despite Macfarlane's assertions, in this respect at the very least, marriage in sixteenth-century English villages was analogous to those marriages in traditional peasant societies, where such corporate concern was a fundamental, indeed a 'typical', feature. Thus far the discussion has been concerned with those marriage processes which preceded the church ceremony. The community, however, might make its opinions known not only during courtship, but also at the point of solemnisation. The calling of banns and the wedding at the church which were presumably intended to be before the congregation, witnessed by the godly folk and under the eye of God, were the most corporate and public expression of control by the community at large. Even though the kin and select-group element were not necessarily dominant at this final stage of marriage, they presumably formed a part of that congregation. The church ceremony may be seen as the religious celebration of the community focused in the parish church.[50] At both

ceremonies, therefore, the involvement of kin and community was manifested. On the one hand was the secularised marriage, community constrained, but dominated it seems by private and special groups. On the other,
was the marriage controlled by ecclesiastical norms, a public event involving
the community at large. And, at both occasions, the feasting and drinking
which occurred, the references to 'marriage dinners' and 'bridales', make it
apparent that marriage was indeed an important social event.[51]

Macfarlane has famously pronounced that 'however one defined
"community" there was relatively little of it in the villages ... as far back as the
sixteenth century'.[52] On the contrary, however, while problems of definition do
arise, there is implicit in the Kentish deposition evidence particular concepts
of a moral and social community.[53] An analysis of these depositions suggests
the ways in which a community defined and expressed itself. Communities
had their particular set of codes and collective values, distinctive internal
groupings and interactions, localised culture, attitudes and sometimes overt
manifestations of collective action. When Joanne Harewood complained of
the 'pitch and tar' in her prospective husband's parish of Folkestone, she may
have been expressing her antipathy to the personal and physical characteristics of the environment as well as to the customs of another parish. Such
expressions are illuminating when treated in the context of changes in
residence at marriage, and alongside notions of acceptance and acceptability.[54]

Evidence of the ritual acceptance of a neighbour which relates directly to
this latter case has already been presented, but collective action could just as
well take on a negative form. In the town of Sandwich, the neighbourhood
demonstrated its displeasure by speaking to the mayor for the reformation of
one Tomlynson's house, where there was likely to have been manslaughter,
complaining 'it is pity that yow shuld suffre horedom and bawdry kept
withowt reformacion and it is pitie that [she] shuld be suffred to dwell in the
towne if she be so evyll as the report is'.[55]

Collective protest could lead to the threat of individuals being expelled, and
to the actual carting of persons out of town. It was said that if one goodwife
Ward of Canterbury was indeed a woman of suspicious life, 'yt ys pitty that she
... ys not carted out of the towne that all other may take example'.[56] Similarly,
in another case of defamation, Joane Clinton shouted to Joane Nowre: 'thow
arte a whore ... and *the* carte comithe for thee'.[57] In voicing such a punishment,
even defamers were invoking institutional forms of collective censure
associated with inappropriate conduct, while traditional images of charivari
portrayed the popular rituals of community sanctions.[58] The slanderous
speech of Arthur Baker, for example, invoked the spectacle of Thomas Argar
'ryd*ing* upon a cow like a cuckold with his face toward*es* the cowes arse and the
cowe taile shalbe his cape and the hornes shalbe his spurres'.[59]

While it is debatable how frequent the occurrence of charivaris were, the bounds of permitted behaviour were nonetheless incorporated and collectively defined in other ways, in libels and in mocking rhymes.[60] Such verses may have been officially regarded as defamatory or illegal, but could still represent a form of social shaming and 'could be used as a vehicle of social control'. In publicising real or alleged misdemeanours, they exposed such behaviour to common judgement, thus influencing the wider opinion and, at the same time, articulating shared values and sensibilities.[61] The early modern period witnessed the growth of libelling,[62] and deposition evidence from Kent would seem to suggest that such forms of expression were by no means uncommon. There are several references to bills 'wherein was shamefull matters wrytten' and read aloud,[63] and to bills displayed, as in the case of *Sprye* v. *Strowde*, on the post of Inckepett's gate, declaring that Sprye had been naughty with Inckepett's wife.[64] Prominent places for finding libels included church doors and pews, gates, fences and stiles, the pillory, maypole and market cross.[65] Other libels imputing ill living were cast abroad in the streets or marketplace for everyone to see. Elizabeth Browne of Lydd devised a letter which she asked to have written for her, in order to disgrace Agnes Evernden, 'and she said she wold disperse and cast abrode into the stretes and houses in the town the same *lettre* and libell to the intent Everndens wife and [John] Patten should be made ashamed of ther ill living together'. It was commonly reported furthermore, that a former letter or rhyme against them had been written at her instruction in order to disgrace them.[66] The making of such libels inevitably involved mischief-makers and rhymes of crude quality and accuracy.[67] Sometimes put to song, they might be performed at fairs and markets and in alehouses.[68] Their derisive and shaming purpose could nevertheless reflect community values and antagonism towards the transgression of communal norms.

The potency of communal opinion is illustrated nicely in the matrimony case of *Turner* v. *Hubbard*. In this case it emerged that one Alice Cheeseman of Aldington, a deponent, had been threatened with expulsion from the community, an extreme form of moral sanction. The case is of particular interest because of what it suggests about communal constraints and godly attitudes and individual reactions to such pressures. The concern expressed by the parishioners over Alice's choice of marriage partner was for reasons that they 'wished her to be preferred to a better marriage'. In 'bearing her goodwill for her behaviour [they] thought her worthy of a better marriage'. Richard Coste's deposition was most informative. He said,

> that the parishioners bear her that goodwill and affection that when yt was reported she shuld be married to Cheeseman they were sore against yt, and stayed the asking of the banns and marriage, and many of the cheefest of the parish counselled her to leave him because the parishioners mislyked of Cheeseman. The which they would not have done without goodwill boorne to the woman for her good behaviour before that time ... [he] saith that although she did offend in carnallye knowing Cheseman

before marriage notwithstanding she made as he thinketh in recompence in that she being persuaded to forsake him bye her freends, she ever said that she should have him and in respecte allso that she hath reconciled herself to god and the world by marrying of her husband.[69]

To deny the existence of community controls, and the pressures which must have been brought to bear on a couple intending marriage, is to deny the evidence. The constraints would have been felt in the 'hinderance' of the marriage, and in the fact that Cheeseman was made to fetch a testimonial of his behaviour. He went to get it from his friends in Sussex, accompanied by Alice and by one of her 'neighbours'.[70] They would also have been felt when 'the parishioners threatened Alice to expell her out of the parish'. Effectively, in prolonging the proceedings, and delaying the church ceremony, 'the child begotten could not be boorne in sufficient cumpas of tyme after marriage'. The delay of two months which was occasioned, coincided with Alice being pregnant for about eight weeks before the church wedding.

It may be argued that the disapproval of an individual's choice of marriage partner, whether by parents, kin or community, might conceivably result in frustrated plans and postponed marriages. Consequently it should not be discounted as a possible factor contributing to prenuptial pregnancies. One cannot, of course, account for all prenuptial pregnancies in this way, given the high national figures for bridal pregnancy in this period. In this case, however, bridal pregnancy may be regarded as a direct consequence of community pressures, and may help to account for the degree of tolerance which the parishioners exhibited towards it. Although premarital sex was legally and theoretically seen as a 'vice', the standards applied to sexual behaviour were ambivalent.[71] It was recognised by the community that the fault in the act was not so great 'in respect of the parishes said hinderance and her towardnes to the matter and in the end marriage'. In John Smith's opinion, in view of the responsibility assumed by the community in the matter, and the fact that the marriage did take place after all, 'he thinketh she ys not so much to be blamed but rather have done sufficiently to reconcile herself to god and the world for the same'.

What is, of course, also revealing is Alice's decision to marry Cheeseman despite parochial opposition and pressure. Retrospectively, her individual decision was vindicated as an act of personal conscience and as a religious act, especially given her pregnant condition. There is the implication that the attempts made to hinder the marriage had been unlawful, and could only be justified on the grounds of genuine goodwill and affection felt for her. The case stands, therefore, as an excellent example of the conflict between individual and collective interests, and the problems of reconciling contradictory elements. What it shows, is that while individuals might follow their own sexual and emotional inclinations, they might have to contend with the potential strength of social opinion, the reality of family and community pressures, the importance of collective sanctions and the very real attempt to control marriage choice.

It may be that we should regard irregular unions and illicit sexual activity as partly an index, and a direct or indirect consequence, of community constraints. There were a variety of ways by which disapproval might be expressed. One of these ways is implied in the deposition of Alice Kyngesnorth of Pluckley. Both William Howell and Richard Wood were suitors to her during her widowhood. As soon as Richard Wood ended his suit, William Howell began his more earnestly, making her an unwitnessed promise of marriage, and from then on lodging with her continually. Alice claimed that she kept him in her house because she was destitute of a servant and that she had every intention of marrying him. She denied that they ever had intercourse, but 'saith she hath been suspected therof howbeit of mallice because she wold not take Wood to her husband'. She reported furthermore that John Richard of Ulcomb said 'that he marvailled whye she marryed not with Howell for that she being so bent to have him answered the parish geve us ill words but if we were so mynded to take that way though we could not wedd yet could wee bedd upon which words so by [her] uttered the parishioners have thought [her] and [Howell] to be evill lyvers and have made compleynt of them'.[72]

Could it be that the widow was prevented from marrying William Howell? In refusing to marry Richard Wood was Alice failing to meet with the expectations of some of the parishioners of Pluckley, thereby incurring their ill will? Whatever the truth of the circumstances, our interest lies in the potential which lay in the hands of the community for coercive action and for the regulation of courtship and sexual behaviour at least through moral, if not legal, sanctioning. The code of good behaviour, the ethic of reciprocity, and the norms of honour and reputation set the bounds of the moral community. Attitudes were complex and behaviour which was theoretically reprehensible might have been tolerated in practice. Certainly, in relation to sexual behaviour, there was scope for ambivalence and for different standards being applied according to particular circumstances. Certain misdemeanours, for example, would seem to have been tolerated provided that marriage was in view. Christopher Selherst, finding his brother lying in a chamber with Joanne Port of Whitstable, was, 'examined whether he was myscontent that they had so companyed together before they were married, he saith no for that he toke them together assured as man and wife'.[73] That there was a degree of flexibility is evident, but it is difficult to gauge at what point the line divided between tolerance and disapprobation. It may be that tolerance was permitted only up to the point of conflict and 'disordre'.[74]

The fact that certain kinds of behaviour were tolerated at particular times, does not, however, undermine the importance of collective values. The concepts of tolerance and control may be seen as alternative sides of the same coin, both operating within the sphere of informal as well as formal sanctions, and effectively limiting social relations. Ample evidence of spying activities exists, incidents where neighbours would 'eavesdrope', would have 'broken a hole in the wall', or put their 'head in at a hole'. Even if they did not lead to formal acts of prosecution, suspect behaviour revealed by such activities could have aroused gossip and 'folkstalk'.[75] Gossip of this sort could act as a powerful regulatory mechanism.

The fact that parishioners sometimes assumed responsibility to arbitrate and reconcile where there was conflict within the family and within the community, suggests another informal means by which the community (at times represented by the parish priest) regulated affairs.[76] In the interests of stability and harmony, the resolution of conflicts was mediated via community scrutiny and intervention. The common recognition of unwritten rules, and the expectation of such informal monitoring gave the community a special role in matters of control and protection.[77] In this sense at least, in terms of the way in which interpersonal behaviour was limited by community norms, an individual must be seen as part of a collective. It is too early, therefore, to abandon notions of community control, or indeed control by kin and other groupings.

The depositions suggest that individuals were defined in terms of their social interactions and the range of their connections. Their reputation both reflected on, and was associated with, the social groups within which they were located. It is important to be able to identify these groups, given their importance as regulatory forces. To uncover the membership of such groups is to reveal those associations of neighbours or kin that might be crucial in the making or breaking of the reputations of courting couples. Such an exercise, however, should really go beyond the evidence concerned solely with marriage cases, since similar social groupings met on many other occasions in village life.

Although marriage provides us with an ideal occasion for identifying these groups, it is as revealing to examine other life-crises. Where childbirth was concerned, for example, the gathering of the company crystallised the existence of a female and gossip network which was a crucial and permanent structure of society.[78] In the defamation case of *Egglestone* v. *Cullembyne*, Joanne Rolf deposed how it was that she happened to be at Elizabeth Browning's house at Burmarsh. She said that it 'fortuned her the goodwif Eglestone and Goodwif Cotterell went to one Browninges wif of Burromershe (she there lying in childbed) a gossoppynge, and to make merry, whether after [she] and her other neighbours had come, and had entered the house, Hellenor Cullembyne and one Hawkes wif followed and came thother a gossoppinge also'.[79] Such childbed 'gossiping transformed a biological event

47

into a communal affair, bonding women among women and incorporating family and neighbours, baby and kin'. Occasions of christening cheer and the churching of women were also renowned for female 'gossipings'.[80]

It should not be imagined, though, that local courtships, individual reputations, domestic goings-on and other matters of communal interest were a subject of concern only to women. A company of gossips was not a purely female phenomenon. Men also formed their own alternative groupings, and seem to have had institutionalised meeting-places. It was said that 'a certayn benche called pennylesse benche towards the waters side in dovor' was 'a place wheare many of that towne use to sitt and talk together', 'being a comon place of resort for men of the towne to meet together to be merry comon and talk'.[81] Arguably these kinds of gatherings provide one means of identifying social groups, but associations could also manifest themselves in a range of specific and ritual activity, of which commensality might be one. A show of solidarity can also be suggestive. The departure from church of a group of 'bretherne' demonstrates such group cohesion. Taking place during morning service at the parish church of Hawkhurst, the curate Mr Mantle expounded the gospel in the pulpit. He digressed and complained 'how that riche men would get their maids with child and then with money marry them to another'. It was said that Mr Culpepper and 'certain other his bretherne' immediately left the church. Mr Mantle, with his hands towards heaven, exclaimed what a state it was that men could not bear to hear their faults.[82]

Precisely how members of social groupings were associated one with another is by no means apparent. It is clear that the language recorded in deposition evidence cannot, when studied in isolation, fully reveal the exact nature of relationships between specific deponents.[83] The descriptive vocabulary used – terms such as 'bretherne', 'brother', 'cousin', 'friend', 'father' – should not be taken as self-explanatory. As well as denoting the exclusivity of groupings, they can equally be inclusive terms, often extended to embrace a range of real and fictive relationships. Only by examining contemporary linguistic expressions and their application are we able to come closer to an understanding of historical structures and early modern concepts of kin, family, household and community.[84] It may be, as I have argued elsewhere, that historians have been too quick to impose arbitrary systems of classification for the purpose of quantitative demographic analysis. The focus on the nuclear unit and the strictly biological and affinal definition of kinship may not accurately represent historical reality or individual experience in the past.[85] Historians' conceptualisation of kinship as a flexible system is arguably not sufficient, and it certainly does not imply that it was individualised. Even if most historians would now reject Macfarlane's view of too simple a dichotomy between kinship on the one hand and individualism on the other, this basic polarisation nevertheless continues to inform discussion of marriage and kinship in sixteenth-century England.[86] In the context of marriage which, as we have seen, might involve much intervention and participation in the interests of stability and mutual obligation, the metaphorical use of kinship would have been particularly relevant. Such usage could invest particular relationships with a moral, if not a practical, purpose, treating them *as if* they were kin, and locating them within an ideological framework of reciprocity and responsibility. To understand courtship behaviour and relationships in the sixteenth century we must explore the social context more subtly. This should be done by appreciating the variety of social groups, networks and social pressures which existed, and by re-examining contemporary perceptions of family, kin and community. The evidence considered here provides fresh insights into the social world within which individuals contemplating marriage had to manoeuvre and the influences brought to bear upon couples in their marriage decisions.

Much evidence exists of constraint coming from a variety of quarters prior to the formal calling of banns and the church wedding. Marriage formation throughout its various stages was affected by the potentially extensive influence of real kin, fictive kin, neighbours and community. Much, if not all, individual expression was subject to external influences and internalised values. The making of marriage was a critical process in the continuous and dynamic restructurings of family, kin and community in sixteenth-century society.

NOTES

1 For new perspectives on the study of kinship, see an earlier published version of this chapter, D. O'Hara, '"Ruled by my friends": aspects of marriage in the diocese of Canterbury, c. 1540–1570', *Continuity and Change* 6 (1991), 9–41.

2 J. Bossy, 'Blood and baptism: kinship, community and Christianity in western Europe from the fourteenth to the seventeenth centuries', in D. Baker ed., *Sanctity and Secularity: the Church and the World* (Oxford, 1973), pp. 129–43 (pp. 130–2).

3 For important comparative discussions of these issues of constraint, parental control, the wider influence of kin, and 'goodwill', see Ingram, 'Spousals litigation', pp. 47–51; Ingram, *Church Courts*, pp. 134–42, 200–5; Houlbrooke, *Church Courts*, pp. 56–64; Houlbrooke, *The English Family*, pp. 63–95; Wrightson, *English Society*, pp. 70–88. The ambivalence of the patriarchal role, and of parental consent, in the law and practice of courtship is further explored in Carlson, *Marriage and the English Reformation*, esp. pp. 74–7, 92–101, 108–9, 117–23, 138–40; and Carlson, 'Courtship in Tudor England', pp. 27–9. Gowing, *Domestic Dangers*, pp. 145–58, sees women as 'more constrained and supported than men' by parents and friends, whether real or 'imaginary'. Her focus on the 'gendered roles of courtship' and the way it governed the part played by parents and friends may not, however, be the most helpful way to view the more complex realities of courtship.

4 See, e.g., Elliott, 'Mobility and marriage', pt iii.

5 (6 Oct. 1505, prob. 22 Nov. 1505), PRC 17/10/43v.–4v.

6 C.C.A.L., MS. X/10/12, f. 97, *Mundell* v. *Filcott* (1564).

7 C.C.A.L., MS. X/10/12, f. 133v., *Bennet* v. *Fletcher* (1564). Such language was not only used in wills too, but in the literature of the day. In *Romeo and Juliet*, for example, Capulet tells Paris, 'I think she will *be ruled*/ In all respects by me', and in *Much Ado About Nothing*, Antonio says to Hero, 'Well, niece, I trust you will *be ruled* by your father.' See Cook, *Making a Match*, pp. 90, 101.

8 C.C.A.L., MS. X/10/6, f. 135, *Hartridge* v. *Morling* (1556).

9 C.C.A.L., MS. X/10/9, f. 7, *Robinson* v. *Baker* (1562).

10 C.C.A.L., MS. X/10/3, f. 1–v., *Rolfe* v. *Jenkyne* (1545–48).

11 C.C.A.L., MS. X/10/11, f. 231v. (1570).

12 C.C.A.L., MS. X/10/10, fos 71v. and 76, *Read* v. *Ladd* (1563).

13 C.C.A.L., MS. X/10/8, fos 205v.–6, *Gaunt* v. *Marsh* (1562).

14 C.C.A.L., MS. X/10/7, fos 168v., 170–1v., *Austen* v. *Rogers* (1567). Stress and abuse might help account for the phenomenon of youthful suicides found in sixteenth-century Kent. See Zell, 'Suicide in pre-industrial England', p. 314; M. MacDonald, *Mystical Bedlam: Madness, Anxiety and Healing in Seventeenth-Century England* (Cambridge, 1981, ppbk edn, 1983), pp. 72–111.

15 C.C.A.L., MS. X/10/7, f. 134v. (1560).

16 The importance of this institution and its demographic, social and economic consequences are well attested to. See, e.g., Macfarlane, *Marriage and Love*, pp. 11, 82–7, 267–8, 276, 334; P. Laslett, *Family Life and Illicit Love in Earlier Generations: Essays in Historical Sociology* (Cambridge, 1977), pp. 12–14, 34, 45–6, 61, 72–5, 163–5, 228; Goldberg, 'Marriage, migration, servanthood and life-cycle'. M. K. McIntosh, 'Servants and the household unit in an Elizabethan English community', *Journal of Family History* 9:1 (1984), 3–23 (pp. 19–21), draws attention to the opportunity which service provided for positive relations between servants, and between servants and their masters. Servants were perceived as belonging to their 'household-family', see N. Tadmor, 'The concept of the household-family in eighteenth-century England', *Past and Present* 151 (1996), 111–40. On the other hand, Chaytor, 'Household and kinship', pp. 47–8, considers that service may have been a bleak alternative to remaining at home for Ryton women. Abuse of authority by masters was a potential danger: S. D. Amussen, 'Punishment, discipline and power: the social meanings of violence in early modern England', *Journal of British Studies* 34 (1995), 1–34 (pp. 15–17). Rushton, 'Property, power and family networks', pp. 212–15, argues that masters might also interfere in the marriage plans of servants and apprentices, particularly those of younger servants. See also, Gowing, *Domestic Dangers*, pp. 150–1, for the role of employers in the marriages of female servants.

17 C.C.A.L., MS. X/10/7, fos 165v.–166, 206v., 208v., 209v., *Haffynden* v. *Austen* (1567).

18 C.C.A.L., MS. X/10/7, fos 257v.–9, 260, 286–7, 292, 293v.–4v., 296v.–7, 298v.–9v., 300v., 302–v. (1567–68).

19 See Sheehan, 'Formation and stability', pp. 240–3 on the abuse of solemnisation.

20 The suggestion that widows might act more independently is also made by Houlbrooke,

The English Family, pp. 211–15; and Macfarlane, *Marriage and Love*, pp. 231–7. According to Gowing, *Domestic Dangers*, p. 158, unlike women's generally receptive role in courtship, widows were more able to offer themselves to men. She does, however, recognise the more complex social and familial networks that might have interests in a remarriage: 'the kin acquired in one union acquires here a say in the next' (pp. 151–2). For widows' and women's property rights, see Macfarlane, *Origins of English Individualism*, pp. 80–4, 131–4. Chaytor argues that though remarriage was not economically necessary for widows in Ryton, women were the objects of transaction between kin, 'Household and kinship', pp. 43–4.

21 C.C.A.L., MS. X/10/8, fos 115v.–16v., 118, 123, 124–8, 141–2 (1561).

22 On the related matter of courtship procedure, Cressy, *Birth, Marriage and Death*, p. 234, sees courtship as a 'deeply patterned activity', where 'most couples passed through a recognizable series of steps'. For interesting courtship narratives derived from the literate and propertied sort, and drawn mainly from the seventeenth century, see pp. 237–52.

23 C.C.A.L., MS. X/10/7, f. 17, *Coppyn v. Richards* (1560).

24 On the simplicity of terminology, see e.g., D. Cressy, 'Kinship and kin interaction in early modern England', *Past and Present* 113 (1986), 38–69 (pp. 65–7); Macfarlane, *Origins of English Individualism*, pp. 146–7; K. Wrightson, 'Household and kinship in sixteenth-century England', *History Workshop Journal* 12 (1981), 151–8 (p. 155); Wrightson, *English Society*, p. 46; and Houlbrooke, *The English Family*, p. 40.

25 The role of masters in the marriages of their servants might also extend to their servants' relatives. The eighteenth-century shopkeeper Thomas Turner, in giving away his servant's relatives at weddings, acted as 'what is commonly known father', Tadmor, 'Concept of the household-family', p. 126, n. 47.

26 Godparents played their part in marriage arrangements, see, e.g., Cressy, *Birth, Marriage and Death*, pp. 156–60.

27 C.C.A.L., MS. X/10/13, f. 44–v. (1570).

28 C.C.A.L., MS. X/10/11, fos 183–6, 187v.–9v., *Kennet v. Dunnye* (1570). In Earls Colne between 1560 and 1660 there was no significant rate of intermarriage between families already linked by marriage or blood, and incest cases as a proportion of other cases in the Essex courts were negligible. See, A. Macfarlane, 'The regulation of marital and sexual relationships in seventeenth-century England, with special reference to the county of Essex' (M.Phil. thesis, University of London, 1968), chs 2–3; and A. Macfarlane, 'The informal social control of marriage in seventeenth-century England: some preliminary notes', in V. Fox and M. Quitt eds, *Loving, Parenting and Dying: the Family Cycle in England and America* (New York, 1980), pp. 110–21. Helmholz points out the absence of marriages involving impediments to marriage within the prohibited degrees, *Marriage Litigation*, pp. 77–87, and Houlbrooke also indicates that there were few suits for annulment of marriage contracted within prohibited degrees, *Church Courts*, pp. 74–5. It is, however, worth suggesting, as Macfarlane has done, that it may be that groups based on some other criterion had a high rate of intermarriage, 'The regulation of marital and sexual relationships', ch. 3. In any case, the concept of intermarriage depends upon the definition of kinship, and may need modification to take into consideration folk ideas of what constituted endogamy.

29 Ingram, 'Ecclesiastical justice in Wiltshire', p. 117, says that 'no definite range of kin

were conventionally accepted as having an interest' in marriage processes. See also, Ingram, 'Spousals litigation', p. 48. Rushton, 'Property, power and family networks', pp. 211–12, concludes that, despite Bossy's suggestion of organised groupings in the late medieval period, there was no observable coherent group of kin, but rather a loosely structured group. As regards the wedding, this was not attended by a specific category of persons, see Macfarlane, *Marriage and Love*, pp. 312–13. This is consistent with Lyndal Roper's findings for Augsburg that wedding ordinances supplied no consistent definition of the kin group, L. J. Roper, '"Going to church and street": weddings in Reformation Augsburg', *Past and Present* 106 (1985), 62–101 (pp. 94–5). See also, Houlbrooke, 'The making of marriage', pp. 342–3, for comparative evidence of who the witnesses were.

30 For recent work on betrothals, see, Cressy, *Birth, Marriage and Death*, pp. 267–81; Carlson, *Marriage and the English Reformation*, pp. 124–7.

31 C.C.A.L., MS. X/10/6, fos 116v.–17, *Lambard v. Harewood* (1556).

32 See, e.g., G. C. Homans, *English Villagers of the Thirteenth Century* (New York, 1970), pp. 175-6; L. Mair, *Marriage* (London, 1977), esp. ch. 7; Van Gennep, *The Rites of Passage*, esp. ch. 7; Gluckman, 'Les rites de passage'; A. R. Radcliffe-Brown, 'Introduction', in A. R. Radcliffe-Brown and C. D. Forde eds, *African Systems of Kinship and Marriage* (Oxford, 1975), pp. 43–60. Wedding rituals are also discussed e.g. in Roper, 'Going to church and street', and M. Segalen, *Love and Power in the Peasant Family: Rural France in the Nineteenth Century*, trans. S. Matthews (Paris, 1980, Oxford, 1983), pp. 11–37.

33 Sheehan, 'Formation and stability', pp. 248–9, suggests a variety of modes of publicity.

34 C.C.A.L., MS. X/10/6, f. 39–v., *Davye v. Wright* (1553–54).

35 C.C.A.L., MS. X/10/8, f. 34 (1562).

36 C.C.A.L., MS. X/10/4, f. 83v. (1549).

37 See, e.g., C.C.A.L., MS. X/10/2, fos 112v.–13, 114–v., *Lye v. Wood* (1544).

38 The probate account of the inventoried goods of Alice Oven of Chislet, for example, referred to money 'paid for bread and beare, and an ewe which was kylled and spent upon her neighbours and kynsfolk that wer at her buryall'. PRC 21/5/233–6. For christening feasts, see, e.g., Cressy, *Birth, Marriage and Death*, pp. 164–72, 201–3.

39 C.C.A.L., MS. X/10/6, f. 128–v., *Austen v. Burrett* (1556).

40 C.C.A.L., MS. X/10/6, fos 115, 116v. (1556).

41 C.C.A.L., MS. X/10/3, fos 19v., 20, 22–v., *Munday v. Parker* (1548).

42 C.C.A.L., MS. X/10/6, fos 118v.–120, 126v., 131–v., *Chinting v. Besbiche* (1556).

43 See the case of *Culpepper v. Mantle*, above, p. 48. For a discussion of concepts of honour and reputation, see Sharpe, 'Defamation and sexual slander'; J. A. Pitt-Rivers, 'Honour and social status', in J. G. Peristiany ed., *Honour and Shame: the Values of Mediterranean Society* (London, 1965), pp. 19–77; J. Davis, *People of the Mediterranean: an Essay in Comparative Social Anthropology* (London, 1977), pp. 89–101; and F. G. Bailey ed., *Gifts and Poison: the Politics of Reputation* (Oxford, 1971), pp. 1–26.

44 E.g. Poos, 'Sex, lies and the church courts', esp. pp. 585–6, 601–5.

45 C.C.A.L., MS. X/10/17, f. 27v., *Hogdekin v. Corbet* (1573).

46 C.C.A.L., MS. X/10/11, fos 161–2v., *Stamner v. Ives* (1569). The importance of reputation, interpersonal trust, and the 'moral language of people's credit and honesty', were con-

sidered integral to all kinds of marketing and economic relations too. See C. Muldrew, 'Interpreting the market: the ethics of credit and community relations in early modern England', *Social History* 18:2 (1993), 163–83; R. Tittler, 'Money-lending in the West Midlands: the activities of Joyce Jefferies, 1638–49', *Historical Research* 67 (1994), 249–63.

47 C.C.A.L., MS. X/10/11, fos 262v.–4v., *Bouche* v. *Cadman* (1569–70).

48 See also, Hindle, 'The shaming of Margaret Knowsley', esp. pp. 392–3, 407; A. Fox, 'Ballads, libels and popular ridicule in Jacobean England', *Past and Present* 145 (1994), 47–83 (pp. 74–5); Gowing, *Domestic Dangers*, pp. 125–33.

49 Macfarlane, *Origins of English Individualism*, p. 29, cites this as a basic feature of peasant society.

50 See also Sheehan, 'Choice of marriage partner', pp. 7–8, 28 and 32–3. Ingram makes the point that emphasis on the openness of solemnisation might bolster the influence of the wider, parochial community, as well as family influence. See 'Spousals litigation', pp. 55–6, and 'The reform of popular culture?' On the calling of banns, see also, Gillis, *For Better, For Worse*, pp. 52–4; Carlson, *Marriage and the English Reformation*, pp. 128–9; Cressy, *Birth, Marriage and Death*, pp. 305–9. The ceremony was important too for publicising the endowment, a matter to which collective values attached, Ingram, 'Ecclesiastical justice in Wiltshire', ch. on matrimonial causes, and Homans, *English Villagers*, pp. 170–2.

51 For wedding celebrations, see, e.g., Cressy, *Birth, Marriage and Death*, pp. 350–76; J. Boulton, '"Economy of time"? Wedding days and the working week in the past', *Local Population Studies* 43 (1989), 28–46.

52 Macfarlane, *Origins of English Individualism*, p. 5.

53 See, e.g., A. Macfarlane, S. Harrison and C. Jardine, *Reconstructing Historical Communities* (Cambridge, 1977), pp. 1–25; A. Macfarlane, 'History, anthropology and the study of communities', *Social History* 2 (1977), 631–52; C. J. Calhoun, 'History, anthropology and the study of communities: some problems in Macfarlane's proposal', *Social History* 3 (1978), 363–73; and C. J. Calhoun, 'Community: toward a variable conceptualization for comparative research', *Social History* 5 (1980), 105–29.

54 C.C.A.L., MS. X/10/6, f. 115v., *Lambard* v. *Harewood* (1556). For courtship horizons, see below, chapter 4.

55 C.C.A.L., MS. X/10/3, f. 32 (1546).

56 C.C.A.L., MS. X/10/14, f. 6v. (1572).

57 C.C.A.L., MS. X/11/1, fos 159–61v., 164–v., *Nowre* v. *Clinton and Clinton* (1587).

58 See also, Gowing, 'Gender and the language of insult', pp. 17–18. For the relationship between popular charivari customs and official customary penalties, see, M. Ingram, 'Juridical folklore in England illustrated by rough music', in C. W. Brooks and M. Lobban eds, *Communities and Courts in Britain, 1150–1900* (London, 1997), pp. 61–82. Discussions of charivari can be found in M. Ingram, 'Ridings, rough music and the "reform of popular culture" in early modern England', *Past and Present* 105 (1984), 79–113; M. Ingram, 'Ridings, rough music and mocking rhymes in early modern England', in B. Reay ed., *Popular Culture in Seventeenth-Century England*, (London, 1985) pp. 166–98; A. Fletcher, 'Men's dilemma: the future of patriarchy in England, 1560–1660', *Transactions of the Royal Historical Society* 6th ser. 4 (1994), 61–81 (pp. 77–8); E. P. Thompson, 'Rough music reconsidered', *Folklore* 103:1 (1992), 3–26.

59 C.C.A.L., MS. X/10/20, fos 191v.–5v., 245v.–68v., *Allenson* v. *Baker*, and *Edmundes* v. *Baker* (1582–83).

60 For example, a form of charivari might be used as a repressive measure to control vagrancy and suppress idleness, as was the case in sixteenth-century Sandwich. See Tronrud, 'The response to poverty', pp. 16–17.

61 Ingram, 'Ridings, rough music and mocking rhymes', *passim*; P. Croft, 'Libels, popular literacy and public opinion in early modern England', *Historical Research* 68 (1995), 266–85 (pp. 283–4); Fox, 'Ballads, libels and popular ridicule', pp. 77–81.

62 Croft, 'Libels, popular literacy and public opinion', p. 284.

63 E.g. C.C.A.L., MS. PRC 39/10/139v., *Webb* v. *Swanne* (1583).

64 C.C.A.L., MS. X/10/11, fos 123–4, 126v.–7 (1569).

65 Croft, 'Libels, popular literacy and public opinion', pp. 271–2; Fox, 'Ballads, libels and popular ridicule', p. 61.

66 C.C.A.L., MS. X/10/19, fos 1–2, 3v.–6, *Evernden* v. *Browne* (1583). See also the libel or rhyme invented by William Stedman against the wives of Smarden, and written by a jerkin-maker at his request to be 'cast abroad'. *Ibid.*, MS. X/10/19, f. 189v., *ar^{lis}* v. *William Stedman* (1584–85).

67 Part of a rhyme concerning one Abigail Parbo and reputedly made by the libel-maker William Harfleet of Sandwich, reads as follows:

> Herein do I write, as best I can Indite to my lover Abigall
> I dare saye for her parte, she loves me at the harte, she loves me veri well,
> Her comely cheare, biddes me draue nere, her bodie to embrace,
> I could behold her still, if I might have my will, she hath so sweete a face;
> Her gowne is full of lace, which make her have a grace, her
> petticote is redd, I would bestowe some monye, so as she had a
> conye, to bigg with me in bedd.

See C.C.A.L., MS. PRC 39/22, fos 169v.–70v., *Harfleete* v. *Tenche* (1599).

68 Fox, 'Ballads, libels and popular ridicule', pp. 66–7, 71–2.

69 C.C.A.L., MS. X/10/11, fos 275–80 (1570).

70 Testimonials might also be used to show that an individual was indeed fit to marry, and was neither pre-contracted nor indebted. See, e.g., C.C.A.L., MS. X/11/1, fos 3v.–4, *Keble* v. *Butler* (1585).

71 See P. E. H. Hair, 'Bridal pregnancy in rural England in earlier centuries', *Population Studies* 20 (1966), 233–43; Carlson, *Marriage and the English Reformation*, pp. 131–2. Macfarlane finds that in Essex in the late sixteenth century, 10 to 20 per cent of brides were pregnant. See *Marriage and Love*, pp. 303–6. He stresses the tolerant attitude shown to bridal pregnancy, and the need for 'sexual conversation' between partners. See also Macfarlane, 'The regulation of marital and sexual relationships', ch. 4. Ingram also concludes that bridal pregnancy did not appear to involve much shame, and that intercourse between a betrothed couple probably went largely uncondemned by the community. He is, however, anxious to point out the ambivalence in attitude towards antenuptial fornication, and an intensification of control from the late sixteenth century. See 'Ecclesiastical justice in Wiltshire', ch. on sexual offences, and 'The reform

of popular culture?' Houlbrooke, however, finds that for the diocese of Norwich, there is little evidence of cohabitation before the church ceremony. See 'The making of marriage', pp. 344–6.

72 C.C.A.L., MS. X/10/12, fos 268–70v. (1556).

73 C.C.A.L., MS. X/10/6, f. 234–v., *Selherst v. Porte* (1558–59).

74 See, e.g., C.C.A.L., MS. X/10/9, fos 21–2, *Tritton v. Saunder* (1563).

75 See, e.g., C.C.A.L., MS. X/11/1, fos 159–61v., 164–v., *Nowre v. Clinton and Clinton* (1587); *ibid.* MS. PRC 39/5/30–v., *Anderson v. Knoll*. See also above, pp. 41–2.

76 Sharpe, 'Litigation and human relations'.

77 S. D. Amussen, '"Being stirred to much unquietness": violence and domestic violence in early modern England', *Journal of Women's History* 6:2 (1994), 70–89.

78 On childbirth rituals and the collective culture of women, see A. Wilson, 'The ceremony of childbirth and its interpretation', in V. Fildes ed., *Women as Mothers in Pre-Industrial England* (London, 1990), pp. 68–107. P. Crawford's work in that collection, on 'The construction and experience of maternity in seventeenth-century England', pp. 3–38, explores the female lore of that culture and women's exchange of support and advice during motherhood. At least up till the mid-seventeenth century childbirth attendants were usually exclusively female. Childbirth could also be an occasion wherein anxieties regarding witchcraft were generated.

79 C.C.A.L., MS. X/10/12, f. 172–v., *Egglestone v. Cullembyne* (1565).

80 Cressy, *Birth, Marriage and Death*, pp. 84–7, 164–72, 201–3.

81 C.C.A.L., MS. X/10/11, fos 13v., 16–v., *Spritewell v. Howe* (1568). See also, Dixon, 'Economy and society in Dover', pp. 397–8, and for a fuller discussion of social and occupational groupings and kinship networks, pp. 376–451.

82 C.C.A.L., MS. X/10/12, fos 185v.–7v., *Culpepper v. Mantle* (1565).

83 To achieve even a little more understanding of the meaning of the terms used would require extensive record linkage and detailed focus on particular communities. Even this time-consuming procedure, however, given the high levels of population mobility in early modern England, would probably only recover, at best, partial and shallow biological kin groupings and, moreover, only those elements of kin universes contained within a restricted boundary. Such an exercise, then, may misrepresent the range and quality of kin relationships available and the metaphorical usage of kin terminology.

84 See, e.g., Tadmor, 'Concept of the household-family', esp. pp. 111–13, 131–40; M. Daunton, 'Introduction', in M. Daunton ed., *Charity, Self-Interest and Welfare in the English Past* (London, 1996), pp. 1–22 (pp. 3–4).

85 For further treatment of this question and an anthropological perspective see, O'Hara, 'Ruled by my friends', pp. 9–11. David Cressy reviews the historical literature on kinship, and provides an extensive bibliography, in Cressy, 'Kinship and kin interaction'. See also, K. Wrightson, 'Kinship in an English village: Terling, Essex, 1550–1700', in R. M. Smith ed., *Land, Kinship and Life-Cycle* (Cambridge, 1984), pp. 313–32; Wrightson and Levine, *Poverty and Piety*, pp. 82–103; Houlbrooke, *The English Family*, pp. 39–62; Wrightson, 'Household and kinship'; Wrightson, *English Society*, pp. 44–51; R. M. Smith, 'Kin and neighbours in a thirteenth-century Suffolk community',

Journal of Family History 4 (1979), 219–56; R. T. Vann, 'Wills and the family in an English town: Banbury, 1550–1800', *Journal of Family History* 4 (1979), 346–67; Laslett, 'Mean household size'.

86 See Macfarlane, *Origins of English Individualism*; A. Macfarlane, 'Modes of reproduction', *Journal of Development Studies* 14 (1978), 100–20, and 'The myth of the peasantry', *passim*.

Chapter 2

The language of tokens
and the making of marriage[1]

I n this chapter the customary significance of gifts and tokens in the making of marriage will be examined. The ecclesiastical court depositions reveal new evidence of crucial bearing on the nature of interpersonal relationships, gift exchange, symbolism and marriage practice in sixteenth-century Kent. Regardless of its legal status, it is argued that the prevalence of such a practice of gift-giving indicates its social and symbolic importance in the traditional rituals of marriage, and in the process of marriage formation. In seeking to demonstrate how a range of gifts demarcated stages of courtship and the progression of personal relations, the chapter focuses attention on the gifts and tokens as a form of articulation and communication in negotiating marriage. Exploring the nature of the gift and the circumstances of giving, it suggests that the gifts themselves, their symbolic and economic value, as well as the occasion, ceremonial and intention of giving, might determine the meaning of particular transactions. As a language for conducting and defining relationships, its versatility was, it seems, appropriate to the essential ambiguity of matrimonial negotiation. Among the deposition evidence presented here, the case of *Divers* v. *Williams* provides unusually detailed information about the ways in which gifts and tokens were used in courtship.

On 12 October 1596 Elizabeth Williams went before the consistory court of Canterbury and brought a case of 'jactitation of matrimony' against William Divers, then of Saints Cosmus and Damian at Blean. She sought to clear herself from the fame of marriage about which he had boasted.[2] In November of the following year, the same William, now resident of Canterbury, complained of her breach of promise and claimed that they were lawfully espoused and contracted in marriage. Like many other plaintiffs who went before the ecclesiastical court, he sought legal means for the enforcement of an allegedly binding marriage which had not been publicly solemnised. Early in 1598 the testimonies of various witnesses were recorded. It would appear that for at least a year and a half, and probably more, William Divers had been a suitor to Elizabeth Williams, and had proceeded so far as to have the banns of marriage published in her home parish of St Paul's, in the suburbs of Canterbury. William Walsall, clerk of St Paul's, and Mr Ralph Grove, a local gentleman, petitioned on his behalf, for Elizabeth's goodwill and that of her elderly widowed mother, Agnes. The process of entreaty was repeatedly beset by changes of mind, so much so that consent given could just as quickly be withdrawn, on the grounds that William Divers 'was not worth so much as he was reported to be'. Some means of coercion may have also been used. Although William Walsall would admit to having worked only with honest persuasions, he was alleged to have said to Elizabeth that he would 'enchaunte' her if she would not take William Divers to her husband, and that 'if he could not do yt hym self he would procure them that should do yt'. The threats to Agnes were apparently no less insidious: 'viz if you meaning the sayd Williams will not geve your consent *that* William Divers shall have your daughter Elizabethe I will be the meanes and so deale wth you *that* your mynd shall never be quiet in the day tyme and in the night you shalbe trubled and vexed wth straunge sightes and noises which you shall se and heare'.

Whether or not Elizabeth Williams and William Divers were freely, and in conscience, bound to each other cannot be resolved easily. The publication of the banns of marriage, and the common voice and fame in St Paul's that they were man and wife before God and contracted in marriage, supported such a claim. Their behaviour together likewise suggested physical intimacy. They were 'continually conversaunt', and 'always or very often kept ech other company', being seen together making a garden out of a piece of ground which Agnes Williams had granted to them. The significance of gifts and tokens, of those *dona sive donaria,* which passed between them, was a further subject of dispute. The case of *Divers* v. *Williams* was not at all unusual in that sense. What is exceptional is the survival among the cause papers of a more detailed schedule of tokens given by the plaintiff, which greatly supplements the evidence contained in the written depositions. It should be stressed that the survival of this exceptional document does not necessarily imply that the social circumstances that surrounded it were in any way unrepresentative. The detail in the schedule demonstrates that depositions would often under-estimate the range, quantity and value of gifts given and received and provide only an incomplete summary of the social context of their exchange. Agnes Williams testified that William Divers had brought many tokens to her house, but said that they were never accepted by her daughter

> in anye consideration of mariage but were there left by Divers, neyther would he carry them awaye with him at any tyme neyther take money for them as namely the russet, wood, potts, candlestick chamber pot, satten and silkelace in the scedule mentioned which with all other the tokens which Divers left at this deponents house

and remayne there for that he wold not carry them away are ready for Divers
whensoever he will call for them.

With the exception of Agnes's testimony, only one other deponent in this case
mentioned the giving of gifts and tokens at all. Michael Coote reported that he
had heard Elizabeth Williams confess to having received gold and also five
pairs of gloves from William Divers 'in tokens of love and goodwill'. That
accompanying schedule is far more informative. As well as identifying the
number, type and worth of gifts and tokens, the document also draws
attention to the circumstances of giving, revealing something about how the
exchange of those items could be represented, and showing how carefully
such objects might be enumerated by the parties involved.[3]

In primis the said william dyvers bestowed and gave to the said ElizabethWyllyams at severall tymes five payer of gloves worth xiis, one payer wherof being to little for, she said that at her day of mariadg with the said dyvers, she would bestowe them one his syster or the like in effecte	xiis
Item he further bestowed on her the said Elizabeth Wylliams two purses worth	iiiis
Item a girdle worth	iiis
Item a payer of knyves worth	iiis xd
Item she hath in her keeping, of the goods of the said william dyvers viii handcarchers a candlesticke a chamber pott, in token of the said matrimonie betwene them, which severall things are worth	xs
Item the said wyllyam dyvers further bestowed uppon her the said Elizabeth wyllyams in tooken of goodwill, or left to her keeping, a pettecoate cloath worth xiiis iiiid a sylver thimble worth iis vid, a scaffe worth xiis, & a peece of sylver being outlandyshe quoyne to the value of xiid	
Item the said wyllyam divers bestowed uppon her the said Elizabeth wyllyams a doosen & an halfe of silke poynts conditionallie to bestowe them at their marriadg, or at the lest, she tooke them & sayd she would bestowe them & distribute them at their maryadg, or promised so to do	
Item the said wyllyam dyvers in tooken of goodwill to the said Elizabeth wyllyams bestowed uppon her mother two payre of gloves, two loads of wood & an halfe, a payer of slippers, iii pounds of stirch, a dosen of temple candles, two temple potts, & a temple wyne pott	
Item he bestowed uppon the said Elizabeth wyllyams certayne satten & silke lace, which her mother tooke & sayd, daughter this I will keepe till yow two (meaning & speaking to the said wyllyam dyvers & Elizabeth wyllyams) have children together, for then yow will have more need of it, & that the said Elizabeth Wyllyams was then and there present & did approve & allowe thereof	
Item in consyderacon of the promisses the mother of the said	

59

Elizabeth wyllyams promised to give him the said wyllyam dyvers &
her said daughter a certayn peece of growne, which thereuppon they
or the one of them digged, dunged & planted, & further more the
mother of the said Elizabeth wyllyams acknowledged that she had
gyven the said peece of growne to the said willyam dyvers & her said
daughter
Item dyvers other gifts bestowed uppon the said Elizabeth wyllyams
by the said william dyvers hereafter to be specifyed to the value of   xls
Item the said Elizabeth willyams gratefullie accepted of the premisses
or sume of them as is deduced in the fowreth article aforesaid, & in
tooken thereof replyed like kyndnes unto him the said wyllyam dyvers

Courtship could prove a costly business. In this case, William Divers presented Elizabeth with an assortment of gifts and offerings on different occasions, whether they were bestowed upon her, left to her keeping, given expressly 'in tooken of goodwill', or allegedly 'in token of the said matrimonie betwene them'. The reciprocity of gift-giving existed not only between the two principal parties, but also between William Divers and his prospective mother-in-law, Agnes Williams.

It is the intention of this chapter to consider more closely the several circumstances and the variety of such objects which were given in the making of marriage. To appreciate better the significance and meaning of those gifts and their giving, we also need to adopt an anthropological perspective, and place the giving of tokens and artefacts in their proper cultural and legal context.

Often treated as an aspect of dowry and bridewealth, the subject of gift-giving is well established as an anthropological field of enquiry.[4] The pioneering work of Mauss and Van Gennep drew attention to the complex interpretation of the rite of giving and the transitional nature of gift exchange. Examining the gift and its function in primitive societies, Mauss considered it as a legal, economic and moral transaction, closely associated with such issues as honour, person and domination. A multiplicity of rights, not least of a sexual nature, pertained to the donor. In seeking to explain the making of a gift and the obligation to make a counter gift, Mauss theorised that the 'spirit' of the gift constrained the recipient to reciprocate. The power of the gift was thus embedded in concepts of magic and in the essentially constraining, obligatory force of exchange. The discussion of the role of the gift in the politics of human relations, extended by Bourdieu, explored further the dialectical import of reciprocity as a means of provocation, equivocation and communication, through strategies of style, timing and choice of occasion.[5] Later anthropological discussions have redressed Mauss's positive, idealised view of exchange as the basis for 'societal integration' by emphasising how exchange might also promote or conceal inequalities and divisions. Other contributions have sought to explain the requirement for return gifts in terms of social and psychological pressures, rather than spiritual sanctions. The role of choice, contingency and human agency, and aspects of hidden exchange, have received more recent attention, and the language of reciprocity itself has been criticised for its ambiguous usage in analytical descriptions. The continued theorising on the subject of gift-giving nevertheless highlights its focal significance in the anthropologist's approach to understanding human relationships, identity, society and gift-based economies.[6]

From a different perspective, surviving artefacts have enriched our understanding of customary marriage practices, and of the economic, social, magical and religious potential of gifts in pre-industrial and modern European society. The long tradition of gift-giving across time and region as a permanent feature of courtship is richly illustrated, with gifts also bestowed upon matchmakers, peers and wedding guests. Differences in ethnographic detail may be seen to reflect aspects of national and local culture. The production, use and distribution of traditional forms of ornament and tokens have chronological, geographical and status associations. However varied the forms might be, they nevertheless express a common rite and symbolic idiom.[7] Antiquarian enquiry, and interest in folklore and matrimonial customs, have focused on identifying the types of object, their artistic and decorative value through motifs and designs, and their functional application as utilitarian, personal, magical or otherwise. The possible influence of cottage industries and crafts has also been observed. Material is abundant for the Victorian era, not least for the fashionable Valentine cards.[8] Above all else, the ring, as a token of great antiquity, has attracted attention. Varied in type but unending in form, it is sometimes inscribed, and has long been imbued with sentimental, legal, religious and magical connotations, used from classical times in ceremonies of betrothal and marriage.[9]

Investigations into the history of sentiments and culture, and litigation studies of dioceses in late medieval and early modern England, have indicated the customary usage of gifts as an aspect of intimate behaviour in the making of marriage.[10] A particularly detailed study, although based upon a small number of depositions, exists for the diocese of Durham in the years 1560–1630.[11] For nineteenth-century rural France, the codified exchange of objects served as an apparently speechless dialogue between courting couples.[12] The custom of offering gifts was evident in the clandestine matrimonial promises made in the province of South Champagne at the end of the fifteenth century,[13] and in the rituals of marriage in sixteenth-century Augsburg.[14] That this was regarded as a characteristic sign of spousals, is best expressed in the work of the lawyer Henry Swinburne, whose contemporary treatise of spousals, although specifically applied to the diocese of York, has more general relevance as an authoritative text of legal interpretation.[15]

Having already observed some of the general problems involved in the use of litigation studies,[16] the more specific issue concerning the legal probity of gifts needs to be addressed in this chapter. It would seem that there was no absolute unanimous agreement among canonists touching the evidential status of gifts and tokens. They were probably generally regarded as a lawful form of demonstrating sentiment at spousals, and of expressing the continuance of mutual consent. Some, however, rejected them along with other 'feeble conjectures' as kissing and embracing, as insufficiently 'evident' and 'urgent', interpreting the practice of giving and receiving gifts, and of ring-wearing, as purely amorous and flirtatious.[17] In the eyes of the law, it was more commonly held that some speech was necessary in contracting spousals, since it constituted better proof of matrimony, although it was admitted that the dumb could contract with signs alone.[18]

The law allegedly regarded the giving and receiving of the ring as 'a sign above all others, and most usual in spousals and matrimonial contracts', to betoken or confirm marriage. The manner of delivery and acceptance was, however, considered crucial in distinguishing a goodwill gift or token, from a 'presumed contract' or 'earnest penny of spousals'.[19] According to the Book of Common Prayer, the ring was used as a 'subarration' in marriages celebrated in the face of the church. If speech was not used, it would appear that the solemnity of ring-giving alone might signify the mutual consent and contract of parties, where endorsed by local custom. Theoretically, it might also be used to resolve a *de futuro* contract into effective matrimony, although such a conclusion was said to be 'not very sound'.[20]

Although, in the sixteenth century, some reformers attacked the use of wedding rings in the marriage service, its association with the fasting of hands and with publicised endowment had long been established within liturgical practice.[21] The ring itself remained as a token of exchanged promises, and its symbolism continued to be recognised.[22] Its essential circularity signified the continuous flow of love, and placing the ring on the fourth finger of the left hand, where love's vein was said to run, could denote the union of the couple.[23]

If the formal position concerning gifts and tokens was somewhat confused, popular interpretation and practice added a further contradictory dimension. For the dioceses of Norwich and Winchester in the sixteenth century, it was found that couples favoured the use of other tokens besides the ring in contracting spousals, delivering them, at times, in a less than solemn manner, and demonstrating the value which they, especially the male suitors, attached to such gifts.[24] In matrimony cases disputed in north-east England, plaintiffs seeking to establish a claim alleged that tokens had been given, most commonly in circumstances where the wording of the contract was vague, and where spousals were insufficiently formal. In those cases, 'the evidence of gifts may have been useful, perhaps crucial, additional testimony'.[25] Judges in Wiltshire probably treated that kind of evidence as a means of gauging the public voice and fame.[26] The law acknowledged that such conduct might contribute to just cause for legal action, and made provision regarding the restitution of gifts and the payment of litigation costs.[27] Nevertheless, at least by the principles of law, it would seem that the testimonies of gifts and tokens constituted only 'supportive evidence',[28] and were seldom used as the sole, legitimate proof of a contract.[29] They have been described as 'a slippery form of evidence'.[30] Although 'pertinent', able to corroborate more formal contracts, and potentially capable of transforming feeble contracts into conclusive facts, the common opinion offered, is that they 'probably did not influence decisions', doing 'little to safeguard contracts', and 'rarely did *they* turn a weak contract into a strong one'.[31]

The principle concerns of this chapter are not, however, with the significance of such gifts and tokens for the legal probity of marriage, but rather with the social importance of those practices. Since we cannot presume to know the full course of litigation procedure,[32] this chapter does not, therefore, consider how legal interpretation of the tokens' evidential power worked in practice to determine the final resolution of matrimonial contract cases. Although the words of consent in the law of matrimonial contract would theoretically have been the principal subject of dispute in marriage cases, the depositions suggest that the gifts were themselves crucial foci of investigation when the validity of a marriage was debated. Whatever the canonical principles, the admission of such testimonies highlights the social relevance of those gifts and tokens even if not, strictly speaking, their legal relevance. It does not seem necessary, therefore, to treat the disputes regarding gifts and tokens as primarily legal controversies. The verdicts of such cases, where they exist, may appear to be legally critical, but they do not alter our perception of the underlying nature of social practice in marriage formation. Contemporary literature and art, folksongs, poems, ballads, posies (described as intended for rings, bracelets, handkerchiefs, gloves, scarves and similar tokens) and the iconography of love, all popularised the tradition of gift-giving, although they should not be valued uncritically as indicative of social practice.[33]

The purpose of what follows, therefore, is to explore the ways in which gifts and tokens were used to conduct and define personal and social relations. It will be suggested that the nature of those gifts and tokens, their symbolic and economic value, and the circumstances, intention and occasion of giving, might all qualify that process of definition and give meaning to the particular transaction. From the evidence of depositions, it would appear that gift-giving was a socially recognised, even psychologically binding custom in a pre-industrial society, often dependent upon non-literate forms of communication.

As well as being a personal and private exchange, it was also a public matter, morally and socially obligatory, regardless of its legal status. Attitudes to giving and receiving, to refusing or returning gifts and tokens, demonstrate the constraints imposed, the repercussions experienced and the implicit significatory force behind the practice. This social significance, it will thus be argued, was independent of the importance at law. While deposition evidence may not suggest that gift-giving was essential in terms of *legally* validating a marriage, it is the intention of this chapter to suggest that the giving of gifts and tokens was a *social* imperative which played a key role in the transacting of personal relationships within the marriage process.

Within the diocese of Canterbury, for the period 1542–1602, just over half of the 301 matrimony cases (172, or 57 per cent) drawn from towns and villages discuss the giving of gifts and tokens.[34] This giving was not limited to the structured occasion of formal betrothal before witnesses, or to the official ceremony of religious celebration, but occurred at various stages in the development of a marriage. The making of marriage should be regarded as an extended and complex process of communication, signalled with gifts from beginning to end, wherein the language of tokens embodied an ambiguous interplay of emotions and behaviour. Usually that dialogue was resolved successfully. In practice its establishment was not simply an individualised exchange of verbal consent, defined by a single event. Rather, it was a process which involved a complex series of formalities observed in varying degrees. The plighting of faith and troth and the rituals of feasting and drinking which occurred at times of formal handfastings, mirrored a whole sequence of privy promises, repeated 'rehearsals' of promises, matrimonial negotiations and conviviality which had taken place before. All of which procedures were accompanied, within their diverse circumstances, with symbols. Marriage, then, should be seen not purely as a legal act, but as a 'social drama' where rituals and symbols, gifts and tokens, played a 'dynamic and creative' role in both its making and its breaking.[35] At all levels of social intercourse and the workings of the Tudor economy, whether in the interests of patronage and stability at Court, as a means of self-protection among the aristocracy, or in the active participation in exchanges among ordinary people, the strategy of gift-giving was a vital cultural, social, economic and political practice.[36] Marriage gifts may be seen as a special case within this wider, more general context of gift-giving, and as taking place in a society which often sought to transact all kinds of relations by means of encoded gestures and symbolic objects.

It was evidently customary for the male suitor to woo with gifts, sometimes referred to in an indiscriminate way as 'divers tokens' or 'small trifles'. Simon Aunsell was said to have bemoaned the fact that 'he had spent many a peny and many tymes hathe had a hevy hart because that she [meaning Agnes Courte] wold not condiscend to marry with him'.[37] The practice of giving was predominantly, although not exclusively, a male ritual.[38] 'Pretty tokens' were generally intended for women, but women might also give in return.[39] Nevertheless, the unevenness of the exchange assigned to women the primarily passive and more obligated role of recipient.[40] Widows were found to be more forthcoming,[41] but women usually acted in response to their suitors, either in returning tokens and, by implication, terminating negotiations, or in reciprocation, reassurance and positive encouragement. In *Lambard* v. *Harewood*, Thomas Lambard suspected that the widow Joanne Harewood was 'fayning things' in order to refuse him. Discontented with her reply, he asked John Geoffrey to speak with her and reclaim all his tokens if she was not inclined to remarry. She insisted that if Thomas Lambard would come to her again he would be even more welcome than before. Upon John Geoffrey's request for a token assuring him of that welcome, she delivered a crown of gold, praying that he might come again.[42] Similarly, the new groat which George Bett carried to Henry Lyon at Challock, was sent by Margaret Cole as a token entreating him to come to her. The significance of the action was made plain. At that time, George Bett told her 'that he wold gladly goo for hym the said Henry Lyon so that he wold not dissemble with hym ... unto whom Margaret answered that she wer a very beast if she wold dissemble *with* hym'. Henry Lyon received the groat very thankfully, and desired to be recommended to her again.[43]

The use of intermediaries as messengers and as deliverers of gifts and tokens was practised frequently.[44] It will be shown that they occupied an important position in the process of matrimonial negotiation and arrangements, and in the testing of emotional response.[45] Commendations from one party to another were frequently carried by them. Gifts might import such conditional messages that the person receiving the gift 'should think so well of the giver as of the gift',[46] a phrase akin to that of some contemporary love posies.[47] While intermediaries assumed representative roles, they might also initiate proceedings by enquiry, serve to vindicate relationships, or even force the issue. As alleged in the case where Margaret Barnes (the intermediary) put a ring into Joanne Stupple's hand, she told Joanne that George More had sent it for a token, 'forsing' her to keep it until such time as she should see him again. It was said that she had 'also in lik order' delivered to Joanne a silver and gilt enamelled button the previous day. Noticeably within three days after receiving the ring, Joanne admitted that she had granted her goodwill to George More, but 'said that she could not tell wherunto she had granted her goodwill'.[48]

Gifts given or taken by force may not have been supported by law, but in practice it seems that such actions were not uncommon.[49] At times the act of giving accompanied the dialogue of marriage promises. At others, its form served as a sexual affront, with gifts stuffed into a girl's bosom, thrust into her hand or pocket, or cast at her. Edward Culling of Upper Hardres claimed that Joan Essex 'said she wold interprete her body by the grace of god as she wold forsake all other men, and submyt herself to [him] to be his wif. And because she promised this, he tooke her a pece of gould at that time valued 13s 4d upon condition that she shold be his wif, which she upon that condition willingly received.' Joan, however, accused him of unjust boasting. By her account he put the gold into her hand 'which she refused to receave and cast it agen after him on a table, and saith that he delivered to her an handkercher to wash wherin was an old grote, and a purse he gave her for a fayring, and the neckercher he thrust into her pockett which she took out and cast to him agen on the ground at Hithe [Hythe] fayer, and an old 6d he gave her also'.[50]

Defendants might plead that gifts were concealed instead of being given openly. Alice Berry, for example, deposed that Serafyn Marketman had taken away one of her gloves and had placed a gold ring and French crown inside it, which glove she received from Sibill Berry. As she was putting on the glove, she felt the hidden ring and crown in it and kept them.[51] In the case of *Longley* v. *Marchant,* Joanne Marchant said that when Longley first began his suit, 'he forced [her] to take of him a token against her will, which she refused, and said she wold not take it, but he nevertheless did put it into [her] bosom being in a paper, which whan [she] went to bed fell from her, and she toke it up, not loking into the paper what it was'.[52] Although, at one level, this seeming lack of curiosity would appear unconvincing, it may be assumed that in her eyes, the very act of revelation and making public would be considered indiscreet. The public wearing of a gift might also transform the personal and initially private nature of giving. Bennet Dunnye allegedly confessed to having worn a pair of gloves given to her by Thomas Kennet,[53] and in *Barrow* v. *Thomlyns*, the widow Thomlyns was given a gown which had formerly belonged to Walter Barrow's first wife. She altered it, made it for herself, and wore it openly.[54]

The circumstances of giving, even in the undisguised context of personal confrontation, were seldom unambiguous. The face-to-face encounter of Agnes Ramruche and William Ottringham proved critical in his relations with Katherine Grigge. The incident occurred shortly before William and Katherine were due to marry, when all three met in the town of Sandwich. Enquiring of Agnes whether or not she had heard the banns of marriage published between himself and Katherine, he added 'yt might have been yor day and yor wedd'. She replied 'it is better as it is', and he thanked God. Taking an orange out of his pocket, he said to Agnes, 'yet for thold love that hath been between you and me, I geve you this orrenge, which she toke at his hands and went away ... And herapon he cam to [Katherine] standing hard by and said to her after Agnes was goon / Com on Katherine, I had loved you well but Anne hathe myn hart.' Katherine, humiliated and perceiving his 'inconstancy and disemblacon', answered, 'yf she have yor hart I wold she had body and all'.[55] The case is rich in its implications, with an even more intriguing development.[56] It would be impossible to interpret accurately the subtleties and nuances of behaviour and sentiment, or recapture those expressions, tensions and tone, which might qualify the meaning of the gift. Nevertheless, the incident was a psychological turning point for Katherine. 'To her great greef of hert', she consequently determined never to marry him.

Attitudes expressed in the giving and receipt of gifts and tokens, on an individual level, and in the public face, affected the progress of relationships. The suitor's expectation was to elicit a response as a starting point for further negotiations and renegotiations. In *Hennikre* v. *Sellar* it was said that Edward Hennikre gave Isadore Sellar two pieces of gold which he desired her to keep, 'and than he asked hyr whye she said nothinge to the matter and she said she colde not tell what to saye. And Hennikre said than to her, you staye for your frends goodwyll do you, and she said yea that I do.' In this instance, although the token in its own right might have effect, it was acknowledged that the influence of Isadore's 'frends' could override that immediate efficacy.[57]

The practice of giving was further elaborated by the offer of gifts which were sometimes made to the relatives of an intended spouse. William Divers, as we have seen, bestowed certain goods upon the girl's mother, Agnes Williams.[58] Transacting relations between potential affines was also evident in the case of *Terrie* v. *Overie*. John Terrie received from Margaret Taylor two pieces of gold wrapped in white paper and tied with silk thread. She delivered the message that they were sent by the widow Elizabeth Overie, who commended herself to him and welcomed him to the village of Littlebourne. John received the message and tokens thankfully, reciprocating with two other pieces of gold wrapped in the same paper. He likewise commended himself to Elizabeth, and promised to be with her shortly. His father also sent Elizabeth a bowed groat for a token and his mother sent her a bowed 3*d*, each with their own commendations.[59]

Such then, were some of the contexts within which the drama of courtship and of ritual exchange were practised. Giving was more commonly a male activity, not necessarily dependent upon reciprocation in kind, but effectively seeking to advance personal and social relations, sometimes with the aid of intermediaries, other times in an open, direct or intimate form, but otherwise secretly, provocatively, even forcibly.

Deponents were not always specific about the kinds of objects which were given and received, usually referring to them as tokens, gifts, or fairings. Those terms were apparently distinctive, but seeking to understand the full range of their contemporary significance exposes their complexity and ambiguity.[60] A gift might be considered to be a 'fre gift', a gratuitous offering, perhaps a fee for services rendered, or one intended to bribe and seduce. The token, indicative of a fact, event or sentiment, had associations with particular rights and privileges. Variously interpreted as evidential, significatory, or expressive it was potentially capable of being religiously, economically and socially symbolic. Complimentary gifts, cakes and sweets sold at fairs, and presents given and bought from there, were described as fairings in contemporary parlance, but even they were subject to various interpretations. A coin by definition may not have been a fairing, yet money could have been given for the purpose of buying fairings. Nicholas King, for example, gave Elizabeth Otway '2s to buy her a fayring' at Lammas fair.[61] Bridal clothes and other wedding apparel were also bought at fairs. The basic purpose of the fair for making commercial transactions, for purchasing, distributing, and socialising, all within the context of gathered communities, gave it a special function in the negotiation of social relations.[62]

Partners in marriage cases attached different degrees of significance and commitment to particular items exchanged between them. In *Frances* v. *Marshe*, Felicity Marshe claimed that, sometime before their talk of marriage, Edward Frances gave her a kerchief for a fairing which she so accepted and not of any other intent. Another time, he offered her a piece of gold of 10 shillings to keep, which she refused. Nevertheless, he persuaded her to 'take it and kepe it till she shuld see further cause, which pece he said he wold take at any other tyme when she shuld redeliver it to hym viz. at Candlemas last past, and then also he required the kercher which he had not because she toke it for a fayring'.[63]

The different shades of commitment and the meaning underlying the transfer of objects might be either initially successfully communicated and revised, or genuinely miscalculated and misconstrued. Such ambiguity could create problems of interpretation for all those involved. Courts had to evaluate the relevance of those objects as contractual marriage symbols as opposed to normal, 'goodwill' presents in courtship or merely other types of transaction.[64] The definition of a marriage token was clearly not predicated solely on the nature of particular objects, whether in kind or value.

The cases demonstrate that the range of goods allegedly given was very wide.[65] The identification of certain objects was not always self-evident. Their nature depended partly upon their function as commemorative, decorative, sentimental or utilitarian. The orange given by William Ottringham, for example, may not have taken the form commonly assumed.[66] Knives might figure as metal trinkets especially if they were inscribed with love posies according to the fashion described in popular literature, but they could also be used as bridal accessories, or as household tools.[67]

The cases provide evidence of 403 givings of different kinds of goods. The number of occasions when gifts were given was noticeably fewer, since more than one item might be given at any one time (Table 1).[68]

Monetary gifts were the most popular type. Athough individuals gave

Table 1 Categories and numbers of gifts and tokens by decade

Categories	1542 –50	1551 –60	1561 –70	1571 –80	1581 –90	1591 –1600	1601 –02	Total	%
Money	13	27	32	37	27	21	2	159	39.5
Clothing and leather	8	24	41	28	13	15	0	129	32.0
Metal and trinkets	9	14	26	13	14	7	1	84	20.8
Written	0	0	0	2	5	6	0	13	3.2
Animals and foodstuffs	2	2	3	2	4	1	0	14	3.5
Household	1	0	1	0	1	1	0	4	1.0
Total	33	67	103	82	64	51	3	403	100.0

Note: 1543–47 is not represented.

different amounts, 10 shillings was recorded frequently (56 times). One-third of the gifts were articles of clothing, leather and textiles. These included all kinds of garments, most commonly gloves (37 times) and, to a lesser extent, a purse or handkerchief. The dominance of rings among the third most popular category of metal objects is hardly surprising, given the symbolic status normally attributed to them. The rings took various forms, and were pre-sumably considered a far more customary choice of gift than knives, mentioned with some frequency, and those other types of jewellery and trinkets which were given occasionally. If the principal items within each of these three categories are compared, the giving of a ring (61 times) would seem to have been most common.

Gifts of animals and food, household items, and the exchange of letters and books, were unusual, but they illustrate the flexibility in the nature of the gift and the custom of giving. Their peculiarity makes it apparently more difficult to determine their significance as gifts bestowed 'in the way or for token of any marriage'. Thomasine Essex straightforwardly denied that the money and bullocks which she received from Thomas Short were taken in that respect. Nevertheless, the importance of consumption and of food exchange, and the element of ceremonial feasting and '[making] merry', should not be under-estimated.[69] Certain foods might also have been valued for their relative rarity, or particular properties.[70] While the more unorthodox gifts may reflect eccentric individual choice rather than, for example, the local economy, they were still regarded as potentially capable of betokening marriage. In *Singer* v. *Smith,* William Singer asked Robert Hilles to take a token, being a raisin of ginger and a nutmeg, to Margaret Smith. It would seem that, at that stage, their relationship was at 'a poynte'. Taking a groat in return, Margaret Smith 'bowed' it and gave it to Hilles to convey on her behalf.[71]

The assortment of gifts and tokens reveals that the nature of the gift was by no means strictly standardised. What was given was probably related to diverse, often intangible, factors including personal preference and practical considerations, status, wealth, occupation and religion. Perhaps not surprisingly, the godly merchant John Hayne gave among his other courtship gifts a puritan tract, a bible and two sermon books.[72] In another context of gift-giving, Elizabeth I received New Year gifts from professionals and craft guildsmen which were tokens of their occupations. Handworked embroideries were also tied to women's status as handmaids.[73] The combination of various influences makes it impossible to draw any rigid distinctions between types of gift and social groups. The upper and more humble classes shared in the emphasis upon customary rituals.[74] Even gifts exchanged among the upper ranks of society might derive symbolic origins from folklore. Again and conversely, the less literate might employ professionals to write love letters. It is, however, likely that the practice of sending such letters was associated more with higher status, literacy and education, perhaps with marriages formed over distance, or protracted due to the absence of either party. Some of the cases which mention such letters were located near the towns of Canterbury, Dover and Sandwich, and the market centres of Faversham and Wye. Others appear to have involved members of the rural elite. The letters are an interesting aspect of pressure applied to particular social groups. Upon receiving a letter from John Mantle, sent from London, Parnell Mereweath declared, 'lettres and more troble yet'.[75] Letters also had the function of making assignations and meetings, furthering or clarifying relationships. By law, they were admitted as a form of proof,[76] and as a means of contracting spousals if they contained words deemed appropriate for matrimony, were delivered by special messenger and were accepted willingly by the other party. It was necessary for the person, upon receipt of the letter, to express mutual consent to the message imported, and for witnesses to prove that the letter was read and understood.[77] The defendant John Beeching of Sandwich admitted that the letters which Alice Pynnocke had in her custody and did 'well accept' were written in his own hand, but he also claimed that there was something contained in the letter which was not true, even though he had written it, viz. the phrase: 'To reveale the love the whiche eche to other by the most sacred and suer knot of contraction ys now associated'. He furthermore alleged that he had merely lent her a prayer book.[78] The testimony of letters might also allude to a language of goodwill. Model love letters were apparently widespread from the sixteenth century,[79] but these cases provide no evidence to suggest that there were standard written forms of proposal or courtship. The extent to which letters might represent a more formal dialogue of love and marriage remains unclear. While it is questionable whether or not letters should be regarded as tokens, they were still an aspect of exchange concerned with the same matters which tokens were intended to symbolise.[80] Indeed it is possible to consider the letter form when fully developed as replacing the need for ritual gift exchanges and symbolic modes of communication. Popular literature suggests that love posies were to be found in letters as well as objects.[81] In Renaissance Europe it was seemingly customary for letters and notes embodying words of love to be worn or kept close to the heart, and to be depicted as associated with love.[82] By the eighteenth century, what were described as love letters in Austria and West Germany may, however, have taken a different form.[83] In sixteenth-century France, the growth in the dedicating of books to friends and family, and the less formal giving of books within personal relationships, reveal that the printed book could play its part in the general exchanges of gifts, compliments and obligation. In a dedication to Pieter Gillis in 1514, Erasmus referred to the 'many jewels in one small book'. Such gifts represented 'presents for the mind and keepsake of a literary description ... tokens of this literary kind'.[84] The Kent depositions show only a few individuals negotiating in the form of letters, or pious books, but the tendency to do so appears to have increased by the end of the sixteenth century, despite the corresponding decline in the number of matrimony cases studied.[85]

The choice of household goods as gifts was even less characteristic. Some time after the plighting of faith and troth, James Philpot gave two chests to Elizabeth Savye, among other things, in token of marriage.[86] In another case, on the very day that the parties joined hands, promised themselves to each other, embraced and drank, the widow Joan Grey delivered to Peter Smyth, upon agreement of the contract, a flockbed and bedding which he carried away to his lodgings.[87] Such goods were, however, rarely bestowed in preference to other types of gift. They were probably more closely associated with the dowry itself, and the goods brought by the bride in the setting up of the household, than with symbolic exchange in courtship.[88]

The unequal distribution of all types of gift, considered together across the period shown in Table 1, directly reflects the number of matrimony cases analysed for particular decades. The highest total of gifts and tokens recorded in the 1560s corresponds with the maximum number of cases. The reverse is true for the 1540s, partly due to the fact that the years 1543–47, as well as 1540–41, are not represented. Comparing the three main categories of gifts as percentages of the total number recorded within each decade, Table 2 confirms, with the exception of the 1560s, the sustained dominance of

Table 2 Percentage of gifts and tokens by category by decade, 1542–1600

	1542–50 %	1551–60 %	1561–70 %	1571–80 %	1581–90 %	1591–1600 %
Money	39.4	40.3	31.1	45.1	42.2	41.2
Clothing	24.2	35.8	39.8	34.1	20.3	29.4
Metal	27.3	20.9	25.2	15.9	21.9	13.7
No. of cases mentioning gifts	16	34	44	35	18	24

monetary gifts over the entire period. It also reveals the fluctuations in gifts of clothing and metal.

Ascertaining their economic values over time was seldom possible where non-monetary gifts were concerned. Occasionally the value of various goods, particularly garments, was recorded, although sometimes only the total cost of different items of apparel was stated.[89] As regards the value of monetary gifts, which was usually specified, the amount given ranged widely from pennies and groats at the lowest end of the scale, to the considerable sum which the widow Elizabeth Godfrey offered John Smyth. Pouring out a bag of gold containing approximately 100 marks, she required him to take it, or as much of it as he would.[90]

It has been said that the giving and acceptance of a gift was more important than the value, although in some societies the value would indicate the seriousness of intention.[91] To a certain extent, the importance of economic value was evidently a matter of context, dependent partly perhaps upon the wealth and status of the parties, and the particular occasion. It was often gold, rather than silver, which was given, most typically (as previously shown), worth 10 shillings. Where more than one coin was given at any one time, the analysis relied upon the combined face value, or stated value, of the gift, since any kind of estimation was complicated by monetary factors and foreign currencies. Joanne Marchant openly professed her own ignorance in identifying particular coins. She deposed that at the time she contracted matrimony with Philip Joyce, he gave her a piece of gold, 'but wither it wer an angel or a royall she remembreth not saying she is not wel skyled in gold, and before that tyme, she received of him an angell also gladly'.[92]

The changing distribution in the value of monetary gifts is shown in Table 3. It suggests an increase in money gifts valued at over 10 shillings, perhaps

Table 3 Percentage value (in shillings) of monetary gifts and tokens by decade, 1542–1600

Value in shillings	1542–50 %	1551–60 %	1561–70 %	1571–80 %	1581–90 %	1591–1600 %
0–1	25	21	18	28	13	13
1–5	17	13	5	6	26	19
5–10	25	25	9	9	13	13
10+	33	42	68	56	48	56
No. of occasions when monetary value was stated	12	24	22	32	23	16

indicating some attempt to keep pace with monetary inflation. Gifts valued at less than a shilling continued to be given even at the end of the sixteenth century. Their continuing use in this inflationary period might indicate their increasingly symbolic nature.

There is some evidence, therefore, of sensitivity in the process of marriage, even at the level of symbolic representation through the giving of gifts and tokens, to economic change. Arguably, in some cases, inflation increased the self-consciousness of gift-giving and, by implication, of matrimonial negotiation. The concept of a 'better gift' is really only meaningful in context, but the case of *Launsfeld* v. *Austen*[93] illustrates how individuals might reconsider the nature and value of their gifts. Robert Launsfeld sought the goodwill of Anne Austen's parents. When Anne refused him, he said to her, 'yf yow cannot so doo let me have such things as yow have of mine and god spede yow well'. Followed closely by her mother and her two sisters, she went to fetch the handkerchief or napkin which he had given her. Her mother, meanwhile, counselled her to have him, for he was an honest man, saying further, 'thou mayest well have a rytcher but never a more gentler fellow'. Returning into the kitchen, she told her husband that Anne could, after all, find it in her heart to keep the handkerchief for longer. He warned that marriage was not for a day or two but for ever, and bade her to advise Anne well. Hearing what was said, Robert Launsfeld added that 'yf she could keep totche, she should have a better gift'. Taking a piece of gold of 10 shillings from his purse, he took Anne about the neck and kissed her, saying that he gave her that piece of gold in the way of marriage, which 'she gentilly receyved *without* any aunswer'.

The versatility in the nature of the gift indicates that the gift or token alone was not the only vehicle of meaning. Interpretation was complex. It was coloured by the timing and ceremonial of giving, the intention and understanding of both parties.Whether or not strong feelings were believed to have had exceptional powers,[94] the binding force of the gift might be affected by the intention of the donor. It has been said that 'a token required an agreement that a gift at a particular point would signify part of a binding marriage contract'. The 'context of the careful establishment of a contract', was, therefore, crucial in the translation of gifts into tokens.[95] Not only the gift then was to be considered. The *occasions* or stages in the marriage transaction might determine its significance. This, in turn, could be modified by the nature of the short-term *strategy* employed by the giver or the receiver. Just as marriage itself was a complex transaction with a multiplicity of economic, social and political implications, so the giving of gifts and tokens reflected that complexity. As the marriage progressed along a line from courtship to church wedding, passing through various more or less clearly defined stages, so gifts and tokens marked that progression. They served to confirm, accelerate, or terminate the developing relationship. In providing a language to express the actual or desired condition of negotiations, they also indicated to family, kin and community, that important stages in the economic, social and political transaction had been reached. As well as being expressive, they might also be constraining, acting progressively to limit the freedom of action of the partners. The language of gifts and tokens was, however, not a simple, direct, symbolic language. It was capable of some subtlety, existing alongside a language of gestures, since even the manner in which giving and receiving was done might alter the significance of the gift, and might be further clarified by some accompanying speech. Such a language possessed a highly versatile symbolism, whose versatility and flexibility may arguably be seen to be ideally suited to the essential ambiguity of the negotiations.

In the case *Packenam* v. *Johnson alias Gybs,* Anne Johnson alias Gybs confessed to having made a conditional contract with Arthur Packenam. She also admitted to receiving a purse and a pair of gloves from him, giving him a handkerchief in return. She maintained, however, that 'all was given and receaved before the words aforesaid and therefore not in the way of marriage'.[96] Such statements implicitly recognise that gift-giving articulated phases in the development of marriage, weighted appropriately with different emotional connotations, and signifying different thresholds of intimacy and obligation. Disputes could arise where the parties genuinely disagreed in their perception of how far the matrimonial communications had progressed. Alternatively, their retrospective redefinition of events, and the way they represented the exchanges in court, provided scope for manipulative play as well as uncertainty by donor and recipient alike. Attempting to identify the timing and stages reached in the establishment of a marriage is evidently problematic, not least because of the wide range of formality and expression in the occasion of betrothal. Nevertheless, it is argued here that there was an underlying procedural pattern of stages in courtship, however vague or loosely interpreted. [97]

In this chapter, the *occasion* within which gifts and tokens were given is defined as the socially identified structure which progresses from a stage of early courtship, to one of pre-betrothal communications of love and marriage, through to a stage of more formal betrothal, and finally to a post-contractual period. The progression towards the church wedding (performed before the public congregation and also accompanied by tokens and symbols), is regarded as a development through a number of stages which often shade imperceptibly into one another. What the giving of gifts and tokens may be seen to do, is conduct the parties through these vulnerable times. All the occasions might be initiated or confirmed by the giving of objects. Complimentary 'fre gifts', and 'fayrings', and the making of certain kinds of exchanges such as loans and reparations would usually suggest relationships located in the preliminary stage of generalised sympathy. Ralph Ryeley's suit for marriage, on the other hand, had allegedly progressed further. He and Jone Pitcher were asked by her brother John to repeat the contract which they had made. Seeing the gold angel which Ralph had formerly delivered to her, John said to his sister, 'let us all see you deliver it'. She consequently delivered it back, they promised themselves to each other and kissed, and Ralph gave her the coin once again.[98] Clearly, the token had passed between them on a previous occasion. Although early promises of marriage are not always easily distinguishable from the stage of formal betrothal, the contractual nature involved in the giving of the token was, at times, made explicit. Upon the conclusion of the contract, John Wanderton gave Agnes Wyld a ring, saying, 'take this as a token that you have confessed and I the like to you, you to be my wife and I to be yor husband if god permytt us life. She receaved it thankfully. They kissed eache the other and drank each to the other.' Wanderton then asked those present to bear witness.[99] In a similar fashion, at the making of a contract between John Atkinson and Helen Wilbore, he gave her 'apon this promise or contract a pece of gold, for shutting up of the bargayn as he said', which was given 'in token of the contract'.[100] Deponents testified also to gifts being given after the establishment of a contract, but did not necessarily indicate the interval. John Alderstone, for example, saw Nicholas Fookes give a service book, certain articles of clothing and other things to Mary Lowes. These were given a 'good space after' the occasion when they had contracted themselves and acknowledged that contract made between them.[101]

While the meaning of a gift or token can be identified in some measure by reference to the occasion, it can also be interpreted in a variety of ways according to the nature of the short-term *strategy* employed by the parties. It is clear from the matrimony cases that gift-giving was important at all kinds of levels. Although at one level it may have been seen and claimed to be non-matrimonial, the circumstances of the exchange could be exploited or transformed and its significance retrospectively enhanced or diminished. The cases reveal that the act of giving was a crucial rite of marriage, enacted at various stages. It is argued here that its meaning would progressively have become more clearly defined, and the sexual–matrimonial obligation increasingly heightened. As the matrimonial context became more carefully established, and more structured by occasion, the ambiguity was likely to decrease, and the problematic notion of a 'fre gift' less possible to sustain. Defendants might, of course, insist that a contract had been involuntarily entered into, and that the gift subsequently received remained purely a 'mere gift', and not binding in conscience. Hence, Alice Cotton admitted that 'she had a pay*er* of hose of Thomas Baxter worth 12*d* and a pay*er* of shoes worth 10*d* being pumpes, which she receaved aft*er* the pretenced contract was made but not in waie of marriage, but of mere gifte'.[102]

In seeking to examine the variety of circumstances in which gift-giving occurred, all the possible alternatives to a matrimonial strategy were considered, whether stated, or implied. The analysis which follows below, therefore, explores the range of alleged intention and of plausible symbolic strategies. Even in cases where the intention was undeclared, or where conflicting claims do not survive, it was still possible to interpret the meaning of unspoken actions such as the putting of a ring on a finger, or the intimate exchange of gifts. Similarly, the plausibility of individual, undisputed statements could still be considered. Some parties provided reasons for bestowing or receiving gifts which were presumably not intended to be matrimonial. In *Badcock* v. *Saunders*, William Saunders deposed that 'he gave her [Jane Badcock] a pair of gloves and some other small trifles apon good will to her as he had to all others'.[103] Another defendant, Juliane Marden, maintained that the silver ring which one Tusnothe sent to her at New Year time, was sent simply as a New Year gift.[104] A distinction also needs to be made between those strategies which were designed to promote the development of a relationship towards a *specific* occasion, and those which were tied to a specific occasion (that is, strategies which were propositional, promising, contractual, nuptial, implicitly matrimonial, sexual–matrimonial, or involving the use of intermediaries). Other strategies, when accompanied by certain words and ceremonial, might also take on the character of having a specific occasional purpose, but they might also occur at *all* occasions and stages, for the promotion, development, maintenance and termination of a relationship.

Beginning with an exploration of some of the strategies, the giving of gifts and tokens in the case of *Marche* v. *Cobbe* provides a vivid illustration of the suitor's methods and intentions. Agnes Cobbe reported how Henry Marche came to see her in the parish of Saltwood. Calling her to the door, he put into her hand an old gold royal which she kept until he came again with his three 'frind*es*'. She delivered back the piece of gold, which he did 'throwe downe in thentrye'. An old woman who was present picked it up and brought it to her again. About a fortnight later, at a time when he was 'very desyerouse and much comoned *with* hir to have hir to consent to marry', he forced her to take two old royals of old gold. A fortnight after, he came to her again, and she offered him his said three pieces of gold and 'told him that she wold not have him nor anie of his gold'.[105]

The case suggests a structured pattern to Henry Marche's courtship in his attempts to promote and develop his suit. His frustration at the time of his accompanied visit and the act of challenge is apparent. Actively soliciting for marriage, he sought to force the issue. The proposition he made is rejected and the return of the coins conveys Agnes's answer that the relationship between them should be ended.

The immediate refusal to accept an offer of gifts, or the subsequent return of gifts, whether considered or provoked, are features commonly shared with several other cases.[106] Clearly, the decision may be made due to various pressures, returned simply upon further reflection, or in order to break off from one another. Alice Fryer had received an angel noble sent to her from Richard Rolf by goodman Weston. She claimed that when they 'had further *communication* of mariage and there brake of because [she] cold not as she saith fynd in her hart to love hym', she gave the angel back to him, saying 'that she was not mynded to have hym'.[107] It was also reported that sundry tokens had passed between Helen Throwley and Thomas Mayhewe, such as sixpenny pieces, a little silver crucifix and a 'jeomey of silver', and that 'apon some falling out between them, the tokens of each were restored'.[108]

The cases illustrate the implicit conditionality often attached to gifts and tokens, and the obligation to return the gifts of undesirable or unsuitable partners. It was said that Jane Bedford was required, under a citation, to take an oath that she was clear from Oliver Symons, for 'the discharge of their conscience'. Her father, Simon Gold of Sittingbourne, answered, 'she shall not appear, for it is a naughty corte', but he was told that her appearance before the spiritual judge was mandatory, she having certain tokens of Oliver's, namely 'a bracelet, a gold ring and other things which she must restore'.[109] Obligation and the return of the gift are here tied intimately to matters of conscience. The public nature of the request dramatises the way in which the token was bound up with aspects of common fame and reputation.[110] Returning gifts may have been the most honourable and guarded policy, but the question of how long they might be kept before being returned was presumably of significance, too, since the timing of the action might effectively transform its apparently reversible nature.[111]

The strategic use of gifts in breaking relations is further suggested, albeit under different circumstances, in Marcia Mace's deposition.[112] The day after Valentine fair, Joan Swift paid Marcia fourpence in order to bring Thomas Wood to Faversham. When he came, they were 'eache frendlie and mutuallie conferring'. After his departure, Joan Swift said that she had a sow and pigs 'which she wold give to [him] condiconallie that he wold forsake her. This deponent saying to her that she was light of love to sell hym awaie so. Swift saying agen that she might have a better then he.' The case is distinctly different from those where gifts which had been received were offered back or demanded back, since there is nothing to indicate that the livestock originally belonged to Thomas Wood. Nevertheless, Joan's conditional offer was apparently intended to compensate for her change of mind. Perhaps this was due to pressure of circumstances (since they were allegedly unable to secure the goodwill of friends), or to the desire for 'worldly gayne' with some other suitor. What may have been perceived as a bribe, may have been experienced by her as an attempt to repair her 'conscience'.

Some gifts were ostensibly given unconditionally, or were otherwise bestowed for purposes of remembrance, goodwill, or reciprocation, serving to maintain a relationship and confirm positive sentiments. The short-term strategy of reassurance was employed at all stages in matrimonial development. As a conciliatory device, gift-giving regulated other aspects of social, political, familial and marital relations. In a case of divorce or separation instigated by Mary Gawnte alias Tresse of Canterbury against her husband, Walter, the sending of a token was interpreted as just such a gesture of reconciliation.[113] Several witnesses deposed that the husband Walter Tresse was reputed to be a violent, incontinent, 'very lewd malicious frayle quarellinge and inconstant fellowe even a mad man in conditions', while his wife was taken to be 'honest and chaste', one who 'did behave herselfe lovingely toward him as a woman ought to doo unto her husband'. She was seen by some to be 'soe beaten about the face', and it was believed that Walter had wounded her with a dagger, and poisoned her. Their neighbour, Jane Newton, heard him say many times since he got out of prison 'that he would cut his wives throt and that he would slyt her nose and marke her for a whore and when he was toward any trouble he would comonly say that he would be avendged uppon his wifes blood', threatening 'that he would kill his said wife and that he would not be contented with her life alone without the losse and damnation of her soul'. Jane's husband Thomas disclosed similar threats, and was told by Mary Tresse 'that she hath bene afrayd at night when she hath gone to bed that she would not live untill morning for she hath said that he ... hath hanged a sword by his bedside which she hath feared he would have killed her withall'. The marriage had evidently deteriorated dramatically since the period of Walter's imprisonment in Canterbury castle. At the time of his incarceration, it was reported that he sent Mary 'a portigue for a token' (a gold coin from Portugal), with protestations of 'great kindnes unto her', 'very earnestly requesting' her to go to him. As a conciliatory strategy, the sending of the token served its function. Mary was finally persuaded to go only, it seems, to find herself verbally and physically abused. Walter Tresse, moreover, was reputed to have seduced the wife of Furner, the keeper of the castle. On one occasion, after showing Furner's wife's wedding ring to Thomas Newton, he declared that Thomas 'had spoiled his sporte in coming to him at that time'. Several other times Walter praised her for being 'a good lustye wench'. In these circumstances the wedding ring symbolised Walter's control over Furner's wife, as he boasted his intention to seduce and flaunted his sexual prowess.

While it is unnecessary to illustrate each of the strategies individually, what is more important is the general impression of the range of options and motives, and the limits of plausibility. The complexity of interpretation meant that other kinds of social and economic relations could be transformed and exploited within a matrimonial context. Acceptance of a gift, in the widest possible sense, might place a constraint on the person receiving it, and create a relationship of indebtedness whether of a moral, emotional, or economic kind. Although the development of matrimony would entail an increasing sense of obligation, its precise nature could be qualified constantly. The aforementioned case of *Ottringham* v. *Grigge* (pp. 66–7) may be seen to demonstrate, albeit in an exaggerated way, the possible coexistence of different degrees of obligation. The form of coercion shown here must surely be accounted an extraordinary one. Katherine Grigge's deposition, which is the only surviving evidence, describes exceptional circumstances, and cannot easily be generalised to infer how economic relations underlay others. Nevertheless it does illustrate the ambiguity in the interpretation of the gift whether as a monetary transaction, purchase, loan, pledge or bribe. It also suggests the potential coercive consequences of such a transaction, dependent upon timing, manner and intention. Katherine, aggrieved at William Ottringham's inconstancy at the giving of an orange to another maid, 'shaked hym of', but he continued to bestow gifts on her. Later on he found the means to have her arrested and placed under the custody of the keeper of Westgate in Canterbury, presumably threatening a charge of debt. Katherine alleged that it was for a flemish angel which he would have given to her, but which she had refused to take. He had said that if she would not have it, that then her father should. Upon delivering it to her, she in turn delivered it to her father. While William was with her, he said that

> she shuld lye till she did rott enforceng her to make promise of marriage unto hym and compelling her to swere ... that she shuld ne*ver* marry ne*ver* with none but hym. And [she] fearing and doubting her imprisonment ther and thinconvenience that

Table 4 Kinds of gifts and tokens given on specific occasions, 1542–1602

Occasion	Money	Clothing	Metal	Written	Animals	Household
Stage 1: Early	9	19	6	1	1	1
Stage 1/2	53	37	36	5	5	3
Stage 2: Pre-betrothal	45	28	26	4	4	0
Stage 2/3	19	4	7	0	1	1
Stage 3: Betrothal	18	0	1	0	0	0
Stage 3/4	1	0	0	0	0	0
Stage 4: Post-betrothal	6	17	9	1	0	0

might follow therof and saying that she wold put her will to godds will and his and that she shuld not be the first that shuld be cast away, she contracted herself to him.[114]

The conclusion to be drawn from the cases cited above would seem to be that the meaning of the gift, and its significance, must be located in the circumstances of giving, in the intention, whether stated or implied, and in the measures taken. Two complementary sets of analyses were carried out, to consider therefore the *occasion* and *strategy* within each case where gifts and tokens were mentioned (Tables 4 and 5). Some degree of clustering was shown in the results. Gifts of clothing and leather were dominant in the preliminary stages, associated with strategies of early courting and friendship. They were also prominent at the end, when wedding preparations were being made, and the relationship had moved beyond that of promise and betrothal. More significant were those stages immediately prior to, and focused on, betrothal, where the element of contract is evident. With some exceptions which usually involved the giving of rings, it was customary, at least within the diocese of Canterbury, to give money. The tolerance and flexibility in the ritual would appear to be least marked at such times. It was as if the progression through the stages of marriage was marked by a movement from personal gifts to financial arrangement, with the money token imitating the economic aspect, and resembling the token payments and exchanges of business transactions.[115] However, within that critical threshold midway between social and personal familiarity, and actual promises of marriage, all kinds of exchanges were made, with various gifts and tokens either bestowed directly, or sent from one party to another. Perhaps the most interesting conclusion to be drawn is the very ambiguity of the negotiation. Individual items were never

Table 5 Kinds of gifts and tokens given according to specific strategies

Strategy	Money	Clothing	Metal	Written	Animals	Household
Complimentary, goodwill, friendship	11	20	9	1	0	0
Personal keepsake/ to remember	6	2	3	0	0	0
Borrow/lend/to buy	4	1	0	1	0	1
Courtship	16	22	14	1	0	3
Proxy	26	13	17	3	4	0
Implied matrimony	35	20	26	3	1	3
Sexual/matrimony	6	2	3	1	0	0
Sexual	3	1	2	0	0	0
Goodwill to marriage	9	7	2	1	0	0
Proposition to marriage	4	1	0	0	0	0
Promise of marriage	27	8	11	0	2	0
Matrimony/contractual	21	1	4	0	0	0
Preparing wedding	0	10	5	0	0	1
Post-contract	6	12	7	1	2	1
End/forsake	0	2	1	1	1	0
Without condition	0	1	1	0	0	0
Other	1	2	2	0	1	0

Note: The number of instances has been restricted to those where identification of motive was possible.

exclusively concerned with any specific occasion or strategy. Instead they were disposed throughout all stages in the development of marriage, and the entire range of strategies employed.

It would also seem to be the case that the manner of giving and receiving further elaborated the complexity. Honest or surreptitious conduct, the use of intermediaries, the behaviour of the giver and the emotional response of the person receiving the gift, even a simple blush, might alter the significance. There are several cases of gifts which were allegedly snatched, 'plucked', deliberately left behind, or taken under pressure from family and kin. Lucy

Newenden alias Terenden deposed that, when Michael Small was at her house in Smarden, the gentleman from London who accompanied him:

> By force tooke [her] weddying rynge of gold worth 24 shillings or thereabouts from her fynger, sayenge he wold see the posy, and when he had it he gave it to Mychaell Small, and Small kept that rynge, and thereupon the gentleman tooke of two small rynges from Mychaell Smalls fyngers and cast them uppon the table, the one with a white stone in it worth 8 shillings and not above, and the other a litle hope rynge of gold worth 2 shillings and not above which said two rings for that Mychaell Small wold not let her have her own ring again, she took from the table sayeng she wold keep them until she had her owne ringes to quyt the said Mychaell Small taking away of her ringe, and not in token of any mariage. And as for the other things mentioned in the schedule, she saith that Mychaell Small left them in her house whether she wold or no.[116]

The ceremonial of giving and the form of words which might accompany such acts, could elucidate the meaning of particular transactions. Certain phrases were repeatedly used: in token of contract, or marriage, in sign of matrimony, by way of marriage, in token of goodwill for marriage, in consideration of marriage, upon that promise, in token of goodwill, by freegift, for a 'fayring', freely, or for 'the love that hath been between you and me'. In the unusual case of *Young* v. *Woolcomber,* the handing over of Michael Woolcomber's 13-year-old daughter to Alice Young was done with a kind of conceit which echoed the language of token giving. About Maytide, Alice and her mother Magdalene of Northgate, Canterbury, were among those invited to dinner at Michael Woolcomber's home in Whitstable. It was said that he bade Alice's guests welcome, and drank to her, calling her the goodwife of the house, and Magdalene 'mother'. Alice was perhaps cautious in her initial reply, saying, 'No not soe to hastie fire will spill the malte.' Later, after lodging there, they gave each other their hands, their faith and troth, and in the presence of the witnesses, Michael delivered his daughter to her using the words, 'here I deliver you my childe as francke and free as god gave her to me'.[117]

Other forms of conduct were capable of altering the meaning of the gift. A treatise published early in the eighteenth century maintained that if a man had a kiss from his betrothed, he could recover at most half of his gifts to her, but 'the female is more favored, for whatsoever she gave, were there kissing or no kissing in the case, she may demand and have all again'.[118] Swinburne, however, established that the rules concerning kissing and the recovery of gifts applied only to Italians and Spaniards who regarded kissing as tantamount to loss of virginity. In England, as in France, civil law apparently took no account of kissing.[119] Whatever its legal status, however, such conduct could be interpreted in the eyes of the participants as some kind of pledge.

While it has been argued that occasion, strategy, and the manner of giving and receiving, might determine or modify the significance of the gift and token, they would seem nonetheless to have been capable of possessing an individual symbolic dimension. Gifts could have recognised symbolic value, but their significance could be redefined within particular contexts to take on specific meanings, and the form of symbols themselves was also capable of adaptation. The problem is that of trying to ascertain the degree of self-consciousness and symbolic awareness which sixteenth-century people displayed, and the extent to which particular gifts were chosen to suit the event, the circumstances and personality of those involved. It is more than possible that certain superstitions surrounded such gifts and their properties. Belief in the efficacy and mechanistic nature of magic, and the role of village wizards and pedlars who distributed love magic and other popular products, may have been more frequent than the recoverable evidence suggests.[120] The quasi-magical dimension of gift-giving should not be ignored. Arguably, the giving of objects might serve to symbolise and effect stages in marriage instead of merely marking its progression. The potential existed for gifts and tokens to take on the character of charms.[121] Superstitions particularly surrounded the ring. Its connotations of pledge, and the seeming constraint imposed by its circularity, gave it a powerful symbolic content.[122] More specifically, the possible symbolism of the type of gemstone, of gimmal rings symbolically shared, and of posy rings, might enhance their significance.[123] In token of marriage, Mary Porredge of Ospringe sent John Colyer 'a weddinge ring with this poysy in yt viz yow have my harte till deathe departe'.[124] The sentimental and superstitious quality of such inscriptions suggests that posy rings were usually intended to be treasured and worn, whether as a pledge, or as a token of remembrance, as in the following messages: 'I am a love token: do not give me away', 'A gadge to love, not to remove', and 'Weare this for a remembrance'.[125] Others might have been bestowed after death. Evidence from wills indicates that some wedding rings were bequeathed by women to their daughters or other relatives. The widow Johane Alarde of Wye, for example, left her 'hoop of gold' which was her wedding ring to her sister.[126]

Inscriptions, love motifs, symbolic designs and imagery could identify the meaning of the gift, so that even utilitarian objects possessed a symbolic repertoire.[127] In Europe, engraving initials on a coin, sticking a coin on to a ring, or decorating caskets, bonnet boxes, money boxes and bags with traditional motifs,[128] were ways of translating the gift from its practical role to an amatory level. The personal crafting of gifts was practised in women's handworked embroidery. Needleworked gifts carried with them the potential for women's self-expression and may be seen to possess a 'particular intimacy, efficacy and authority'. Evidence of elaborate handmade gifts given and received by Elizabeth I reveals one of the means by which women actively participated in cultural production and symbolic exchanges.[129] How exten-sively handmade gifts featured among the courtship exchanges of ordinary people is uncertain. In the Kent depositions, one Joan Parker admitted that William Monday 'delivered her tenne pens to by napkins wherwith she bought him two napkins and market them and delivered them to him'.[130] She claimed it was 'not in tokyn or favour of any matrimonie', but her action would presumably have been interpreted as indicative of intimacy. In another case it was deposed that the letter which was sent by Thomasyn Lee of Canterbury to Thomas Sething at Sandwich, contained within it 'a litill handkercher wrought with black works, and he sent to hir agayn a silk lace or point with a true love knot'.[131] Highly personalised gifts were obvious symbols of affection and promise. They served to forge a signifying link between the giver and the gift for the purpose of effecting a particular relationship with the recipient.[132]

Expressions of intimacy and sexuality could also be found in particular items of clothing such as the garters and hose, with their associative patterns and colours,[133] and an entire array of clothing might suggest the change of identity with marriage. The giving of gloves, perhaps an embodiment of handfast or the challenge of the gauntlet, and the gift of knives, which possibly evoked the sexual symbolism of cutting or that of domestic labour, were among those objects which also had a decorative function and could serve as accoutrements in wedding attire.[134] It is conceivable that certain spices such as ginger were thought to be aphrodisiacs, that other foodstuffs like oranges represented fertility,[135] and that food gifts were generally considered an important aspect of ritualised exchange. At times, in circumstances of remarriage, the exchange of gifts was symbolic of a partner's former marital status.[136] The personal nature of the giving was related to the previous marriage. The widow, Joan Bridger, had a silver goblet belonging to William Nightingall. She recalled the time when he visited her and 'sitting at table dryncking, he having a goblet of sylver in his hand which he brought with him drank to her saying this goblet was a token betwixt me and my first wife and I do drinke to you in the same on condicon you shalbe my wife. She answered that she wold pledge hym, but not upon any such condicon.'[137] The circulation of particular gifts upon remarriage presumably betokened the transfer of sentiment and expectations to the new spouse, although some prospective brides may have been wary of accepting such recycled gifts for various reasons. The same day after a contract was made between the widower George Bell and the widow Juliane Mason, he gave her 10 pieces of linen, a cap and a hat, a new waistcoat and a cassock. The cassock, it was said, 'she would not permit to be brought into her house for fear it was Bell's wife's, who died of the plague'.[138]

The giving of household goods can be interpreted as anticipating and symbolising the transfer of property at marriage, while alluding to domestic relations and the formation of a household. In the diocese of Canterbury, as has been seen, such objects were, however, rarely incorporated into the symbolism of courtship gifts and tokens. Where monetary gifts were concerned, their associations with payment, purchasing power, dowry and jointure, may be perceived as economic. They might express the economic status of the parties involved, but they also possessed explicit symbolic value when 'broken', 'bowed', or 'bent'. Witnesses reported that Thomas Kennet gave Bennet Dunnye a 6*d* piece, 'bendying yt once, as a tooken and pledge of the bargen and promis passed betwene them'.[139] Likewise, at such time when William Warde and Catherine Tench contracted themselves, he did 'brake [a] peece of gould a sunder and gave her one halfe and kepte the other himselfe'.[140] Coins, like gimmal rings, symbolically shared, may have recalled the making of an indenture.[141] An interesting tension existed between the real economic value of the gift bestowed and its symbolic nature, between the act of purchase on the one hand, and that of mutual promise on the other. Thomas Kennet would have given Bennet Dunnye a 10 shilling piece of gold, 'which she would not receave, saying that a les pece should serve thoughe yt were but a pennye'. In another instance, after financial matters had been negotiated satisfactorily, John Comb gave Anne Smyth a penny saying, 'take this it is as muche to bynd up the bargain betwixt us as a thousand pound'.[142] Attitudes expressed to symbolic value as opposed to economic worth were, in part, fashioned by the idealism of romantic love. That there was also a desire to impress upon a partner financial generosity is implied in the case of *Awsten* v. *Rogers*. William Awsten asked Marian Rogers 'if she wold have anye monye and wold have geven hyr some and offeryd hir hys purse and all that was in it, and she answered and said I will take you some monye of myne if you will and I will have none of yours and said further that she had rather to be at home and continue together with him in hys house than to have all the money that he had'. Upon taking leave of each other, with a kiss she 'byd hym farwell and said that he shold have hyr harte whersoever he went and he lykewyse said the same to her'.[143]

Money gifts exemplify the duality of real and symbolic value, and illustrate the flexibility of objects as exchanged items. Certain gifts could express a range of personal, domestic and sexual relations, or might have been associated with particular stages of courtship. Many objects, however, may have possessed a significance which is either now lost or difficult to recover, and whose symbolic status remains ambiguous. Returning to the case of *Ottringham* v. *Grigge*, and William's gift of the orange to Agnes, what is so perplexing is the precise significance of both the gift and its giving. The giving may have been intended as a generous one, a touching sentiment, or personal remembrance. If it was meant as a parting gift, it could also be perceived as a keepsake or token of unending love. William's motives were ill defined. The strategy to end a former relationship was complicated by his miscalculated remarks, in which he spoke in the present tense of his love for Agnes, yet expressed his love for Katherine, whom he was on his way to marry, in the past tense. In Katherine's eyes, the personification of the orange and the sexual implications were apparent. For Katherine, the distinction between 'hart' and 'body' was a false one. William's words and action amounted to Agnes having his heart, his body and all.[144]

If the ambiguity and the problem of ascertaining the significance of the orange are highlighted in this case, the giving of letters between parties, in other cases, could arguably become a statement of clarification. Jane Hardes, 'gentlewoman', testified that when William Alcocke was at her father's house, he

> importuned her ... for her resolution as tuching maryadg to be had betwene them, signifieng further to [her] that yf she would not give him a resolute answeare he would set his love on some other and named both place and person whereunto [she] answeared him that she was contented therewith, with which her answeare the said William Alcocke [was] not contented but desyred her for an answeare in writing under [her] hand.[145]

In another case, the note given to Judith Symons, which John Spayne had written himself signifying that he was contracted, was later to be returned and burned. Frances Hicks or Higges deposed that, at Judith's request, he went to John Spayne with the following message. She feared that she could never have his friends' goodwill and that she might match herself well with another. She entreated him to come to talk with her, and if he were so contented, to end the matters between them:

> And yf he could not come unto her that then he should signifie unto her by some pryvye token that he was contented to surcease and leave her the said Judyth to her further choyse which message [Hicks] forthwith delivered unto the said John Spayne whoe thereuppon willed [Hicks] to goe unto the said Judyth with this token that she the said Judyth had a note in writing which he willed her to send unto him, And soe [Hicks] with the same token went unto the said Judyth whoe delyvered a certeyne note unto [him] whereunto was subscribed the said John Spaynes name and the said Judyth Symons name which [Hicks] sawe taking in the same note and the contents of the same note were concerning matrimony betwene the said John Spaine and the said Judyth ... which note [Hicks] burned as he sayth.[146]

Taken in its entirety the symbolism of gifts and tokens in the transaction of marriage may be seen to possess a complex duality. The symbolic import of gifts and tokens might be most obviously experienced on clearly defined occasions when their significance corresponded with the purpose of the occasion. On the other hand, as has been seen, individual tokens might be given over the whole range of occasions leading to marriage, and it seems likely that the function of the symbolism in these non-specific instances was to provide a flexible language of initiation, promotion, development, confirmation, or termination of relations. The case of *Haffynden* v. *Awsten* illustrates contemporary awareness of this versatile symbolism. Constance Awsten alleged that James Haffynden offered 'to geve her a payer of gloves, whiche she in no wise wold receyve, James saying, Why Custaunce you may take them if it were of one that you never saw, And therapon she answering, and receaving the gloves said, I take them at yor handes as thoughe you were but a straunger towards me'.[147]

All transactions entered into by individuals or groups in the sixteenth century were multi-dimensional whether primarily economic, familial, social, political, or religious in intention. The transaction that led to marriage was simply a special case, crucially involved, as it was, in the reproduction of the community. In seeking to incorporate the complexity and ambiguity of changing relationships and interests, a language was developed by means of which change might be expressed and accommodated. It has been suggested that the language was the versatile and deliberately ambiguous symbolic language of the giving of gifts and tokens within the structured progression from early courtship to wedding. This language was part of the wider language of reciprocal exchange, of favours and compliments, of feasting, ceremonial, visiting, courtesy and other contexts of gift-giving. It was part of a range of elaborate processes which served also to enhance the value of important relationships and social institutions.[148] At the personal, familial and community level, the giving of gifts and tokens, on closer examination, was a vital, sustained code of popular practice. Such exchanges of gifts were sometimes channelled through intermediaries. The next chapter argues that the use of such go-betweens was an equally important and significant part of the making of marriage in the sixteenth century.

APPENDIX: TYPES OF GIFTS AND TOKENS

MONEY

angel[a]	flemish; gold; noble; old; old/15 shillings; quarter; of 10 shillings in gold
crown[b]	english; french; gold; half
ducat[c]	of gold
gold	angel of; bag of; crown of english/french; ducat of; great piece of; pieces of; and silver; small pot of; tokens of; two shillings and sixpence of; five shillings of; 10 shillings of; 13 shillings and fourpence of; 20 shillings of
groat[d]	new; old; old/threepence
money	amounts: twopence; threepence (bowed); fourpence; sixpence (bowed); 10 pence; 12 pence; two shillings and sixpence; three shillings; three shillings and 10 pence; five shillings; six shillings and eightpence; 20 shillings; 26 shillings

penny	bent; silver
pistolet[e]	of six shillings
royal[f]	*(ryall)*: half; old; old/15 shillings; spurr(?)/15 shillings
silver	and gold; penny; spanish; of two shillings and sixpence
sovereign[g]	*(sufferaine)*: half
teston[h]	
white	10 shillings of

CLOTHING AND LEATHER

apparel	
apron	of buffins[i]
calles (?)	
canvas	ell of
cap	coif[j]
cape	
cassock	of woollen cloth
christening smock	
cloth	gown; jerkin;[k] linen
cotton	
facing of frock	
fringe	
garments	
garters	pair of
girdle	riband; silk
glove(s)	knit; pair of
gown	cloth; kirtle with sleeves;[l] wedding
handkerchief	
hat	felt; silk
heading	
hose	pair of
jerkin	cloth
kerchief	
kirtle	worsted – nether bodice for
lace	little penny; satin and silk; silk
linen	cloth; ell of white
napkin	
neckerchief	
partlet[m]	
petticoat	russet
point[n]	silken
purse	and all in it; of black velvet; of red sarcenet; of silk

raiement	
riband	girdle; silk
scarf	silk
shadow°	
shoes	pair of
sleeves	gown kirtle with; pair of
stockings	jersey
stomacher[p]	
waistcoat	
wedding	garments; gown

METAL GIFTS AND TRINKETS

bracelet	
button	enamelled; silver and gilt
crucifix	silver
eyes	of silver
goblet	silver
hooks	gilted; silver
knife	pair of knives
nutmeg	gilded
picktooth	silver
pin	silver
ring	bagguage;[q] copper; gimmall/gemmey of gold/jeomey of silver;[r] of gold of the value of a crown with a stone; hoope;[s] little hoope ring of silver; jet; with ruby; of silver; signet ring of gold; of silver and gilt; wedding
tokens	of gold (?)
whistle	silver

WRITTEN

book
letter
note
prayer book
testament/psalter

ANIMAL AND FOODSTUFFS

bullocks	
cake	spice

cattle
cony
fish
ginger   raisin of
nutmeg
orange
peas   bushel of
pigeons
sow and pigs
strawberries   basket of

HOUSEHOLD GOODS

basin
candlestick
chamber pot
chests
coverlet
ewer
flockbed
pot
wood

NOTES TO APPENDIX

a   English gold coin, originally called angel-noble and coined in the reigns of Edward IV–
    Charles I, varying in value between 6s 8d and 10s. In 1552 it was worth 10s.

b   English crown worth 5s, issued in 1551.

c   Gold coin of varying value. In 1387 said to be half an English noble, and later worth 7s
    6d. Loosely refers to a piece of gold.

d   4d. Old groat could be 5d.

e   Foreign gold coin. In sixteenth century valued between 5s 10d and 6s 8d.

f   Gold coin, originally 10s. In 1526, 11s 3d, and in 1556, 12s.

g   Gold coin, minted in Henry VII's reign at 22s 6d. In 1542 was the greatest English coin,
    and worth 4$^{1}/_{2}$ crowns, but by 1591 worth only 10s.

h   In English, first applied to a shilling of Henry VII's reign. Sank from 12d in 1543
    successively to 10d, 9d and 6d, and recalled in 1548. Said to be 6d in 1577. Counterfeit
    testons which remained in circulation were rated even lower at 4$^{1}/_{2}$d and 2$^{1}/_{2}$d in 1560,
    their red colour described as a 'blushe for shame'.

i   A coarse cloth in use for the gowns of the middle class in Elizabeth I's time, or a
    garment of that material.

j   Close cap covering top, back and sides of head.

k   Sleeveless jacket.

l   Woman's gown or outer petticoat, alternatively a man's tunic or cloak.

m   Worn about the neck or upper chest, originally a neckerchief of linen, otherwise a collar or ruff for women.

n   Piece of lace used as a kerchief in the seventeenth century.

o   Woman's head-dress, appliance for shade.

p   Worn by women under the lacing of the bodice, and by men as a waistcoat.

q   Possibly bague.

r   The term may have been more generally used for rings bearing clasped hands, but specifically refers to two or more separate rings joined together (Kunz, *Rings for the Finger*, pp. 218–20).

s   Possibly a variant of the puzzle ring.

Note: Unless otherwise stated all definitions come from the *Oxford English Dictionary*.

NOTES

1   An earlier published version of this chapter appeared in *Rural History* 3:1 (1992), 1–40.

2   Causes of 'jactitation of matrimony', although less common, were often associated with the more familiar type of spousal suits, see above, pp. 12, 16. Matrimonial litigation could be complicated by the interests and claims of other parties. In this case it was one Jerman Seliborne. See C.C.A.L., MS. X/11/3, fos 18–19v. The following account of the case of *Divers* v. *Williams* has been pieced together from the depositions, loose cause papers and Act books: C.C.A.L., MSS. X/11/5, fos 223–5, 233v.–4, 248v.–9, 258–v.; J/J 3, 37 and 38; Y/3/15, f. 271v.; Y/3/2, f. 42.

3   The merchant John Hayne of Exeter enumerated the costs of the many gifts and tokens which he bestowed on Susan Henley. He travelled repeatedly over 35 miles in order to visit and court her. Cressy, *Birth, Marriage and Death*, pp. 240–1.

4   J. L. Comaroff ed., *The Meaning of Marriage Payments* (London, 1980), 'Introduction' and pp. 161–95; Mair, *Marriage*, ch. 4; Radcliffe-Brown, 'Introduction', pp. 44–54. For a discussion of the historical development of marriage gifts with its associated bundle of rights and obligations, see D. O. Hughes, 'From brideprice to dowry in Mediterranean Europe', *Journal of Family History* 3:3 (1978), 262–96.

5   M. Mauss, *The Gift: Forms and Functions of Exchange in Archaic Societies*, trans. I. Cunnison (London, 1954, 1980 edn); Van Gennep, *The Rites of Passage*; P. Bourdieu, *Outline of a Theory of Practice*, trans. R. Nice (Switzerland, 1972; 1st English trans. Cambridge, 1977), pp. 5–8, 12–15, 191–5.

6   E.g. G. MacCormack, 'Mauss and the "spirit of the gift"', *Oceania* 52:4 (1982), 286–93; G. MacCormack, 'Reciprocity', *Man* 11 (1976), 89–103; E. Bercovitch, 'The agent in the gift: hidden exchange in inner New Guinea', *Cultural Anthropology* 9:4 (1994), 498–536. For a new representation of the gift in Melanesian society, see M. Strathern, *The Gender of the Gift: Problems with Women and Problems with Society in Melanesia* (Oxford, 1988, ppbk edn, 1990); M. Strathern, 'Partners and consumers: making relations visible', *New Literary History* 22:3 (1991), 581–601. Reciprocity in an historical context is

discussed in G. McCracken, 'The exchange of children in Tudor England: an anthropological phenomenon in historical context', *Journal of Family History* 8 (1983), 303–13 (esp. pp. 304–6). See also, L. M. Klein, 'Your humble handmaid: Elizabethan gifts of needlework', *Renaissance Quarterly* 50:2 (1997), 459–93 (pp. 464–9); N. Z. Davis, 'Beyond the market: books as gifts in sixteenth-century France', *Transactions of the Royal Historical Society* 5th ser. 33 (1983), 69–88 (p. 70).

7   *Aspects of Folk Life in Europe: Love and Marriage*, International European Exhibition organised by the Ministry of French Culture and the Ministry of Flemish Culture (Musée de la Vie Wallonne, Liège, 4 July–5 October 1975). I am grateful to Richard Wall for bringing this book to my attention.

8   J. Brand, *Observations on Popular Antiquities: Chiefly Illustrating the Origin of our Vulgar Customs, Ceremonies, and Superstitions* (2 vols, London, 1813), ii, 19–121; J. Strutt, *A Compleat View of the Manners, Customs, Arms, Habits and of the Inhabitants of England from the Arrival of the Saxons Till the Reign of Henry VIII* (3 vols, London, 1775), i, 74–8; ii, 23–4; iii, 151–8; M. Baker, *Discovering the Folklore and Customs of Love and Marriage* (Aylesbury, 1974), pp. 15–18; C. Bloxham and M. Picken, *Love and Marriage* (Devon, 1990); S. Bury, *An Introduction to Sentimental Jewellery* (London, 1985), pp. 15–32; E. Porter, *Cambridgeshire Customs and Folklore* (London, 1969), pp. 37, 48; E. Bradford ed., *Roses are Red: Love and Scorn in Victorian Valentines* (London, 1986); *Love Spoons from Wales* (Cardiff, 1973); *The Story of the Love Spoon* (Cardiff, 1973); *Victorian Valentine Cards*, Temporary Exhibition at the Heritage Centre (Canterbury, February 1988); J. Jones and K. Ames, *Love Tokens* (Devon, 1992).

9   J. Evans, *English Posies and Posy Rings* (London, 1931); G. F. Kunz, *Rings for the Finger* (Philadelphia, 1917, republished New York, 1973), pp. 193–248; H. Newman, *An Illustrated Dictionary of Jewellery* (London, 1981); S. Bury, *An Introduction to Rings* (London, 1984), pp. 15–17; J. Cherry and M. Redknap, 'Medieval and Tudor finger rings found in Wales', *Archaeologia Cambrensis* 140 (1991), 120–9.

10 R. Chartier ed. *Passions of the Renaissance* (trans. A. Goldhammer, Massachusetts, 1989), pp. 246–8, 258; Chaytor, 'Household and kinship', p. 42; J. R. Gillis, 'Peasant, plebeian, and proletarian marriage in Britain, 1600–1900', in D. Levine ed., *Proletarianization and Family History* (Orlando, 1984), pp. 129–62 (p. 132); Gillis, *For Better, For Worse*, pp. 31–4, 38, 51; Houlbrooke, *Church Courts*, pp. 60–2; Houlbrooke, 'The making of marriage', pp. 344–6, 350; Ingram, 'Spousals litigation', pp. 46–7; Ingram, *Church Courts*, pp. 196–8; Macfarlane, *Marriage and Love*, pp. 300–3; D. Woodward ed., *The Farming and Memorandum Books of Henry Best of Elmswell: 1642*, Records of Social and Economic History, n.s. 8 (London, 1984), pp. 122–3. For more recent references to tokens and courtship gifts, see P. J. P. Goldberg, *Women, Work and Life-Cycle in a Medieval Economy: Women in York and Yorkshire c. 1300–1520* (Oxford, 1992), pp. 238–40; Carlson, *Marriage and the English Reformation*, pp. 111–12, 127, 136; Carlson, 'Courtship in Tudor England', pp. 24–5; Gowing, *Domestic Dangers*, pp. 159–64; Cressy, *Birth, Marriage and Death*, pp. 263–6; A. Wall, 'For love, money or politics? A clandestine marriage and the Elizabethan Court of Arches', *Historical Journal* 38 (1995), 511–33.

11 Rushton, 'The testament of gifts', *passim*; Rushton, 'Property, power and family networks', p. 205.

12 Segalen, *Love and Power*, pp. 18–19.

13 Gottlieb, 'Clandestine marriage', pp. 49–53, 70.

14 Roper, 'Going to church and street', pp. 81–3, 89, 96.

15 Swinburne, *Treatise of Spousals*, pp. 1, 21, 27, 31–3, 39–43, 203–12, 229–30; J. D. M. Derrett, 'Henry Swinburne (?1551–1624) civil lawyer of York', *Borthwick Papers* 44 (1973).

16 See above, pp. 12–16.

17 Swinburne, *Treatise of Spousals*, pp. 6–7, 21, 31–3, 41, 209; Conset, *Practice of the Ecclesiastical Courts*, p. 255.

18 Swinburne, *Treatise of Spousals*, pp. 203–5; Helmholz, *Marriage Litigation*, pp. 33–4.

19 Swinburne, *Treatise of Spousals*, pp. 10, 39–43, 71, 209–10; Derrett, 'Henry Swinburne', p. 25.

20 See also, Houlbrooke, *Church Courts*, pp. 60–2, and 'The making of marriage', pp. 344–6, who finds only one Norwich case of its conclusive effect.

21 M. M. Sheehan, 'The influence of canon law on the property rights of married women in England', *Medieval Studies* 25 (1963), 109–24 (p. 114); Burn, *The Ecclesiastical Law*, p. 479; Sheehan, 'Choice of marriage partner', pp. 31–2.

22 Carlson, *Marriage and the English Reformation*, pp. 44–7.

23 Swinburne, *Treatise of Spousals*, pp. 207–9; Roper, 'Going to church and street', p. 81. Posies also alluded to the ring as 'round and hath no end'. See Evans, *English Posies*, pp. xxi, 98.

24 Houlbrooke, *Church Courts*, pp. 60–2.

25 Rushton, 'The testament of gifts', p. 28.

26 *Ibid.*, p. 31, n. 23, citing Ingram.

27 Houlbrooke, *Church Courts*, pp. 60–2; Houlbrooke, 'The making of marriage', pp. 344–6; also Conset, *Practice of the Ecclesiastical Courts*, p. 271.

28 Helmholz, *Marriage Litigation*, pp. 45–7.

29 Rushton, 'The testament of gifts', p. 28.

30 Ingram, *Church Courts*, pp. 196–8.

31 Ingram, 'Spousals litigation', pp. 46–7; Houlbrooke, *Church Courts*, pp. 60–2; Houlbrooke, 'The making of marriage', p. 346. Further discussion of gifts as circumstantial evidence can be found in Carlson, *Marriage and the English Reformation*, pp. 127, 136. He is critical of Rushton and Gillis, and argues instead that there was *no* uncertainty regarding the meaning of gifts in litigation. Carlson claims that contemporaries could recognise and understand the difference between betrothal tokens and courtship gifts. 'Ultimately, it was simply the responsibility of each individual to make intentions clear when giving and receiving gifts. People did not need the church courts to assist them in that. Litigation in church courts which involved gifts was not about gifts; it was about words' (p. 136).

32 See above, pp. 12–16.

33 Rushton, 'The testament of gifts', p. 25; *Love and Courtship in Renaissance Prints*, Temporary Exhibition at the Fitzwilliam Museum (Cambridge, March–June 1989). For love posies of the sixteenth and seventeenth centuries, see, A. H. Bullen ed., *Some Shorter Elizabethan Poems: an English Garner* (Westminster, 1903), pp. 269–310; R. Thompson ed., *Samuel Pepys' Penny Merriments* (London, 1976), pp. 114–15; and for courtship gifts

in small merry books, see M. Spufford, *Small Books and Pleasant Histories* (London, 1981), pp. 168–9. Numerous examples of gifts and tokens span the works of Geoffrey Chaucer, William Shakespeare, George Herbert and John Donne, and later writers such as Charles Dickens, Jane Austen and Thomas Hardy, to name a few. Elizabethan structures of exchange, and the viability and dynamics of exchange practices, are explored in plays; see e.g., M. T. Burnett, 'Giving and receiving: *Love's Labour's Lost* and the politics of exchange', *English Literary Renaissance* 23:2 (1993), 287–313; K. Newman, 'Portia's ring: unruly women and structures of exchange in *The Merchant of Venice*', *Shakespeare Quarterly* 38 (1987), 19–33.

34 The figure is approximate because of circumstances of multi-contract, and because matrimony can only be inferred in certain cases. Cf. Rushton, 'The testament of gifts', p. 25, where 29 out of 81 actual or inferred matrimony cases provided such testimonies, and Houlbrooke, 'The making of marriage', pp. 344–6, where references to gifts were found in 25 per cent of the cases.

35 Gillis, *For Better, For Worse*, pp. 6–7, 17.

36 For New Year gifts at the Elizabethan Court, see e.g., Klein, 'Your humble handmaid', esp. pp. 459–64. The Lisle correspondence reveals the regularity of giving. See, M. St Clare Byrne ed., *The Lisle Letters* (London, 1983), *passim* and esp. pp. xiv–xv. In France, the public gift of a dedicated book used in the search for patronage and other more general social purposes is discussed in Davis, 'Beyond the market', pp. 69–81.

37 C.C.A.L., MS. X/10/9, f. 64, *Aunsell v. Courte* (?1563).

38 See also, Houlbrooke, 'The making of marriage', p. 344; Rushton, 'The testament of gifts', p. 26; Carlson, *Marriage and the English Reformation*, p. 111.

39 Bullen ed., *Some Shorter Elizabethan Poems*, pp. 279–306.

40 See also, Gowing, *Domestic Dangers*, pp. 160–1.

41 Houlbrooke, 'The making of marriage', p. 344.

42 C.C.A.L., MS. X/10/6, fos 115v.–16, *Lambard v. Harewood* (1556).

43 C.C.A.L., MS. X/10/7, f. 102v., *Lyon v. Cole* (1560).

44 For the role of intermediaries, see below, chapter 3.

45 See also, Houlbrooke, 'The making of marriage', p. 344.

46 C.C.A.L., MS. X/11/5, f. 121, *Stringer v. Sturman* (1596); but in this case, Thomas Sturman delivered the gift himself.

47 E.g. Evans, *English Posies*, p. 85; 'Not the guift, but the giver' (1596).

48 C.C.A.L., MS. X/10/18, fos 154v.–5, *More v. Stupple* (1579).

49 See also, Houlbrooke, *Church Courts*, p. 60, and 'The making of marriage', p. 344; Macfarlane, *Marriage and Love*, pp. 300–1.

50 C.C.A.L., MS. X/10/16, fos 277–v., 283, *Essex v. Culling* (1577); also e.g. MSS. X/10/18, fos 213v.–14v., *Balden v. Brokwell* (1580); X/10/17, fos 88–96v., *Levet v. Willyams* (1574).

51 C.C.A.L., MS. X/10/21, f. 81v., *Marketman v. Berry* (1581).

52 C.C.A.L., MS. X/10/12, f. 287v., *Longley v. Marchant* (1566).

53 C.C.A.L., MS. X/10/11, f. 183v., *Kennet v. Dunnye* (1570).

54 C.C.A.L., MS. X/10/9, f. 59, *Barrow v. Thomlyns* (?1563).

55 C.C.A.L., MS. X/10/15, f. 161–v., *Ottringham* v. *Grigge* (1567); cf. Evans, *English Posies*, p. 30, 'Take hand take heart take body and all'.

56 See above, pp. 79–80 and pp. 85–6.

57 C.C.A.L., MS. X/10/11, f. 126, *Hennikre* v. *Sellar* (1569).

58 See above, pp. 59–60.

59 C.C.A.L., MS. X/11/1, f. 2–v., *Terry* v. *Overie* (1585).

60 For sixteenth- and seventeenth-century usages, see *Oxford English Dictionary*.

61 C.C.A.L., MS. X/10/19, f. 264, *King* v. *Otway and Wood* (1584).

62 See chapter 4, below, pp. 138–43.

63 C.C.A.L., MS. X/10/8, fos 68v.–9, *Frances* v. *Marshe* (?1561).

64 Houlbrooke, *Church Courts*, p. 60; Rushton, 'The testament of gifts', pp. 26–7.

65 See Appendix, above, pp. 87–91. Rushton, 'The testament of gifts', p. 26, concludes that there were no fixed rules regarding type, although rings were often given. Houlbrooke, 'The making of marriage', pp. 344–6, similarly cites the frequency of rings associated with pledge, but also the popularity of coins, ornaments and trinkets. For gifts such as flowers, mirrors, 'conceited toys and novelties' like whistles, lockets, thimbles, etc., see Goldberg, *Women, Work and Life-Cycle*, pp. 238–40; Carlson, 'Courtship in Tudor England', p. 24; Carlson, *Marriage and the English Reformation*, p. 111.

66 Cf. the 'orange' cited from eighteenth-century Belgium in the form of a heart, being a sweet-dish in orange peel covered with papier mâché: *Aspects of Folk Life in Europe*, p. 121.

67 Bullen ed., *Some Shorter Elizabethan Poems*, pp. 291–306; Bloxham and Picken, *Love and Marriage*, pp. 76–82; Brand, *Observations on Popular Antiquities*, pp. 54–61.

68 Categorising the gifts and tokens by type is inevitably somewhat arbitrary and simplified. The cases also often make unspecific allusions to gifts exchanged. Conservative estimates have been used throughout the analysis.

69 C.C.A.L., MS. X/10/6, f. 213v., *Short* v. *Essex*, and e.g. MS. X/10/8, f. 205v., *Marshe* v. *Gaunt* (?1562).

70 E.g. the unicorn's horn may have been thought to possessed a special property, see, Byrne ed., *Lisle Letters*, pp. 242–3.

71 C.C.A.L., MS. X/10/3, f. 25, *Singer* v. *Smith* (1546).

72 See above, p. 91, n. 3.

73 Klein, 'Your humble handmaid', esp. pp. 462, 464.

74 An example of gifts exchanged in the courtships of the upper class can be found in Wall, 'For love, money or politics?', pp. 527–9.

75 C.C.A.L., MS. X/10/18, f. 24–v., *Mantle* v. *Mereweath* (1577).

76 Conset, *Practice of the Ecclesiastical Courts*, pp. 146–51.

77 Swinburne, *Treatise of Spousals*, pp. 178–89.

78 C.C.A.L., MS. X/10/14, f. 99–v., *Pynnocke* v. *Beeching* (1572).

79 Macfarlane, *Marriage and Love*, pp. 301–3. The Derbyshire yeoman Leonard Wheatcroft (1627–1707) modelled his letters on romantic literature. See Cressy, *Birth, Marriage and Death*, pp. 243–4.

80 The exchanges of letters 'in the symbolic economy of *Love's Labour's Lost*, are perceived as presents': Burnett, 'Giving and receiving', p. 295.

81 Thompson ed., *Samuel Pepys' Penny Merriments*, pp. 114–15.

82 Chartier ed., *Passions of the Renaissance*, pp. 246–8; N. P. Meyjes, *Character and Beauty of Dutch Painting in the Seventeenth Century* (Netherlands, 1957, English–Dutch edn), nos 36/37: Jan Vermeer's *The Message* or *The Love Letter*.

83 *Aspects of Folk Life in Europe*, pp. 172, 177, 210. The later spate of Valentine cards, and postcards of matrimony maps, illustrates the communication of love by literate means (matrimony maps are geographical representations of the emotional and material advantages and disadvantages of entering into marriage). *Ibid.* pp. 149–50; Bloxham and Picken, *Love and Marriage*, pp. 22–3; Bradford ed., *Roses are Red*.

84 Davis, 'Beyond the market', esp. pp. 77, 81–2.

85 It is perhaps worth noting that book ownership and literacy generally were increasing in Kent in the later sixteenth century. See P. Clark, 'The ownership of books in England, 1560–1640: the example of some Kentish townsfolk', in L. Stone ed., *Schooling and Society* (Baltimore, 1976), pp. 95–111.

86 C.C.A.L., MS. X/10/2, f. 33, *Savye* v. *Philpott* (1542).

87 C.C.A.L., MS. X/10/15, f. 209–v., *Smyth* v. *Grey* (1567).

88 See above, p. 84 and below, pp. 191, 201.

89 E.g. C.C.A.L., MS. X/10/7, fos 85v.–6, *Lyon* v. *Cole* (1560); MS. X/10/16, f. 300, *Hannyng* v. *Knowler* (1577).

90 C.C.A.L., MS. X/10/12, f. 44v., *Smyth* v. *Godfrey* (1564).

91 Gillis, *For Better, For Worse*, p. 31.

92 C.C.A.L., MS. X/10/12, f. 286v., *Joyce* v. *Marchant* (1566).

93 C.C.A.L., MS. X/10/12, fos 151–2, *Launsfeld* v. *Austen* (1565).

94 Gillis, *For Better, For Worse*, p. 33.

95 Rushton, 'The testament of gifts', pp. 26–7.

96 C.C.A.L., MS. X/10/11, fos 255v.–6 (?1569).

97 Stages of courtship are also exemplified in the seventeenth-century account of Henry Best of Elmswell. See, Woodward ed., *Henry Best*, pp. 122–3. The later, nineteenth-century maps of matrimony would also seem to illustrate the course of love, betrothal and marriage, representing the process pictorially as a narrative. E.g. *Aspects of Folk Life in Europe*, p. 158; Bradford ed., *Roses are Red*.

98 C.C.A.L., MS. X/10/18, fos 276v.–8, *Ryeley* v. *Pitcher* (1580).

99 C.C.A.L., MS. X/10/20, f. 176, *Wanderton* v. *Wyld* (1583).

100 C.C.A.L., MS. X/10/9, fos 50, 51v., 53, *Wilbore* v. *Atkinson?* (?1563).

101 C.C.A.L., MS. X/11/1, f. 215–v., *Fookes* v. *Lowes* (1588).

102 C.C.A.L., MS. X/10/17, f. 152v., *Baxter* v. *Cotton* (1574).

103 C.C.A.L., MS. X/10/12, f. 297 (1566).

104 C.C.A.L., MS. X/10/12, f. 182–v., *Tusnothe* v. *Marden* (1565).

105   C.C.A.L., MS. X/10/12, fos 103v.–4 (1564).

106   See also Rushton, 'The testament of gifts', p. 28; Gillis, *For Better, For Worse*, pp. 32–3.

107   C.C.A.L., MS. X/10/9, f. 28, *Rolf* v. *Fryer* (1563).

108   C.C.A.L., MS. X/10/12, fos 173, 175–6, *Mayhewe* v. *Throwley* (1565).

109   C.C.A.L., MS. X/10/6, fos 200v.–1, *Symons* v. *Bedford* (1558).

110   For legal recovery of marriage gifts, see, Houlbrooke, *Church Courts*, p. 60; Swinburne, *Treatise of Spousals*, pp. 229–31.

111   Bourdieu, *Outline of a Theory of Practice*, pp. 5–8.

112   C.C.A.L., MS. X/10/16, fos 56–8, *Wood* v. *Swift* (1575).

113   C.C.A.L., MS. Y/3/14, f. 47v.; X/11/6, fos 198v.–201, 215–17, 220v.–IV., 223–4, 227v.–8, 229v.–30, *Tresse* v. *Tresse* (1593–94).

114   C.C.A.L., MS. X/10/15, fos 161v.–2v. See above, pp. 66–7 and pp. 85–6.

115   For earnest money in the North Riding, see Gillis, *For Better, For Worse*, p. 29.

116   C.C.A.L., MS. X/11/2, fos 160v.–1, *Small* v. *Newenden and Terenden* (1586–87).

117   C.C.A.L., MS. X/11/6, fos 167–9v. (1593).

118   Gillis, *For Better, For Worse*, p. 51; Strutt, *Manners, Customs, Arms, Habits*, iii, pp. 151–8.

119   Swinburne, *Treatise of Spousals*, pp. 229–31.

120   K. Thomas, *Religion and the Decline of Magic: Studies in Popular Beliefs in Sixteenth- and Seventeeth-Century England* (1971, ppbk edn, Harmondsworth, 1973, repr. 1980), pp. 277–9; Thompson ed., *Samuel Pepys' Penny Merriments*, pp. 130–1; *Aspects of Folk Life in Europe*, pp. 19–23, 245, and *passim*; Cressy, *Birth, Marriage and Death*, pp. 265–6.

121   E.g. Baker, *Love and Marriage*, pp. 15–18; Gillis, *For Better, For Worse*, p. 33.

122   Swinburne, *Treatise of Spousals*, pp. 207–8; Burn, *The Ecclesiastical Law*, ii, 479; Van Gennep, *The Rites of Passage*, p. 134; Roper, 'Going to church and street', p. 81. For sexual symbolism in the rite of bestowing the ring, see Segalen, *Love and Power*, p. 27.

123   Bloxham and Picken, *Love and Marriage*, pp. 60–5; Evans, *English Posies, passim*; Bury, *Introduction to Rings*, pp. 16, 33.

124   C.C.A.L., MS. J/J2 18, *Colyer* v. *Porredge* (1596–97).

125   Evans, *English Posies*, pp. 2–3, 106; Bury, *Introduction to Rings*, p. 25.

126   PRC 17/21/110v.–12 (15 Oct. 1536). Also, e.g., PRC 17/43/192v. (will of Alice Mantell, widow, of Wye, 28 Mar. 1576).

127   See also, e.g., Bloxham and Picken, *Love and Marriage*, pp. 32–41, 44–9; Bury, *Introduction to Sentimental Jewellery*, pp. 15–16, 28; *Aspects of Folk Life in Europe*, pp. 149–50, for a later vogue.

128   *Aspects of Folk Life in Europe*, e.g. pp. 172, 177, 185.

129   Klein, 'Your humble handmaid', esp. pp. 462, 471, 483–5. For a reference to the gift of a needleworked waistcoat, see, Wall, 'For love, money or politics?', p. 527.

130   C.C.A.L., MS. X/10/3, f. 19, *Monday* v. *Parker* (1546).

131   C.C.A.L., MS. X/10/12, fos 173v.–4v., *Lee* v. *Sething* (1565).

132   For examples of mnemonic gifts, see, Klein, 'Your humble handmaid', pp. 472–4.

133 Also Macfarlane, *Marriage and Love*, p. 301. The judge Jean de Coras in Toulouse sent his wife 'a naughty dress' among other gifts, and she sent him homemade garters from their home in the country, see, Davis, 'Beyond the market', p. 82.

134 Bloxham and Picken, *Love and Marriage*, pp. 43, 76–82.

135 *Ibid.*, pp. 18–19.

136 Gowing, *Domestic Dangers*, pp. 163–4.

137 C.C.A.L., MS. X/10/18, f. 144–v., *Nightingall* v. *Bridger* (1579).

138 C.C.A.L., MS. X/10/16, fos 196–8, *Mason* v. *Bell* (1576).

139 C.C.A.L., MS. X/10/11, f. 183–v., *Kennet* v. *Dunnye* (1570).

140 C.C.A.L., MS. X/11/5, fos 225–6v., *Warde* v. *Tench* (1598).

141 See also Rushton, 'The testament of gifts', p. 26, which suggests that the custom of bending was optional.

142 C.C.A.L., MS. X/10/18, fos 98–100v., *Smyth* v. *Comb* (1578).

143 C.C.A.L., MS. X/10/7, f. 187–v. (1567).

144 See above, pp. 66–7. Lady Lisle sent a gift of 'fine oranges' to Oudart du Bies. He thanked her for 'these fine presents', see, Byrne ed., *Lisle Letters*, p. 286.

145 C.C.A.L., MS. X/11/3, f. 5v., *Alcocke* v. *Hardes* (1598); *ibid.*, MS. Y/3/2, f. 66.

146 C.C.A.L., MS. X/11/5, f. 255, *Symons* v. *Spayne* (1598).

147 C.C.A.L., MS. X/10/7, fos 165v.–6v. (1560–61).

148 For the wider notion of reciprocity in exchange, see also, Muldrew, 'Interpreting the market', *passim*.

Chapter 3

'Movers', 'sutors', 'speakers' and 'brokers' of marriage: the role of go≀betweens as a 'means' of courtship

In a moment of self-reproach and self-realisation, the widow Whiter confessed to John Payne of Seasalter and his wife, her fault in 'drynckyng and making merye amonge yonckers'. She firmly acknowledged the mutual unsuitability of a match with such a one as 'woulde littell regard [her] hereafter'. Choosing instead the elderly William Rolf, 'a man well broken in the world', one evidently 'fytt for me and I for him', she urged John Payne to make a six-mile return journey to find him and bring back a definite answer of marriage. This was a moment of crisis. 'If ever thowe wilte do for me, do for me now' she pleaded.[1] While she and William Rolf appear in the record as the principal protagonists in the marriage dispute, the mediation of the 41-year-old Payne, himself a presumably established and reputable fellow parishioner, was of timely significance in the complex management of personal relationships. In this case, his going between the parties was in order to confer about marriage and determine, once and for all, the matrimonial intention.

In sixteenth-century English society, the making of a match was inextricably tied, among other things, to circumstances of family, fortune and place, and the necessity of forging 'a good match'[2] was a matter of pressing consequence. For this reason, the process of finding appropriate partners often involved not only the 'twoo doings' of the parties concerned, but also the machinations of other 'makers of a marriage'.[3] The earlier examination of parental, kin and community participation has already thrown some light on the concept of the marriage-maker.[4] As will be shown in the following chapter, choice of marriage partner was to some extent also dependent on the environmental limitations of locality and residence, and on the opportunities made available to individuals living in close proximity or coupled from further afield. The unions which did ensue, temporary or permanent though they may have been, were arguably, however, not simply a matter of fortuitous occurrence. Even where geography made or hindered relations, or where situations for courtship manifested themselves in a range of coincidences, the apparent spontaneity might itself have disguised the underlying possibilities for other kinds of influential arrangements. One institution which acted as a 'means' of courtship, with varying degrees of formality, was the intermediary.

It will be the purpose of this chapter to consider more closely than historians have hitherto attempted, the role of those who, in some capacity, acted as agents, spokesmen, negotiators, intercessors, or messengers, in the course of matrimonial proceedings. In so doing, it will seek to gauge part of 'the collective aspect of making a match'.[5] Alan Macfarlane has expressed the opinion that 'courtship was a game [which], on the whole, people played for themselves', although he made some allowance for 'interested spectators, perhaps an umpire', and certain 'customary rules'.[6] To qualify his analogy, it may alternatively be said that all games, of necessity, incorporate beside the basic rules, crucial moves, checks and procedures, which furthered or hindered their development. In Kentish courtship, the so-called 'movers' and 'medlers', 'utterers' and 'brokers', may have been crucial not just in the interests of publicity and attestation.[7] Such persons, at the same time, might fulfil a more active function as 'not onelye a wytnes but allsoe an actor'.[8]

Within aristocratic society and among the more privileged status groups, their use and influence in marital negotiations and solicitations have been observed. Go-betweens served an identifiable purpose as part of the etiquette of courtship, not least in the interests of financial matters.[9] Even Macfarlane has acknowledged the matchmakings of leading men like Lord Burleigh, and the brokering activities, among rich merchant families, of so-called 'matrimonial bawds'.[10] Beneath those levels, the lesser (though still propertied) families might also seek the assistance and expertise of outsiders in the preliminaries to marriage.[11] For the middle class of early modern London, introductions to courtship might entail considerable brokerage fees. As Peter Earle observed, 'How common such brokerage fees were one does not know, but given the mercenary nature of much of the London marriage market it seems probable that they were far from unusual. Some people certainly made a business of marriage broking.' They might include scriveners, 'experienced matrons', or a neighbourhood matchmaker 'who knows to a title the exact rates of the market and the current prices of young women that are fit to marry'.[12]

Reluctant nevertheless to accredit any very real significance to this form of behaviour, even for those of titled or wealthy rank, Alan Macfarlane has been less prepared to admit the possibilities of a more general employment of go-betweens. Seeking to distinguish the courtship and marriage system of early modern England from those of 'peasant societies', he argued that the institution of marriage brokerage existed only in the latter. 'In most peasantries, whether in China, India or Europe, there are professional marriage "brokers" or "match-makers". Such people are experts in finding suitably endowed partners: they know the field, and who is a good "investment". They may arrange meetings and terms, and generally act as a kind of matrimonial agency.'[13] The type of marriage broker which Macfarlane identified as a characteristic feature of most peasant societies was very specific, and was also strictly concerned with the initiation of marriage rather than with the more general conduct of courtship. Indeed, he employs the kind of polemical device apparent in his earlier works, proceeding via negative evidence – in this case, the absence of any such 'instituted role' in early modern England – to further support his theory that a highly individualistic marriage system and social system developed precociously in England.[14] Convinced of the absence of matchmakers in England, he argued that 'below the level of the upper gentry and merchant families, there is little evidence of marriage brokers. They are not mentioned in ecclesiastical court cases about broken engagements, they are not visible in accounts of courtship in diaries, they do not appear in letters, they are not referred to in accounts of courtship.'[15] He presumes, as in his earlier works, that societies can be easily classified into ideal archetypes, the familistic, peasant societies, as opposed to the individualistic, capitalistic ones. Such models have little place for diversity, change or caution. If one allows for greater flexibility in defining the intermediary, the depositions from the consistory court of Canterbury provide overwhelming evidence of their existence. The custom of 'deputised courtship', which figures so prominently in the contemporary literature, and particular entries in English diaries and autobiographies of the seventeenth century likewise demonstrate their widespread use.

The well-known diary of Samuel Pepys (d. 1703) shows Pepys actively engaged in arranging a marriage for the daughter of his patron, helping in the discussions, giving advice, making various visits, even instructing the inexperienced young man in the business of love matters and the art of amorous wooing.[16] Lovers themselves would rely on others in their plots and intrigues. Lady Elizabeth Livingston (d. 1717), ashamed of her vanity and flirtations, confessed the 'little subtleties' she played with a 'particular knot of friends' to discover the secret thoughts of her admirers.[17] The autobiography of the sixteenth-century musician Thomas Whythorne (d. 1596) illustrates, too, the use of 'oblique approaches through allies and intermediaries'. His quest after a 'twenty-pound widow' reveals the nature of courtship among gentle quarters as a joint project, which was very likely to have been dependent upon the help, broachings and introductions of third parties.[18] Further down the social scale, the Derbyshire 'yeoman'/tailor Leonard Wheatcroft (d. 1707) began his courtship of Elizabeth Hawley at the prompting of a mutual friend, who informed him of her eligibility and attractiveness. His informant acted as a go-between, and other 'friends' later served as carriers of love letters, and supported him in his endeavours.[19] On more than one occasion, Roger Lowe, an apprentice shopkeeper (d. *c.* 1679), allowed others to intercede for him. They acted in accompanying him, and devised strategies for him in various aspects of personal diplomacy.[20] As well as the evidence of diarists and autobiographers, gentry correspondence can likewise expose the activities of intermediaries in courtship, in soliciting and promoting a marriage.[21]

Several of the Shakespearean comedies and tragedies make play with the intricate complexities and problems attendant upon courtship. The proverbial figure of the go-between is employed in diverse ways as a device in dramatic complication or resolution. In situations such as that of geographical separation, clandestinity, or perhaps deception, the familiar character variously termed 'go-between' or 'goer-between', 'spokesmate', 'attorney', 'agent' and 'messenger', features unmistakably in the plot, performing or subverting the customary role of a marriage intermediary in Elizabethan England.[22]

In the study of contemporary historical records pertaining especially to the courtships of the middling and lower classes, the importance and prevalence of this cultural practice, and its implications, have not received the appropriate critical recognition. As noted earlier, Macfarlane's overemphasis upon *traditional* models of marriage brokers has effectively limited the historical identification of these matchmakers or middlemen. The kind of marriage brokers he identified are found in societies geared towards universal, early and formally arranged marriage, where often paid professionals who specialised in finding partners of desirable status and connections were commissioned to initiate and conclude matrimonial arrangements.[23] It is argued here, that, in order to evaluate the strength of this cultural phenomenon and its relevance in the regulation of matrimony in sixteenth-century English society, it is necessary to extend one's definition to accommodate a more flexible range of intermediary types.[24]

Proceeding therefore in a less rigid manner of interpretation, this chapter seeks to examine the diverse forms of mediation which existed in the management of courtship. It suggests that the activity of the more traditionally recognisable type of go-between is indeed hinted at in the ecclesiastical court depositions. More commonly, the various introductions, investigations, recommendations, arbitrations, intercessions, persuasions and negotiations which frequently took place, might generally be regarded as part and parcel of the customary role of the intermediary. From the more definable model, to the more informal manifestations of their functions, the identity of the go-between deserves close attention. Even where historians have acknowledged that 'matchmakers, go-betweens, brokers and attorneys played their part',[25] the importance of their conduct in marriage transactions has not been explored adequately. The making of property transfers which they directly or indirectly effected and which, as will be seen in a following chapter, were fundamental to marriage, invests their position in courtship with a conservative as well as a dynamic significance. Who they were; of what age, status and relationship to the parties; their place of residence; the nature of the tasks they performed and their apparent motivation; the ambiguity of their role; and their many guises, will be discussed here.

The legal specifications regarding the employment of matrimonial agents would seem to suggest that the practice was a familiar one. Provision was made for betrothal and marriage to be contracted through sufficiently appointed persons. According to Swinburne, the mediation of proctors, of messengers, or of letters, allowed for contracts to be made on behalf of parties. Legal strictures set limitations, however, on the mediation employed. The validity of an agreement was dependent upon its being made in due form by a person with a sufficient mandate to act, provided also that there was no alteration in the mind of the sender. Such a proviso applied, too, in circumstances where the messenger was employed simply for the delivery of a message or letter. In those cases the consent of the recipient ratified the contract. Canon law sought to protect the intentions of both parties by restricting the mediator's exercise of authority. All messengers had to be *specially sent*, and might not validly contract in another's name of their 'own accord and motion'. A messenger who was sufficiently authorised to do so, came not in his own name, but in the name of the sender, and was regarded as 'the voice of the others mind, and the picture of his person'. Even those without any such authority still had to act specifically as another's representative. By law, therefore, mediators did not have unlimited licence. They had to adhere to their client's agenda.[26] Notwithstanding the legal restrictions on their role and on their ability to negotiate independently or make overriding decisions, what is clearly significant is the ample recognition of this custom in the eyes of the law. The implication that certain persons might well transgress those limits, and the legal distinction between various forms of intermediaries, are also of significance.

The evidence recorded by church court officials for the diocese of Canterbury suggests a common contemporary nomenclature for intermediaries. Although individuals were never specifically referred to as 'go-betweens', certain terms which were often used identified the range of mediatory doers. Some were said to be 'persones *indifferently chosen*'[27] or '*indifferent* men' sent 'to enquire what she was' to see if she was 'fite to match'.[28] The aged Peter Bellingham was '*a sutor*', on Robert Cousen's behalf, to a reputedly rich widow 'that he might obtayne her in mariage to be his wife'.[29] Richard Dennys of Kennington, a 30-year-old bricklayer, likewise represented himself as a *sutor* to Katherine Richards, speaking for Edmond Coppyn in expectation of securing 20 nobles 'yf he coulde brynge yt to passe'. In the event, neither he nor Henry Lodge who had been acquainted with both parties for four to five years, could prevail as 'an ernest *sutor*'.[30] Some described simply as 'messengers' were sent to convey some communication, dispatch a letter, or to otherwise expedite matters. When Margaret Cole's parents were sent for to the bedside of Henry Lyon, 'the *messinger* [declared] that if ever they wold see hym alive they shuld com out of hand'.[31] Even messengers with apparently limited authority might, however, act as disruptive or compromising agents. Evidence which was tangential to the case of *Simons* v. *Spayne*, recalled the elopement of Mary Hale. Important enquiries were disclosed as to whether or not her mother, and stepfather William Tanner, 'both or one of them did not as much as in them was both by themselves their *servantes* and *messengers* seeke by all meanes to hinder and breake the same mariage'.[32] At times the terminology of brokerage would appear to have been used. William Hawsnothe, for example, a weaver residing in Frittenden, was voiced to be 'the first *broker* of the mariage between Julian Barnes and Bridgeman'.[33] More common, was the general suggestion of self-styled intermediaries. Thomas Mussred claimed that he accompanied Richard Harker of Whitstable at the start of his suit, 'to be a *means* to break the matter' to John Lawrence and his wife and to Jone Young, the defendant.[34] In a different case contended between Mark Giles of Selling and Katherine Wyborn of Sheldwich, several individuals were called upon to act as negotiators. Among them, Christopher Sowthouse of Selling, aged 63 and well known to both parties, deposed that 'he hathe been a *meane* and persuaded with the parties and Paramor [her uncle] that there ought to be some good end made without swyte in law'. Edward Songar, a middle-aged yeoman from Boughton-under-Blean, sought 'to confer' with Paramor and 'mytigate his anger'. He described himself as 'a *meane* to Paramor to grant his goodwill', and Hugh Hall of Woodnesborough, Katherine's cousin, was reportedly requested likewise 'to be a *meane*' to Paramor for his consent.[35]

The language employed in identifying more formal designations of spokesmen and substitutes, is cogently expressed in a lengthy deposition made by the proxy, Regenold Smith. He was deputised to act for the widow Alice Porter of St Mary-in-the-Marsh. A yeoman living in the adjacent parish of Dymchurch, he was sufficiently acquainted with Alice after six years, but professed a far longer-standing relationship with the opposing party, Regenold Aderyn, who resided about 13 miles away. He testified that after some initial private talk of matrimony, he was duly 'appointed and made by her, Alis Porter to be *an utter and speaker or mover* of all suche promis and contractes as she did make to [him] in behalf of Regenold Aderyn to be uttered to Aderyn, and also that [he] should have and receave of Aderyn all such promis, faith and trouth, and contractes as he would make to him, in behalf of Alis Porter'. Upon further entreaty, she promised him to take Aderyn to her husband, to bestow herself and her goods and, in her words, 'perfoorme to him that I do promis yow for him'. Immediately afterwards, everything was repeated to her brother who was called to witness, with Smith rehearsing how she had specifically 'ordeyned [him] to be a *speaker and utterer*'. Taking her subsequently by the hand for confirmation of her consent, he asked 'yf the woords aforesaid wer not her mynd. And [she] said yes and gave [him] her hand.' While she was later to deny ever having made any promise to Regenold Aderyn, she did acknowledge the making of a faithful promise to Regenold Smith on Aderyn's behalf.[36] In this case, what is demonstrated is the role played by a specific type of empowered go-between in the making of a contract.

The constituting of a proxy invested with the potential authority to make such a match between absent parties, marks one of a number of intermediary types who were involved as matrimonial agents in the sixteenth century. Allowing for a certain latitude in their features and functions, a typology of different characters presents itself. They include the more traditional and official mediators such as the parish priest[37] and church court officers, the letter-writers, midwives, bawds, busybodies and medlers, and dealers in magic existing on the margins of social and legal respectability, not to mention the neighbours, friends, relations and patrons of either party concerned. Seen from a literary angle, it has been suggested that 'go-betweens may come from any segment of society'.[38] In what follows, some analysis of the above said kinds of characters will be attempted as they emerge from the historical records of matrimonial cases.

While the conventional role of the parish priest officiating at a marriage ceremony may be an assumed part of his ecclesiastical duty, the functions of religious-type intermediaries in the affairs of courtship were not limited to the stage of contract making.[39] Enquiries regarding the marriage plans of the couple, the intended place of wedding, and careful examination of their appropriate consent were professionally called for.[40] The very act of clarification encouraged the expedition of proceedings and the affirmation of promises. Instrumental in the role of pacifying and arbitrating, they gave advice and comfort in the interest of harmonised relations,[41] and might also serve as advocates to a particular cause. Acting on behalf of the defendant William Saunders, the curate of Minster, Thanet, sought to 'pacifie the displeasure' of William's father, and 'persuaded Edward Saunders to receave his son into favor again'.[42] In a separate case, as we have seen, the intercessionary help of the clerk William Walsall was called upon by William Divers to treat for marriage with Elizabeth Williams. Whether by fair means or foul, he solicited for the goodwill and consent of both Elizabeth and her mother. Persuasions, threats and the alleged invocation of magic, were the tactics he may have employed to make a match between the parties.[43] Even after contracts were made, clerics were asked to resolve problems and assuage doubts. The curate of Stodmarsh, Peter Bennet, went at the request of his fellow 'countrywoman' Isabell Parker to Thomas Tanner's house in Herne. There he conferred with him 'about certeyne doubts' which he had, and assured him of the falsity of certain reports made of her which had prompted his change of mind.[44]

Somewhat less conspicuous in his professional capacity as a type of intermediary, the legal agent nevertheless figured as witness, mandate and envoy. He acted indirectly at times, it would seem, outside the expected call of duty. Edmond Arundell of Wootton, a distant relation of the plaintiff John Mantle, might have served the office of summoner at the time when he visited the Mereweath household in Sheperdswell, although he denied bringing any citation with him to command Parnell Mereweath's presence in court. In the course of his apparently unauthorised visit, the neutrality of his position was immediately transformed to a role of confessor, confidant, secret messenger and conspirator, at the instance of Parnell's emotional and private declaration. Affirming 'with weaping teares to him' her love for John Mantle, with whom she was contracted, she spoke despairingly of the misery she suffered under her parents' and brother's spite. She claimed that she was fearful of her father's intense anger and readiness to kill her if he should learn of their conversation, seeking to elope rather than endure her present life, and beseeching Edmond to convey her commendations and everything she had spoken, to John Mantle. Having consequently written down his deposition on paper for his better remembrance, as he claimed, Edmond Arundell was able to report that she had said to him in secret, 'I pray you have me comended unto him, and tell hym that whensoever he will serve any citacon upon me that I will com furth to my answer although I dye within an hour after for it'.[45]

Some characters appearing in the depositions who were sufficiently literate, although not necessarily public notaries of any kind, were employed to write letters in the name of one party and see to their safe delivery. As previously indicated, the mediation of letters was a legally recognised means of contracting between absent parties.[46] The 55-year-old deponent, Thomas Ridley of Herne, on the other hand, may have had some pretensions of professional legal expertise. In the case of *Hannyngs* v. *Cockman*, he was allegedly appointed by Richard Cockman to bring Thomasina Hannyng to his house 'by any meanes possible', and in so doing witnessed their promise of marriage. His credibility as a witness and his role as an intermediary were, however, suspect and his dabblings in the law did not stand him in good repute among his neighbours. He was described as 'a medler of everymans', and such a one as having 'no other meanes to lyve by but as a *broker* of mens matters in law being no lawyer, takethe monney of men for whome he neither can doo good, ne yet is able to help them to their right'. Generally he was regarded as a false 'sutor', a dissembler, and a goer-between people with ill tales, making debate between them.[47]

With local talk and the spreading of reports being, in some measure, a controlling factor in courtship, it is important to recognise the very act of intermeddling as a form of intermediary behaviour. This was so regardless of whether or not the intervention which was made helped to forward or obstruct a particular suit. Intermediaries had the capacity to interfere in negative, as well as positive means. The witness Cicely Goodstone, for example, wife of a Littlebourne labourer, was taken by Ralph Cole to be a 'buysybody and a comonly medler in meny folkes maters'. He told the court that, at the time when he was a suitor to Anne Hall of Littlebourne, whom he subsequently married,

> Cicely was and wold ever be against his sute, saying reporting him to be a nawghty and lewde fellow, and wheare as the mayd had made a promise to him of mariage ... Cicely would give her counsaill not to marry ... persuading her to forsake him and that she would provide her of an honest man and as riche, and this manner of evill talk she had ... And herapon [he] perceyving her ill tongue and disposition against him, desired her to be contented and that he might have her goodwill, and to that ende he promised to give her som reward, as ... 2s ... and promised her an apron besides ... and over that he had her to the alehouse divers times ... And thyen ever after she did give him a good report to the mayde night and day.[48]

The goodwill and support of Cicely Goodstone in Ralph Cole's courtship, obtained as he said 'by reason of giftes', strongly parallels the desire felt by William Witherden 'at that tyme of his sute to have ... mother Butterwickes favor and goodword'. The elderly Agnes Butterwick, appointed by the will of alderman Starkey of Canterbury to be a stay and bedfellow to his wife, presided at the wooing dinner for widow Starkey's hand in marriage. She was also, it seems, the means whereby William Witherden was brought and allowed to enter the widow's bedchamber. William acknowledged having promised Agnes at other times 'that if it wer his fortune to spede of the widow or place hymself with her, meanyng thereby to marry with her, and that she wold speake a good word for hym he would recompence her paynes'. Agnes Butterwick was later to complain that 'for her good will she was negentilly rewarded'. When she asked to have 'a good torne' of him for that cause, (being a gown of Mr. Starkey's to make a frock for herself), William 'bad the said Agnes walk like a bawde and get her out of the house for ther she shuld no longer loge nor have anything of him'.[49]

Mother Butterwick, as she was known by some, was by profession a midwife in the community. A midwife was an agent of social contact within a predominantly female network, and might act as an informal broker. Although also regarded as potentially subversive, far from occupying a peripheral position, 'the midwife's office allowed her to pass thresholds and open doors ... occasionally perform[ing] a priest-like function'.[50] In this case, possessed of a complex identity which also incorporated images of a disreputable past, Mother Butterwick was perhaps as much an ideological construction of conflicting opinions, as a real definable personality.[51] A practitioner on the one hand, she was a so-called 'bawd' on the other.[52] A character, perhaps, not unlike those 'goer-betweens' who appear in Shakespeare, the 'bawd' representing 'the final debasement of the Shakespearean agent in courtship'.[53]

Existing also on the fringes of lawfully recognised culture, semi-professional quack doctors practised their knowledge of physic and magic to intercede on behalf of their customers. The experience of Thomas Fanshaw of Canterbury with his patient Alice Suttill highlights their intermeddling role. It was said that Thomas Fanshaw visited her house on several occasions, during which time they held long conferences. Both he and his wife received food, money, cloth and a ring from Alice in return for physic, in particular a bill or scroll with 'dyvers prayers' in it to cause her husband, William Suttill, to love her. Alice was seen by her household servant to wear a piece of paper about her neck night and day. Whether or not the failure of his intervention in the cause of love was later inverted to predict or divine death, remains uncertain. He was later charged for the use of 'witchcrafte and socerye to know as yt was said how long William Suttill should live and be her husband'. William Fanshaw confessed that Alice did 'intreate [him] to gyve hir something or to do somwhat for hyr to make hir husband to love hyr, and that he did give her a prayer or a charme', which was 'a certen bill of socerye concernyng William Suttill but said that bill could not do any harme to [him] only he did yt to please Alice Suttill because until he had so done he could not be in quiet'. By the report of others, he served her as a reluctant intercessor, experiencing acutely the dilemma of doing 'that he could not do'. As he told the warrant bearer at the time of his arrest, 'Suttills wife would have me do that for her that I cannot do and by no meanes I cann be quiet for she is so importunate upon me.'[54]

It has been suggested so far, that different kinds of intermediaries may have been customarily employed in the activities of courtship and in the making of matches in the sixteenth century. Both the contemporary literature and the law might be seen to confirm the use of this social custom. Some attempt has been made, moreover, to develop the concept of the intermediary by identifying specific intermediary types as they are variously termed in the marriage cases. Those with more traditional, and professional, or marginally professional roles have been represented here. The intention now will be to examine the profile of the go-betweens, their geographical proximity and association with the couple concerned, and their means of acting on the behalf of either party or of other interested parties.

Of all the marriage cases found in the consistory court depositions for the period concerned, approximately one-quarter (82) of those cases provide evidence for use in this study. This proportion clearly underestimates the much more extensive involvement of outsiders in the conduct of courtship, their participation in contract making, the intervention of parents as marriage-makers or hinderers, and group interference in individual choice.

This being said, the 145 persons treated here as intermediaries were living in parishes located throughout the Canterbury diocese, representing therefore a generally unbiased geographical distribution. Where there was clear evidence to indicate the place of residence of the marriage partners concerned, and of the intermediary employed in those particular cases, it was possible to examine the degree of residential proximity between all three. Of the sample, 35 per cent of marriage partners lived in the same parish. In such situations, the go-between was almost always another fellow parishioner. Clearly, it was far more common in this study for couples to live at some distance from each other although, as we shall see in the next chapter, the distance was unlikely to have been very great. It may be argued that this sample favours cases where partners were predominantly separated by distance, implying too that such separation might encourage a match to be negotiated by means of others. However, it is also very noticeable that under those circumstances it was just as likely for the intermediary to reside in a totally different locality, as to reside in the same parish as either one of the parties. Measuring the distance between the intermediary and the closer of the two marriage partners, it would appear that they were largely drawn from within an area of three to 10 miles, otherwise from adjacent parishes, and at times up to 20 miles away. Given, however, that these distances represent the minimum estimate, since one of the parties would be living further away, the field of courtship activity and matrimonial negotiation within the diocese would have been more extensive and complex. What is also suggested is that the conduct of courtship was neither haphazard nor simply dictated by situations of convenience. A careful and conscious use of outside intervention was at play.

Plaintiffs in disputed matrimonial cases were usually men, and since intermediaries generally acted on their behalf, it is not surprising that they too were usually male. Although men were more likely to find allies in other men, there was no absolute gender discrimination. Male suitors employed the services of both men and women, and so did their female partners.

Precise information regarding the status of the parties concerned is hard to come by. They included widows, servants, virgins, or young people, a gentle-man, a weaver, a shoemaker's daughter, a scholar and other literate persons. More can be gleaned about the intermediaries themselves, whose depositions provide better clues and often specify their age, occupation and personal knowledge of both parties in the marriage case. Of the eighty-four ages mentioned, only three were under 21 years, with nineteen more under 30 years. Forty-four were between the ages of 31 and 50, another twelve were in their fifties, and six intermediaries were 61 years of age or more. Assuming that the average age of marriage in early modern England as shown in family reconstitution studies applies here too,[55] it would appear that intermediaries were generally older than the parties themselves. Some were evidently very senior, implicitly bearing the hallmarks of respectability and experience. In terms of age, at least, there may have been little question of parity between the parties and the choice of intermediary. Marriage partners opted instead for sobriety, decorum and a more authoritative means of conveying their matrimonial intention.

The professional and economic status of these intermediaries may also confirm this conclusion. Certain professional groups, by virtue of their calling, were ideally positioned for mediating and negotiating relationships. Several of religious rank, of 'gentle' and predominantly 'yeoman' status, served as some form of go-between. Artisans, those in the building, clothing and food trade, which included the Buckland butcher Edward Reade, with 'learninge enough' to oversee a marriage,[56] were likewise involved. Among the women, the midwife, widows, and particularly wives as opposed to single girls, acted as channels of communication between partners. Those who were, however, merely servants, were usually stated to be under the age of 25. Although a few of them served in important households, many were either fellow servants, former fellow servants to the parties concerned, or servants in the household of their kin. Almost invariably, their task was more restricted, and their authority limited to the delivery of tokens or messages. Occasionally they also delivered the appropriately desired commendations, wrote letters on behalf of one party, or in the course of their own business, served as contacts and bearers of news. Nevertheless, even those servants who ranked lower down the social scale were qualified in other ways to act as agents in courtship. As trusted servants in one's household, whether the place of work or home, they were relied upon as messengers, informants and as discerning representatives in marriage.

If age and status were two of the criteria which probably governed the choice of intermediary, the third was likely to have been forged on the basis of personal kin ties or on the strength of mutual acquaintance. Of those who were neither servants, nor churchmen, we have evidence of personal ties for 73 individuals. At least 15 intermediaries specifically identified themselves as being 'kin' or 'cosyn' to one of the parties, with 13 others termed 'friend', 'felowe', or 'neighbour'. In some cases, relationships based on work and property incorporated those who were clearly masters, tenants and, in one instance, a nurse to the household. Intermediaries who simply specified the number of years they had known the parties, might well have included blood relatives or affines. They were evidently known to at least one of the marriage partners for a minimum of two to three years, more often four or five years, and in several cases up to 12 and even 20 years. Some intermediaries professed a knowledge dating back from childhood, or described their relationship as one of many years standing. Even in circumstances where they were not related through blood or marriage, the durability of fictive ties, of work, property and place, and the credibility gained out of personal knowledge, would appear critical in motivating action.

Examining more closely the issue of motivation, it is possible not only to determine who the instigating party may have been at a particular time, but also, in some instances, the stated reasons for intervention given by the intermediaries themselves. Laurence Taillor of Frittenden, who had known Juliana Barnes and Ralph Cole of the same parish for approximately five years, described his relationship with Ralph as being one 'a good while together of acquayntence and freendes'. They often went to visit Juliana together, and he was often present when Ralph declared the matrimonial purpose of his visits. He deposed that in

> perceyving the good will that she did beare towards hym the said Rauf that way, [he] fayned to be a sutor for hym selfe thereby to understand and trye her constancy towards Ralf Cole/ Julian declaring to [him] that she had made a promise to Ralf Cole and that she wold have hym only and forsake all other with which her aunswer [he] percyving her mind so bent towards Ralf Cole said to her, Than I have my aunswer Juliane, and I will trouble ye no more but will geve place unto Rauf of whome I percyve you be well spell.[57]

Other intermediaries similarly gave testimony to their familiarity, affection and goodwill for a particular party. The 60-year-old John Hudson had known Edward Longley of Boughton Maleherbe since childhood, and Joanna Marchaunt of Hartlip (the servant of his kinsman Thomas Blechinden) for eight years. He acted out of 'the love and familiarity that he of long tyme had borne towardes Edward Longley and knowing hym to be a very honest and frendly man brought hym to Thomas Blechindens house ... wher the said Edward was never but ones afore ... of intent to make merry' during which time the couple were able to talk together privately.[58] In another marriage case, Margery Overye's ex-master, Robert Austen, a Littlebourne yeoman of 44 years, acted as 'a meanes to get her freinds goodwill'. He earnestly solicited for the consent of her stepfather John Rigdon, 'very much endevoring to make up a maryage' between Margery and Thomas Launsfield, the 'cause of which his endevour [Rigdon] beleveth to be the great affection he beareth unto Launsfield'.[59] Being 'moved of goodwill' for the man was also the reason professed by the tailor John Rolf for helping Robert Sloden to win his sister's hand. He claimed that he 'hath been a meanes to Robert Sloden for that he hath alwaies seamed to be a very honest man and well able to lyve of hymself, to be a sutor unto Silvester Witherden to wyne with her in conference of talke of mariage. Wherapon [Sloden] folowing [his] advice attempted his sute unto the wedowe.'[60]

Some go-betweens acted, as we have seen, in the interest and expectation of financial reward or other means of remuneration. Richard Dennys was promised 20 nobles, Agnes Butterwick expected to receive a gown, or at least appropriate recompense for her efforts,[61] and Cicely Goodstone some reward such as money, clothes and drink.[62] Small payments were occasionally made for more restricted tasks. The widow Marcia Mace, who had been known to both parties for three years, was asked by Jone Swift to fetch Thomas Wood to her house, and was offered 4*d* for doing so.[63] Perhaps what is more interesting is the moral sense of indebtedness incurred, and the desire for some kind of reciprocal behaviour, as expressed in the allegations made against William Beale. He wrote and delivered a letter on Judith Symons's behalf which appointed the time wherein she and John Spayne made a privy contract. It was at about the same time that William Beale was secretly married to Mary Hale. During his interrogation, he was asked

> wether he did promise to Judith Simons that if it coulde so be broughte to passe that he mighte marrye with Mary Hale his now wife, that then he woulde be the meanes and in such sorte he would compasse and bring to passe that she should marry with John Spaine ... [and] whether not long before or ymediatly after he was married to his nowe wife he would have procured and so much as in hym was did procure the sayd John Spaine to have contracted hymself in mariage to Judith Simons.[64]

Thus far, we have seen intervention borne out of an official capacity, motivated by an openly declared personal affection, or prompted at least in part by material incentives or the promise of future obligation. Seldom, it seems, did intermediaries act entirely independently. Legally at least, in terms of making a contract, they were not entitled to act without specific recommendation, and without being specially sent. Usually it was the parties themselves, and as already stated, predominantly the men, who requested their services, but arguably, the crucial point is not merely a matter of who the instigating party was. It is the fact that it was customarily necessary for others to be called upon to manage the courtship and, moreover, the effect of their actions, which might exceed the initially desired task.

In some situations, however, neither of the parties was responsible. Masters, kindred and particularly parents sought to use go-betweens for specific ends. Edward Saunders, unwilling to grant his consent for his son William to marry with Susan Woollet, and believing, as he said, that 'she was no wife for his son, and dyvers matters were against her', claimed that he had sent 'indifferent men' to make formal enquiries regarding her suitability, and had received 'answere that she was in no sorte fite to match with his son'.[65] Less formally, parents and kin relied upon others to inform them of what was going on between the parties. 'At the biddinge of John Wyse', father of Katherine, Edward Sowgate went to speak 'secretly' with Edward Clynche to demand an acknowledgement of his promise to her. Although Edward denied it at first, he soon confessed that they were indeed sure together, but because she 'protracted and prolonged allweys the marriag tyme', he said 'that he would be no longer pynned to her sleeve, but would marrie otherwise with one that did not so lynger the tyme'.[66] Probing to understand what the matter was, and the intention of the parties, was only one of the several tasks which intermediaries were assigned to perform. Edward Williams, the brother of the defendant Joan Williams of St Alphege, Canterbury, was persuaded by his mother and father to, in turn, persuade his sister to favour Peter Levet. He acted therefore as 'a meanes unto her ... to allure her goodwill', declaring the 'goodwill and fervent love that Peter ought to her, and also the willing consents of his father and mother'.[67] By contrast, the cleric Thomas Wilson was sent for by old Collye, father of Thomas Collye, to confer about the dissolving of a promise between Thomas and Elizabeth Baker and, by his advice, 'the matter grewe to be dissolved'.[68] In another case, the efforts of John Colen were prompted by Agnes Wills's parents as well as by Richard Benet. They were designed to ensure that Agnes might clear herself from James Lambart in order to marry with Richard Benet. James communicated his consent that she might 'marie where she woulde'.[69]

It now remains to be seen what roles the intermediaries actually played in the conduct of courtship, the problems they caused and in turn faced, and the general significance of their position in the moves and stratagems of marriage. According to John Gillis, they were employed in order that all procedures should be witnessed and publicised for whensoever the need for confirmation arose.[70] For the man to bring someone with him to bear witness of the woman's promise, or to hear matters of marriage discussed was quite common.[71] Richard Randall recalled how he had been sought and asked by his brother-in-law, Philip Joyce, to accompany him to Hartlip to hear just such a matter. At that time Richard said to Joanne Marchaunt, 'I have brought you here my frende to whom I perceyve by hym you bear goodwill, and to hear what answer you will give him and stand to'.[72] The function of the intermediary in bringing together parties in clandestine situations was as apparent in the court cases as in Shakespearean drama.[73] The aforementioned Edward Reade was informed by Thomas Kennet and Judith Simons of their intention to marry. He kept their secret, and soon after Thomas was expelled from Mr Tanner's service, Edward was asked by both parties to 'be a meanes to bring them together to some place from Mr Tanners house where they might meette and talke together, and to that end he ... carried tokens from eche to other.'[74] In circumstances where the go-between acted at the man's behest, approximately half of the cases involved the delivery of a token, compared to a third of the cases where women were the instigators. The task, however, was often not restricted to the mere delivery of a token. The person carrying the token in his or her name, was charged with declaring commendations, reporting back to the sender, questioning the recipient, testing his or her conscience and reminding either of their promise.[75]

Whether at a frivolous or perhaps irreverent level, it is not clear if Judith Simons really did rehearse the marriage ceremony with a female proxy. It was asked whether 'at such tyme as she hath byne pleasant and merrye ... [she] hath taken a booke of comon prayer and taking unto her a mayden hath said unto her these wordes or the like in effect viz thow shalt be the man and I wilbe the mayde ... and we wilbe married, and therupon taking or ioyning handes together she hath reade of mariage'.[76] If proxies were used in the parodies of courtship which young people acted out, they were employed more seriously throughout every stage of courtship. Numerous instances demonstrate cogently the importance and diversity of their role. They were used as a means of recommendation, arbitrating in some cases, soliciting in others, making investigations, giving their opinion, advice and assistance, seeking to confirm one's intention, trying to bring matters to a conclusion, and generally intervening at any time in the course of matrimonial proceedings. Some intermediaries such as Peter Bellingham facilitated introductions,[77] or accompanied the man at the beginning of his suit.[78] Thomas Colly, the kinsman of the defendant also named Thomas Colly, prepared the way for future marriage entreaties by testing the ground in the preliminary stages. He reported to Mary Oldfield's mother the goodwill which existed between the couple, indicating that Thomas had sent him 'to know whether he should be welcome or not' to her house.[79] Go-betweens were employed no less at the end of a suit. At Oliver Symons's request, the gentleman Christopher Gay, for example, went to the house of Jane Bedford's father requiring her to speak with him to discharge their conscience.[80] In between the early and final stages they acted in a variety of ways, both positive and negative, going to bridge the physical or psychological distance between the couple and between the parties and their kin.

It has been shown that certain intermediaries were required to speak a good word, do a good turn, entreat for the goodwill of party or kin, alleviate any displeasure incurred, carry messages and gifts, help to arrange a rendezvous, act as chaperone, confidant, confessor, arbitrator, counsel, informer and investigator. The practical assistance they provided in terms of financial assurance was also evident. Anne Philpott, who wept at thinking herself 'undone' because Thomas Funell was 'worthe nothing', was given an assurance by James Boykett that he would be worth £10 at the day of marriage and that she need not be afraid to marry him. Upon that promise she desired James to bid him to come to her again.[81] The aged carpenter John Taylor was likewise responsible for moving matters forward, performing the duty of financial arrangement considered so crucial as a basis for marital security. He was asked by Elizabeth Overie to speak to old Terry in order to get as much as he could off Terry for her and for her children if she was to marry his son John.[82]

It is, however, important to realise that whatever the apparently definable nature of the task specifically required of the intermediary, the effect of the actual confrontation might also have been significant. Some intermediaries, after all, were unlikely to have been impassive communicators, especially given their probable acquaintanceship with the party concerned. Opinions which might be expressed were themselves a manner of advertisement, admonition, challenge or provocation. The nurse and widow Dorothy Fittell who was asked by John Spayne to 'helpe him to speak with Judith Simons' lying sick at that time in the house, began to talk with him herself. She 'told him that he must nowe trye himselfe a man or a boy', either to stand to his promise or else to leave her to her other suitor.[83] George London, having known Nicholas Fookes and Mary Lowes to have been very familiar in his house, and having been told by Nicholas that Mary had forsaken him, spoke to her at his request. Riding to Fordwich and calling upon her, he reminded her of the trouble which had fallen out between herself and Nicholas. Testing her conscience, he warned 'it wer best that you did advise with yorself whither you wer man and wife'.[84] Certainly so far as communication via tokens was concerned, the mere delivery of a token by an agent stimulated a response. Christopher Bridge, asked by his late household servant, Thomasine Lee, to deliver a letter and handkerchief, returned to report what 'he perceyved', and also delivered to her a reciprocated gift of love.[85]

The perceptions, opinions and reports of go-betweens cannot always be assumed to have been correct, whether due to misinterpretation, misguidance, or wilful falsity of representation. Contemporary fiction illustrates some of the problems caused by the abuses, vexations and plots of 'ambassadors', 'friends' and agents, and the potential for deception which existed. Writers of conduct books on matrimony also warned against the dangers of relying upon intermediaries, expressing the suspicions which surrounded a much practised custom.[86] At times the accounts given in court cases depict the craftiness of their behaviour through the medium of false reports, disguised gifts, or cunning pretexts. When Katherine Richards refused to accept the pair of knives which Richard Dennys offered her, he confessed to having 'tolde her that he gave them to [her] hymself as his owne gyfte, and not as the gyfte of Edmund Coppyn which Edmund willed hym soo to doo yf she wolde not receive them',[87] a form of deception which, however intended, might have significant repercussions. More ingenious was the bizarre tale of the hole-in-the-wall contract between Dorothy Hocking and Richard Edmundes. It took place in the parish of Holy Cross near Westgate, Canterbury, in 1564, between the backyards of Hocking's house and the house of Robert Holmes. By her own deposition, Dorothy maintained an apparent innocence in the contrivances worked out by Holmes's wife. She claimed that while she was busy with her mother's affairs in the backside of the house, Holmes's wife called her to come and speak with her through the hole in the wall, on the pretext of showing her how Dorothy's dog had entered their backyard and stolen their conger fish. Encouraging Dorothy to kneel down so that they could speak secretly at the hole, she took Dorothy's hand through the hole. Richard Edmundes, who was present, thereupon had her by the finger, and sought to contract matrimony with her.[88]

While there may have been some justifiable misgivings regarding the motives and activities of intermediaries, they too placed themselves at risk and were subject to abuse. There was the dilemma of Thomas Fanshaw, coerced into acting beyond his means in order to 'be ride of' his patient and customer, Alice Suttill.[89] One Dionisia Archer also took a gamble when she was charged with delivering a silver ring and a pair of shoes from John Bonham to Margery Ellet, then a servant in the house of Salmon Wilkyns at Tonge. In so doing she met with her aunt, Mistress Wilkyns, in the cherry garden. She 'told her that she had a ring to deliver to Madge her maide, which ring [Dionisia's] awnt toke away from her, and did beate [her] for bringing the same'.[90] In another case, it was alleged that Mary Rolf was a 'principall partie' in procuring the marriage between William Beale and Mary Hale, the stepdaughter of William Tanner of Dymchurch. It would appear that she gave her consent 'to the stealing or taking away of Mary Hale by William Beale and his confederates', and for her role was whipped and scourged by Mr Tanner or his wife before certain of their neighbours of Dymchurch, and turned out of their service.[91]

Although the use of intermediaries in the game of courtship, and the playing of that role, were in part recognised as a gamble, the whole area of courtship represented a field of testing, negotiation and experimentation between the single and married state. The go-between was one popular means of bridging the gap. Some parties required several intermediaries to woo on their behalf, or depended upon the same person repeatedly to see to the conclusion of the suit. Intermediaries were not only important at the moment of crisis, but at various encounters; indeed, as we have seen, at every stage of courtship from beginning to end. They acted in the presence of both partners as well as in the absence of one. John Hudson, for example, was specifically asked by Edward Longley after he left Joanna Marchant's company, to deliver a ring of gold to her 'whan he was goon ... and to ask her the question whether that she were the same woman and of the same mynde that she was towards him the last tyme that she and he had talk together, and to examyn her of the talk'. John Hudson did so, and she declared 'that there was faith and trouth between her and Longley of marriage, and sayd that she wold never forsake hym so long as she lyved'. She accepted the ring 'very gladly and willingly of herty goodwill without any forcement seaming very willing to have hym to her husband, and apon the receipt of the ring required [Hudson] to have her commended to him'.[92]

The importance of intermediaries in the process of courtship was not only a recognised, and frequently employed, cultural phenomenon, it involved the use of prime and secondary movers with different degrees of influence, and suggests the existence of a hierarchy of intervention, albeit a flexible one. The 58-year-old yeoman John Beere feared himself unable to speak on William Saunders's behalf to his father. He believed that 'he could do nothing with his father', and spoke instead to the curate of the parish, desiring him to solicit for the goodwill of Edward Saunders in the marriage between his son and Susan Woollet.[93] While John Beere transferred his given responsibility to a higher authority, Margery Overye sought the help of Robert Austen. She asked her intended, Thomas Launsfield, to obtain Robert's consent to their marriage 'because she sayd she thought that noe man was soe likely or more likely to get her freinds goodwill then [he]'.[94] The need to acquire the favour and goodwill of intermediaries such as Robert Austen, and even of less reputable characters like Agnes Butterwick and the meddlesome Cicely Goodstone,[95] testifies to their implicit power to help make a match or obstruct it.

Most of the go-betweens, as we have seen, were unlikely to have been professionals, and were also unlikely to have conformed to the precise model of formal, expert marriage brokerage outlined by Macfarlane. They ranged instead from the aged and respectable, to the marginal characters at the other end of the spectrum. Experienced negotiators, semi-professionals and neutral intermediaries, parties interested in deriving some material reward, and kindred and friends with a personal interest in the marriage, were all involved in matchmaking. All may be regarded as go-betweens in some sense. The pervasiveness of their use suggests a degree at least of formalised procedure in marriage negotiations, even among less prosperous rural folk in the communities and provinces of sixteenth-century Kent. Although, *pace* Macfarlane, they were seldom formally constituted, and were less vital in the initiation of matches, thereafter such agents were integral to its making, and played an important role in promoting, sustaining and developing matrimonial relationships. The existence of such a diverse range of go-betweens operating in Kentish courtship suggests that, in this respect, courtship in Kent differed significantly from the highly individualistic model posited by Macfarlane for England. It may, therefore, have wider implications for Macfarlane's definition of English marriage, which rests on the relatively crude distinction between peasantries and their supposedly characteristic familistic courtship patterns on the one hand, and the individualistic courtship system of pre-industrial England on the other. Such categorisation of societies proves to be highly misleading and the testing for distinctive features appears both intrinsically flawed and too rigid. It would be difficult, for example, to argue that Kentish courtship was based on out-and-out individualism. Far from being a game played solely by the courting couple, the extensive employment of go-betweens suggests that, on the contrary, courtship was very often a game with many players, a mediated and delegated joint effort. That this was so, however, does not necessarily mean that Kent's economy and society resembed very closely that of a classic peasantry.

What the widespread use of intermediaries does demonstrate is the fact that the making of marriage was a matter too important to be left to the individual and his or her sentiments alone. By interposing themselves between prospective partners, go-betweens acted to moderate the emotional temperature of courtships and of individual passion. The significance of go-betweens was not, however, confined to the conduct of courtship. In the highly personalised and negotiable state of the 'moral economy', where every relationship might be considered polyvalent, intermediaries (like gifts and tokens) were used to negotiate all kinds of relationships and transactions. It is suggested that their participation in the conduct of courtship shows that their role was not random but purposeful, and in some respects regulatory. In courtship, they served when couples lived in close proximity, but they were also prepared to make the necessary journeys to bridge physical distances between prospective partners. In so doing they performed a vital function in the maintenance of liaisons between couples who may not have lived as near neighbours for the total duration of their courtship. The following chapter will attempt a fresh examination of such courtship horizons since questions of distance and location were further mechanisms and determinants that might facilitate or hinder the making of marriage.

NOTES

1 C.C.A.L., MS. X/10/4, fos 52, 60, *Rolf* v. *Whiter* (1549).

2 E.g. C.C.A.L. MSS. X/10/8, fos 126–8, *Rayner* v. *Chamber* (1561), and X/10/11, fos 213–14v., *Richards* v. *Cockes* (1570), give contemporary opinions on the suitability of particular matches.

3 C.C.A.L. MS. X/10/12, fos 173v.–4v., *Lee* v. *Sething* (1565).

4 See above, chapter 1.

5 Cook, *Making a Match*, p. 104.

6 Macfarlane, *Marriage and Love*, pp. 293, 295.

7 Gillis, *For Better, For Worse*, p. 34.

8 E.g. C.C.A.L., MS. X/11/3, fos 56v.–7, *Alcock* v. *Hardes* (1598).

9 Cook, *Making a Match*, pp. 107–8.

10 Macfarlane, *Marriage and Love*, pp. 294–5.

11 Stone, *Family, Sex and Marriage*, p. 72.

12 Quoted in P. Earle, *The Making of the English Middle Class: Business, Society and Family Life in London, 1660–1730* (London, 1989), pp. 193–4.

13 Macfarlane, *Marriage and Love*, p. 294.

14 See above, Introduction, p. 5.

15 Macfarlane, *Marriage and Love*, p. 295.

16 R. A. Houlbrooke ed., *English Family Life, 1576–1716* (Oxford, 1988), pp. 22–7.

17 *Ibid.*, pp. 27–8.

18 Cressy, *Birth, Marriage and Death*, pp. 237–9.

19 *Ibid.*, pp. 243–4; Houlbrooke ed., *English Family Life*, p. 257.

20 Houlbrooke ed., *English Family Life*, p. 20; Gillis, *For Better, For Worse*, pp. 36–8.

21 Cressy, *Birth, Marriage and Death*, pp. 252–3. For further examples in diaries and autobiographies, see pp. 239–40, 248–9. The concept of a 'mean' person can be found, for example, in Byrne ed., *Lisle Letters*, p. 68.

22 Cook, *Making a Match*, pp. 110–19.

23 Macfarlane, *Marriage and Love*, pp. 247, 294; and for other historical examples of brokerage, see C. Klapisch-Zuber, *Women, Family, and Ritual in Renaissance Italy*, trans. L. G. Cochrane (Chicago and London, 1985), p. 183; Segalen, *Love and Power*, p. 22; M. A. Kaplan ed., *The Marriage Bargain: Women and Dowries in European History* (New York and London, 1985), pp. 126, 129–30.

24 For an interesting parallel discussion of social intermediary types and the problems of definition, see 'Cultural Intermediaries', in M. Vovelle, *Ideologies and Mentalities*, trans. E. O'Flaherty (Oxford, 1990), pp. 114–25.

25 Cressy, *Birth, Marriage and Death*, p. 235.

26 Swinburne, *Treatise of Spousals*, sect. xiii, 'Of contracting spousals either betwixt parties present or absent', pp. 154–92, esp. pp. 162–7, 178–82. Cook, *Making a Match*, pp. 109–10, for a summary of the laws. J. A. Brundage, *Law, Sex, and Christian Society in Medieval Europe* (Chicago and London, 1987), pp. 436, 497–8.

27 E.g. C.C.A.L., MS. X/10/9, fos 46v.–8, *Hopkinson v. Philippes* (1563).

28 C.C.A.L., MS. X/11/2, fos 41v.–2v., *Woollet v. Saunders* (1590).

29 E.g. C.C.A.L., MS. X/10/12, fos 97v.–9, *pro partem John Parkes of New Romney* (1564).

30 C.C.A.L., MS. X/10/7, fos 134v.–5, 326v.–7, *Coppyn v. Richard* (1560–61).

31 C.C.A.L., MS. X/10/7, f. 83, *Lyon v. Cole* (1560).

32 C.C.A.L., MS. J/J3 38 (1598).

33 C.C.A.L., MS. X/10/8, f. 24v., *Cole v. Barnes* (1561).

34 C.C.A.L., MS. X/11/6, fos 251v.–2v., *Harker v. Young* (1594).

35 C.C.A.L., MS. X/10/18, fos 49v.–53, 67–9v., 81–4v., *Giles v. Wyborn* (1578).

36 C.C.A.L., MS. X/10/14, fos 229–31v., *Aderyn v. Porter* (1573).

37 See also Carlson, *Marriage and the English Reformation*, pp. 124–5.

38 See also Cook, *Making a Match*, p. 119.

39 For an example of the curate's role in the contract, see C.C.A.L., MS. X/10/10, fos 3–4v., 9, *Bircheley v. Pelland* (1562–63).

40 E.g. C.C.A.L., MSS. X/10/6, fos 115v.–16, *Lambard v. Harewood* (1556); X/10/11, f. 231–v., *Turner v. Hubbarde* (?1570).

41 E.g. C.C.A.L., MS. X/11/4, fos 91–2, *Pigeon* v. *Hastling, Taylor* (1601).

42 C.C.A.L., MS. X/11/2, fos 41v.–2v., *Woollet* v. *Saunders* (1590).

43 C.C.A.L., MS. X/11/5, fos 223–5; MS. J/J3 38, *Divers* v. *Williams* (1597–98); see above, chapter 2, pp. 57–60.

44 C.C.A.L., MS. X/11/4, fos 161v., 162v.–4v., *Parker alias Parr* v. *Tanner* (1602).

45 C.C.A.L., MS. X/10/16, fos 333–6, *Mantle* v. *Mereweath* (1577).

46 E.g. C.C.A.L., MSS. X/10/18, fos 14v.–15v., *Mantle* v. *Mereweath*; X/11/5, fos 243–5, 246v.–7, *Symons* v. *Spayne* (1598). See above, pp. 70–1.

47 C.C.A.L., MSS. X/10/9, fos 56v.–7v., 62–3; X/10/10, fos 23–8v., 30v.–2 (1563).

48 C.C.A.L., MS. X/10/15, fos 240v.–2v., *Smyth* v. *Gray* (1567).

49 C.C.A.L., MS. X/10/8, fos 134–8, 161–2v., *Coppyn* v. *Richard* (1560–61); see below, chapter 4, for the wooing party, p. 149.

50 Cressy, *Birth, Marriage and Death*, p. 61.

51 See above, Introduction, p. 14.

52 Cf. the term 'matrimonial bawd', in Macfarlane, *Marriage and Love*, p. 295.

53 Cook, *Making a Match*, p. 118.

54 C.C.A.L., MS. X/11/2, fos 215–17, 232–4v., 247–8, 249v.–50, 256, *Suttill* v. *Blackborn alias Suttill* (1591).

55 See below, chapter 5, pp. 163–5.

56 C.C.A.L., MS. X/11/5, fos 250–2, *Symons* v. *Spayne* (1598).

57 C.C.A.L., MS. X/10/7, f. 155–v., *Cole* v. *Barnes* (1560–61).

58 C.C.A.L., MS. X/10/12, fos 280v.–2, *Longley* v. *Marchaunt* (1566).

59 C.C.A.L., MS. X/11/4, fos 125–7, 130v.–2v., *Launsfield* v. *Overye* (1601).

60 C.C.A.L., MS. X/10/8, fos 47v.–9v., *Edmonds* v. *Witherden* (1561–62).

61 See above, p. 107.

62 See above, p. 107. For an example of an intermediary who was promised £20 for negotiating a marriage, and who subsequently instigated a case to prove the contract in order to claim her reward, see, Wall, 'For love, money or politics?', p. 514.

63 C.C.A.L., MS. X/10/16, fos 56v.–7v., *Wood* v. *Swift* (1575).

64 C.C.A.L., MSS. X/11/5, fos 243–5, 246v.–7; J/J3 58 (25), *Symons* v. *Spayne* (1598).

65 See above, p. 103.

66 C.C.A.L., MS. X/10/11, f. 208–v., *Wyse* v. *Clynche* (?1570).

67 C.C.A.L., MS. X/10/17, fos 95–6v., *Levet* v. *Willyams* (1574).

68 C.C.A.L., MS. X/11/4, f. 13–v., *Off.* v. *Collye* (1600).

69 C.C.A.L., MS. X/10/3, fos 78v.–9v., *Benet* v. *Lambart* (1548).

70 Gillis, *For Better, For Worse*, p. 34.

71 E.g. C.C.A.L., MS. X/10/7, fos 154–7, *Cole* v. *Barnes* (1560–61).

72 C.C.A.L., MS. X/10/12, fos 284–6v., *Joyce* v. *Marchaunt* (1566).

73 Cook, *Making a Match*, p. 110.

74 See above, p. 110.

75 E.g. C.C.A.L., MSS. X/10/6, fos 115v.–16, *Lambard* v. *Harewood* (1556); X/10/7, fos 326v.–7, *Coppyn* v. *Richard* (1561); X/10/12, fos 280v.–2, *Longley* v. *Marchaunt* (1566); X/10/18, fos 23–5, *Mantle* v. *Mereweath* (1577).

76 C.C.A.L., MS. J/J3 58 (24), *Symons* v. *Spayne* (1598).

77 See above, p. 103.

78 See above, p. 104.

79 C.C.A.L., MS. X/11/3, fos 136v.–7v., *Oldfield* v. *Colly* (1599).

80 C.C.A.L., MS. X/10/6, fos 200v.–1, *Simons* v. *Bedford* (1558). See above, chapter 2, p. 77.

81 C.C.A.L., MS. X/10/7, fos 174–5, *Funell* v. *Philpott* (1567).

82 C.C.A.L., MS. X/11/1, fos 1–3, 8–9, 12–14, 336–v., *Terry* v. *Overie* (1585).

83 C.C.A.L., MS. X/11/5, f. 241v., *Symons* v. *Spayne* (1598).

84 C.C.A.L., MS. X/11/1, f. 218–v., *Fookes* v. *Lowes* (1588).

85 C.C.A.L., MS. X/10/12, fos 173v.–4v., *Lee* v. *Sething* (1565).

86 Cook, *Making a Match*, pp. 105–6, 110–11, 117–18.

87 C.C.A.L., MS. X/10/7, fos 134v.–5, *Coppyn* v. *Richards* (1560–61). See above, pp. 103–4.

88 C.C.A.L., MS. X/10/12, fos 122v.–3, *Edmunds* v. *Hockings* (1564); see also, W. Urry, *Christopher Marlowe and Canterbury*, ed. A. F. Butcher (London, 1988), pp. xxxii–xxxiv.

89 See above, p. 108.

90 C.C.A.L., MS. X/10/7, f. 74–v., *Bonham* v. *Ellet* (1560).

91 C.C.A.L., MS. J/J3 58 (20, 28 and 33), *Symons* v. *Spayne* (1598).

92 C.C.A.L., MS. X/10/12, fos 280v.–2, *Longley* v. *Marchant* (1566).

93 C.C.A.L., MS. X/11/2, fos 62v.–3v., *Woollet* v. *Saunders* (1590).

94 C.C.A.L., MS. X/11/4, fos 130v.–2v., *Launsfield* v. *Overye* (1601).

95 See above, p. 107.

Chapter 4

———◆———

Courtship horizons in the sixteenth century: distance and place as factors in marriage formation[1]

The testimonies given by litigants in matrimonial suits are often expressive of the sentiments and activities of courtship, but are more vague and reticent about the precise *origins* of specific relationships. Although a range of possibilities and circumstances are suggested, the significant moment and location when a couple actually met and where a courtship began, may sometimes be inferred, but are less easy to identify. That there were 'numerous and varied occasions where courtship began and took place' was, in part, associated with the degree of geographical mobility.[2] This chapter offers a discussion of distance and place as factors affecting where courtship might begin and continue. Previous studies of marriage horizons have focused on place of residence at the time of marriage using figures calculated from parish registers. This chapter, however, provides a unique quantification of place of residence during courtship itself. The distances over which potential marriage partners initiated and conducted their affairs will be examined first, using the records of ecclesiastical court Act books. Secondly, the likely auspiciousness of time and place occasioned by such interactions will be explored more closely. Assuming that courtship horizons are partly indicative of marital choice, this chapter seeks to elucidate some of the mechanisms involved in choosing a partner, through an understanding of the spatial context within which personal relationships were developed.

That physical mobility was the common experience of most people living in pre-industrial England has been widely shown. Such studies have also revealed that the structure and dynamics of mobility was a complex one.[3] Nevertheless, movement between places was, characteristically, highly local-ised and 'circular', with 'servants, apprentices, would-be spouses, and others out to better themselves, travelling fairly limited distances, to a neighbouring town or village, usually within an area defined by traditional notions of a sub-regional "country"'.[4] Often contained within the county, moves which were largely restricted to horizons of 10–15 miles were pervasive from the late Middle Ages to the early nineteenth century.[5] The post-Restoration movement of servants in husbandry, although frequent, was geographically circumscribed,[6] while in the sixteenth and seventeenth centuries their urban counterparts in East Anglia usually migrated from distances of eight to 20 miles.[7] London's immigrants in the seventeenth century, in common with other towns, included many of marriageable age.[8] More generally, the fact that the most mobile element of the population comprised a workforce significantly made up of young, unattached men and women, meant that a fund of marriage partners was continually in circulation between residences, and provided circumstances which ensured opportune moments for courtship to proceed.[9]

The experiences of single women in the London marriage market would seem to indicate that mobility was indeed one factor which might affect the timing and finding of suitable partners and the extent to which courtship was supervised.[10] For some, the expectation of marriage may have motivated moves to and from towns,[11] while also predisposing those engaged in agricultural service to change their place of residence in search of a spouse.[12] Small parishes, in particular, offered fewer eligible partners of appropriate standing and interest. The lack of marital opportunities in such places, and the problem of unlawful marriage within prohibited degrees, might have prompted exogamous matches.[13] At the same time, the countervailing pressures of family and other ties, considerations such as cost[14] and travel,[15] perceptions of distance and locality, and restrictions imposed by natural and cultural frontiers,[16] could have encouraged choices made in geographical proximity.

The distance over which regular personal contact might be maintained was inevitably determined by what was feasible, and by just how far, and how often, suitors, intermediaries and lovers could and would journey. In his autobiography, Leonard Wheatcroft estimated the amount of travelling that he had undertaken during his courtship. 'How many times I went a-wooing you shall find so many slashes upon an ash tree at Winter town end, and how many miles I travelled for her sake was 440 and odd.'[17] Living within close range of one another *at the time of marriage* would have been predictable, but it did not necessarily mean that this had hitherto been the case. 'Marrying someone who has always lived a mile or two away' was quite different from 'marrying someone whom one has only known for a year or two because he or she has recently moved from elsewhere'.[18] As regards urban relations, and the marriage choices of St Saviour's inhabitants, it has been recognised that 'place of residence does not tell us anything about period of residence and it is possible therefore that many brides and grooms may have been inhabiting the parish for only a short time, as servants, apprentices or lodgers before their marriage'.[19] Using parish registers to understand marriage horizons, therefore, might be misleading, since the place of residence recorded solely on the eve of wedding would obscure previous moves. Furthermore the custom of marrying in the bride's parish, meant that it was usually only immigrant husbands who would be recorded.[20]

With these reservations in mind, conclusions regarding marriage horizons which have been derived from local studies, confirm that most marriages occurred over a short distance. At Easingwold, between 1644 and 1812, the majority of chosen partners were resident in the parish.[21] Eversley stated that 'generally speaking, marriages between persons resident in the same parish, and those involving a partner from an adjoining parish or one within a five-mile radius, account for 75–80 per cent of all marriages, and if we extend the radius to fifteen miles, we are likely to include all except an insignificant fraction of places of origins of partners'.[22] As late as 1800, about 90 per cent of Lancashire villagers who were of labouring or artisan status, chose brides 'from within 10 miles, and all but a negligible proportion from within 20 miles', while the Midland parish of Claybrooke had a parochial endogamy rate of about 85 per cent between 1771 and 1841.[23] Calculations from East London, and from the parish register of St Saviour's, Southwark, similarly reveal heavily circumscribed marriage horizons in the seventeenth century.[24]

Such a pattern of marrying within a limited radius may have existed 'not only in the age of parish registers where such figures are calculable, but also probably long before'.[25] For the fifteenth century, using the evidence of medieval Act books, Helmholz identified that 38 of 78 marriage contract cases in fifteenth-century York, and 21 of 42 cases in Canterbury between 1411 and 1420, concerned partners who came from the same parish, but he was doubtful about the meaning of those findings. He remarked that 'they may be unrepresentative of marriage in general, and I have not been able to calculate the average distance between parishes'.[26]

The aim here is to pursue this very enquiry through a detailed study of such evidence for the Canterbury diocese between 1475 and 1600. Basing the analysis upon precisely the kind of calculation which Helmholz did not attempt, the Act books will be used to explore further the question of what may more appropriately be considered horizons of *courtship*, rather than those of marriage. The analysis which follows is restricted to the use of litigants' place of residence in actions styled as matrimonial or spousal cases, and to the spatial relationship between places where the record is complete for each party.

The Act books were examined in conjunction with the corresponding church court depositions in order to clarify the relevance of the places identified. The complementary study of the two sources revealed that the parish named in the Act books referred to the litigants' place of domicile as opposed to that of origin. The widow Thomasine Rayner, for example, was recorded as being of Lydd, where she and her father evidently resided, but she was born in the parish of Woodchurch.[27] The record of deponents' mobility experience which prefaced individual witness accounts is unfortunately not given for the plaintiffs' or defendants' testimony. The parties were sometimes stated to be of a particular parish, but often such information has to be deduced from the circumstantial details found in the narratives, which touch upon their place of habitation, of work, of courtship, of common fame, or their family's parish of residence. The varied situations of independent or shared accommodation, of residence with either or both parents, or with relatives, masters or mistresses were all embraced. At times, the peripatetic nature of service made it difficult to establish any clear parochial identity. Richard Bonnam, household servant to William Gybbes of Sturry, deposed 'that he ys of that parryshe most commonly where he may gett woorke, and not certeyne in any one parryshe but ys subiecte to my lorde of Can*terbury* jurisdiction'.[28] Place of residence did not, of course, necessarily correspond with place of service, in circumstances where employees did not live with their employers, and the retrospective character of deposition evidence which recalled former residences and intermediate moves, would further account for discrepancies in the otherwise concurring series of records. Very occasionally there was some internal contradiction. Marion Rogers was apparently living with her uncle in Tenterden at the time of the incident deposed, and in one deposition it was stated that she 'was of p*arishe* of Faversham, but now ... is dwellinge in the p*arishe* of Tenterden'. In another account she was said to be lately of Tenterden, and now of Faversham.[29] Changes in residence between the time recollected by individuals in their depositions and the time when a particular case came to court and was recorded in the Act books meant that, theoretically at least, the information provided in the latter was more contemporary. Elizabeth Hatche of Pluckley, for example, had evidently moved from the parish of Rainham where she had dwelt as John Mendam's maidservant.[30] Some litigants moved even during the course of court proceedings. Among them, Joan Williams was found to be of St Andrew's, Canterbury at the time of citation, and later of St Peter's parish.[31] The Act books themselves, however, might not always have specified the most recent changes. Joan Parker, who 'since the last court day', was of the parish of Adisham, was nevertheless recorded as being of Sandwich.[32]

The locations given in the Act books may be seen to represent at least a terminal point of contact in what might have been an extended, and shifting, courtship scene. The evidence as to the whereabouts of potential marriage partners at a critical time in their relations enables us to examine the geographical ambit of social interaction framing the activities of courtship. Such an examination complements the demographer's preoccupation with duly completed marriages recorded in parish registers. While such registers may be effectively used to estimate the proportion of parochial in-marriage and

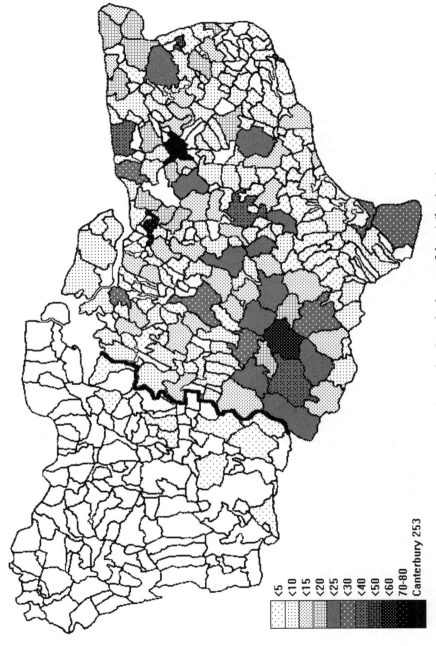

Map 2 Frequency distribution of data, 1474–1601 (only where both sets of domicile given)

Canterbury 253

<5
<10
<15
<20
<25
<30
<40
<50
<60
70-80

Table 6 Distance between domiciles of matrimonial litigants measured over time, 1475–1599. (Distances in miles, expressed as a percentage of total per quinquennium)

Miles	0 %	<5 %	<10 %	<15 %	<20 %	<25 %	<30 %	<35 %	>35 %	Total no. of cases
Date										
1475–79	40.0	32.3	10.8	6.2	1.5	3.1	1.5	1.5	3.0	65
1480–84	46.5	30.2	9.3	14.0						43
1485–89	60.4	8.3	16.7	6.3	2.1	2.1			4.2	48
1490–94	55.2	13.8	15.5	8.6	3.4				3.4	58
1495–99	36.8	31.6	15.8	7.9	5.3	2.6				38
1500–04	42.0	28.0	14.0	8.0	4.0	4.0				50
1505–09	50.6	20.7	12.6	6.9	2.3	2.3	1.1	1.1	2.2	87
1510–14	47.8	24.4	16.7	4.4		3.3	1.1		2.2	90
1515–19	47.3	23.7	16.1	7.5	4.3		1.1			93
1520–24	53.6	21.8	10.9	7.3	1.8	3.6			1.8	110
1525–29	49.1	24.1	10.7	8.0	5.4	0.9	0.9		0.9	112
1530–34	48.8	25.0	11.9	8.3	2.4	2.4	1.2			84
1535–39	46.7	26.7	6.7	20.0						15
1540–44	38.1	42.9	7.1	7.1	2.4			2.4		42
1545–49	48.8	26.3	11.3	10.0		2.5	1.3			80
1550–54	53.5	21.0	9.3	7.0	3.5	5.8				86
1555–59	51.6	24.2	8.1	11.3	4.8					62
1560–64	48.6	18.6	14.3	12.9	1.4	2.9			1.4	70
1565–69	36.1	29.5	16.4	8.2	4.9	1.6	1.6		1.6	61
1570–74	32.3	25.8	16.1	19.4	6.5					31
1575–79	42.6	21.3	13.1	11.8	3.3	4.9			3.2	61
1580–84	32.6	28.3	10.9	21.7	2.2	2.2	2.2			46
1585–89	37.9	27.6	27.6	3.4	3.4					29
1590–94	35.0	15.0	30.0	15.0	5.0					20
1595–99	60.0	4.0	12.0	20.0	4.0					25
1475–1599	47.0	23.8	13.1	9.2	2.9	2.1	0.6	0.2	1.1	1506

out-marriage, the Act books can be used further, to ascertain the normative perimeters of courtship.

Map 2, which plots the frequency distribution of the evidence, shows how nearly every parish is represented within the diocesan boundaries.[33] The primacy of the city of Canterbury, and the lesser, but still substantial, significance of some other market towns and of parishes in the generally populous parts of the Weald, would seem, to some extent at least, to reflect regional

Table 7 Fifteen-year moving averages of courtship distances

Miles	0	<5	<10	<15	>15
1475–89	49.0	23.6	12.3	8.8	6.3
1480–94	54.0	17.4	13.8	9.6	5.2
1485–99	50.8	17.9	16.0	7.6	7.7
1490–1504	44.7	24.5	15.1	5.5	10.2
1495–1509	43.1	26.8	14.1	7.6	8.4
1500–14	46.8	24.4	14.4	6.4	8.0
1505–19	48.6	22.9	15.1	6.3	7.1
1510–24	49.6	23.3	14.6	6.4	6.1
1515–29	50.0	23.2	12.6	7.6	6.6
1520–34	50.5	23.6	11.2	7.9	6.8
1525–39	48.2	25.3	9.8	12.1	4.6
1530–44	44.5	31.5	8.6	11.8	3.6
1535–49	44.5	32.0	8.4	12.4	2.7
1540–54	46.8	30.1	9.2	8.0	5.9
1545–59	51.3	23.8	9.6	9.4	5.9
1550–64	51.2	21.3	10.6	10.4	6.5
1555–69	45.4	24.1	12.9	10.8	6.8
1560–74	39.0	24.6	15.6	13.5	7.3
1565–79	37.0	25.5	15.2	13.1	9.2
1570–84	35.8	25.1	13.4	17.6	8.1
1575–89	37.7	25.7	17.2	12.3	7.1
1580–94	35.2	23.6	22.8	13.4	5.0
1585–99	44.3	15.5	23.2	12.8	4.2

economic and demographic conditions.[34] The assumption that people living in a centre like Canterbury and seeking partners within the city did not have to travel at all, is of course inaccurate, and renders the notion of zero miles somewhat misleading. Calculations of distance which were undertaken probably underestimate the number of miles separating potential couples. Since the actual route was also seldom ever straightforward, measurements made 'as the crow flies' between parish churches marked on an Ordnance Survey map are inevitably approximate.[35] Distances of less than five miles seldom, in fact, exceeded three miles, and very often comprised parishes adjacent to one another.

Throughout the period considered, 47 per cent of litigants were apparently resident in the same parish, with just over 70 per cent forming relationships within a five-mile radius. Extended to 10 miles, the figure rose to 84 per cent, and stood at 93 per cent for contact under 15 miles (Table 6). That there was

Figure 2 Fifteen-year moving average showing endogamous courtships, where distance = o miles

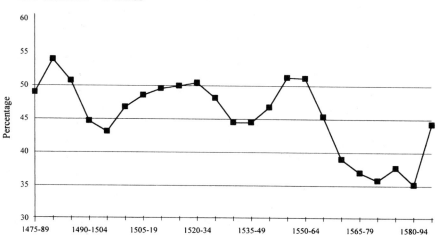

clearly a marked emphasis upon highly localised courtship pursuits, is consistent with previous studies of marriage horizons, and may also indicate that the evidence derived from church court records was not atypical. Identifying the apparent outer limits within which marriage communications were spatially circumscribed is also important. Figure 2 and Table 7 show some expansion in courtship horizons in the second half of the sixteenth century. Over time, it would appear that it became less common to choose partners from within the same parish.

The picture of a possible transition from more insular, static communities, to one of enlarged contacts and theoretically a wider pool of available spouses, should be set against the backdrop of deposition evidence surviving from the mid-sixteenth century. Significantly, the detailed testimonies which were recorded concern a period of apparently increasing fluidity in the marriage arena. The much noted 'common fame', which deponents attested to, often referred to more than a single parish, reflecting perhaps the potential for a growing nexus of connections, and for the geographical spread of reputation and regulation. The difference between a radius of say two miles and 20 miles might be considerable in terms of family, social, economic and work relations. Geographical bounds, which were themselves changing, could affect the strength of external pressures on marriage choice, the maintenance of per-sonal relations and the continuance of courtship. Short distances, then, proved little obstacle to lovers but might be more visible. In their account of Martha Sowtherne's suspected incontinent behaviour with one Mount (the keeper of Mr Edward Boyse's mill in Nonington), witnesses drew attention to the silk girdle which she had received from him, and to the fact that she had sent a pair of garters and brought him a basket of strawberries. It was often reported that Martha, who served Mr Stace of Upper Hardres, resorted to the mill, and it was believed that 'the mill and Mr Stace's house are 4 miles asunder at least'.[36]

As already shown, travelling distances of a few miles was commonly part of the pattern of courtship. Although contemporaries may have envisaged the likelihood of making longer journeys, the normative structures implicit in the Act book material would seem to accord with the kind of expectations deduced from the depositions. In the complex unfolding of Judith Symons's case against John Spayne, allegations were made that John Spayne's mother sought to prevent the love match between them. Instead she did 'privilye' but purposefully 'practize to make a match' between Thomas Kennet and Judith. The widow Dorothy Fittell of Dymchurch claimed that Mistress Spayne had told her 'she would finde a remedy' for the love between her son and Judith, 'and set them further asunder'. Both parties were said to have lamented their parting. Judith wept when he 'was gone away from hir', and John was heard to confess 'that yd did soe greeve him that he was about to go out of the country'. Although his parents' house was situated in the parish of Dymchurch where Judith worked as a servant in the custody of William Tanner, John was probably living at that time in Hinxhill, within reasonable distance for courtship to be maintained, and for planned meetings to take place. It was, however, presumed that beyond a certain point the intervening distance might be sufficient to hinder further marriage communications. In his deposition, Thomas Bryant, who was himself a suitor to Judith Symons, recalled his conversation with Mistress Spayne concerning the relationship between his rival and Judith. She answered 'that she would break that match well enoughe & she would set them far enough asunder and so afterward placed her son at Battell in Sussex being 20 miles from Dymchurche or thereabouts'.[37]

The treatment of distance as a psychological experience as well as a matter of physical practicality, may in this case have been coloured by some sense of regional identification, the perceived threshold being the boundary separating the counties of Kent and Sussex. For an outsider entering another county, adjustments may have been particularly marked. Dorothy Browne of the city of Canterbury testified that Thomas Brooke declared his intention to marry her if he could 'have his frynds good will to marry with a Kentishe mayd and to dwell in Kent'.[38] Coming from Bristol,[39] he was allegedly doubtful about his chances of success in the matter, 'howbeyt he said that at his next coming into this countrye he wold tell hyr how his fryndes liked of yt'. The ritual incorporation of incoming marriage partners into communities, and the necessity in certain instances for testimonials to be procured by outsiders,[40] also suggest a mental construction of notional barriers.

Discussing frontier restrictions on physical mobility, Phythian-Adams remarked that 'where shire and or ancient diocesan boundaries coincide with geographical obstacles, the existence of cultural barriers will also be likely'. He further remarked that the 'shire divisions of this country (and, indeed, sometimes their major subdivisions, as possibly in the cases of East and West Kent) are extraordinarily ancient'.[41] At times, deponents expressed their recognition of particular territories. One deponent, for example, referred to the appointment of a convenient meeting place for Mark Giles's friends to confer with Katherine Wyborn's 'frendes of East Kent'.[42] In another case, evidence was given that 'a ring out of Est Kent' was brought from Bartholomew Pigden to Mary Willard in Benenden.[43]

When courtship contacts formed outside the county or the diocese are examined in the Act books, it would seem that the eastern half of Kent was relatively self-contained. The coincidence of the River Medway with the diocesan boundary would seem to have created an effective, although not absolute partition. Despite the potential influence of county divisions, marriage partners were perhaps more likely to be found in the neighbouring county of Sussex than in western Kent.[44] If so, this might help to confirm Phythian-Adams's concept of an 'inter-mixed buffer zone' between counties, being an 'area of "overlap" ... conspicuous where continuous stretches of homogeneous countryside, like the wealden region of Sussex and Kent cut across the county divisions'.[45] Kent's strategic geographical position in relation to London and the continent presumably fostered the marriage connections with the metropolis, and with the port of Calais,[46] but what is apparently exposed in the previously cited case of *Tusten* v. *Allen*, is the still tenuous nature of communications maintained at that distance. Before the solemnisation of her marriage with Simon Aunsell in Mersham, the widow Godlen Allen, residing approximately four and a half miles away at Wye, received tokens 'for a remembrance' sent to her from Richard Tusten. Richard was then temporarily away in London. Lamenting his absence, and fearing the machinations of others, Godlen was said to have weepingly declared her fervent wish for his return home.[47]

In overall statistical terms, the rather marginal significance of attachments made with partners from outside the county and, in particular, the apparent dissociation between the eastern and western halves of Kent, provide a methodological justification for studying the diocese of Canterbury as a regional entity. Examining the range of courtship contacts by individual parishes, the total numbers (now based on *persons* rather than cases[48]) recorded within each category of distance were calculated as percentages. The aggregated results are presented in the last row of Table 8.[49] Such figures have also been reworked to take into account the size and character of particular places, and the possible existence of economic and cultural sub-regions.

Table 8 The courtship horizons of selected areas and communities (percentage)

Miles	0 %	<5 %	<10 %	<15 %	<20 %	<25 %	<30 %	<35 %	>35 %	Total no. of persons
Traditional urban centres	64.7	9.6	9.1	9.7	2.1	3.2	0.7	0.3	0.5	711
Market towns[a]	48.3	19.9	13.9	9.2	4.0	2.2	1.2	0.2	1.0	402
High Weald[b]	52.5	21.0	11.5	7.1	3.8	2.9	0.6	0.0	0.6	480
Wealden Vales	37.6	29.4	15.3	8.2	5.9	1.2	1.2	0.0	1.2	85
Romney Marsh area[c]	52.8	18.1	11.9	9.8	2.1	3.6	1.6	0.0	0.0	193
Isle of Thanet	62.6	14.5	11.5	6.9	1.5	3.1	0.0	0.0	0.0	131
North Kent coast	44.9	29.9	12.9	8.2	2.0	1.4	0.7	0.0	0.0	147
Rural parishes in the North Downs[d]	35.6	32.2	17.8	11.0	1.7	0.4	0.0	0.0	1.2	236
Total of *all* Kent courtship horizons	47.2	23.9	13.5	9.2	2.8	2.3	0.5	0.1	0.6	3015

Notes

[a] The list of market towns, by no means exhaustive, is based upon Thirsk ed., *The Agrarian History of England and Wales*, IV, p. 474. Only those within the Canterbury diocese, with the exception of the traditional urban centres, are included. The population of these market towns in the mid- to late sixteenth century could vary considerably from about 500 in Ashford in 1570; 600 or 700 in Milton near Sittingbourne in 1570; to about 1500–2000 in Cranbrook in this period. See e.g. Chalklin, *Seventeenth-Century Kent*, pp. 30–2; Collinson, 'Cranbrook and the Fletchers', p. 174.

[b] Parishes in the High Weald have been analysed separately from those located in the Wealden Vales and have been taken from the map found in Robert Furley's, *A History of the Weald of Kent*, 2, ii (Ashford, 1874), p. 701; compared with K. P. Witney, *The Jutish Forest: A Study of the Weald of Kent from 450 to 1380 AD* (London, 1976), p. 323. For the demographic experience of different districts in the Weald, see, Zell, *Industry in the Countryside*, especially pp. 52–87.

[c] Includes parishes bordering on the Weald and Marsh; Romney Marsh proper and Walland Marsh; and the Isle of Oxney.

[d] These parishes may be classified as located in the North Downs, in the area predominantly south of Canterbury, and in the area stretching north of the scarpland towards West Kent, but not all the parishes in this region have been included.

Every now and then deponents did, after all, voice their tolerance of, or lack of immunity towards, their environment. Joanne Harewood of Mersham claimed that 'she could not abide' the air in Folkestone.[50] In another case, the defendant Richard Bonnam may have had more just cause for being apprehensive and suspicious of Prudence Bramelo's desire to marry him so hastily. As household servants to William Gybbes of Sturry, both she and her master were anxious to dispatch the affair. Richard included in his account how William Gybbes had declared to him 'that Prudence was syckly and coulde not well a waye, *with* thayer there at Sturrey', commanding him as his servant, and indeed threatening to have him imprisoned if he would not obey, to carry her off into her own country.[51] Such sensitivity to the environment may have been used as fabricated excuses in these cases, but they might, however, in other circumstances, be interpreted as a matter of acculturation or allegiance to a community. Such a sense of belonging, by implication, differentiates between places and particularises peculiar features. Not only did contemporaries express a conscious sense of their present or future surroundings, they also indicated their identification of distinctive regions. In one instance, Richard Russell of Northgate, Canterbury, and his wife Elizabeth, describing the company of men gathered at evening supper in the house of the recently widowed Mistress Starkey, referred to there being 'divers Weldishe handsom men of the wealld of Kent'.[52]

The type of *pays* was one factor which might affect the geographical pattern of marriage choices. It was found, for example, 'that the large well-populated wealden parishes, which contained numerous dispersed settlements, were likely to be more endogamous than the small under-populated parishes of the wolds', in the early seventeenth century.[53] Previous work on migration fields and marriage horizons, has considered the relationship between demographic and socio-economic criteria, and the distance of interaction or 'catchment area' of particular places. Jeremy Millard predicted that parishes with large populations would have low *proportions* of extra-parochial marriages but would, paradoxically, form more distant marriage contacts in *absolute terms*. While it has been established that 'urban migration was more geographically extensive', it has also been shown that the individual character of specific urban communities and their hinterland, produced different migratory responses. Nonetheless, 'in principle, the larger the town, the wider its catchment area', as comparisons between Canterbury, Maidstone and Faversham in the period 1580–1640 demonstrate.[54]

Making distinctions between types of community immediately raises problems of definition and classification.[55] Peter Clark has suggested that settlements with a population of 1000 or more were seen by contemporaries to possess an urban identity.[56] In formulating a hierarchy of communities from the Act books, on the twin basis of population size and the complexity of

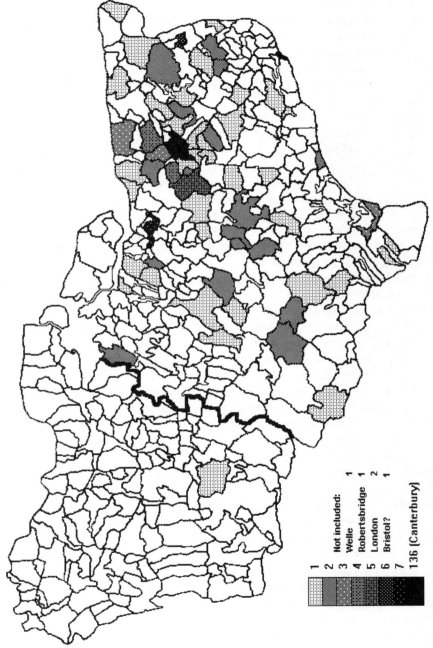

Not included:
Welle   1
Robertsbridge   1
London   2
Bristol?   1

1
2
3
4
5
6
7
136 [Canterbury]

Map 3 Canterbury's courtship horizons, 1474–1601 (frequency of courtship connections)

Table 9 Canterbury's courtship horizons, 1474–1599 (percentage)

Miles Date	0 %	<5 %	<10 %	<15 %	<20 %	<25 %	<30 %	<35 %	>35 %	Total no.
1474–79	75.0	12.5	6.3	6.3	0.0	0.0	0.0	0.0	0.0	16
1480–89	82.1	7.7	5.1	2.6	0.0	0.0	0.0	0.0	2.6	39
1490–99	44.4	11.1	22.2	22.2	0.0	0.0	0.0	0.0	0.0	18
1500–09	64.9	10.8	5.4	2.7	2.7	8.1	0.0	2.7	2.7	37
1510–19	71.4	9.5	4.8	4.8	2.4	4.8	2.4	0.0	0.0	42
1520–29	79.2	5.7	3.8	5.7	1.9	3.8	0.0	0.0	0.0	53
1530–39	71.4	0.0	0.0	21.4	0.0	7.1	0.0	0.0	0.0	14
1540–49	62.9	8.6	11.4	14.3	0.0	0.0	0.0	2.9	0.0	35
1550–59	77.8	11.1	2.8	8.3	0.0	0.0	0.0	0.0	0.0	36
1560–69	64.3	10.7	0.0	14.3	0.0	7.1	0.0	0.0	3.6	28
1570–79	64.0	16.0	8.0	4.0	4.0	4.0	0.0	0.0	0.0	25
1580–89	60.9	4.3	13.0	17.4	4.3	0.0	0.0	0.0	0.0	23
1590–99	72.7	4.5	4.5	18.2	0.0	0.0	0.0	0.0	0.0	22
1474–1599	70.1	8.8	6.2	9.3	1.3	2.8	0.3	0.5	0.8	388

socio-economic functions,[57] two underlying assumptions were made. First, that marriage choice was determined to some extent by economic relations, and second, that marketing patterns might influence courtship distance.

The cathedral city of Canterbury, with an estimated population of over 3000 in the mid-1520s, which by the seventeenth century had nearly doubled, was examined first on its own (see Map 3 and Table 9). More than two-thirds of Canterbury's marriage litigants would seem to have had partners resident within the city. Of the remaining 30 per cent, contacts were most marked with other towns, with villages in the immediate vicinity and along the coast. For a centre which might be expected to form the most distant courtship connections, while also sustaining much larger numbers of internal marriage competitors, Canterbury's horizons were still predominantly provincial, and it was just as common for women as for men living outside the city to court its inhabitants. Courtships undertaken within the locality of Canterbury itself seem to have been a little less common between 1560 and 1589, in line with the possible expansion of courtship distances detected for the diocese as a whole.

Grouping the principal urban communities together, and comparing their pattern of courtship distance with that exhibited for market towns, the differences and similarities in the scales of interaction become apparent. The smaller market towns were usually less endogamous than larger urban centres, often making up for the shortfall with partners living nearby. Otherwise there were broad similarities with the pattern between types of town, unlike the more marked urban–rural distinction.[58] Individuals in rural parishes in the North Downs were far less likely to find partners within their parish boundary than those living in urban settlements. Such rural inhabitants, however, made significantly more contacts within a five-mile radius (see above, Table 8).

While the courtship characteristics of parishes in specific regions of Kent may be tentatively examined, any strict demarcation between the physical landscape of weald, downland, marshland and the mixed areas of wood and arable in the diocese, is inevitably an abstraction.[59] Ascertaining a particular sub-regional boundary could be perplexing, as the contemporary topographer William Lambarde implied. He remarked on the 'diversity of opinions touching the true limits of this Weald; some affirming it to begin at one place and some at another'.[60] Parts of the Weald were not only particularly populous, they contained significant market towns and, by the mid-sixteenth century, were sufficiently prosperous to undermine the primacy of traditional urban communities. The expansion in the cloth and iron-making industries in several of the parishes there, ensured the growing economic attraction of the High Weald.[61] It is thus unsurprising that the courtship horizons of the area were nearly identical to those encountered for market towns, although the pattern for parishes located in the Wealden Vales would appear to have displayed more rural characteristics (see Table 8 above).

Residents of the Romney Marsh region, which comprised the southern coastal marshlands of Romney and Walland Marsh, the Denge promontory and the Isle of Oxney,[62] frequently paired themselves with those living in the Weald. Noticeable attachments were also formed with Ashford and its environs, with coastal parishes from Hythe to Dover, with Canterbury and its neighbourhood, and less frequently with places in the salt marshes to the north of the county. For these southern marshes, the courtship arena extended to approximately 30 miles. The geographical range of interconnections shown in courtship for the area is similar in size to that of the hinterland of Romney town.[63] The other regional marshlands of the Isles of Thanet and Sheppey, and the salt marshes of Kent's north shore were geographically less extensive in their courtship ties (see above, Table 8). The parishes contained within this area often interacted with each other, with the Cinque Ports, Canterbury, the Stour river parishes and villages in the North Downs, and with neighbouring market towns. It was probably marketing links with Faversham and Milton near Sittingbourne which mitigated the otherwise insular mentality displayed by Sheppey islanders in their partnerships which never exceeded a distance of 10 miles.[64]

Indeed, the exogamous matches of the Isles were probably, in part, a consequence of their not possessing any obvious market town of their own.

This implies that marital contacts and the circumstances promoting marriage choice were, to some degree, dependent upon an economic determinism and local market structure. According to Alan Everitt's calculations on market areas in eastern England, 60 per cent of people going to market travelled 1–5½ miles, a further 25 per cent up to 9½ miles, 13 per cent between 10 and 19½ miles, and only 2 per cent over 20 miles.[65] The similarities between market distance and the courtship distances calculated from the Act books for the Canterbury diocese, suggest that marketing activities, and the patterns of movement generated by them, provided an economic framework and a communication apparatus within which other kinds of social interchange were likely to occur, and in which personal relationships could be facilitated.

In sum, the matter of geographical context was clearly one variable which might affect actions, decisions and, most importantly, opportunities for courtship. The courtship distances uncovered in the Act books are a measurement of exploratory personal contact, of relationships in the process of communication and compromise. As evidence of courtship horizons, they are particularly suggestive, because they are not centred on any one location, and may actually serve to qualify the quantitative use made of marriage registers. It should also be said that the Act books need not be regarded as a record of marriage failure, but, more appropriately and significantly, as indicative of possible contacts, and of provisional liaisons in an experimental phase. The high degree of essentially localised contact in courtship, anticipates the pattern of marriage horizons studied by demographers, and helps to refute any claim which might be made that disputed court cases simply emphasise marriage breakdown and longer-distance relationships. The results would seem to indicate some correlation between courtship distances and the character or size of individual communities. Perhaps what was also crucial was the general influence of marketing functions, as courtship horizons would appear to have been largely tied to a marketing radius. Although, on the whole, partners in courtship were often found within reasonable proximity, and although much of the mobility in the sixteenth century was short distance, in the course of that century those courtship horizons may have been changing. By implication, the vexed issue of choice and control within marriage would constantly have adjusted its meaning. The contacts of a parish, the ties of kin and neighbourhood and the spatial bounds of a community, which were partly dependent upon the general demographic background and upon the particular experience and features of individual places, were nevertheless expanding. Whether or not the increased travelling served to sever contacts and lessen the power of constraints, or alternatively extended the regulation of marriage to assimilate wider influences, must be considered an open question. Another possibility is that, to the extent that intermediaries helped bridge geographical distance, their role in sixteenth-century courtship might actually have increased as courtship horizons widened. Such then was the overall spatial context of courtship in the diocese of Kent. Where parties met, how they met, the occasion and timeliness of meetings, and the liminality of negotiating relationships, will be considered next.

As has already been mentioned, the enfolding drama of courtship, re-enacted through the testimonies of church court deponents, seldom specifically locates the *earliest* point of encounter between partners. Although numerous incidents of fortuitous meetings or assigned rendezvous may be rehearsed, the frequent failure of the testimonies to recall plainly and unequivocally the initial circumstances of contact, represents a gap in the narratives, stories without an obvious beginning. As such, they are more likely to evoke succeeding stages in a sequence of events, serving as episodic snapshots, open to imaginative interpretation. While the use of literary and autobiographical evidence may offer further clues concerning the first manner of meeting or awareness,[66] the reading of depositions can nevertheless go a long way in exploring the context and opportunities, by chance or design, of marriage choice.

The occurrence of fairs and markets has been recognised, in passing, as a favourite venue for much social activity, and for intermingling between the sexes.[67] Of the opportunities for social contact afforded by English medieval fairs, it has been said that 'not only in the variety of goods and services they attracted, but also and especially in the interactions they provided between people of different regions and social groups, were fairs such an important institution of the high middle ages'.[68] In the Elizabethan period, servants in the manor of Havering, Essex, were found to be a mobile group, often travelling on errands during work time, while 'in their free time, they went to meet their friends commonly at Romford market'.[69] Deposition accounts confirm this picture of sociability, and the role of fairs and markets as a meeting-place. Meeting at Tenterden fair a little before St George's day, John Spayne reportedly protested his solemn intention to marry with Judith Symons. In the company of servants gathered together in the inn that fair day, he 'wished that his fleshe might rotte from his bones yf he meant not as he sayd'.[70] The leverage for clandestine reunions too is illustrated in the case of *Cullen* v. *Cullen*. It followed Stephen Smith's expulsion from service, as a consequence of his unseemly behaviour towards his mistress, Mildred Cullen. She was alleged to have wept upon learning of his departure, begging leave of her husband to go to the Christmas fair at Canterbury where they had secretly agreed to meet. Both were accused of continuing to frequent each other's company, of 'appoynted meetings ... in blynde alehowses and suspicious places ... and especiallie at a *m*arkett kept at dover, or in her returne by the way as she came from dover *m*arkett'. On diverse occasions, Mildred 'made arrand*es* to market*tes* and fayres to meet with the said Smith', revealing the same to two housemaids in Thomas Cullen's service.[71] As the case suggests, travelling to and from market may, at times, have been as eventful as the actual marketplace scene or fairground. For Mildred Cullen and Stephen Smith, the meeting was reputedly already planned, but in other instances, some degree of coincidence, or at most of heightened expectation, was equally possible. Not long before her death, Agnes Butterwick, the key witness in Edmond Coppyn's suit for marriage, provided evidence of just such an encounter. She testified that while she was *en route* 'to old Mr Coppins dwelling without the walles of Canterburie ... at the torne pike at St Austens wall, in the afternone, Katherine Richards comyng to the towne and Edmond Coppyn from London mett togither by chaunce in the place aforesaid'.[72] Another deponent verified the meeting 'alongist the wall', and observed the basket which Katherine carried on her arm as she made her way to the market. Katherine herself admitted that 'she being at the *ma*rket at Canterburie, and going to her mestres house chaunced to speake w*ith* Edmond Coppyn at the further end of St Austyns wall without the city, who offrid to her a pair of gloves',[73] described by Agnes Butterwick as 'a pair of new faire gloves'.

Conceptualising the journey to fairs and markets and the point of juncture as a 'territorial passage' may enhance our understanding of the potential significance of the marketplace. Adopting that notion to establish a framework for his discussion of rites of passage, Van Gennep proposed 'that the passage from one social position to another is identified with a territorial passage, such as the entrance into a village or a house, the movement from one room to another, or the crossing of street and squares'.[74] The idea of a delimited territory, and the image of crossroads, gates, or other 'kinds of entrance', symbolising a threshold,[75] are perhaps worth elaborating upon. That many markets would have occupied religious spaces, often attached to church property or located next to religious portals,[76] suggests that they were special places. It is indeed possible to imagine the marketplace as a liminal zone within formally bounded areas, where people from different communities met together outside their normal, daily pattern of life. They were often protected in their coming to market and in their transactions by special rules to govern that particular occasion, rules which provided new boundaries for their temporarily unbounded existence. Although participants in the market were ostensibly engaged in economic exchange, the marketplace with its own social ambience was also the territory where social transactions were conducted. There, the communication of ideas, gossip, news, and the experience of exceptional levels of noise and activity, might mediate changes in social relations and permit the negotiation of new relationships. The circulation of libels and their performance would also occur on market days and at fairs.[77] Travelling pedlars were also oral communicators of tales and gossip.[78] In writing about the role and language of the marketplace and fairs of the Renaissance, Bakhtin described the 'certain extra territoriality' of that space, and its 'atmosphere of freedom, frankness, and familiarity'. The marketplace relationship was regarded as 'a special type of relationship', pertaining to 'a peculiar second world within the official medieval order'.[79] Bakhtin's interpretation of the market or fair as the festive representation of the traditional, folk community outside the 'official order and official ideology' may overemphasise the populist domain. In seeking to offset the conceptualisation of the fair as exclusively the site of popular, unofficial celebration, it has been argued elsewhere that the fair should instead be seen as 'a point of economic and cultural intersection'. The 'crossing of ways', the 'interconnection' of different 'languages, images, symbols and objects', was thought to be more significant. Emphasising that 'the market square was a crossroads, and if it was the focus of "community" it was also the point of intersection of different cultures', it was also said that 'even the smallest fair juxtaposed both people and objects which were normally kept separate and thus provided a taste of life beyond the narrow horizons of the town or village'.[80] Whichever interpretation is deemed the more appropriate, the theme common to both is the central idea that the fair or marketplace possessed a special status. It constituted a dangerous, vulnerable and energetic space, in which cultural, social and economic aspects were interrelated, and in which a heterogeneous collectivity manifested itself. There, the participants, spectators and commodities merged and crossed roads.

The kind of activity which occurred during fair-time, as is evident from the circumstantial details given by deponents, suggests that such an occasion was often instrumental in the making of marriage, serving in a variety of ways as a forum for courtship. The depositions recall events in Canterbury, Faversham, Sittingbourne and Hythe fairs, in the several fairs attached to market towns such as Ashford, Wye, Lenham, Elham and Cranbrook, and to rural parishes like Elmstead and Warehorne. Alongside their special quality, the multiplicity of sites and times when they were held made that institution all the more commonly experienced.

Even if fairs are regarded predominantly as marts for economic transactions, the kind of commodities which were advertised, sold and bought might include items used as wedding accessories, objects given as tokens of love or for amorous solicitation.[81] It was reported that sometime after the contract between Stephen Hannyng and Godline Knowler, at Midsummer or Canterbury fair, he bought 'a red pettycot cloth for Godly as for his wif, and so muche tuffed mokado as made a pair of sleves and other things'.[82] The purchase of bridal clothes at fairs or markets was likewise evident in the testimony given by Clement Knoll, a tailor from Appledore. He deposed how he met with William Gabriell and Martha Burche 'at the market of Ashford upon purpose to helpe buy the wedding apparell for Gabriell and Burche, where the same at that time was boughte by them both together, whiche being bought Martha Burche asked [him] against what day he could make yt readye and he promised her against the next Thursday then following, wherof she desired [him] not to fayle'.[83] Thomas Yomanson, a capper normally resident in St Mary Magdalene parish in Canterbury, provided a more detailed account of when he first became acquainted with the parties Margaret Cole of Lympne and Henry Lion of Challock. He recalled

> that he was at Wye fayer kept upon Saint Gregories day last to make sale of his wares there/ And Valentyne Nott and his wife with Lion and Cole came to him standing in the said fayer to buy a wedding capp for Henry and a wedding cap for Margaret as Valentyne Nott and his wife shewed [him] declaring that it shuld serve for Henry and Margaret after Easter/ And so Henry Lion bought a cap for himself of this deponent of the price of 4s and appointed the maide to com another tyme to Canterburie for her cap because he had not at that tyme non fyne enough to serve her ... And this deponent said that Henry and the parties being at his stall aforesaid had a fardell of cloth and other things to the value of 8li or above as he judgeth, which Henry said that he had bought for the mariage apparell of him and Margaret. And this deponent said that then and there Henry shewed him a wedding ring of gold and a pair of hooks of silver and gilt that he had bought.[84]

The 'boothe or standing place' occupied by a glover may have been frequently visited on a fair day by men intending to purchase a pair of gloves for their desired or prospective partners. Ralph Cole of Frittenden was seen standing at a glover's stall on St Giles's day at Cranbrook fair. According to Thomas Dogett, a clothier of Cranbrook, and Laurence Taillor, a friend of Ralph Cole's, it would seem that the defendant, Juliane Barnes of Frittenden, received a pair of gloves that afternoon upon promise of marriage, both deponents being present to witness the same. Thomas Dogett deposed how he

> by chaunce mete with Raufe Cole in the fayer/ who desired him to tarry with him to hear communication of matrimony betwene hym and Juliane Barnes for the which Juliane he did loke to speke with in the fayer/ And the same Rafe Cole perceyving that she cam not to the fayer according to his expectation told this deponent that he wold goo before to Frittenden to the house of William Hawsnothe unto her wher she dwelt ... desiring this deponent after his buysynes in the fayer doon to com to Frittenden unto hym.

All three men appointed to meet at Frittenden church, and after drinking together in 'the church taverne', proceeded to the house, where they found Juliane willing to stand to her promise of marriage and to accept the gloves which Ralph offered her.[85]

In admitting only to having received the gloves 'of hym for fayringes', Juliane implicitly denied their contractual significance but, like many other women in those circumstances, she also drew attention to the close association between fairs, gifts and the practice of courtship. Mary Hubbard, similarly protesting that she never made Richard Turner any kind of promise, did nevertheless confess, that 'at one faire the said Turner gave [her] and one of her fellowes eather of them a pair of glooves'.[86] The purchase of fayrings at fairs, and the giving of such presents at that time, whether they were the gloves which Benedict Dunnye of Mersham received from her two suitors, Thomas Kennet at the fair of Warehorne and Peter Wattle at Wye fair,[87] or the pair of knives which Mary Wraight of Swingfield accepted at Elham fair,[88] meant that such occasions might indeed serve to stimulate and intensify personal familiarity.

The kinds of goods advertised in fairs which Rabelais may have observed in his time, probably included herbs for sexual potency,[89] sold by itinerant quacks, if not by tradespeople on open stalls. A pedlar's wares, according to an early seventeenth-century ballad, invited buyers to 'view the Fayre' of fashionable cosmetics.[90] Even when seen in terms of personal intimacy, fairs were not simply concerned with the exchange of items of beautification and bridal adornment, or with arousing new desires. Unofficially they may have been timely occasions for pronounced sexual and verbal licence, as couples were seen behaving in unchristian manner, and gossip became less restrained.

In the process of courtship, fairs were also appropriate times for keeping appointments. They were situations which allowed for the discovery and searching out of partners, for further communications of marriage, if not for the renewal or making of promises. In the case of *Frid* v. *Chawker*, witnesses testified to having heard John Frid claim that, at Lenham fair, he and Alice Chawker 'eche to other had renued repeated and confirmed the self-same promises and cove*nan*tes or contracte', and that upon making 'themselves sure and betroughted by faith and trouthe eche to other ... did break a sylver ring yn two peeces yn token of the faith and trouthe then given'.[91] Other instances suggest that the fair day itself provided some kind of opportune justification for rekindling relationships, and that going to the fair together was somehow celebratory as well as practical. It was 'apon the fayer kept at Rochester', that John Norman 'as sutor by appointment' was said to have gone to John Mendam's house in Rainham. He 'challenged a promis of marriage' of Mendam's maidservant, Elizabeth Hatche, and the following day 'they two went to Rochester fayer'.[92] The diary of the Sussex merchant Samuel Jeake (d. 1699) reveals that he journeyed to various fairs and markets for an opportunity to communicate with Mary Weeks and her family.[93]

As courtship merged with traditional forms of popular recreation, so the fair focused the celebrative mood of marriage with the conviviality of social intercourse. It was not uncommon for contracts to be made on a fair day among a company found drinking together. On Michaelmas day, Geoffrey

Cooke 'being at Sittingborn fayer went up into a chamber of one Allen's house in Sittingborn to drink which for the fayer time William Croxon had hired', and found John Jenkyns and Barbara Adams, who had gone to the Kingshead 'to drink together being at the fayer there kept', talking of marriage and concluding a contract.[94] More specifically, in the case begun by Henry Den against Margaret Cole, the testimonies given by Edward Carden, James Ilchinden and William Cole, who were all residents in Lympne parish, described an incident which occurred at Elmstead fair kept on St James's day. Having 'chaunced to repair thither as ... doth accustemally use at that place in tyme of faires to buy certain neicessaries/ And chaunced to goo into a barne aside the place of the fair situate/ to recreat ... and to drinck/where many resorted for like cause', they ate and drank in the company of Henry Den and Margaret Cole. After which repast, they witnessed the promise made between the parties. According to William Cole, 'a pair of new gloves and a silken riband of the value of 4*d* or 6*d* ... she toke at his hands'. He further deposed that about a fortnight later, when he came from the church 'with them in company, Henry asked her if she would stand to her promise at the fair. And she said she was content.'[95]

The cases cited dramatise the importance of drinking places as centres of communal activity, where merriment might lead to slanderous talk[96] or to marriage entreaties. It would appear, for instance, that Thomas Hawkins was at Faversham with Mathew Rayner and Henry Ady 'at the Signe of the Ship, of intent and purpose to comon of a mariage with Henry Adee to be had betwene his daughter viz. goodwife [Elizabeth] Chamber and Mathue and to have his goodwill therin'.[97] Emphasising the popularity of drink as a 'social lubricant', Keith Wrightson noted those 'specific occasions of heavy indulgence, such as at fairs, wakes, festivals and "rites of passage", but also less formal occasions on which drinking was bound up with the establishment and re-establishment of mutual relationships'.[98] Apart from bringing together partners and their relatives in the negotiation of marriage, the alehouses of the sixteenth century, whether licensed or unlicensed and however rudimentary, had a significant role to play in the process of social integration and mediation.[99] It was at the Sun tavern in Canterbury that the vicar of Tenterden united the two parties, Thomas Bennet and Henry Smith, who were in dispute over a matter of defamation, making 'annmytie and agreement betwixte them'.[100] In the case of *Symons* v. *Spayne*, a letter of appointment sent from Judith Symons to John Spayne led to a meeting together at a victualling house in Hythe. Anxious to speak with him to understand his intention, and 'eyther to be assured of him or els utterly to leave one another', the couple met there on St Barnabas's day together with John Wilson and William Beale, and 'they four being so all met together spent there in drink and shared pyes and bread about 18*d*', before any more serious talk of marriage.[101] The deposition of Thomas Bryant of

Dymchurch exemplifies the way in which alehouse gatherings served to reconcile conflicting interests and mitigate tense situations. As a rival suitor for Judith Symons's hand in marriage, he recalled the confrontation he had had with John Spayne. John had warned him

> that if he would not surcease his suite unto Judyth that then he would be revenged of him, and so afterwards Spayne challenged and dared [him] to fight, and on the 2 May they fought together appon the same quarrell at a sluice between Dymchurch and Romney after which their fighting [he] and Spayne went together to St Maryes in the marshe unto a victualing house there where they drank together and were good freinds.[102]

The need for local taverns and tippling houses as meeting-places was presumably partly due to the fact that private homes were often ill equipped for much social activity.[103] They provided a refuge from the cramped environment and scrutiny of domestic houses, and were also commonly associated with illicit sexual liaisons and clandestine unions.[104] We are reminded of the appointed meetings between Mildred Cullen and Stephen Smith in the 'blind' alehouses.[105] In *Coppyn* v. *Richards*, we are informed about Agnes Butterwick, reputedly once the wife of one Best, dwelling in Ashford and keeping a little blind alehouse, the haunt and resort of many 'light people', 'suspected personnes' and 'nawghty' women.[106] The common tippling house may have principally served the needs of single and married men, particularly among the less well-to-do, but they were not simply a male domain.[107] Besides serving an important function in the ritual procedure of matrimony,[108] groups of young people of both sexes might entertain themselves in such surroundings. An example from Lancashire in the 1660s shows how rambles could end in an alehouse,[109] and it was precisely the society of young people, frequently servants, which 'gave the alehouse something of a role in courtship'.[110]

Social gatherings, whether of mixed company or not, encouraged playful, provocative and arousing behaviour. The presence of a group of men making merry and playing at cards, is illustrated richly in a case which smacks of blasphemy and appears to mock the solemnity of marriage.[111] Certain of the deponents in the case 'chanced to come' to John Woodland's house, a tippler in Benenden. Others went there upon 'hearing that dyverse of Goodherst aboute the nomber of eyght yowng men were come to Benenden to make merrye', while some, 'among other yonge men of Benenden [were] invyted and desyred upon a certen day appoynted to meet' there. Apart from the men of Goudhurst, there were several others of Benenden, at least a dozen, plus men in blue coats, and men of Cranbrooke, Horsmonden, Hawkhurst and Brenchley, playing cards and laughing. They decreed among themselves 'that who so ever had loste all his money shoulde bee searerd upon the buttockes with a hott yron', a fate which befell Thomas Grymmell of Cranbrooke.

Grymmell was reported to have said repeatedly 'that he thoughte hym selfe so symple th*at* wolde no body have him', and that he would rather marry himself to George Sowtherden's mare than be branded again with the iron. (One William Willard had shortly before that time sold the mare to Sowtherden in jest, for 18*d* and two pots of beer.) The mare was thereupon escorted into the room in between two men, the sight of which, 'so bare and impotente', was said to have moved the company to great laughter. Those who were present recalled how Thomas Grymmell stood on a table or stool and asked the banns of marriage between himself and Mildred Willard of Benenden. According to the company, George Sowtherden forbade it, and then dinner was served. They denied, however, knowledge 'of eny maryage of the mare or of eny rynge gyven or hanged on the mares eare', or of 'eny takyng of the mare by the hoofe in stede of the hand*es*'. Explaining why it was that the men of Goudhurst should have rung two peals in the church of Benenden, Stephen Mannocke claimed that it was 'not for solemnyte' nor 'in yoye of eny suche foolishe maryage'. Rather, it was in reciprocation and fulfilment of promised hospitality, 'for that they of Benenden were abowte a fortenyght before at goodherst in makyng merrye, and there theym of Benenden dyd rynge a peale or two, and so lykewyse the men of goodherst dyd desyre to rynge a peale at Benenden'.

From the event narrated above, it would not be difficult to imagine similar circumstances of courtesy visits, the communal reception of 'strangers' from another parish, the various ways in which individuals came together to fraternise, and the kind of conversation, camaraderie and foolery which might ensue. News spread by word of mouth that guests were expected may well have stimulated the interest of those seeking eligible partners, temporary unions, or other forms of introduction. Even if the presence of parties of youths did not lead to direct encounters, the situation might encourage the development of future relationships, or at least be conducive to sexual dalliance. Wherever groups formed, whether at play, or at work, there was greater scope for sexual relations, close friendships and courtship. Times of village celebrations and amusement[112] were propitious for broaching the question of marriage whether for the first time or for confirmation. In *Bonham* v. *Ellet*, it was 'among a great multitude of company' gathered at the forestall beside Teynham vicarage house watching the May dances, that John Bonham was heard asking Margery Ellet openly if she would keep to her promise.[113] The working environment likewise created opportunities for initiating and pursuing desires. The deposition of Anne Beane, for 10 years a servant to Mr Thomas Brodnex of Godmersham, indicates moreover the potential influence of seasonality and labour in the timing and effecting of personal relationships and sexual liasions. Testifying to the alleged sexual exploits of one Christopher Carter, she maintained that he never attempted to seduce her except once, 'in a harvest tyme the young men and bachelers of godmersham coming to Mr Brodnex ... to reap corne [she] went up to make a bed in a chamber of her masters house [and he] came up after her and was there playeng and toyeng with her and at length ... did put out the candle and still contynued jesting and playeng with her untill som of his company called him awaye'.[114]

Of the various contexts in which social bonds were formed and intimate relationships likely to develop, it is probably easiest to document the experience of those in service and infer, as Brodsky Elliott does, 'that the most common meeting ground for potential spouses was in the households which brought together unmarried men as apprentices and women as servants'.[115] The physical proximity of young people in households promoted emotional ties and nourished sexual appetites. Peter Laslett highlighted the features of 'courtship, sexual experimentation and exploitation' among the servant population.[116] Flirtation between servants was to be expected. Frank Kelsam, discounting any obligation to Parnelle Norton, said that his attentions were 'not seryously' meant, 'but as servants use somtyme to iest one with another'.[117] William Kemsley also only admitted to having had communications with Mildred Mason 'meryly (as servants together in one house use sum tymes to do) of marriage in iest'.[118] Those attachments which developed could become intense and companionate. One of Mr Leede's household servants said that Richard Nashe and Anne Colyar were her fellow servants in the house at that time, that she often heard them talk of marriage, and that 'thone favored thother muche, and wold be together, and for the most parte [Anne] wold kepe hym company in the house wheresoever Richard went'.[119] The atmosphere of close contact could prove claustrophobic if relationships foundered.[120] Even a change of service did not always provide an escape for those who did not fancy the assiduous pursuit of their admirers. Katherine Grigge professed that when she and William Ottringham were household servants to William Norwood of Sampson Court in Thanet, he often courted her but she, 'not favoring him, desired him to acquiet his mind, saying she'd never have him'. Nevertheless, about two years later, while she was in the service of the victualler Richard Wynter of Wingham, being at that time somewhat sickly, William Ottringham resorted to her, seeking to renew his love and his earnest suit for marriage.[121] In households where several servants were in attendance, or where employees frequently came and went, the situation clearly existed for jealous rivals, for the making of multi-promises and a number of close partnerships. Both Sara Paramor and Jane Mussered, for example, who were together in service in David Hole's house in Ash, appear to have had some claim on one Lawrence Claringboll who also dwelt there for nearly a year.[122] Returning to the case of *Symons v. Spayne*, the competition for Judith Symons, William Tanner's servant-in-trust, has already been shown in the challenge between John

Spayne and Thomas Bryant who 'then being Mr Tanners man was greatly in love with [Judith]'. Although John Spayne was never actually in Tanner's service, he had presumably succeeded Tanner's former servant, Thomas Kennet, in her affections.[123]

At the same time as introducing servants to their peers, being in service provided the opportunity for some male servants such as Robert Launsfield to seek to marry their employer's daughters, in this case, Anne Austen of Ickham.[124] Female servants also found themselves in situations which furnished similar relationships. Barbara Baull, a servant to Mistress Filpot of Faversham, was heard to affirm that she should have her mistress's youngest son, William Filpot, to her husband. She 'confessed that she was bounden to sett downe on her knees to geve god thankes that ev*er* she cam to her mestres ... declaring ... that she was a mother to her and a spe*ci*all good frend to kepe her as she did'.[125] Alternatively, the depositions expose the vulnerability of some servants in the machinations of courtship. Alice Cotton, who served Henry and Elizabeth Baxter in Sandwich, would have had little to be thankful for. In her testimony, she appealed to the judges to dissuade her master and dame from abusing her with stripes and threats. Afraid of returning to her service 'she saith she hath had such a miserable lif with her dame and master and partlie for that she was alwaies unwilling to consent to marrye with Thomas Baxter that she wishe her dailie out of her lif and she is assured that if she go home to her masters house agen she shalbe sharpely punished the rath*er* for the disliking of his son'. She deposed how she wept at being constrained to fulfil a contract with Thomas Baxter which she said was done only out of fear, and not out of any love or goodwill towards him.[126]

Partnerships might also originate between servants and their employer's other relatives. It was while she dwelt with Mr Coppyn, the alderman of Canterbury, that Katherine Richards frequently encountered Edmond Coppyn, who resorted several times to his uncle's house.[127] As for John Davye's suit for marriage to Marion Wright, her master, Thomas Davye of Eastchurch, claimed that 'he himself was the first mover' of the contract made between his servant and his kinsman.[128] It is seldom clear precisely how much initiative employers took in negotiating relationships of this character, but what is apparent, is that the conditions and fortunes of service cultivated the possibility for certain kinds of personal contacts to materialise. If not with fellow servants, or with their master's immediate family or kin, some servants later found themselves wedded to their former employer.[129] Especially in circumstances where the intention was, presumably, primarily sexual, relationships between employers and their subordinates were predictable. We have, for example, already glimpsed the suspected pregnancy of William Gybbes's maid, Prudence Bramelo.[130] In the parish of Hackington, it was commonly reputed 'among women', that either the widower William Johnson, or one of his men, had got his servant Benet Hutchyn with child. While women may generally have believed that to be the case, Johnson claimed 'that the men [did] not thinke so', reflecting perhaps deep-seated gender divisions over particular issues.[131]

Although employment within a household has been portrayed as a common environment for uniting people of the opposite sex, in situations where relationships developed outside the domestic setting, the experience of service could inhibit the frequency of meeting, or indirectly encourage parties to depend upon alternative meeting-places. Thomas Tanner, who lived and worked in Herne, sent a message to Isabel Parker alias Parr at Stodmarsh, in which he requested 'that she would not take his absence unkindly for that he was a servant and could not come to her soe often as he could afford'.[132] In the case of *Symons* v. *Spayne*, the place appointed for Thomas Kennet and Judith Symons to meet in secret lay in the highway leading from Dymchurch to Eastbridge. At a later time when Judith was being courted by both John Spayne and Thomas Bryant, she went in the company of Dorothy Fittell, 'unto the seae syde at Dymchurche wall', and there they met with John Spayne who promised to marry her.[133]

The meeting at Dymchurch wall, and the fight between the two men at the sluice between Dymchurch and Romney,[134] provide dramatic focal points, and may well be understood to possess symbolic relevance. When perceived as a barrier or bridge – like rails, gates,[135] stiles or crossroads – such topographical features might also represent areas of liminality. Katherine Richards, as we have seen, met Edmond Coppyn at the turnpike at St Augustine's wall.[136] In another case, William Keble and Suzanne Butler were seen sitting together 'on the thresholde of the bine dore' before promising each other marriage 'at a rayle under the peare tree'.[137] References in the depositions to people sitting upon their 'threshold doore' and the 'entry' of private homes, and the fact that incidents of defamation so often occurred when parties were poised at their own doors,[138] may likewise indicate the significance of the doorstep as a marginal space. That institutionalised meeting-places existed for courting couples, in addition to the traditional popularity of alehouses and other customary social gatherings, may be recognised in Sampson Marshall's advice to Simon Aunsell and Agnes Court. As they approached a stile joining the highway between the parishes of Wye and Boughton Aluph, he asked them if they could both be contented to conclude a marriage bargain there, saying further 'that at that stile bargagnes of Cli or twoo have been made'.[139] Although such evidence is impressionistic, it is nevertheless highly suggestive of places and areas which might occupy special significance in the experience of courtship.

In exploring some of the contexts and places of meeting which brought together individuals often residing in the same household, or parish, or within reasonable distance of each other, it has been presumed that the economic and social circumstances of work, marketing and leisure pursuits stimulated that process. The encounters depicted in the depositions at various stages of courtship, reflect in part the prevailing opportunities in marriage choice. Without further detailed knowledge of social networks and how they operated, we have to depend primarily upon such situations for our information regarding first meetings. Very occasionally we may glimpse other means by which couples first met. Nowhere is this more apparent than in situations where the widow proved herself a marketable asset.[140] A large proportion of the deposition cases are concerned with the marriage of widows, and in several instances the competition for widows would appear to have been pronounced. The widow Elizabeth Chamber was heard to declare to her suitor Mathew Rayner, 'many doo com hither to see and speak with me, but I doo use to kepe in, and speake with none except with suche as I doo well know, but that with you specially I am well contented to speak withall'.[141] That many men sought the hand of Margery Dennys of Faversham was aptly expressed by her neighbour. Being in his own house, and hearing 'a great talking noyse in Dennys' house, he went thither, and seing her said, goodwyf dennys you are a foole, for you have a great sort of sutors come to you, and if you will do as I wold have you do I wold take hym that I love best by the hand and take him to my husband, and wold set all the rest out of dores'.[142]

When confronted with so many suitors, the criteria upon which choice was made were evidently most pertinent. Instead of a possible succession of suitors, the presence of a wooing party assembled at one time in widow Starkey's house in Canterbury has already been observed.[143] The incident described, occurring as it did only eight weeks after the death of her husband, a late alderman of the city, may hardly have allowed a sufficient period for mourning, but the reception of the handsome and substantial men who came from the Weald of Kent demonstrates the active lure of the widow with position or wealth. They were all gathered together at supper 'of intent of wooing the said Mistress Starkey and for marriage'. It was, however, the man seated silently at the end of the table who that night lodged in the widow's house, and who later married her. The situation whereby the widow found a spouse was apparently created by the opportune coming of a group of eligible partners. However, the reason for the final choice of one William Witherden, who 'shuld have the wedow from them all', a man who was then resident in the nearby parish of Wingham, barely five miles away, is more difficult to discover. Agnes Butterwick's role in 'bringing the marriage to passe' may have been crucial. At that time she declared, 'here sitt a merry company and yet I see one among them all that sitteth still and saieth never a worde that may putt all the rest of the company out'. There is no indication in this case of the kinds of social mechanisms which prompted the coming of the Weldishmen, but one of the ways in which such knowledge might spread and in which such introductions might be made, is hinted at finally in the deposition of Peter Bellingham of Willesborough. He had known the widow Agnes Ely of New Romney, daughter of William Baker of Willesborough, for 30 years. He testifed that Mr Brent's miller had told him one day, as he was grinding the corn, 'that reporte was made at Mr Brents table of a riche wedowe and a handsom woman that had well where withall to lyve dwelling at New Romney requesting [him, Peter Bellingham] to be a sutor for him to the said wedowe'.[144]

The role of intermediaries in the activities of courtship and marriage has already been shown, and so too the geographical compass of their negotiations. In this chapter, we have seen that courtship horizons more generally were relatively contained, although its limits were possibly expanding towards the end of the sixteenth century. In rural areas they were usually confined to the more immediate locality, with more distant connections occurring with and between towns. It is suggested that the potential for longer-distance courtship was partly a factor of the greater size and more complex functions of urban communities. It may be, in fact, that the extent of courtship horizons corresponded in some measure with the range of social and economic interests of particular communities. The social interaction of young people, then, may have been affected by the extent of social and economic interaction of parents, families, households (both parental and service) and communities.

As the depositions show, the places and opportunities for relationships to develop were varied. Such bonds could clearly develop in the work-regulated environment of service. Whether within the master's household, in the course of work as servants outside the household, going as a servant to other households or as a servant between households, there were stolen opportunities for friendship and intimacy, and conditions which must have encouraged other flows of information. On special occasions, and at particular times and places, further opportunities manifested themselves. Some of the places could permit social interaction which was otherwise not possible, as in the tavern or alehouse. These institutions were often socially marginal and subversive, with their own networks of communication, common knowledge and gossip. Others gave licence to unusual degrees of intermingling, such as markets and especially fairs, where relationships would be initiated, tested, explored, flirted with, or confirmed. Such occasions were regular, complex social gatherings of marked importance within the locality, and may conceivably have provided a kind of secular sanction for courtship activities, observing and permitting the development of potential relationships.

Tavern, alehouse, market and fair may be seen to represent, in different ways, social experience beyond the conventional, ideologically sound, moral regulation of the community. They possessed a distinct liminality, inhabiting a domain which had its own rules and providing the opportunity for licensed and unlicensed transgression. Both liminality and transgression were crucial in the negotiation of courtship and in the pursuit of personal relations. Other less formal kinds of social institution or practice, such as the private assignation, intimate meetings by stile, gate or other specified barriers, and the activities of identifiable youth groups, and parties of young people, might have similar functions. They might also have possessed their own rituals of set times and places, and ways of behaving, ritualising their activities along traditional lines, or borrowing ritual to invest the occasion with significance. Not only then was courtship itself liminal, as Van Gennep emphasised, poised between the unmarried and married condition. Within its area of social activity, courtship employed other liminal states for its exploration.

NOTES

1 The term 'courtship horizons' was used by C. Phythian-Adams, *Re-thinking English Local History*, Department of English Local History Occasional Papers, 4th ser. 1 (Leicester, 1987), p. 41.

2 Macfarlane, *Marriage and Love*, p. 296.

3 E.g. P. Clark and D. Souden eds, *Migration and Society in Early Modern England* (London, 1987); P. Clark, 'The migrant in Kentish towns, 1580–1640', in P. Clark and P. Slack eds, *Crisis and Order in English Towns 1500–1700: Essays in Urban History* (London, 1972), pp. 117–63; H. Hanley, 'Population mobility in Buckinghamshire, 1578–1583', *Local Population Studies* 15 (Autumn 1975), 33–9; M. Siraut, 'Physical mobility in Elizabethan Cambridge', *Local Population Studies* 27 (Autumn 1981), 65–70.

4 P. Clark, 'Migration in England during the late 17th and early 18th centuries', in Clark and Souden eds, *Migration and Society*, pp. 213–52 (p. 215).

5 For continuities in the migration pattern, see L. R. Poos, 'Population turnover in medieval Essex: the evidence of some early-fourteenth-century tithing lists', in L. Bonfield, R. Smith and K. Wrightson eds, *The World We Have Gained: Histories of Population and Social Structure* (Oxford, 1986), pp. 1–22 (p. 4). For references to localised mobility within territorial boundaries, see Phythian-Adams, *Re-thinking English Local History*, pp. 32–4. In particular Clark, 'Migration in England', pp. 223, 228, suggests a radius of little more than 10 miles in the period 1660–1730, and Hanley, 'Population mobility', pp. 35–6, found that 68 per cent of his sample moved 15 miles or less. For short-range residential mobility within London in the seventeenth century, see, J. Boulton, 'Neighbourhood migration in early modern London', in Clark and Souden eds, *Migration and Society*, pp. 107–49. For the localised mobility of the Kent Wealden population, see, Zell, *Industry in the Countryside*, pp. 80–5. Credit relations usually operated within a similarly restricted radius, see, Tittler, 'Money-lending in the West Midlands', pp. 256–7.

6 A. S. Kussmaul, 'The ambiguous mobility of farm servants', *Economic History Review* 2nd ser. 34 (1981), 222–35 (pp. 228, 233–4).

7 J. Patten, 'Patterns of migration and movement of labour to three pre-industrial East Anglian towns', in Clark and Souden eds, *Migration and Society*, pp. 77–106 (pp. 86–7).

8 Boulton, 'Neighbourhood migration', p. 109; Elliott, 'Single women', p. 90. For age at migration, see also, Goldberg, 'Marriage, migration, servanthood and life-cycle', p. 148; Clark, 'Migration in England', pp. 226–7; Clark, 'The migrant in Kentish towns', p. 124.

9 For service and child-exchange between households, see McCracken, 'The exchange of children in Tudor England', *passim*. The importance of service in the maturation of youth is treated by I. K. Ben-Amos, 'Service and the coming of age of young men in seventeenth-century England', *Continuity and Change* 3:1 (1988), 41–64, and I. K. Ben-Amos, *Adolescence and Youth in Early Modern England* (New Haven and London, 1994).

10 Elliott, 'Single women', esp. pp. 84, 97.

11 E.g. Goldberg, 'Marriage, migration, servanthood and life-cycle', p. 148; Siraut, 'Physical mobility', p. 68. For marriage as a means of effective integration into an urban community, see P. Clark, 'Migrants in the city: the process of social adaptation in English towns, 1500–1800', in Clark and Souden eds, *Migration and Society*, pp. 267–91 (pp. 270–1). Cf. Laslett, *Family Life and Illicit Love*, p. 70, on marital migration in the villages of Clayworth and Cogenhoe.

12 Kussmaul, 'The ambiguous mobility of farm servants', p. 225. Also on settlement of servants, see Hanley, 'Population mobility', p. 37.

13 P. Clark and D. Souden, 'Introduction', in Clark and Souden eds, *Migration and Society*, pp. 11–48 (p. 13); Carlson, 'Courtship in Tudor England', p. 24.

14 For parish fees, see, J. Boulton, 'Itching after private marryings? marriage customs in seventeenth-century London', *London Journal* 16:1 (1991), 15–34 (pp. 16–19).

15 R. Phillips, *Putting Asunder: a History of Divorce in Western Society* (Cambridge, 1988), p. 6.

16 Clark and Souden, 'Introduction', pp. 26–7; Phythian-Adams, *Re-thinking English Local History*, esp. pp. 30, 35–6.

17 Cressy, *Birth, Marriage and Death*, p. 244.

18 Macfarlane, *Marriage and Love*, pp. 261–2. For a hypothetical local scale of interaction, see, J. Millard, 'A new approach to the study of marriage horizons', *Local Population Studies* 28 (Spring 1982), 10–31 (p. 13).

19 J. Boulton, *Neighbourhood and Society: a London Suburb in the Seventeenth Century* (Cambridge, 1987), p. 234.

20 E.g. Boulton, 'Itching after private marryings?', p. 18; B. Maltby, 'Easingwold marriage horizons', *Local Population Studies* 2 (Spring 1969), 36–9 (p. 36); E. A. Wrigley, 'Age at marriage in early modern England', *Family History* 12 (1982), 219–34 (pp. 229–30); Wrigley and Schofield, 'English population history', p. 163.

21 Maltby, 'Easingwold marriage horizons', pp. 37, 39.

22 Cited in Macfarlane, *Marriage and Love*, p. 261.

23 Stone, *Family, Sex and Marriage*, p. 51; Phythian-Adams, *Re-thinking English Local History*, pp. 40–1.

24 Boulton, 'Neighbourhood migration', p. 135.

25 Phythian-Adams, *Re-thinking English Local History*, p. 34.

26 Helmholz, *Marriage Litigation*, pp. 80–1. The figures are, however, provided to suggest that spouses were commonly sought from outside.

27 C.C.A.L., MS. X/10/18, fos 45, 62v.–3, *Dale* v. *Rayner* (1578); MS. Y/3/16, f. 129.

28 C.C.A.L., MS X/10/11, f. 35, *Bramelo* v. *Bonnam* (1568). In the Act books, he is described as being from Chilham; *ibid.*, MS. Y/2/25, f. 445v.

29 C.C.A.L., MSS. X/10/7., f. 188; X/10/15, f. 249v., *Austen* v. *Rogers* (1567).

30 C.C.A.L., MSS. X/10/12, fos 36v.–9v.; X/2/26, f. 135, *Norman* v. *Hatche* (1563).

31 C.C.A.L., MSS. X/10/17, fos 89, 92v.; Y/2/30, f. 252, *Levet* v. *Williams* (1574).

32 C.C.A.L., MSS. Y/2/16, f. 40; X/10/3, f. 19, *Mondaye* v. *Parker* (1546).

33 See, O'Hara, 'Sixteenth-century courtship', Appendix 2, Table A2.1, pp. 268–70, for the figures for individual places, and the numbers of exogamous relationships.

34 See above, Introduction, Map 1, p. 18.

35 See also Clark, 'The migrant in Kentish towns', pp. 124–5, and 'Migration in England', p. 223.

36 C.C.A.L., MS. X/11/6, fos 191–v; 194–5, 198–v., *Stace* v. *Mount* (1593).

37 C.C.A.L., MSS. X/11/3, fos 25v.–27v.; X/11/5, fos 236, 240, 241v., 243v., 255, 256v., 266v., 269v. *Symons* v. *Spayne* (1598).

38 C.C.A.L., MS. X/10/15, fos 246–7, *Brooke* v. *Browne* (1567).

39 C.C.A.L., MS. Y/2/27, f. 118v.

40 See above, chapter 1, pp. 39, 45.

41 Phythian-Adams, *Re-thinking English Local History*, pp. 36, 47.

42 C.C.A.L., MSS. X/10/18, fos 67–9v.; Y/3/16, f. 106, *Giles* v. *Wyborn* (1577–78).

43 C.C.A.L., MS. X/10/12, f. 114, *Pigden* v. *Willard* (1564).

44 For the location and distance of extra-county and extra-diocesan links, see, O'Hara, 'Sixteenth-century courtship', Table 4.3, p. 140.

45 Phythian-Adams, *Re-thinking English Local History*, p. 36. Regarding the mobility of the Kent Wealden population, migrants rarely came from beyond the county and Sussex, see Zell, *Industry in the Countryside*, p. 85. For further evidence of the importance that county boundaries might have for marriage horizons, see M. Carter, 'Town or urban society? St Ives in Huntingdonshire, 1630–1740', in C. Phythian-Adams ed., *Societies, Cultures and Kinship, 1580–1850: Cultural Provinces and English Local History* (Leicester, 1993), pp. 77–130.

46 For links with London and Calais, see, Clark, *English Provincial Society*, p. 11.

47 See above, chapter 1, pp. 35–6.

48 Both parties in any one case are included in their respective parishes.

49 A detailed breakdown of courtship horizons by individual parish, and by settlement type and region, can be found in O'Hara, 'Sixteenth-century courtship', Appendix 2, Table A2.2, Table A2.3., pp. 271–81.

50 See above, chapter 1, p. 43.

51 C.C.A.L., MS. X/10/11, f. 34v., *Bramelo* v. *Bonnam* (1568).

52 C.C.A.L., MS. X/10/8, fos 134–5v., 136v.–8v., *Coppyn* v. *Richard* (1560).

53 Phythian-Adams, *Re-thinking English Local History*, p. 35.

54 Millard, 'A new approach to the study of marriage horizons', pp. 11, 14; Patten, 'Patterns of migration', p. 102; Clark, 'Migration in England', p. 230, and 'The migrant in Kentish towns', p. 126.

55 See, e.g., A. Everitt, 'The market towns', in P. Clark ed., *The Early Modern Town* (London, 1976), pp. 168–204; W. G. Hoskins, 'English provincial towns in the early sixteenth century', in *ibid.*, pp. 91–105, and J. F. Pound, 'The social and trade structure of Norwich, 1525–1575', in *ibid.*, pp. 129–47.

56 Clark, 'The migrant in Kentish towns', p. 132.

57 Some approximate population figures for individual shire towns, head Cinque Port municipalities and other boroughs in the sixteenth and seventeenth centuries, can be found in Clark, *English Provincial Society*, pp. 8–9; C. W. Chalklin, 'A seventeenth-century market town: Tonbridge', in M. Roake and J. Whyman eds, *Essays in Kentish History* (London, 1973), pp. 89–99 (p. 89). For market towns, see Everitt, 'The market towns', pp. 178–9. For further population estimates of Canterbury, Faversham, Maidstone, Sandwich, New Romney, Dover and Hythe, see also, Chalklin, *Seventeenth-Century Kent*, pp. 30–1; Tronrud, 'The response to poverty', p. 10, n. 2; Tronrud, 'Dispelling the gloom', pp. 10–11; Clark, 'The ownership of books', pp. 97–8.

58 This may be seen by comparing the pattern shown here with that for certain rural parishes in the North Downs in Table 8.

59 See above, Introduction, pp. 17–19.

60 Furley, *History of the Weald*, p. 699.

61 Thirsk ed., *The Agrarian History of England and Wales*, pp. 57–9; Clark, *English Provincial Society*, pp. 7–8; Jessup, *Kent History Illustrated*, p. 43; *Victoria County History of Kent*, III, pp. 384–9, 403–12; Zell, *Industry in the Countryside*.

62 For parishes located in the Romney Marsh area, see, J. Eddison and C. Green eds, *Romney Marsh Evolution, Occupation, Reclamation*, Monograph 24 (Oxford University Committee for Archaeology, 1988), pp. 92–3, and Fig. 0.1.

63 A study of the origins of Romney freemen in the late fifteenth and sixteenth centuries demonstrated that the radius of its hinterland approximated to 30 miles, see Butcher, 'Origins of Romney freemen'.

64 The total number for the Isle of Sheppey (26) proved too small for any meaningful percentage calculation.

65 Everitt, 'The market towns', p. 193.

66 E.g. Macfarlane, *Marriage and Love*, p. 296; Houlbrooke ed., *English Family Life*, pp. 15–51.

67 Houlbrooke, *The English Family*, p. 72; Boulton, 'Neighbourhood migration', p. 127; Carlson, 'Courtship in Tudor England', p. 24; Carlson, *Marriage and the English Reformation*, p. 110; Ben-Amos, *Adolescence and Youth*, p. 200. For the attendance at fairs instead of at church, see Emmison, *Elizabethan Life*, pp. 82–3. On the possible connection between fairs and sexuality trends, see E. Lord, 'Fairs, festivals and fertility in Alkmaar, North Holland, 1650–1810', *Local Population Studies* 42 (Spring 1989), 43–53.

68 E. W. Moore, 'Medieval English fairs: evidence from Winchester and St Ives', in J. A. Raftis ed., *Pathway to Medieval Peasants*, Papers in Medieval Studies 2 (Pontifical Institute of Medieval Studies, Toronto, 1981), pp. 283–99 (p. 283).

69 McIntosh, 'Servants and the household unit', p. 16.

70 C.C.A.L., MS. X/11/5, fos 238–41, *Symons* v. *Spayne* (1598).

71 C.C.A.L., MSS. X/11/5, fos 26–8v.; J/J1 146, J/J1 150 (1595).

72 C.C.A.L., MS. X/10/7, f. 17–v., *Coppyn* v. *Richards* (1560).

73 C.C.A.L., MS. X/10/7, fos 130–1, 332v.

74 Van Gennep, *The Rites of Passage*, pp. 15–25, 192.

75 M. Douglas, *Purity and Danger* (London, 1966, 1984 edn), ch. 7, esp. p. 114.

76 I am grateful to A. F. Butcher for this information.

77 Fox, 'Ballads, libels and popular ridicule', pp. 58, 61, 66–7.

78 M. Spufford, 'The pedlar, the historian and the folklorist: seventeenth-century communications', *Folklore* 105 (1994), 13–24 (pp. 15–16).

79 M. Bakhtin, *Rabelais and His World,* trans. H. Iswolsky (Cambridge, Massachusetts, 1968, 1984 edn), ch. 2, 'The language of the marketplace in Rabelais', pp. 145–95 (esp. pp. 153–4). For further discussion of the marketplace as a 'ritually circumscribed', 'ambivalent' and 'marginal space', and for seventeeth-century images of the market as a festive place, a place for discovery, intrigue, negotiation and risk, see, L. Hutson, 'The displacement of the market in Jacobean city comedy', *London Journal* 14:1 (1989), 3–16 (pp. 7–9).

80 'The fair, the pig, authorship', in P. Stallybrass and A. White, *The Politics and Poetics of Transgression* (London, 1986), pp. 27–43, (esp. pp. 27, 29–30, 36–8).

81 See above, chapter 2, p. 68.

82 C.C.A.L., MS. X/10/16, fos 295–303v. (1577).

83 C.C.A.L., MS. X/11/4, fos 26v.–7, *Greenway* v. *Burch et Gabriell* (1600).

84 C.C.A.L., MSS. X/10/7, fos 85v.–6, *Lyon* v. *Cole* (1560); Y/2/22, f. 53v.

85 C.C.A.L., MS. X/10/7, fos 152, 154–7, 346–7v., 352v., *Cole* v. *Barnes* (1561).

86 C.C.A.L., MS. X/10/11, f. 229–v., *Turner* v. *Hubbard* (?1570).

87 C.C.A.L., MS. X/10/11, fos 179v.–82, *Kennet* v. *Dunnye* (1570).

88 C.C.A.L., MS. X/10/18, fos 152v.–3, *Hogben* v. *Wraight* (1579).

89 Bakhtin, *Rabelais and His World*, p. 186.

90 Stallybrass and White, 'The fair', p. 39.

91 C.C.A.L., MS. X/10/13, fos 84–6v. (1571).

92 C.C.A.L., MS. X/10/12, fos 36v.–7v., *Norman* v. *Hatche* (1563).

93 Cressy, *Birth, Marriage and Death*, pp. 245–7.

94 C.C.A.L., MS. X/10/18, fos 46–8, *Jenkyns* v. *Adams* (1578).

95 C.C.A.L., MS. X/10/7, fos 123v.–7v., *Den* v. *Cole* (1560).

96 E.g. C.C.A.L., MS X/10/6, fos 34v.–7, 38v., *Wood* v. *Crispe* (1553). Words of defamation spoken in a 'chaffering' house. For railing rhymes and the alehouse society, see, Fox, 'Ballads, libels and popular ridicule', p. 72.

97 C.C.A.L., MS. X/10/8, fos 126–8, *Rayner* v. *Chamber* (1561).

98 K. Wrightson, 'Alehouses, order and reformation in rural England, 1590–1660', in E. and S. Yeo eds, *Popular Culture and Class Conflict, 1590–1914* (Hassocks, 1981), pp. 1–27, (p. 6).

99 Also Clark, 'Migrants in the city', pp. 280–1.

100 C.C.A.L., MS. X/10/2, fos 20–1, *Bennet* v. *Smyth* (?1542).

101 C.C.A.L., MS. X/11/5, fos 243–4, 246v.–7 (1598).

102 C.C.A.L., MS. X/11/5, fos 256–8.

103 See Boulton, 'Neighbourhood migration', pp. 126–7, 131, for social activity outside the dwelling-place.

104 P. Clark, 'The alehouse and the alternative society', in D. Pennington and K. Thomas eds, *Puritans and Revolutionaries: Essays in Seventeenth-Century History Presented to Christopher Hill* (Oxford, 1978), pp. 47–72 (p. 60).

105 See above, pp. 138–9.

106 C.C.A.L., MS. X/10/8, fos 43v.–4v.

107 Wrightson, 'Alehouses, order and reformation', p. 7; Clark, 'The migrant in Kentish towns', pp. 140–1.

108 See also Clark, 'The alehouse and the alternative society', p. 62, and P. Clark, *The English Alehouse: a Social History, 1200–1830* (London, 1983), pp. 127–8, 147–53.

109 Houlbrooke, *The English Family*, p. 72.

110 Wrightson, 'Alehouses, order and reformation', p. 8.

111 Paragraph based on C.C.A.L., MS. PRC 39/6, fos 89v.–90, 93–5, 97–9 (1571).

112 For wakes, revels, group gatherings, love-ales and other communal pastimes, see, S. Hindle, 'Custom, festival and protest in early modern England: the Little Budworth wakes, St Peter's Day, 1596', *Rural History* 6:2 (1995), 155–78 (esp. pp. 157, 164–5).

113 C.C.A.L., MS. X/10/7, fos 73v.–4 (1560).

114 C.C.A.L., MS. X/11/5, f. 90, *Carter* v. *Maverlye* (1596).

115 Elliott, 'Single women', p. 96.

116 P. Laslett, 'Notes and queries: the institution of service', *Local Population Studies* 40 (Spring 1988), 55–60 (p. 56).

117 C.C.A.L., MS. X/10/18, f. 94v., *Norton* v. *Kelsam* (1578).

118 C.C.A.L., MS. X/10/18, f. 165–v., *Mason* v. *Kemsley* (1579).

119 C.C.A.L., MS. X/10/7, fos 71–2v., *Nashe* v. *Colyar* (1560).

120 See above, chapter 1, p. 34, *Haffynden* v. *Austen*.

121 C.C.A.L., MS. X/10/15, fos 160–2v., *Ottringham* v. *Grigge* (1567).

122 C.C.A.L., MS. X/11/6, fos 192v., 193v., *Claringboll* v. *Mussered* (1593).

123 C.C.A.L., MS. X/11/5, fos 240, 241v., 242v., 250 (1598); see above, pp. 130, 143–4 and above, chapter 3, p. 113.

124 C.C.A.L., MS. X/10/12, f. 150–v., *Launsfield* v. *Austen* (1565).

125 C.C.A.L., MS. X/10/16, fos 70–5v., 81v.–3, *Filpot* v. *Baull alias Cruttall* (1575).

126 C.C.A.L., MS. X/10/17, fos 150v.–5v., *Baxter* v. *Cotton* (1574).

127 C.C.A.L., MS. X/10/7, fos 17–v., 131, 332v., *Coppyn* v. *Richards* (1560).

128 C.C.A.L., MS. X/10/6, fos 39–40, *Davye* v. *Wrighte* (1554).

129 E.g. McIntosh, 'Servants and the household unit', p. 21; Elliott, 'Single women', p. 89.

130 See above, p. 133.

131 C.C.A.L., MS. X/10/14, f. 40–v. (1572).

132 C.C.A.L., MS. X/11/4, f. 162v., *Parker alias Parr* v. *Tanner* (1602).

133 C.C.A.L., MS. X/11/5, fos 241v., 250–3v. (1598).

134 See above, p. 144.

135 E.g. Riding gate in Canterbury, where John Jackson and Rebecca Odert met, C.C.A.L., MS. X/11/3, fos 81v.–3, *Jackson* v. *Odert alias Simons* (1598).

136 See above, p. 139.

137 C.C.A.L., MS. X/10/19, fos 250v.–1v., *Keble* v. *Butler* (1585).

138 Gowing, 'Gender and the language of insult', p. 18.

139 C.C.A.L., MS. X/10/10., fos 29–30, *Aunsell* v. *Court* (1563).

140 On the high premium attached to widows in the London marriage market, see V. Brodsky, 'Widows in late Elizabethan London: remarriage, economic opportunity and family orientation', in L. Bonfield, R. Smith and K. Wrightson eds, *The World We Have Gained* (Oxford, 1986), pp. 122–54.

141 C.C.A.L., MS. X/10/8, fos 121v.–3, *Rayner* v. *Chamber* (1561).

142 C.C.A.L., MS. X/10/16, fos 266v.–7v., *Jefery* v. *Dennys alias Cook alias Read* (1577).

143 See above, chapter 3, p. 107.

144 C.C.A.L., MS. X/10/12, fos 97v.–9 (1564). See above, chapter 3, p. 103.

Chapter 5

The timing of marriage: constraints and expectations

The previous chapter discussed how distance and place might provide some underlying determinants or parameters of courtship. Apart from the matter of *where*, the question of *when* marriage was supposed to commence posed a further constraint over courtship. Instead of concentrating, as historical demographers have done, on computing the ages at which people actually married, this chapter aims to offer a different kind of perspective on the dynamics of nuptiality. It seeks to examine the social and cultural assumptions about appropriate marriage ages which lay behind the actual timing of marriage.

Expected or prescribed ages of marriage could inform the behaviour and attitudes both of courting couples and of the family and friends who sought to influence and guide their choice. Moreover, the ages at which they married or perhaps, just as significantly, perceived the possibilities of marriage, have more than the mere demographic consequences which have been studied so far. Such ages might also be seen to represent the crucial, ultimate threshold of adult status in a complex process of maturation and coming of age. Any evidence which can be gleaned about the identification and recognition of ages which contemporaries thought proper for the timing of marriage tells us a great deal about prevailing notions of youth, competence and stages of life. These notions could provide an important framework for courtship in the past, and for the definitive transition and integration into adult life.[2] The appropriate age at which to marry was not necessarily thought of solely in terms of economic self-sufficiency although, as we shall see in the following chapter, earning power, employment opportunities, and financial resources and prospects, were critical prerequisites for marriage to proceed. For many participants in courtship, a subtle blend of customary attitudes and values, as well as an evident attachment to those economic considerations, would seem to have been displayed.

In the Wiltshire court cases, Ingram found some antagonism towards the marriage plans of unknowing, inexperienced adolescents, and at the same time, a collective dislike of excessive age-differences between partners. He also remarked upon the flexibility revealed, concluding that it was 'not law but social custom, internalised as a sense of what was "fitting", [which] thus largely governed marriage age'.[3] Canon law did, of course, set minimum legal ages of 'discretion' and consent, when binding marriage contracts could be made, at 14 years for boys and 12 for girls,[4] accrediting the young with some judgement and legal rights before the 'full age' of 21 years.[5] In the course of the sixteenth century, proposals were made to reform the canon law in England which, if effected, would have raised the minimum ages of contract, and invalidated the marriages of dependants made without parental consent.[6] Along with efforts directed at constitutional changes, piecemeal legislative proposals, such as that 'by which young men should be restrained from marriage till they be of potent age, and tall and puissant persons stayed from marriage of old widows',[7] demonstrate both the pressure to change current legal thresholds, and the disagreement over when precisely such thresholds should be reached. That disagreement existed is hardly surprising, given the fact that there was no single, uniform age at which adult competence was reached in all the spheres of social, economic, religious and political life.[8] Contemporaries then had their own disparate ideals regarding the timing of marriage, at what ages one was considered to be psychologically, physio-logically, socially and economically mature enough to marry. Opinion differed too on the kind of age-gap between spouses deemed reputable and most desirable for a successful union. Such ideals turned on contemporary age definitions, the notional threshold of adulthood, legal limitations, past experiences, appropriate means, and a host of formal and informal recommendations. The 'gerontocratic ideal' outlined by Thomas for the early modern period ascribed maturity, wisdom and self-government to increasing age, contrasting those capacities with the irrationality and foolishness of youth, often represented as 'a slippery age, full of passion, rashness, wilful-ness'.[9] According to Macfarlane, there was the common assumption that men matured only after 25 and women after 20, an assumption which both 'reflected and checked age at marriage'.[10]

From the Kent depositions, there is some evidence to show that the restraints upon too early marriages were internalised by the parties them-selves. When 'the yonge man' John Austin asked the 'vyrgyn' Suzanne Parker if she would marry him, she answered 'that she mynded not to marry with anny before she shuld attayn to be of thage of twenty yeres. And [he] said agayn to her that she was of yere sufficient to marry yf that she wold and that there were lesse in yeres than she that have marryed, but she answered that she did not care for that, and said she wold not marry with any otherwise then as afore she answered hym.'[11] Suzanne may thus have been expressing her own sense of unpreparedness for marriage. Other girls who rejected their suitors indicated the seeming untimeliness of their proposals. Amy Colyer discussed marriage with Richard Nashe, but told him that 'she was but a child and wold not marye yet'.[12] The servant Mary Hubbard's response was 'that she would not marrye yet and that she was not meate bye reason of her age'.[13] Upon being asked by William Amys to forsake all other men for him, Elizabeth Fayreman said 'she would not, because she was not of yeers to proceede that way, and he said, that ther were as young as her which did marry and that she might leekewise, but she said no'.[14]

Some partners, though, were clearly still adolescents when they got married or at least contemplated marriage.[15] One Mary Hale, for example, was said to have been just 13 or 14 when she eloped with the 20-year-old Beale to marry at London, contrary to the wishes of her mother and stepfather, William Tanner.[16] As for the projected marriage between his servants, Thomas Kennet and Judith Spayne, the same Mr Tanner was heard to object strongly, 'the said Judyth being but a gyrle committed to his custody'.[17] Further cases similarly suggest that contracts were made among young people in their mid- to late teens.[18] For the 'smale' Godlina Knowler of Herne, it was commonly reported that her stepfather 'sold' her in marriage at the early age of about 14 years. Although she would have been legally eligible for marriage at that age, the opinion of the cleric John Bridges may have been more representative of prevailing social assumptions regarding the proper time for marriage. Declaring to Godlina's mother, 'his disliking ... that they [Hannyng and Knowler] should kepe company together the maid being so yong ... the mother told him that Hannyng had promised her that they should not accumpany together till her frendes thought good that they should accumpany so together'.[19]

Occasionally, deponents disclaimed any dealings in the marriage plans of their children on the assumption that they had sufficient maturity of judgement. The yeoman John Prowd of Ash called upon his daughter 'to answer for herself, for quoth he, she is of age to make choyce herself'.[20] Unfortunately, the deposition statements alone seldom make it clear just what that perceived threshold in age was. What they do reveal is, on the one hand, the expressed apprehension towards marrying too early. While some marriage litigants appeared to be self-conscious of their juvenility and, like Juliane Marden, professed 'that she was to younge to marry, and that she would not marry without the consent and goodwill of her frendes',[21] there were those whose marriage objectives were specifically said to hinge upon the timing of their inheritance. John Fulcombe alleged that he could not marry Margery Graves until he was 21 years, when his goods were to come to his hands in one and a quarter years' time, to which one John Knightsmyth replied, 'that maketh no matter, for you be yonge both and may tarry a while'.[22]

On the other hand, the depositions also suggest that ageing litigants might have their own misgivings about their marriageability. John Eddredge asked Dionisia Rede, 'canne you fynde in yor harte to love me as I canne love you for I am sum what aged'.[23] As Keith Thomas has pointed out, cultural conceptions about age and the behaviour thought appropriate to the age, applied accordingly to the old as well as the young. Contemporaries mocked the sexual passions of the elderly for being socially inadmissible for that age-group.[24] Regarding the famed incontinency of one Richard Abarrow, seen running naked out of a certain woman's house, and generally suspected of incontinent behaviour with other women, the 60-year-old deponent William Collye believed him to be 'clear from the vice, for he beleeveth that a man of that age and yeers hath little or no desier to comit any suche acte'. He added that he 'taketh Richard Abarrow to be 70 years and not able to get a child, to be so weake of body that he ys not provocable to fleshely lust'.[25]

Just as the excessive youth or age of couples might be seen as an obstacle to marriage, transgressing the acceptable norms of proper marriage age, some litigants also felt conscious of the need to avoid excessive differences in age between themselves and their future partners. The widow Joan Whiter, as we have already observed, sought a more elderly man whom she regarded as more suitable for her in contrast to the carousing 'yonckers'.[26] Those who ignored such customary constraints of age-parity might risk a certain degree of mockery and ridicule by their fellow parishioners, for although disparities in age may not have been uncommon in the early modern period, their acceptance remained questionable.[27]

In the case of *John Estland* v. *Mary Barrow* of Ash in 1580,[28] it would appear that the publication of the banns of marriage between the parties in Ash church precipitated some kind of crisis for Mary Barrow. At the time she was living as a servant in the house of her uncle, John Chapman, a middle-aged husbandman and long-established parishioner. None were 'sayeing agenst it', and Mary was apparently absent when the banns were first asked, but when one Mr Brooke of Ashe 'found fault' with John Chapman for permitting the asking of the banns between Mary, 'being of some yeres and Estland who is but a boye', he thereupon chided her and put her out of his service, 'somewhat disliking' the liaison. Not knowing where else to go, Mary went to live in the house of old father Estland, during which time John Estland was also present. There she received free board for four to six weeks. At the third time of asking of the banns, perhaps the most critical, there was again no formal impediment expressed. 'None spoke up against it', and Mary later claimed to have been sitting 'far off, and also thick of hearing', although it was said that she seemed to consent to it since she also said nothing. As soon as the service was completed, however, the parishioners began to utter 'sondry speaches ... agenst her' in the churchyard, 'marvelling that she wold have suche a boy to her husband', and believing that 'she did folishly to matche with such an one as Estland was'. Angered by all the gossip, Mary was heard to reply:

> My bak is brod enough to beare all your moks and flowts (turnyng herself specially to a kynswoman of her own called goodwif Wacher). But though Estland be a boy, he may be a man and I will not forsake hym whilest breath is in my body. Goodwyf Wacher answered that she was sory and ashamed to understand that she Mary had so misused herself as she did. Mary said that she cared not, for quoth she I am nether whore nor thef, and I will never forsake hym while breath is in my belly.

Mary's own account is somewhat less pointed, but interesting nevertheless for being so defensive. If, as she alleged, there was never any agreement of marriage between herself and John Estland, and if she never did consent to the publication of the banns, her own rejoinder would have been an impulsive response occasioned by the jeers of her neighbours and kin. According to her, whatever her intentions towards Estland, they were justifiable, for 'though he is now but a boy yet he wilbe a man one daie by the grace of god'. Certain persons who stood by her applauded her stance, prompting her to repeat, 'those words I've said ... I will never denye'. Within an hour after the incident, Mary went with Johanna Robinson and Mary Cork to drink together. In the company of several others, Johanna Robinson drank to John Estland, with Mary answering, 'I pledge you ... I will never forsake him ... and all present comended her for her constancy and so incoraged her to be still'. That same night, Mary Cork lay with her in old Estland's house, at which time Mary Barrow told how 'that she might and she wold marry with a wydower namyng hym goodman Mustred. But quoth Mary, I will never have hym. And I think ... my uncle Chapman wold rather consent I should marry hym then with this fellow that now I shall have (viz) John Estland. But ... thys mans labor is going away (viz) Mustred, and the other though he be but a boy his labor is comyng.'

The ambiguities in the case are clearly revealing. If no lawful impediment existed then the objections raised derived principally from social attitudes. Such informal pressures might, in the short-term, provoke the breaking of norms, but sustained over a long period, could ultimately influence and check the considered marriage decision. In countering such opposition, Mary Barrow may have been forced to take a particular rhetorical stand, resembling those moments of conflict in cases of defamation where parties hardened their respective positions. The allusion to defamation is no less real in the assertions of honour and loyalty. The case may express contemporary disapproval of the implicit sexual appetite of women for younger men, and represents the possibilities for Mary Barrow in her choice of partner by the pitted polarities of the 'widower' as opposed to the 'boy', the ebbing strength of the one, in contrast to the potential physicality of the other. From the voices of discontent, the limits of toleration are exposed, such 'gossip' accusations presumably depending for their making, their reception and their effectiveness, upon the prevailing social, economic and demographic conditions. But the nature of informal control proved itself to be ambiguous and conflicting, as the case demonstrates the influence of positive as well as negative pressure. Keith Thomas may rightly have identified the gathering of particular social and age-groups after church services.[29] Mary Cork was likely to have been Mary Barrow's bedfellow and confidante, and Johanna Robinson clearly a neighbour-at-hand. Both were also 'virgins', unmarried, aged 26 and 41 respectively, sharing in female sociability, supportive and positively encouraging of Mary's choice. But perhaps their intimacy and sympathy with her as friends and drinking companions transcend the real opinion and perception of what was generally acceptable. More likely, the negative voice of goodwife Wacher reveals more about the social and cultural constraints and notions regarding marriage age and age-parity.

Such assumptions about the appropriate age at which couples should embark on married life must have played a key role in reinforcing and bolstering the prevailing marriage regime. In particular, in sixteenth-century England, where measurement of age at first marriage is difficult and patchy, appreciating the existence of such attitudes is crucial in arriving at an informed understanding about changes, or perhaps the relative lack of change, in the prevailing age at which most couples chose to marry.

It has long been recognised that age at marriage has basic demographic as well as social and cultural significance. Together with the proportion ever marrying, it was one of the prime determinants of fertility, although recent research has placed greater emphasis on the incidence of marriage. In affecting the community's capacity to reproduce itself, age at marriage influences the size of families, household and age structures, and overall population trends.[30] Serving as both a demographic indicator and an index of changing attitudes and experience, it is also essentially tied to various kinds of socio-economic and cultural processes such as migration, modes of property transmission, the regional culture and economic system, and the general 'performance of the economy'.[31] Marriage age thus possessed a 'high strategic significance ... in relation to a wide range of economic, social and demographic questions'.[32]

Its measurement is, however, problematic. Some sources do give stated ages at marriage, namely marriage licence allegations, but this material is socially and in other ways biased, and the ages reported sometimes rounded.[33] Moreover, such licences, although procured, did not necessarily mean that the marriages actually took effect. In the case of *Hannyng* v. *Knowler*, it is clear that Stephen Hannyng did indeed obtain a licence to marry Godlina Knowler, but when he carried her off to Hackington to be married, she resolutely refused to proceed and wept bitterly.[34] Accurate ages at first marriage can be calculated from parish registers using the technique of family reconstitution. However, the evidence suffers from several disadvantages. Registers do not commence until 1538 at the earliest, the calculated ages are distorted by the effects of migration, and reconstitution cannot recapture the entire local population, but only that possibly unrepresentative 'reconstitutable minority'. All this means that we have no reliable national age at marriage figures until the last decades of the sixteenth century. For the earlier period there are virtually no sources that shed direct light on this crucial variable. Marriage licences, although useful for the seventeenth century, cannot be depended upon to supply age information for the preceding century. Some medieval historians have used other sources, such as church court depositions, to derive a rough estimate of the prevailing demographic regime, and to infer likely marriage regimes from proportions in service or mobility statistics, but the empirical evidence is scanty.[35] Poos remarked that 'no source or methodology has yet been discovered that can conclusively yield reliable data for marriage ages in rural England before 1500'.[36]

For the early modern period, England is thought to have been part of the wider north-west European household formation pattern. This consisted of a late average marriage age for both men and women, typically in the mid- to late twenties, and a substantial proportion of women who remained celibate. Such a pattern was closely associated with predominantly nuclear households, and the institution of service which allowed children to leave home in their mid-teens who would then save up property to help establish their own independent households.[37] The Cambridge Group's study suggests that, for 13 reconstituted parishes in the early Stuart period, the mean age at first marriage for women was 25.6 and for men 28.1.[38] Earlier reconstitution evidence, based on one 12-parish sample, implied that in the period 1550–99 age at marriage for single women lay between 26.4 and 26.1, and for men, between 29.3 and 28.2.[39] That there was considerable variation in the actual range in marriage ages found within parishes has also been shown in local studies. Between 1566 and 1597 in Hunstanton, Norfolk, for example, the range in ages for women lay between 16 and 34 years, and for men between 19 and 38 years.[40] Average figures themselves were variable across regions and parishes, and between urban and rural areas, highlighting the absence of a 'clear pattern in the age of marriage' and instead a 'crazy-quilt of individuality' in their experience.[41] In the sixteenth century, several parishes in the Weald of Kent which were linked to rural industry were characterised by an average age at first marriage which was lower than the national findings.[42]

While late entry into marriage was by no means universally practised in early modern England, its general prevalence has been reasonably well established. Its origins are more obscure, and for the late medieval period the age and frequency of marriage are much debated. According to Hajnal, the distinctively 'European' regime he described did not exist in England in the later fourteenth century, but originated in the post-medieval era.[43] Historians who emphasise continuity between the late medieval and early modern period, argue instead that marriage in the later fourteenth and fifteenth centuries was 'companionate', relatively late and 'compatible with the West European model'.[44] However, the phenomenon of teenage marriage is also recognised as a very real one, particularly among more elevated social groups.[45]

One's social status was among the most pronounced of the several variables which might have affected age at first marriage. Early marriage was much more common among the British peerage and squirearchy in the sixteenth century, although not all children within those social echelons would have married early.[46] In seventeenth-century London, on the other hand, status did not greatly influence variations in male marriage age, but it did affect the pattern of age-difference between spouses. It was other important factors, such as migration and parental mortality, which could affect age at marriage there.[47]

Marriage opportunities were influenced by changes in the sex ratio and social composition of the population, by the state of local marriage markets and the amount of female employment available.[48] Besides such determinants the timing of marriage impinges upon other more social issues. It affects the age-gap between husband and wife, and hence the possible equality or patriarchalism within marital relations.[49] Marrying young is usually equated with a greater degree of parental control over the marriage decision, particularly for women, and child marriages are often identified with the union of families, rather than individuals.[50]

As we have seen then, deponents in marriage cases made it clear that their age was indeed a factor to be taken into consideration when making marriage decisions, and demographers are agreed that the age at which such decisions were made played an important part in regulating population growth. What needs to be examined now is any supporting evidence we might have which could add to what we already know about the ages which contemporaries thought suitable for marriage to commence, their perceptions of age categorisations and their use of numerical ages. Such material supplies a fresh perspective on the timing of marriage in the late fifteenth and sixteenth centuries.

Where depositions can be said to reveal something about contemporary self-awareness of their age at marriage and about the various expectations governing the timing of marriage, parish registers show the pattern of marriage age for at least a proportion of the population which was followed in practice. Evidence from wills may be used to indicate the existence and significance of notional minimum ages, by representing statements of intention in the transmission of property, the perception of when such

transmission would occur and possibly, therefore, the time at which independence and competence for marriage were expected to begin.

General problems concerning the nature of the source and the limitations
of the wills as evidence are already familiar to the historian. Aside from the
legal requirements and restrictions upon will-making, how pervasive the
institution was in practice both as a social phenomenon and as a male
prerogative is problematic.[51] Much work has been devoted towards the
question of status groups among testators, the family circumstances which
necessitated the making of a will and other underlying motives and pressures.
The formal structure of the will and its implications for authorship, religious
persuasion and personal intention have also been studied.[52]

As to the general level of testation among local populations, there is some
significant variation in historical findings. Michael Zell suggests that in the
Kent Weald, there was probably an increase either in the popularity of will-
making, or in the practice of enrolling wills in the late fifteenth and early
sixteenth centuries. Fluctuations coincided with changes in mortality levels,
but the growth was maintained until a plateau at the end of the sixteenth
century.[53] In the Lincolnshire town of Grantham, on the other hand, the
evidence points to an increase in testation in the later sixteenth century,
thought to be characteristic of the general experience.[54] In early modern
England, the proportion of the dying adult local populations represented by
testators may have ranged between 5 per cent and 45 per cent.[55] Certainly, it
was not typical of most men to leave a testament, and for women, far less
likely.[56] Erickson concluded that 'family situation, wealth and local economy
seem to have had some impact on men's will-making (although the
relationship is not yet clear) but none of these factors is a good predictor of a
widow's likelihood of making a will. Although wealth caused prosperous
people to think of making a will more often than poor people, it was also
important to many poor people, especially women, to make a will.'[57]

Of the several predispositions to make a will which have been identified
among male testators, factors of wealth and status may have been of some
significance. In Banbury, will-making tended to come from the richer,
propertied classes, although all social classes with the exception of paupers
were represented.[58] Hunstanton testators comprised a reasonably wide
economic and social cross-section of the community, but with certain groups
either not represented or under-represented.[59] Other findings indicate that
prosperity alone may have been rather less causative than is usually assumed,
the actual nature of property itself being a likely factor.[60] In Grantham in the
later sixteenth century, the lower socio-economic groups were increasingly
prevalent among will-makers. While the middling rich strata remained most
prominent, 'will-making by the late sixteenth century was becoming a socially
downward process'.[61] It would seem that by the mid-sixteenth century, a

proportion of landless men in the Kent Weald were more disposed to make a will.[62] Spufford's and Howell's explanation for will-making argues against any clear correlation between absolute wealth and property ownership, and the tendency to greater testacy. Of the 49 will-makers in Willingham at the end of the sixteenth century, most came from the poorer ranks. Singling out family responsibilities instead, Spufford showed that the dominant motivation behind will-making was the need to provide for under-aged and unestablished dependants.[63] Similarly, for the inhabitants of Kibworth Harcourt, 'the decisive factor was not class or family, but the age and family responsibilities of the testator at the time when he made his will'.[64]

In recognising the significance of the demographic status of testators and their stage in the life-cycle,[65] it has also been observed that most wills were usually made close to death. An analysis of the sixteenth-century wills of rural Leverton and Grantham showed that half of the testators made their wills on their deathbed and that, despite the moral and legal recommendations, will-making was often delayed until death was imminent.[66] A glance at the testamentary cases in depositions would reveal some of the family, kin and community pressures brought to bear on men in such circumstances, seeking themselves to salvage their conscience and declaring their ultimate intentions.[67] To what extent the conditions of will-making might have determined the attitudes and strategies of testators can only be surmised, for 'the will ... was the testator's ultimate public act representing the final conscious statement of his intentions prior to decease. In some ways, as Ariès has suggested, it was part of the ritual preparation for death. The proximity of death sometimes prompted deathbed penitence, anxiety for proper burial, or hasty provision for surviving dependants.'[68] Moreover, the ways in which wills were produced could introduce further problems of interpretation. The authorship of wills has been much disputed, since the influence of scribes, professional notaries and clergymen in will formularies could affect the originality of the will.[69]

For the majority of people, will-making was not necessary in circumstances where the existing local, manorial and ecclesiastical customs required no modification.[70] Furthermore, the transmission of property was often a gradual process, and non-testamentary, pre-mortem gifts and settlements were a frequent occurrence.[71] As Bonfield emphasises, inheritance by will in early modern England was only one stage in an extended system of inter-generational property devolution. Various 'strategies of inheritance' were in operation, and the will might serve as 'a supplement, the means of correcting biases in lifetime transfers or creating them at death'. His study of inheritance among Preston copyholders illustrates the alternative and preferred means of property transmission, and the non-exclusivity of testamentary provision. Nevertheless, Bonfield argues for a close connection between inheritance and household formation. He suggests that, 'for some families the marriage of the child was the juncture at which commitments regarding inheritance were undertaken', that 'admittance to a future rather than a present possessory interest in property was related to marriage ... [and] that it was the assurance of resources rather than actual possessory transfer that was crucial'.[72]

Given that there is some relationship between the transmission of property and the timing of the decision to marry it is clearly important to investigate this complex subject. Although wills can tell us only part of the story of property transfer, they can, nonetheless, yield important new evidence about the practice and its links with marriage.

Relating paternal death to the age of first marriage of the succeeding generation is, as Vann points out, problematical precisely because of the significance of pre-mortem transfers and the establishing of married children during one's lifetime.[73] Indeed, Levine has argued that there is no connection between inheritance and marriage age, since the majority of marriages preceded paternal death. In rejecting the 'inheritance–marriage' model, however, he narrowly restricts his definition of inheritance to post-mortem transmissions.[74] The findings of the Cambridge Group also indicate that there is no evidence in the reconstitution data that the survival status of fathers had any influence on age at marriage.[75]

Nonetheless, the absence of any simple correlation between paternal death and marriage age does not preclude a link between property devolution and the timing of marriage. If we were to consider those familial circumstances where fathers died leaving under-aged, unmarried legatees, the evidence of wills may be used to reveal something about the *minimum* ages generally thought opportune to commence married life, or at least to begin independent property holding. They could indicate, therefore, the potential influence of property transmission upon marriage decisions and their future timing.

No study of wills as yet has given much detailed consideration to the range and meaning of the ages specified by testators. Some mention has, however, been made of age stipulations. In the case of daughters, especially, historians implicitly equate marriages with the provision of legacies. Aristocratic daughters in the late seventeenth century were being paid their portions between the ages of 17 and 21, most commonly at 18.[76] Middle-class testators in London usually provided for their daughters at marriage or at the age of 21, depending upon which event occurred first,[77] and a number of local studies in the early modern period have also indicated such age specifications in wills. In the parishes of Earls Colne and Kirkby Lonsdale, daughters were automatically paid at the age of 18 or 21.[78] In Banbury, payment was normally tied to the age of 18, even 16, or marriage, whichever was earliest, with the range in age between 16 and 25,[79] while in Kibworth Harcourt, children were allowed their share of inheritance at the stipulated ages of 16, 18, or 21, or at the time of marriage.[80] Ages prescribed for sons were usually somewhat later. In the parish of Orwell, compared to daughters who were provided for at 18 or at marriage, and sometimes between the ages of 19 and 21, sons did not usually receive their legacies until they were 21.[81] Similarly in Hunstanton, bequests to sons were made over slightly later, although both sons and daughters did not acquire their parts till their early twenties.[82] According to a more recent study, based on a large sample of Ely diocesan wills in the period 1545–1602, it was commonly found that legacies were made conditional upon attaining a specified age. Although many testators allowed their children to receive their inheritance if they married before that age, the proportion leaving bequests solely at marriage and irrespective of any age, was small. Unfortunately, despite the invaluable size of the sample and the evident frequency of age specifications, no further analysis was undertaken in that study and the actual age specifications were not presented.[83]

References to age qualifications such as these do not, by themselves, aid our understanding of their significance. It has been suggested in these studies that the testamentary means of property transfer did not function to retard or control the marriages of children since legacies might be paid before, or irrespective of, any marriage. However, although it may well be the case that these clauses were not intended to delay or dictate marriage behaviour, it is argued here that the specifications of ages may imply that testators were intent upon prescribing at least some lower boundary to marriage age, and/or minimum limitations upon when their children might start to hold property independently. A thorough examination of such ages, therefore, could tell us when young people were customarily reckoned to be both financially capable and maritally eligible. Given the significance of this question, the remainder of this chapter presents the first systematic analysis of notional ages as prescribed by testators. Such an exercise reveals much about those social and cultural preconceptions that permeated and determined those times thought most fitting for marriage and maturation.

All the registered wills probated in the archdeaconry and consistory courts of Canterbury for the chosen parishes of Tenterden, Wye, Whitstable, Chislet and Sturry have been used in this analysis.[84] They cover the period from the mid-fifteenth to the end of the sixteenth century. These communities were selected[85] partly because of the sheer number of their surviving wills, particularly in the case of Tenterden. In total, 1304 wills were consulted for all five parishes combined.[86] A further 501 wills for the period 1503–09, which were geographically more representative of the Canterbury diocese, were also used, but since they served as a pilot study, their findings are supplementary.[87] Detailed statistical treatment will be confined to the individual parish studies. Although the status of testators would appear to have been more commonly provided from the mid-sixteenth century, such details are largely insufficient for the identification of social groups in any systematic way. As Zell's study of

Figure 3 Number of wills in Kentish parishes

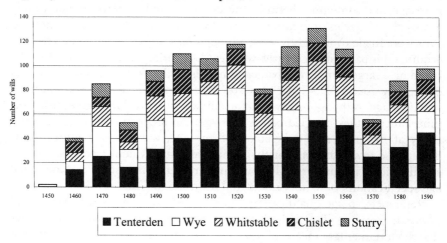

surviving sixteenth-century wills from the Kent Weald also showed, while the number of extant wills is certainly ample, the occupational information found within them is less than satisfactory. He therefore concluded that it is 'not possible to derive a valid measure of occupational diversity and of local trades from the wills alone'.[88]

Compared to other local findings, the proportion of the dying population represented by testators may generally have been somewhat on the low side.[89] Tenterden, for example, had a total of 209 wills in the period 1550–99 when 2389 burials were recorded, suggesting a ratio of will-makers to burials of 1 to 11. In Whitstable, the ratio in the period 1560–99 was approximately 1 to 17.[90] It is clear that the total number of wills which survive varies considerably for each of the parishes, as does the decadal pattern in their distribution. However, the overall trend in the five parishes combined indicates an increase in the level of testation from the late fifteenth to the mid-sixteenth century, peaking in the 1550s, with a decline at the end of the period (Figure 3).[91] Even in the parishes of Chislet and Sturry where the populations may have increased in the course of the sixteenth century, there was no apparent corresponding growth in will-making at the end of the century.[92]

In examining the age data provided in the wills, all the ages prescribed by testators principally for their children but also for specified kin, and for legatees bearing their surname, were included. Other forms of timed bequests were specified in wills, such as those contingent upon maternal or sibling death, or the widow's remarriage. Alternative time measurements included provision within a period of years after the testator's death, when apprenticeship came to an end, when a son could work, or when an elder sibling received an

Figure 4 Percentage of wills giving ages in all five parishes

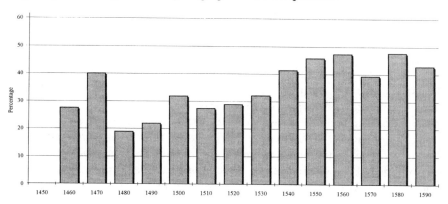

inheritance. Several references to 'nonage', 'minority', 'within age', 'age of discretion', 'age of maturity', 'lawful age', 'full age', 'age of puberty or marriage', 'lawful age or marriage' and 'age of marriage' were also to be found but these could not be used in the quantitative analysis despite the implications for attitudinal thresholds. Hence the actual numerical ages specified in the wills represent one definable time limit on the transfer of property, by far the most predominant when dealing with young, unmarried children, but nevertheless, one of a range of possible stipulations.

Overall, approximately 36 per cent of all the wills for the five sample parishes provide such evidence on numerical age. Apart from Tenterden, with the highest proportion of 43.1 per cent, the other parishes mentioned ages in about one-third of their wills for the entire period studied.[93] Despite the apparent fall-off in the total number of surviving wills in the latter part of the sixteenth century, the proportion of wills giving ages appears to have risen although the increase was uneven. This means that the quantifiable evidence presented in this chapter is generally best in the second half of the sixteenth century (Figure 4).[94] Perhaps this reflects the burgeoning 'awareness of their numerical age' and their increasing 'social relevance', as suggested by Keith Thomas for the population of early modern England.[95] There was, however, a surprising consciousness of it, in Tenterden and Wye at least, in the 1470s.

Seeking to understand what the prescribed ages in wills actually meant and represented is far more complex and problematic. While it is possible to speculate about the significance of particular numerical ages, on the basis of legal and religious precepts, economic and political activity, and social and biological maturations, the milestones of independence, adulthood and marriageability were, as suggested earlier, themselves subject to modification.

There was no universal consensus of opinion regarding certain ages,[96] and 'the very meaning of numerical age was still ambiguous'.[97]

In those earlier studies where the evidence of ages in wills has been used, the ages have generally been accepted uncritically as those of inheritance and/ or ages of majority. From the Ely diocesan wills, Carlson seemed to conclude that the age denoted was unquestionably that of inheritance age, and that 'testators assumed that marriage would not normally precede the specified age of inheritance'. Their intention was to enable their children to be possessed of independent resources, and thus allow them the freedom to marry independently as they chose.[98] With lawful age of majority presumed to be 21, any inheritance which did not occur at that time was either under-age, or over-age.[99] Even where such interpretations may be correct, the treatment and recognition of ages specified deserve greater attention. As regards the meaning of 'majority', Mitterauer pointed out that 'the details given about ages of majority do have their importance for social history, for they reflect social conceptions about minimum age limits for growing up with respect to different areas of life'.[100] In relation to inheritance ages, Keith Thomas stressed that 'the age of inheritance envisaged by will-makers ... varied considerably and cries out for more investigation'.[101] Moreover, a close examination of the Kent wills would suggest that the precise meaning of the various ages stipulated by testators, be they of inheritance, majority, discretion, maturity, service, puberty, or marriage, were in fact far from easily identifiable, nor necessarily exclusive.

One complicating factor was the possibility of having separate ages prescribed for a particular beneficiary. The testator James Robyns of Tenterden bequeathed a chest to his son at the age of 12, other household goods, oxen, cash, lands and appurtenances at 21, and an annual sum of 5s from the age of 15 until 21 years.[102] With the exception of Sturry where none was recorded, sons, daughters, and other male relatives might receive some form of annuity, or land profits, often as part of their legacy, and often prior to their main inheritance. This was particularly so for sons in Tenterden. Stephen Davy was to be endowed with lands at 26 years, for his 'marriage or worship and profits', but was to take the profits from the age of 16.[103] Such forms of early provision meant that some teenagers entered service already partly endowed with a small income and annual expectations. In Tenterden, boys and girls were ideally thought to enter service at 14 years, boys sometimes at 15 or 16 years. The ages prescribed generally coincided with the termination of school and maternal upkeep, from 12 to 16 years, but usually at 14 years. The clothier Edmund Lewkenor, for example, provided for his three sons to come to their lands at 21 years, with the land profits used towards the upkeep of all his children until 14 years, 'and as they grow to that age, they be put to service, and each have per annum 20s until their full age'.[104] In her study of service and adulthood in the seventeenth century, Ben-Amos also found that 'the wills of some craftsmen and tradesmen ... make it clear that there was an age in which children were considered sufficiently grown up to be bound apprentices'.[105]

That there were definite conceptualisations of age contained within the wills, and strategies formulated to accommodate them, is itself significant. Wills then do not just contain retrospective statements of marital, family, social and economic relationships. They were also prescriptive documents, including important age specifications or sets of ideal strategies which might conceivably have limited the behaviour of the succeeding generation. Their particular social relevances and the actual extent of their determinative influence may be uncertain. However, the extent to which the ages prescribed might be interpreted as notional ages at marriage and represent perceived minimum thresholds in the timing of marriage and independent property-holding, potentially capable of affecting the proportions marrying beyond certain age categories, should be considered.

The association between provisions for female beneficiaries and dowry payments was particularly strong and frequently quite explicit, the timing of their legacies being often specifically linked to marriage.[106] It was not uncommon for testators like John Peake of Wye to leave equal cash portions to his two daughters, Alice and Agnes, 'to be paid to them at the age of mariage'.[107] John Pett, a Tenterden clothier, referred to his daughter coming to the 'age of discretion and marriage', providing for her 'at age of marriage',[108] while John Edward senior of Whitstable intimated an 'age of puberty or marriage'.[109] In some wills, therefore, there was a definite concept of an age of marriage. Robert Robard of Hougham stipulated that (los) bequeathed to each of his two daughters should be invested in the hands of his wife and brother, 'unto such tyme as they be maried or come to the age of mariage. And if either die before thei be maried or cume to the age of mariage then the other to enjoy the hole XXs with thencrease of the same.'[110] Testators were generally far more flexible in the timing of provisions for daughters than for sons, allowing for legacies to be paid at the time of marriage whensoever the event occurred, at 'lawful age of marriage',[111] at a specified age or at marriage, or simply the age prescribed, although they were also more disposed in particular circumstances to attach restrictive or conditional clauses.[112]

For male beneficiaries, the specifications tended to be less flexible, and were usually of particular ages only. Nevertheless, given the set of rules and ages formulated, testators showed some recognition of the fact that their sons might marry, or require advancement, before the time or age specified. Some made provision for this eventuality, especially where the ages prescribed were already in the twenties. Henry Pellond of Tenterden left certain lands to his son John at 22 years, but provided that 'if John befor that age mary as it may be to his profite and worship after the discretion of my executor and feoffees, then I will that he have to his marriage the said lands and tenements or part thereof after ther discrecions'.[113] The three sons of Robert Davy were each to receive the land profits and the estate at 26 years, but if they married before 26, then 'for ther promocion' the feoffees were to 'make and grant such resonabull joyntor to thuse of his wife'.[114] To grandsons, as well as to sons, such prior provisions made to their 'advantage', or 'rather if it seem necessary for their use', might apply,[115] decisions being left to the testator's executor and feoffees.[116] In certain instances, the inheritance received was not only subject to age stipulations, but also to further qualifications. Simon Smethe of Wye willed that his son Roger should come to his lands at 22, 'provided he be ruled and guided by his mother'.[117]

Although the relationship between marriage and the timing of property disposition is far less self-evident and much more tenuous where males were concerned, the importance of marriage in this regard was still embedded in contemporary consciousness. Some testators were more explicit in their intentions. Thomas Cok bequeathed his lands to his son William at 24 years, 'in wey of maryage', or 'to his profit and worship',[118] and Thomas Pyrkyne of Chislet specifically referred to an 'age of mariage' in relation to both his sons and daughters, devising a reversionary clause 'if any of my said children die before they come to thage of mariage'. Particularly referring to his son Thomas inheriting certain land, he added a further clause should Thomas die before he come 'to age of mariage'.[119] In most wills, however, the connection between the ages prescribed for males and the timing of their marriages may be deduced from the interchangeable terminology used, such as the equation of 'age of marriage' with 'being of age' or of 'lawful age'. There was also the implicit tendency to assign equal status and meaning to the 'day and time of marriage' of daughters with the stipulated ages of their brothers, and the general presumption of testators that the ages prescribed would generally either coincide with, or precede, the marriages of their children. Seen in this light, the ages specified in wills may be perceived as the recognised minimum ages for marriages to occur, or at least, for property to be transmitted, thus enabling economic resourcefulness and competence for marriage. Thomas Reade of High Halden provided for his daughter Johane, to 'have to her mariage when she comyth to XX yers of age', £10 in 'mariage money' and a parcel of land,[120] and Simon Hokkyng of Whitstable willed that when his youngest son John 'shalbe married after he cometh to the age of 20 years', he should enjoy certain lands.[121] In both circumstances, the testator apparently considered his child as marriageable only at that age or after.

The ages mentioned in the wills then, may provide an invaluable insight into contemporary notions of the lower bounds of marriageability in the fifteenth and sixteenth centuries. They do not, of course, necessarily represent

Table 10 Percentage distribution of ages specified in wills for all men and women

Men (ages)	1449–74 %	1475–99 %	1500–24 %	1525–49 %	1550–74 %	1575–99 %
10–14	4.7	3.9	2.2	5.1	3.5	0.7
15–19	37.2	24.7	17.4	17.2	19.8	11.9
20–24	51.2	59.7	73.9	75.8	74.9	80.6
25–29	4.7	9.1	4.3	1.9	1.8	3.7
30–34	2.3	2.6	2.2	0.0	0.0	3.0
	100.0	100.0	100.0	100.0	100.0	100.0

Women (ages)	1449–74 %	1475–99 %	1500–24 %	1525–49 %	1550–74 %	1575–99 %
10–14	18.2	0.0	6.3	4.1	2.5	0.8
15–19	18.2	18.2	46.9	35.1	43.3	57.5
20–24	63.6	81.8	46.9	60.8	52.9	40.9
25–29	0.0	0.0	0.0	0.0	1.3	0.8
30–34	0.0	0.0	0.0	0.0	0.0	0.0
	100.0	100.0	100.0	100.0	100.0	100.0

the actual ages at which beneficiaries married, since marriage could have taken place earlier or more often later than envisaged, or not at all, according to a variety of individual circumstances. Nevertheless, the numerical ages specified in wills provide potentially important evidence about the social, legal, economic and customary landmarks which could affect courtship behaviour and it is to an analysis of them to which we should now turn.

The findings are presented in Table 10. Immediately apparent is the discrepancy between the ages specified at which property was transferred by will (and possibly the ages at which testators perceived the minimum age at marriage), and the average age of marriage generally thought to be characteristic of English society in the early modern period.[122] Unfortunately the reconstitution data do not really consider the social status of the brides and grooms or the mortality of their parents, and measurement of marriage age distributions among the will-making sector and the parish register population is not therefore strictly comparable. Moreover, the diversity disguised by averages makes it difficult to identify similarities in the range of ages. Nevertheless, the results suggest that there were nubile men and women already endowed with property for some years before the age when most of those who married actually did so. There is, anyway, no contradiction between early property transmission and a predominantly late marrying regime. The aspiration to marry at a particular age need not have coincided with the actual timing of marriage. Testators may also have sought to provide for their orphaned children early, in an attempt to give them better prospects, and the financial opportunity to make responsible matches appropriate to their means and status.

For sons and other male relatives, the teenage years specified in the fifteenth century are quite striking. Over time there appears to have been a disappearance in the proportion of teenage bequests, with an increasing tendency in the sixteenth century for a consolidation in the age category of 20–24 years. Throughout the period, too, it was relatively uncommon for legacies to be received beyond the age of 25. For women there was, perhaps, a gradual decline in the specification of very young ages (less than 15 years) and a shift instead to the later teens, although fluctuations in the overall teenage distribution and the smaller number of beneficiaries involved renders inter- pretation more problematic. The late fifteenth century (while based on only a handful of wills) does, however, seem significantly different to the later period in this regard. From 1525, when there are just under a hundred or more female legatees in the samples, there appears to be a steady increase in those aged 15– 19 years, and a corresponding decrease in the early twenties. As for those over the age of 24, it was extremely rare for them to be still financially unprovided for at any time from the mid-fifteenth to the end of the sixteenth century.

To understand more fully, though, the pattern in age categorisations shown in Table 10, we need to examine in greater detail the concentration by testators on *particular* numerical ages. Tables 11 and 12 display the percentage distribution of each individual age specified in the wills.

Where male ages were prescribed, it is quite clear that certain ages were distinctive. Sixteen years was commonly mentioned until 1549, and that of 18 figured in wills throughout the period. Few testators ever stipulated the years 15, 17 or 19. Despite the frequent use of ages 20 to 22 years and the relatively common occurrence of 24 until the late sixteenth century, age 23 was insignificant, and no age over 24 can be identified as possessed of any legal or customary prominence.

As to the changing distribution of ages over time, the period witnesses the decrease of property transmission to men aged 16 and, to a lesser extent, to those at 18 years. In contrast there was an extraordinary concentration on the age of 21 in the late sixteenth century which may help to explain the diminution in bequests below the age of 20. Between 1500 and 1550, the ages

Table 11 Percentage distribution of ages, all five parishes (men)

All men	1449–74 %	1475–99 %	1500–24 %	1525–49 %	1550–74 %	1575–99 %	1449–1599 %
10	0.0	2.6	1.1	0.6	0.0	0.0	0.5
11	0.0	0.0	0.0	0.0	0.0	0.0	0.0
12	4.7	1.3	1.1	0.0	1.8	0.0	1.1
13	0.0	0.0	0.0	1.3	0.4	0.0	0.4
14	0.0	0.0	0.0	3.2	1.3	0.7	1.2
15	0.0	0.0	2.2	2.5	1.8	2.2	1.8
16	14.0	9.1	7.6	9.6	3.5	1.5	6.2
17	0.0	3.9	0.0	0.6	0.0	0.0	0.5
18	23.3	11.7	7.6	4.5	14.1	8.2	10.4
19	0.0	0.0	0.0	0.0	0.4	0.0	0.1
20	7.0	20.8	20.7	24.2	17.6	9.7	17.7
21	16.3	6.5	23.9	21.7	33.0	64.2	31.4
22	18.6	16.9	19.6	21.0	9.3	3.7	13.4
23	0.0	1.3	0.0	1.9	3.5	1.5	1.9
24	9.3	14.3	9.8	7.0	11.5	1.5	8.6
25	0.0	3.9	1.1	0.0	1.3	1.5	1.2
26	4.7	5.2	0.0	0.6	0.4	2.2	1.5
27	0.0	0.0	0.0	0.0	0.0	0.0	0.0
28	0.0	0.0	3.3	1.3	0.0	0.0	0.7
29	0.0	0.0	0.0	0.0	0.0	0.0	0.0
30	2.3	2.6	1.1	0.0	0.0	3.0	1.1
31	0.0	0.0	0.0	0.0	0.0	0.0	0.0
32	0.0	0.0	1.1	0.0	0.0	0.0	0.1
	100.0	100.0	100.0	100.0	100.0	100.0	100.0
Number	43	77	92	157	227	134	730

20, 21 and 22 were favoured nearly equally by testators, but by 1575–99, 64.2 per cent of the male legatees would have anticipated their age of 21 as a landmark, compared to only 8.2 per cent at age 18. Even the preferred upper age limit of 24 specified for about one in twelve men, virtually disappeared by the end of the sixteenth century, making the growing importance of the age of 21 for men the most marked feature of the period.

The evidence for women displayed in Table 12 is based on a smaller sample size. Nonetheless, a focus on the age of 16 is clearly discernible and, after 1474, on 18 years. Otherwise, as with male beneficiaries, testators chose the ages 20, 21, 22 and, to a lesser extent, 24, that of 20 years being especially noteworthy. When examined over time, the growing popularity of 18 as a

Table 12 Percentage distribution of ages, all five parishes (women)

All women	1449–74 %	1475–99 %	1500–24 %	1525–49 %	1550–74 %	1575–99 %	1449–1599 %
10	0.0	0.0	3.1	0.0	0.0	0.0	0.2
11	0.0	0.0	0.0	0.0	0.0	0.0	0.0
12	18.2	0.0	0.0	0.0	0.6	0.0	1.1
13	0.0	0.0	0.0	1.0	0.6	0.0	0.4
14	0.0	0.0	3.1	3.1	1.3	0.8	1.5
15	0.0	0.0	3.1	0.0	3.8	1.6	2.0
16	18.2	4.5	21.9	10.3	10.2	8.7	10.7
17	0.0	0.0	0.0	1.0	1.3	0.0	0.7
18	0.0	13.6	21.9	22.7	28.0	43.3	28.7
19	0.0	0.0	0.0	1.0	0.0	3.9	1.3
20	9.1	27.3	31.3	39.2	29.3	7.9	24.5
21	9.1	4.5	9.4	8.2	9.6	26.0	13.6
22	18.2	18.2	3.1	6.2	8.3	2.4	6.8
23	0.0	13.6	0.0	4.1	1.3	0.8	2.2
24	27.3	18.2	3.1	3.1	4.5	3.9	5.7
25	0.0	0.0	0.0	0.0	0.0	0.0	0.0
26	0.0	0.0	0.0	0.0	1.3	0.8	0.7
27	0.0	0.0	0.0	0.0	0.0	0.0	0.0
28	0.0	0.0	0.0	0.0	0.0	0.0	0.0
29	0.0	0.0	0.0	0.0	0.0	0.0	0.0
30	0.0	0.0	0.0	0.0	0.0	0.0	0.0
	100.0	100.0	100.0	100.0	100.0	100.0	100.0
Number	22	22	32	97	157	127	457

Note: Numbers in Tables 11 and 12 refer to each individual legatee with a specified age.

perceived milestone (as against the decline in age 16), and a gradual increase in the age of 21, are immediately observable. While 20 years had been stipulated for approximately one-third of all the women in receipt of property between 1475 and 1574, the specification switched thereafter to 21, marking the age of 21 as a phenomenon of the late sixteenth century, although never with the same overriding significance with which it was attached to men. For women the age of 24 years had lost much of its relevance by the sixteenth century.

The above findings, then, illustrate not only the pattern within certain age-categorisations and the general range of age specifications contained within the wills, but more precisely, the apparent distinctiveness of particular numerical ages. The priorities attached to the ages 16, 18, 20–22 and 24, for both sexes (with some mention of 12, especially for women in the mid-fifteenth century), would suggest their identification as conceptual structural landmarks. At the same time, the evidence, for example, of an increasing concentration on the age of 21 for men, and the growing popularity of 18 for women, serves as an important reminder that the values attached to particular ages were *not* necessarily constant throughout the period. Historians bemoan the imprecision and difficulty of exploring contemporary age definitions given the diversity and variation according to context. However, in his treatment of the problem, Thomas earmarks some of the same numerical ages as points of especial significance for boys and girls, and discusses their specifications according to a host of legal and economic criteria. The gradual standardisation of the legal age of majority at 21 and, in the Tudor and Stuart periods, the increasing practical applicability of numerical age,[123] may well be substantiated by the will evidence cited here. The apparently growing integration of, and consensus about, particular ages as demonstrated in Kentish wills by the end of the sixteenth century, might give some indication of how changing contemporary concepts of numerical maturation could have some effect on marriage age, in ways not yet envisaged by historical demographers. Such legal and cultural notions were, perhaps, just as, if not more, effective than any subconscious response to the prevailing level of economic resources. Likewise, although the relationship is speculative, the decline in teenage bequests to men over time, coupled with the decline in very early age specifications for women, might be associated with a disappearance of child marriages. This implies that whereas in the fifteenth century a greater proportion of single young people might have been endowed at a more youthful age, by the end of the sixteenth century, the minimum limits of marital eligibility may have been higher, and generally more uniform.[124]

Certain qualifications to this growing consensus of opinion on age specifications do, however, need to be addressed. The results of the analysis presented in Tables 11 and 12 have so far amalgamated the findings of all five Kent parishes. Further tentative conclusions may be drawn if the sample is broken down by parish. The general pattern exhibited in the parishes was for women to be prescribed ages somewhat younger than those for men, the age-gap being usually one of a few years.[125] In all parishes, individual testators commonly, but not invariably, allocated similar ages to each surviving son or daughter, irrespective of their birth order. In only three parishes – Tenterden, Wye and Whitstable – however, were sons also more routinely given bequests later than their sisters. In the other two parishes, where the statistical evidence is thinner, gender disparities within families appear far less, if at all. Inevitably, some diversity is to be expected, since individual circumstances, the familial context and the personal predilections of testators, necessitated appropriate strategies.

It was also found that while testators in all five parishes most commonly prescribed the age of 21 and, to a lesser extent, the ages of 20 and 22 for men, there were some noticeable differences between the parishes where other age specifications were concerned. In Tenterden, property was rarely envisaged as being transferred in the teens (except in the form of annuities), whereas in Wye, Whitstable and particularly Chislet, mention of age 18 was evident, and of age 16 in all the parishes except Tenterden. Furthermore, some emphasis on age 24 was discernible in Tenterden, Wye and Whitstable, but not in the remaining two parishes. Nevertheless, despite these differences, the recognition of particular ages for men showed a significant degree of regional consistency and homogeneity.

By contrast, the previous discussion has already established that for the whole sample, there was a greater variety of experience for women, making it harder to identify the pattern over time. This might suggest that there was more regional variation in the prescription of ages for women than for men. An examination of the most favoured ages within individual parishes confirms that this was the case. Throughout the period, 20 was the prominent age in Tenterden. The ages 21 and 18 were equally favoured in Wye. In Whitstable and Chislet it was overwhelmingly 18 years, and in Sturry (although numbers are few), the age of 16 was preferred.[126] Whereas the oldest age of property receipt in Tenterden was 24, and 26 in Wye, there was an apparently greater emphasis on the transmission of property to teenagers in the other parishes, where none of the ages specified exceeded 22. If the *mean* age of property transfer for women is considered, it lay between 18 and 22 years in Tenterden and Wye, comparatively higher than it was for Whitstable, Chislet and Sturry, which was invariably the mid-to-late teens in the whole period.

The findings of this chapter, then, suggest that there may have been some differences in the age strategies adopted by individual testators for their dependent children and relatives, and in the experiences of young men compared to women. There could also have been some local variation in the ages so prescribed. Moreover, there is evidence of some change over time, the decline in the teenage specifications for male beneficiaries and the greater numerical agreement among testators as the ages converged. The increasing concentration upon the age of 21 as the established landmark for men was most pronounced.

Just as important as the differences and changes over time discerned here, is the *significance* of prevailing ideas of appropriate age in the process of maturation and marriageability, and the enduring nature of these norms. To the extent to which age of marriage was linked to the process of social maturation, the information on ages contained in wills can identify some of the perceived social, legal and customary thresholds in property-holding, maturation and competence for marriage. While in some circumstances, the wills seemed to imply a definite concept of 'age of marriage', more generally, the age specifications may be understood as representing the notional minimum limits of marriageability. It is, of course, a mistake to imagine that we can derive from the results presented here, a mechanical mirror of the demographic ages of marriage, precisely because the age at which individuals got married was not simply a response to environmental pressure or population growth rates, nor independent of a host of other constraints and expectations. The evidence of such attitudes may, however, assist in explaining some of the findings of historical demographers, for example local variations in the age at first marriage, or the pattern of male marriage age being generally higher than that for women, or even the relative rigidity in marriage ages in our period.

Ingram's statement of marriage age as being something thought of as 'fitting', thus conceals a far more complex reality.[127] As the deposition evidence indicated, contemporaries possessed their own notions about the ages appropriate for courtship and marriage. It is clearly extremely difficult for historians to identify what these ages actually were, especially since the perceptions of appropriate age must have been governed by a sometimes conflicting range of moral and legal recommendations, external forces, economic and cultural factors and personal desires. Clearly, there was no single determinant to age at marriage.

Demographers may calculate the actual ages of marriage on the basis of parochial registration, but such calculations are virtually impossible before the later sixteenth century and any other available sources on marriage age are therefore invaluable. That wills yield information from the late fifteenth century is clearly of major significance to those interested in the marriage regime of the late medieval period. Furthermore, the evidence presented here serves to promote the importance of male age in any discussion of nuptial dynamics. Men, too, after all, participated in the setting up of households at marriage and whatever information we can derive about male ages should complement the demographers' concentration on female ages and female fertility.[128]

Direct evidence about the customary restraints on age of marriage, above and beyond the simple questions of economic sufficiency, is hard to come by, and notional ages of marital eligibility are a relatively unconsidered aspect of early modern courtship. What the evidence culled from the wills can supply, is the ages which testators thought appropriate for the transmission of property to the younger generation, ages which were theoretically, at least, usually tied to marriage. They reveal those particular numerical ages which might have represented milestones in the achievement of personal, legal and economic maturity. In examining those symbolic ages systematically for the first time, the implicit connections between the timing of inheritance, majority, courtship and marriage can be appreciated more fully. The transmission of property was crucial in the negotiations of courtship and this will be demonstrated in the next and final chapter which considers one important aspect of that property transfer, namely the provision of dowries.

NOTES

1 See above, p. 163.

2 For the conceptual link between marriage and adulthood in European society in the past, see, e.g., K. Thomas, 'Age and authority in early modern England', *Proceedings of the British Academy* 62 (London, 1976), 1–46 (esp. p. 24); M. Mitterauer, *A History of Youth*, trans. G. Dunphy (Germany, 1986, Eng. trans. Oxford, 1992), esp. pp. 31–3, 38, 59, 79–86; Ben-Amos, 'Service and the coming of age', pp. 58–60; Carlson, *Marriage and the English Reformation*, p. 106.

3 Ingram, *Church Courts*, pp. 129–30, 140–1. For hostility towards early marriage, see also, Ben-Amos, *Adolescence and Youth*, pp. 32–3.

4 Burn, *The Ecclesiastical Law*, ii, pp. 434, 455.

5 Ben-Amos, 'Service and the coming of age', p. 44. For the age of majority of 21, see also, Thomas, 'Age and authority', pp. 19–21, 25–6.

6 Some of the proposals were of doubtful legal force. Thomas, 'Age and authority', pp. 24–5, cites those made in 1571 to raise the ages to 16 and 14 respectively, and the proposal of 1552 to make void teenage marriages made without parental agreement. The former was in reality a canon agreed upon in convocation without Queen Elizabeth's authorisation. Carlson's book, *Marriage and the English Reformation*, shows how the European reformation of marriage made parental consent indispensable for the marriage of dependants, while the English church continued to uphold 'pre-Tridentine rules', remaining even more 'Roman' in its rejection of marriage reform (pp. 3–8). For some of the rejected proposals regarding the minimum age limits for contracts, and requirements for parental consent, see pp. 72–81. Further reforms proposed in 1563 surfaced in parliamentary debate over marriage licences (pp. 92–6, 138).

7 Carlson, *Marriage and the English Reformation*, p. 81.

8 For the diversity of milestones in youth and adulthood, and the variety of numerical timing, see Thomas, 'Age and authority', pp. 12–30; Mitterauer, *A History of Youth*, pp. 45–87; Ben-Amos, 'Service and the coming of age', pp. 45–6, 58–9; M. Pelling, 'Child health as a social value in early modern England', *Social History of Medicine* 1 (1988), 135–64 (esp. p. 138 and notes). For limitations set by the 1563 statute, see, Stone, *Family, Sex and Marriage*, p. 44; Houlbrooke, *The English Family*, p. 68. The age at sexual maturation is discussed by Laslett, *Family Life and Illicit Love*, pp. 214–32. I am grateful to Dr Ralph Houlbrooke for pointing out that, among the upper classes, 16 years was generally considered the minimum age for girls to engage in sexual relations, even in child marriages. It was also the normal age for the termination of female wardship. The traditional ending of male wardship, on the other hand, would seem to have depended upon types of tenant, with 21 being the normal age of knightly majority, but several years earlier for certain other tenancies.

9 Thomas, 'Age and authority', pp. 5, 16. The alternative depictions of youth also show

that early modern perceptions were controversial and ambivalent. See Ben-Amos, 'Service and the coming of age', pp. 42–5.

10 Macfarlane, *Marriage and Love,* pp. 211–16. Cook, *Making a Match,* pp. 17–38 (esp. p. 23), cites the ages 17–22 for women, and 20–25 for men, as recommended ages at marriage.

11 C.C.A.L., MS. X/10/11, fos 93–4, *Austin v. Parker* (1569).

12 C.C.A.L., MS. X/10/7, f. 65v., *Nashe v. Colyar* (1560).

13 C.C.A.L., MS. X/10/11, f. 229–v., *Turner v. Hubbard* (?1570).

14 C.C.A.L., MS. X/10/14, fos 46–7, *Amys v. Fayreman* (1572).

15 Nevertheless, Ingram, *Church Courts,* p. 194, claimed that most spousal litigants in the period 1570–1640 were in their twenties or early thirties, with only a small number under 21 years.

16 In C.C.A.L., MS. X/11/5, fos 236v., 241, 242v., 248, *Symons v. Spayne* (1598).

17 *Ibid.,* f. 27v.

18 E.g. C.C.A.L., MSS. X/10/3, fos 19–23, *Munday v. Parker* (1546); X/10/12, fos 116v.–18v., 122v.–3, *Edmonds v. Hocking* (1564). Joan Parker of Sandwich was thought to be about 15, and Dorothy Hocking of Canterbury between the ages of 16 and 20.

19 C.C.A.L., MS. X/10/16, fos 312v.–16, *Hannyng v. Knowler* (1577).

20 C.C.A.L, MS. X/11/1, fos 279v.–85, *Prowd v. Gibs* (1589). Also, MS. X/11/5, f. 223, *Divers v. Williams* (1598).

21 C.C.A.L., MS. X/10/12, f. 182–v., *Tusnothe v. Marden* (1565).

22 C.C.A.L., MS. X/11/6, fos 14v.–17, *Graves v. Fulcomb* (1592).

23 C.C.A.L., MS. X/10/6, f. 174, *Eddredge v. Rede* (1557).

24 Thomas, 'Age and authority', p. 41.

25 C.C.A.L., MS. X/10/14, fos 219–21v., *Abarrow v. Hawke* (1572–73).

26 See above, chapter 3, p. 99.

27 See also, Ingram, *Church Courts,* pp. 140–1; Thomas, 'Age and authority', p. 42; Cook, *Making a Match,* pp. 24–38.

28 C.C.A.L., MS. X/10/21, fos 11v.–13, 40v.–46v., for full references to the case.

29 Thomas, 'Age and authority', p. 7.

30 Wrigley and Schofield, *Population History.* For references to age at marriage and proportions never marrying, see pp. 255–65, 423–4; Wrigley and Schofield, 'English population history', p. 161; Schofield, 'English marriage patterns revisited'.

31 J. Hajnal, 'European marriage patterns in perspective', in D. V. Glass and D. E. C. Eversley eds, *Population in History* (London, 1965), pp. 101–43 (esp. pp. 132–3).

32 Wrigley, 'Age at marriage', pp. 219–20.

33 For the use made of marriage licences, see Elliott, 'Mobility and marriage'; Elliott, 'Single women'; P. Laslett, *The World We Have Lost: Further Explored* (London, 1983), pp. 82–4; Ingram, *Church Courts,* p. 129; Chalklin, *Seventeenth-Century Kent,* p. 37. On the growing awareness of numerical age, see Thomas, 'Age and authority', pp. 3–5. As he pointed out, 'In Tudor times such awareness was far from universal' (p. 3).

34 C.C.A.L., MSS. X/10/16, fos 326v.–9, 336v.–7; X/10/18, fos 6v.–8v., 10v.–11v. (1577). Licence dated 21 September 1576, J. M. Cowper ed., *Canterbury Marriage Licences, 1568–1618* (Canterbury, 1892).

35 Goldberg, 'Marriage, migration, servanthood and life-cycle', pp. 154–5; P. J. P. Goldberg, 'Female labour, service and marriage in the late medieval urban North', *Northern History* 22 (1986), 18–38 (esp. pp. 25–6); Goldberg, *Women, Work and Life-Cycle*, pp. 8–9, 205–9, 225–32; R. M. Smith, 'Human resources', in G. Astill and A. Grant eds, *The Countryside in Medieval England* (Oxford, 1988), pp. 188–212 (esp. pp. 200–12).

36 L. R. Poos, *A Rural Society After the Black Death: Essex, 1350–1525* (Cambridge, 1991), p. 145.

37 Hajnal, 'European marriage patterns', p. 108, suggests that the mean age at first marriage for women should be at least 23+ years, usually 24+, for an identifiable European pattern. A non-European pattern would imply one below the age of 21 years.

38 Wrigley and Schofield, 'English population history', p. 162.

39 Wrigley and Schofield, *Population History*, pp. 423–4. Figures drawn from a smaller 10-parish sample suggest that the mean age at first marriage for women in the same period was only 24.8, and 27.2 for men, Wrigley, 'Age at marriage', pp. 221–2. For the parish of Colyton, Devon, see also, Laslett, *Family Life and Illicit Love*, p. 127; P. Sharpe, 'The total reconstitution method: a tool for class-specific study?', *Local Population Studies* 44 (Spring 1990), 41–51. For some early modern European examples of a late marrying regime, see, S. C. Ogilvie, 'Coming of age in a corporate society: capitalism, pietism and family authority in rural Wurttemberg, 1590–1740', *Continuity and Change* 1:3 (1986), 279–331 (p. 321); M. Segalen, *Historical Anthropology of the Family*, trans. J. C. Whitehouse and S. Matthews (Cambridge, 1986), pp. 116–19.

40 The average age of first marriage for women and men was 26.2 and 27, C. Oestmann, *Lordship and Community: The Lestrange Family and the Village of Hunstanton, Norfolk, in the First Half of the Sixteenth Century* (Woodbridge, 1994), pp. 174–5. See also, Macfarlane, *Marriage and Love*, pp. 216–17.

41 For differences between market and rural communities, see, e.g., M. K. McIntosh, *A Community Transformed: the Manor and Liberty of Havering, 1500–1620* (Cambridge, 1991), p. 73, n. 179. For regional variation and for the early marriage age of native-born London brides, based on marriage licences, see Elliott, 'Mobility and marriage', pt iii; and Elliott, 'Single women', pp. 86–9. A concise statement regarding the wide range of individual experience can be found in D. Levine and K. Wrightson, 'The social context of illegitimacy in early modern England', in P. Lastlett, K. Oosterveen and R. M. Smith eds, *Bastardy and its Comparative History* (London, 1980), pp. 158–75 (esp. pp. 159–61).

42 In Brenchley, the mean for women and men was 23.7 and 25.3, and in Staplehurst, 23.5 and 26.3, in Zell, *Industry in the Countryside*, pp. 69–76. Relatively early marriage ages have also been found for the parish of Terling, Essex, and for late sixteenth-century Stratford-upon-Avon. See, Wrightson and Levine, *Poverty and Piety*, pp. 47–8; Laslett, *Family Life and Illicit Love*, p. 218.

43 Hajnal, 'European marriage patterns', esp. pp. 119, 134.

44 Also Houlbrooke, *The English Family*, pp. 63–5.

45 Goldberg, *Women, Work and Life-Cycle*, p. 231; Houlbrooke, *The English Family*, pp. 65–6; Oestmann, *Lordship and Community*, p. 175; F. J. Furnivall ed., *Child Marriages, Divorces and Ratifications etc. in the Diocese of Chester, A.D. 1561–6*, Early English Text

Society, original ser. 108 (London, 1897); Carlson, *Marriage and the English Reformation*, pp. 96, 107–8.

46 T. H. Hollingsworth, 'The demography of the British peerage', *Population Studies*, suppl. to 18:2 (Nov. 1964), i–iv, 3–108 (esp. pp. 15, 25–7, Tables 5–6, 17 and figs 1–2); L. Stone, *The Crisis of the Aristocracy, 1558–1641* (Oxford, 1965, abridged edn 1967, repr. 1977), p. 294; Stone, *Family, Sex and Marriage*, pp. 40–5; Laslett, *The World We Have Lost: Further Explored*, pp. 82–4.

47 Elliott, 'Mobility and marriage', *passim*; Elliott, 'Single women', pp. 82–6. A study of the middle class in London confirms Elliott's findings, see Earle, *Making of the English Middle Class*, pp. 180–4. For differential marriage ages between occupational groups, see e.g., Poos, *Rural Society*, pp. 63, 157; Sharpe, 'The total reconstitution method', pp. 47–9; Chalklin, *Seventeenth-Century Kent*, p. 37; M. Drake, 'Age at marriage in the pre-industrial West', in F. Bechhofer ed., *Population Growth and the Brain Drain* (Edinburgh, 1969), pp. 196–207.

48 Sharpe, 'The total reconstitution method', pp. 47–50; Wrigley, 'Age at marriage', p. 231; Wrigley and Schofield, 'English population history', p. 163; A. Kussmaul, *Servants in Husbandry in Early Modern England* (Cambridge, 1981), pp. 110–11; Goldberg, 'Female labour, service and marriage', *passim*; Goldberg, *Women, Work and Life-Cycle*, pp. 324–61; Smith, 'Human resources', p. 211.

49 At the end of the sixteenth century the average age-difference between spouses was 2.4 years, with a trend towards a declining age-gap during the seventeenth century. See Wrigley, 'Age at marriage', p. 223; Wrigley and Schofield, 'English population history', pp. 166–8; A. Laurence, *Women in England, 1500–1760: a Social History* (London, 1994), p. 32. For the companionate nature of medieval marriage, see, Goldberg, *Women, Work and Life-Cycle*, pp. 226–32, where the average age-difference found among urban couples was 2.9 years and among rural couples, 3.8 years.

50 Stone, *Family, Sex and Marriage*, p. 42; Stone, *The Crisis of the Aristocracy*, p. 294; Houlbrooke, *The English Family*, p. 66.

51 For the non-testamentary capacity of particular groups such as minors, married women and excommunicants, see, e.g., M. M. Sheehan, *The Will in Medieval England from the Conversion of the Anglo-Saxons to the End of the Thirteenth Century* (Toronto, 1963), esp. ch. 6; S. Coppel, 'Wills and the community: a case study of Tudor Grantham', in P. Riden ed., *Probate Records and the Local Community* (Gloucester, 1985), pp. 71–90 (p. 73); Burn, *The Ecclesiastical Law*, iv, pp. 44–498, esp. pp. 44–63.

52 C. Howell, 'Peasant inheritance customs in the Midlands, 1280–1700', in J. Goody, J. Thirsk and E. P. Thompson eds, *Family and Inheritance: Rural Society in Western Europe 1200–1800* (Cambridge, 1976, ppbk edn, 1978), pp. 112–55; M. Spufford, 'Peasant inheritance customs and land distribution in Cambridgeshire from the sixteenth to the eighteenth centuries', in *ibid.*, pp. 156–76; B. Capp, 'Will formularies', *Local Population Studies* 14 (Spring 1975), 49–50; E. Poole, 'Will formularies', *Local Population Studies* 17 (Autumn 1976), 42–3; M. Spufford, 'Will formularies', *Local Population Studies* 19 (Autumn 1977), 35–6; M. Spufford, 'The scribes of villagers' wills in sixteenth- and seventeenth-century Cambridgeshire and their influence', *Local Population Studies* 7 (Autumn 1971), 28–43; Matlock Population Studies Group, 'Wills and their scribes', *Local Population Studies* 8 (Spring 1972), 55–7; R. Richardson, 'Wills and will-makers in the sixteenth and seventeenth centuries: some Lancashire evidence', *Local Population Studies* 9 (Autumn 1972), 33–42; Vann, 'Wills and the family',

passim; L. Bonfield, 'Normative rules and property transmission: reflections on the link between marriage and inheritance in early modern England', in L. Bonfield, R. Smith and K. Wrightson eds, *The World We Have Gained: Histories of Population and Social Structure* (Oxford, 1986), pp. 155–76; S. Coppel, 'Will-making on the deathbed', *Local Population Studies* 40 (Spring 1988), 37–45; A. L. Erickson, *Women and Property in Early Modern England* (London and New York, 1993), pp. 32–9, 61–97, 129–51, 204–22; Zell, *Industry in the Countryside*, pp. 20, 55–6, 114–15; Oestmann, *Lordship and Community*, pp. 185–7, 191–3.

53 Zell, *Industry in the Countryside*, pp. 20, 55–6. A detailed discussion of will registration in the Prerogative Court of Canterbury, compared to provincial courts, is given by M. Takahashi, 'The number of wills proved in the sixteenth and seventeenth centuries: graphs, with tables and commentaries', in G. H. Martin and P. Spufford eds, *The Records of the Nation* (Woodbridge, 1990), pp. 187–213.

54 Coppel, 'Wills and the community', p. 77.

55 Erickson, *Women and Property*, p. 32. For calculations of the rates of will-makers to intestates, or 'potential testators', see Bonfield, 'Normative rules', pp. 164–6. In Banbury, testation ran at 25 per cent of males and 10 per cent of females; the parishes of Terling and Orwell show a comparable rate of will-making, with testation being slightly higher in Willingham. In Grantham, between 1581 and 1610, it was on average 10 per cent; in Earls Colne between 1610 and 1640, only 8 per cent; but in one chapelry in Kirkby Lonsdale, approximately one-third. See Coppel, 'Wills and the community', pp. 78–9. Finally, in Hunstanton, the proportion was roughly a quarter in the sixteenth century, see, Oestmann, *Lordship and Community*, p. 185.

56 Erickson, *Women and Property*, p. 204. She finds that men were six times more disposed to will-making than women. Also Bonfield, 'Normative rules', p. 161, and Vann, 'Wills and the family', p. 347, emphasise the point that most men didn't leave wills.

57 Erickson, *Women and Property*, pp. 207–8.

58 Vann, 'Wills and the family', pp. 352–6.

59 Oestmann, *Lordship and Community*, pp. 185–6.

60 Bonfield, 'Normative rules', pp. 167–9.

61 Coppel, 'Wills and the community', pp. 77–8.

62 Zell, *Industry in the Countryside*, p. 20.

63 Spufford, 'Peasant inheritance customs', pp. 169–73.

64 Howell, 'Peasant inheritance customs', p. 141. See also, Oestmann, *Lordship and Community*, pp. 191–3. He, too, identifies the provision for dependent children as determinative, and connects it with the need to protect the family's property rights where primogeniture failed.

65 Vann, 'Wills and the family', p. 347.

66 Coppel, 'Will-making on the deathbed'. This finding applies where the dates of burial of testators are known. See also, Oestmann, *Lordship and Community*, p. 187.

67 J. Addy, *Death, Money and the Vultures: Inheritance and Avarice, 1660–1750* (London, 1992), *passim*.

68 Coppel, 'Wills and the community', pp. 80–1.

69 For will formularies and scribes, see above, p. 185. Also, Coppel, 'Wills and the community', pp. 82–7; Collinson, 'Cranbrook and the Fletchers', p. 187.

70 Bonfield, 'Normative rules', p. 161; Oestmann, *Lordship and Community*, pp. 189–90, where the custom of primogeniture was so strong as to require no ratification. Erickson, *Women and Property*, p. 78, where will-making may have been designed to modify the effects of primogeniture and allow for the provision of other dependants. See also, pp. 26–8, for rules of inheritance in intestacy.

71 Vann, 'Wills and the family', pp. 347, 361–2; Spufford, 'Peasant inheritance customs', pp. 173–6; A. Macfarlane, *The Family Life of Ralph Josselin: A Seventeenth-Century Clergyman: an Essay in Historical Anthropology* (Cambridge, 1970, New York, 1977 edn), pp. 64–7; Erickson, *Women and Property*, pp. 32–3.

72 Bonfield, 'Normative rules', esp. pp. 160–1, 171–6.

73 Vann, 'Wills and the family', pp. 361–3.

74 D. Levine, '"For their own reasons": individual marriage decisions and family life', *Journal of Family History* 7:3 (Fall 1982), 255–64 (esp. pp. 255–9). Levine also suggests that paternal death delayed marriage.

75 Jim Oeppen, private communication. Its effect on the proportions ever marrying, however, cannot be ascertained.

76 Stone, *The Crisis of the Aristocracy*, abridged edn, p. 274. By that period, the portions were paid irrespective of marriage. Carlson, *Marriage and the English Reformation*, p. 100, uses the Elizabethan wills of Essex gentry and merchants to show that only a small proportion of testators who provided for their unmarried daughters placed restrictions on their daughters' marriages after the age of 21 years (adulthood). See also, below, chapter 6, pp. 194–5.

77 Earle, *Making of the English Middle Class*, p. 187.

78 Macfarlane, *Marriage and Love*, p. 269. This payment was made, regardless of whether or not a marriage occurred.

79 Vann, 'Wills and the family', pp. 357, 362–3.

80 Howell, 'Peasant inheritance customs', p. 145.

81 M. Spufford, *Contrasting Communities: English Villagers in the Sixteenth and Seventeenth Centuries* (Cambridge, 1974, ppbk edn, 1979), p. 112.

82 Oestmann, *Lordship and Community*, pp. 195–6.

83 Carlson, *Marriage and the English Reformation*, p. 139, where 2500 or so wills provided for unmarried children.

84 The proving of wills in all five parishes came under the jurisdiction of the archdeacon's official, with the commissary general exercising jurisdiction only in particular circumstances. For a discussion of jurisdiction, see, Woodcock, *Medieval Ecclesiastical Courts*, i, 'the jurisdictions'.

85 See above, Introduction, pp. 9, 19–21.

86 The number of wills for each parish is as follows: Tenterden, 1449–1600 (506); Wye, 1464–1600 (288); Whitstable, 1455–1600 (217); Chislet 1460–1600 (176); Sturry, 1464–1600 (117). For a full list, chronologically arranged by parish, see, O'Hara, 'Sixteenth-century courtship', pp. 285–311.

87 For a list of these wills, see, O'Hara, 'Sixteenth-century courtship', pp. 312–22, and for maps showing their geographical distribution, *ibid.*, between pp. 185–6.

88 Zell, *Industry in the Countryside*, pp. 114–15.

89 See above, p. 166.

90 The ratio is something of an underestimate since the burials recorded also include that of women and minors, those who were legally excluded from making a will. It should also be noted that the ratio tended to vary between decades, the period 1570–79, for example appearing to be one of an exceptionally low rate of testation coupled with a generally lower mortality level. See C.K.S., P 364/1/1 (parish register of Tenterden) and C.C.A.L., U3/131/1/1 (parish register of Whitstable).

91 The decades when the highest number of wills were made are as follows: Tenterden 1520s; Wye 1510s; Whitstable 1540s; Chislet 1550s; Sturry 1540s.

92 See above, Introduction, p. 20.

93 The percentages were Wye 30.2 per cent; Whitstable 31.8 per cent; Chislet 34.7 per cent and Sturry 31.6 per cent.

94 The number of wills with prescribed ages is as follows: Tenterden (218); Wye (87); Whitstable (69); Chislet (61); Sturry (37); total 472. For comparison, only 82 of the 501 wills in the period 1503–09 specify ages (16.4 per cent).

95 Thomas, 'Age and authority', pp. 3–5.

96 See above, p. 159.

97 Thomas, 'Age and authority', p. 4.

98 Carlson, *Marriage and the English Reformation*, n. 278 (p. 244). The term 'age of inheritance' is also used by Thomas, 'Age and authority', p. 20, n. 2 (citing Stone).

99 See above, p. 159.

100 Mitterauer, *History of Youth*, p. 59.

101 Thomas, 'Age and authority', p. 26.

102 PRC 17/30/166–v. (1555).

103 PRC 17/3/365–v., Richard Davy of Tenterden (1481).

104 PRC 17/23/26–7v. (1541).

105 Ben-Amos, 'Service and the coming of age', p. 46.

106 See below, chapter 6, pp. 193–4.

107 PRC 17/12/254–v. (1512).

108 PRC 17/5/152v. (1490).

109 PRC 17/1/125 (1463).

110 PRC 17/9/354–v. (1509).

111 E.g., see, PRC 17/6/305v., Thomas Consant of Chislet, 1497; PRC 17/4/170v.–2, Richard Elmere of Whitstable (1488).

112 See also below, chapter 6, pp. 194–6.

113 PRC 17/3/217–v. (1479).

114 PRC 17/6/110–11, Tenterden (1494).

115 E.g., see, PRC 17/48/55–v., Agnes Frye, widow, Tenterden (1590).

116 E.g., see, PRC 17/2/290v.–1, John Lucas, Tenterden (1473); PRC 17/6/177v.–9, William Gybon, Tenterden (1495); PRC 17/39/288–9, John Clarke, Sturry (1566).

117 PRC 17/10/63v. (1505).

118 PRC 17/2/148–v., Tenterden (1473).

119 PRC 17/29/265–6 (1549).

120 PRC 17/9/73v.–4v. (1504).

121 PRC 17/12/338 (1514).

122 See above, p. 164.

123 Thomas, 'Age and authority', esp. pp. 5, 14, 19–26.

124 The disappearance of some early bequests may be partly due to a decline in kin bequests over the period, see below, chapter 6, pp. 197–9, 211, although most of the legatees were sons and daughters. It should also be noted that provisions in the form of additional cash annuities or small livestock bequests went disproportionately to teenagers, so that a reduction in the number of teenage bequests, if that occurred, could conceivably be related to a decline in bequests of that nature.

125 If the *mean* age for men and women in each parish is compared over time, the difference between genders was usually between one and three years. Such an age-gap is also apparent in family reconstitution populations. See, Wrigley and Schofield, 'English population history', p. 162.

126 The three most significant ages for women in each parish follow in order of preference: Tenterden, 20, 18, 21; Wye, 21, 18, 20; Whitstable, 18, 16, 21; Chislet, 18, 20, 16; Sturry, 16, 21, 18.

127 See above, p. 159.

128 My thanks to Keith Wrightson for this comment.

Chapter 6

Material girls?:
dowries and property in courtship

Introducing the study of dowry in European history, Marion Kaplan emphasised its widespread importance in matters such as inheritance and property, courtship, household and group formation, the position of women in the family and economy, and their marriageability. At the same time, she drew attention to the historians' relative neglect of the subject.[1] The essays in her collection discuss the fluctuating significance of dowries from the medieval period and their heightened importance in times of economic and social instability. Dowries were a means of conferring status, of building alliances, and of transferring and redistributing wealth. They could also influence social and family relations and symbolise the role of women and their property rights. Perhaps most significantly they could affect women's marriage bargaining power, their partner and prospects, by determining who, when and whether they married.

The groom's financial contribution to a marriage was also of significance. In her recent work on women, property and marriage settlements in early modern England, Amy Erickson has pointed out that although early modern England has been described as a 'dowry culture', payment of dowry did not exclude other forms of marriage payments. Unlike Macfarlane, who emphasised the absence in England of 'bridewealth' or 'brideprice' payments, Erickson suggests that 'in actual practice ... Dowry and bride price operated simultaneously, except that the bride price went not to the bride's family but to the new marital household.'[2] Her work also seeks to redress the over-concentration by other historians on the upper classes and their marriage settlements, and on the common law.[3]

By that common law, women were entitled to a lifetime right of dower in a third of their husband's freehold during their widowhood. Increasingly, however, from the later Middle Ages, marriage agreements specified the portion brought by the bride and, in return for her dowry, a settlement in the form of a jointure to maintain her if her husband died first. The provision of a 'contractual jointure' – either as a lump sum, an estate, or an annuity arising from it – which became the usual alternative to common law dower by the sixteenth century, aimed to protect women's rights and material interests.[4]

What needs to be addressed is the question of just how far down the social scale the practice of making such settlements extended. Whereas in some European countries, the financial management of dowries was a municipal concern and notarial evidence of portions is profuse, the information about dowries and jointures in early modern England is much more difficult to come by.[5] Hence, until very recently, discussion of this central topic has been restricted to the social elite whose marriage bargains are better recorded and more visible to the historian. As their studies show, the size of portions, and the size of jointures thought appropriate to them, were matters of intense negotiation among the landed classes. The changing balance between the two have important implications for the aristocratic marriage market in the sixteenth, seventeenth and eighteenth centuries.[6]

As Stone and Outhwaite suggest, several factors might influence the size of marriage portion. These could include family circumstances, parental love, the number of daughters, their individual characteristics and any necessary compensation made for personal defects or status discrepancy.[7] There is some disagreement about the estimated average size of aristocratic portions in the early sixteenth century and the rate of nominal and real increase in the course of that century and the next. However, historians agree that a massive dowry inflation well in excess of aristocratic income and the general price rise, was experienced by the social elite in the early modern period. Both Stone and Cooper maintain that portions were nominally 12 or 13 times higher in 1675–1729 than in 1525–49. Outhwaite argues that by 1625–49 average portions had probably risen to at least seven times their level in 1475–1524, compared to the six-fold rise in the general price index and the three-fold rise in the industrial one. Nevertheless, he notes that the 'rise in dowries before the early seventeenth century remains largely unexplained'. Estimating in her article a doubling or tripling of marriage portions between 1600 and the early eighteenth century and, in her book, a more dramatic four- to five-times rise in portions of the English peerage, Erickson was cautious to observe that 'the actual increase relative to prices is problematic'. It was, however, 'substantially more' than any contemporary price inflation. According to Stone, it was after 1600 that the then nominal inflation of dowries gained momentum in *real* terms, and surged ahead of agricultural prices.[8] With inflated dowries valued typically at several thousand pounds among the aristocracy in the seventeenth century, the charge on the parental estate, worth perhaps the equivalent of up to three years' income, became increasingly burdensome as the century progressed.[9]

As well as demonstrating the phenomenal rise in the level of bridal portions within that social class, historians have also sought to calculate the ratio of portion size to jointure size in assessing the balance of financial exchange at marriage. They have found that the average ratio of £5 of portion to £1 of jointure that existed at the start of the seventeenth century (and possibly before in the mid-sixteenth century) had changed to a 10:1 ratio by the end of the century.[10] This implied that the balance of the matrimonial market was weighted decisively against aristocratic women who may have found themselves appreciably disadvantaged in the course of the seventeenth century.

A number of explanations have been put forward as to what might have caused those trends, some more convincing than others. It has been argued that the sex ratio of the aristocratic marriage market was affected by an increasing, although inexplicable, tendency for eligible aristocratic males to remain celibate. Social and demographic developments – among them the loss of adult males from emigration, war and falling male survival rates, the rise in the number of heiresses and the surplus of status-seeking girls – created a situation which supplied increasing numbers of marriageable women and fewer men to meet their demand. Economic changes such as a decline in interest rates which allowed for easier borrowing or mortgaging, and inflation coupled with growing expenditure, may also have contributed to the inflation of dowries.[11] Moreover, it has been suggested that aristocratic women faced increasing competition from mercantile and financiers' daughters, from the daughters of the squirearchy, the daughters and widows of City aldermen, and from other wealthy widows. Explaining the causes of dotal inflation in Europe, Hughes suggested that it was 'its use as a mechanism for alliance and mobility in a status-conscious yet mobile world that may have encouraged the dowry to rise dramatically in value'.[12] Where she drew attention to the imbalance between wealth and status, Erickson emphasised the significance of dowry as a symbol of social status in itself, pointing out that it 'must surely be one reason why truly massive inflation was limited to the highest echelons'.[13]

Inflation of portions on a less massive scale has also been identified among social groups beneath the level of the aristocratic elite, that of the gentry and knightly class. For the sixteenth century, knightly families studied by Cooper offered portions averaging £286 in the first half of the century and £859 in the latter half. This represented a trebling in value comparable to increases for the peerage in the period 1475–1524 and 1575–99.[14] In the early seventeenth century, where aristocratic portions were often in excess of £5000, those among the upper gentry ranged between £1000 and £5000, and among county gentry, between £500 and £1000. Erickson's Chancery litigants, who mostly comprised wealthy yeomen and tradesmen, but also gentry, knights and baronets, experienced a three-fold increase in their median portion from £200 in the later sixteenth century to £500–£600 at the end of the seventeenth. In connection with the three-fold rise in gentry portions and those involved in Chancery suits, the portion:jointure ratio followed a similar but less marked trend from that experienced by the aristocratic elite.[15]

Moving yet further down the social scale, the evidence about bridal portions is more difficult to find. Peter Earle remarked on the paucity of information for analysing middle-class contracts. He was, however, convinced that among the middle classes too, 'there must have been rules and conventions, as well as market pressures, which determined the approximate size of the portion a girl would have to bring to her marriage with men of different fortunes and expectations and so determined in turn the parameters of the bargaining process'.[16] For the vast majority of yeomen, tradesmen, craftsmen, husband-men and labourers, surviving probate documents give some evidence of the making of marriage settlements and of portions bequeathed towards marriage, although, as Erickson found, they are sometimes less than inform-ative. From her examination of probate accounts, she was able to demonstrate that marriage settlements were commonly made among those status groups normally regarded as 'propertyless'.[17] Her study of wills in Yorkshire, Lincoln-shire and Sussex revealed that few testators provided details concerning an already married daughter's portion. Only a small number even specified a marriage portion as such, and then only from the later seventeenth century, giving portion sizes which were disproportionately wide-ranging. Neverthe-less, the wills do allow an examination of bequests to unmarried daughters which may at least be suggestive of the size of portions. Such values would of course 'represent minimum marriage portions since they rarely take into account bequests from grandparents or uncles or aunts, they only sometimes mention previous gifts in the parent's lifetime, and there is no reason for them to consider the young woman's earnings'.[18]

In addition to Erickson's work, other local studies have used wills to make assessments of the size of dowries. Macfarlane based his calculations for husbandmen's daughters on 39 portions mentioned in wills from Lupton for the period 1550–1720, and on 13 portions bequeathed in Earls Colne between 1550 and 1800. He indicated that such portions were 'not specifically tied to marriage', and that it was extremely difficult to uncover evidence for dowries at the level of labourers.[19] Cicely Howell's study of Kibworth Harcourt analysed a total of 207 wills to track the movement in the value of cash legacies between 1520 and 1720 and the shift from legacies in kind to legacies in cash. Although her sample was sizeable, her method of analysis was not confined to marriage portions for daughters, but included all the portions of younger and unmarried children, irrespective of sex.[20]

It is perhaps questionable whether or not legacies given to unmarried daughters should necessarily be regarded as dowry payments. Historians who have used wills would seem to have treated them as such, assuming that the portions provided for daughters as their inheritance were expected to be used for marriage. It has been recognised that there was a close, almost indistinguishable, relationship between dowries or specific marriage gifts, and the daughter's natural, ordinary female inheritance. Hughes saw the relationship as pertaining particularly to less wealthy folk. Howell equated the marriage portion with a child's portion; Erickson noted that the portion inherited was intended to become a dowry, although many never actually married; and Macfarlane justified the use of wills as evidence, 'since the portion was both an anticipation of inheritance and a marriage gift'.[21]

The preceding chapter has already examined the significance of notional ages of marriage and inheritance, and the synonymous use of such terms as 'day of marriage', 'being of age', 'lawful age and marriage' and 'lawful age of marriage'.[22] The wills often stipulated that provisions made for women, particularly daughters, were to be received at their 'time of marriage', when they 'be married, or come to the age of marriage'. Alternatively, it was at a given age or whensoever they married, depending on which event occurred first. William Graunte of Chislet (prob. 1545), for example, bequeathed £10 to each of his three daughters at their day of marriage, with specific reversions if any died before coming 'to the age of marriage'.[23] Likewise, William Collin of the same parish (prob. 1559) left his daughter a feather-bed and £6 13s 4d at the day of her marriage, willing that she be kept with the profits from his land and moveables by his executor 'till she com to thage of mariage'.[24] The frequency of bequests specifically tied to marriage alone, or to either marriage or a notional age, helps to validate the assumption that the portions willed to unmarried daughters were genuinely intended as payments of dowry. For the parish of Tenterden between 1449 and 1600, 150 daughters were to be endowed at a specified age or at marriage, 97 were to receive portions at marriage, and the remaining 28 at an age stipulated by the testator. In Wye, during a similar period, of 115 portions, the numbers were 20, 70 and 25 respectively.[25]

Historians have also indicated that the arrangements prescribed by testators for their daughters rarely imposed sanctions designed to control their marriages. In Banbury, stipulations or inducements which aimed at ensuring approvable marriage choices did appear in some wills, but they were infrequent, and largely irrelevant upon children attaining the age of 21 years.[26] For the middle classes, Peter Earle has claimed that fathers were generally lenient and seldom imposed a threat of disinheritance, providing few sanctions even against daughters who were under age.[27] According to Erickson, any requirements which were made in ordinary men's wills, when at all, for children to marry with their mothers' or guardians' consent, were as applicable to sons as to daughters, and were usually limited to persuading them to take heed of their elders' advice.[28] Even Stone suggested that among aristocratic classes, the maxim of strict compliance by daughters was, between 1560 and 1640, becoming increasingly more liberal. With the changing attitudes reflected in the nature of testamentary bequests, 'fierce disposition' became the exception rather than the norm by the end of the seventeenth century.[29]

Nevertheless, although the majority of testators did not attempt harsh regulation of their daughters' behaviour post-mortem through the will, it remains the case that where such control was attempted, the wills can reveal exceptionally well the provision of portions tied to marriage, and contemporary attitudes to their payment.[30] John a Bere, of Chislet (will 1499), left a portion of 10 marks to each of his daughters towards their marriage, with the general condition that they be married by the consent and goodwill of their mother, otherwise they were to receive only half their portion.[31] Other testators were more specific about their daughters' marriage choices. Andrew Hawker, elder of Wye (will 1498), anticipating his daughter's desire to marry John Alcy, butler of the college of Wye, and evidently disapproving of the match, willed that his executors 'pay to her mariage no more in money and stuff but onely to the valew of 40s'. Moreover, he added, that 'if Thomasyne wilbe rewlid and governed by my will and be thadvise of my feoffeis and executors and mary with some other man that it is my will that my executors pay to the mariage of Thomasine be good advyse 20 marke of money, and stuff of household'. Thomasine was thus urged not only to accept parental advice, but also the advice of other kin and of neighbouring parishioners.[32] By contrast, the widow Johana Alarde, also of Wye (will 1536), sought to promote the marriage of her daughter Alice to one Mr Tucker. Having bequeathed to her sons William, John and Robert a 'silver salt', 13 silver spoons with images of God and his apostles, and her best mazer (drinking bowl), she willed to her daughter, among other things, the following:

> that if she marry with maister Tucker as my wyll is god helpyng thereto that then the salt of silver bequeathed to William and the spones and masers before assigned ... be utterly void, and all the said silver salt spoon and masers to remain to Alice my daughter, and for the £30 given to her by her fathers wyll, I wyll she have all my sheepe for and in recompense of the same £30. Also if Maister Tucker have her to wyff then I will to Alice all my housholde stuff, and if that maryage breake and take not effect then I will all my said housholde stuff be evenly devyded.

If the marriage was to proceed, Alice was also to acquire the best chest, and five other chests originally intended for her brothers.[33] What emotive pressures may also have operated besides the material inducement can only be inferred but it may have been difficult to flout a parent's deathbed wish. Although the number of these cases is small, their relative significance could well have been greater. This is because direct post-mortem intervention in daughters' marriages would presumably have been more likely if a parent died during their daughters' courtship, and particularly when a prospective marriage was on the immediate horizon. Some testators, it seems, might have seen their final days as a time for reconciliation with daughters. The yeoman Richard Smith of Tenterden gave by his will nuncupative (1599), to his daughter Anne, the then wife of John Howlte, butcher, 'who as he said married against his will, in token of his free pardon of her said faulte the sume of 13li 6s 8d'.[34]

Revealing though such qualitative evidence is, the true value of the material found in wills lies in the indication it provides about the size of marriage portions among the will-making population. It can therefore be used to shed light on the crucial question of changes in dowry over time. An approach to these questions must inevitably be a quantitative one. The study of dowries which follows is based on the wills used also in the preceding chapter,[35] and involved recording the nature and value of legacies bequeathed to each unmarried daughter.

Although the wills occasionally referred specifically to children's 'portions', the actual term 'dowry' as marriage payment for daughters was not used.[36] Instead, the words 'dowrye', 'dower', 'joynter' and 'widdowright' were seen in connection with a widow's provision.[37] Legacies were only recorded in this analysis where they were clearly stated to be bequests 'towards marriage', given 'at marriage', or at a specified age, usually implying that the daughters were then minors. The possibility of an increase in the size of portions following reversions from immediate members of the family, particularly unmarried sisters, could not be accounted for here. As Cooper observed, 'in general wills may tend to understate the amount actually given in portions, because they often provided that, if a child died underage and unmarried, the portion should go to the survivor, or be equally divided among survivors'.[38] Conversely, the amount of legacy might be diminished in the event of another child being born. William Gybon of Tenterden (will 1495) assigned 10 marks each to the marriages of his daughters Johane and Eleanor, but arranged for the portions to be reduced to 7 marks and no more, if another daughter should be born subsequently.[39] Where testators apportioned a given amount to an unborn child, irrespective of gender, as it was common for them to do, that amount was not considered, since it applied to sons as much as to daughters.[40]

Some other forms of marriage payments have not been included in the main quantitative analysis. There were times when testators left marriage gifts to women whose relationship was unspecified. In 1549, Katherine Churche of Sturry bequeathed to one Alice Bewman, certain household goods and her wedding ring at the day of her marriage, to Margery Chapman, more household goods at her marriage day, and to Katherine Farmor, the additional gift of lambs, when she married.[41] Charitable bequests to pauper marriages were usually in the form of small money payments. Hughes has pointed out that the dowering of poor maidens in Mediterranean societies was to guarantee female chastity. Although those societies placed more emphasis on the symbolic importance of dowries and its moral connotations for women, the provision made for the marriages of poor girls was common in England from at least the Middle Ages, and continued in the sixteenth and seventeenth centuries.[42]

In addition, testators provided portions for the marriages of other female kin and of resident female servants. Such portions, although far fewer in number and often worth substantially less than the provisions made to unmarried daughters, were still not negligible, particularly in the earlier part of our period. Other historians have commented upon the contributions which girls could expect from relatives, friends and employers in funding their marriages. That received from parents constituted the main source of dowry, but there was, nevertheless, a variety of sources of inherited and accumulated means.[43] Erickson referred to those 'small gifts' which 'provided a steady flow of contributions to portions'. Although she did not distinguish between female and male legatees, she found a significant proportion of godchildren, siblings, grandchildren, other relations and servants among them. Women (in particular single women) were found to favour female recipients and the preference extended to all kinds of bequests. Young girls entering into marriage could thus probably also expect to find a 'benefactress' in the form of a sister, aunt, mistress or grandmother.[44]

In the Canterbury diocese, for the period 1503–09 surveyed, of the 69 testators who mentioned portions, 11 gave cash bequests to the marriages of their granddaughters and god-daughters (16 per cent). As for the five parishes studied from the mid-fifteenth to the end of the sixteenth century, testators provided for the dowries of 130 women other than their daughters. At the same time they provided for 480 daughters altogether, a ratio of roughly 1 to 4. Bequests to non-daughters came disproportionately from female testators, and included a range of female kin, both real and fictive. In Tenterden, 56 per cent were granddaughters; nieces and great-nieces 16 per cent; unspecified female kin 10 per cent; god-daughters 9 per cent; 'cousins' 5 per cent, and the small remainder were sisters and affines.[45] Although the proportions varied between the parishes, vertical blood-ties were most prominent, indicating a generational obligation to provide something for the marriages of maiden relatives. Recognition of kin obligation was particularly marked in the absence of single young daughters. Of the 46 testators from Tenterden who mentioned female kin, only 9 made provision for unmarried daughters too. In those circumstances, the dowering of relatives was much less generous than that of the immediate family. The yeoman Thomas Smythe gave £20 to his daughter at her day of marriage but only 5 marks to his granddaughter at her marriage.[46] Likewise, the widow Anne Love left nearly 10 times as much to her two daughters at their age of 18 or day of marriage, as to her nine grand-daughters at 18 or 15 years.[47] Testators who provided for more than one kinswoman did not always give equal amounts to each.

Among all the non-daughters receiving cash bequests, the amount received ranged from under 10s to as much as £25. Such variation is to be expected, given that we are not always dealing with the same kind of relationship or familial circumstances, but for the entire period, the average was 76.7s and the modal value 40s. While marriage gifts for kinswomen were mostly cash payments, some testators bequeathed items of household such as bedding, silver, pewter and brass utensils. Personal clothing and occasionally livestock were also given. In 1519, William Edward of Whitstable willed that his grand-daughter Eleanor should have to her marriage or when she attained the age of 18 years, a cow, certain bedding and 10 marks in cash.[48]

At times the provisions made towards the marriages of kinswomen were clearly conditional. Juliane Scott could hope to receive from her brother, Richard Castewesill of Tenterden, 5 marks at the time of her marriage or at 21 years, provided she married 'by discretion of parents and friends'.[49] The yeoman William Bodell left £10 to his cousin's daughter, but only 'upon condition she keep herself honest and be ruled' by his wife.[50] Other examples illustrate restrictions imposed upon female relatives and servants. The single cow and the small sum of 13s 4d was willed by Thomas a Deale to his niece in 1525, 'if she wilbe gided and ruled ... unto the tyme she be maryed', otherwise the gift was to be void.[51] Grandparents could seek to reinforce parental authority in marriage choices. Thomas Serles, the elder of Wye, bequeathed £6 13s 4d to his granddaughter Rose on the day of her marriage, and a further £6 13s 4d a year later, 'so that she be rulyd by her father and mother'.[52] Other testators who provided for the marriages of female servants attempted not only to regulate their marriages, but also their mobility, by ensuring continued service for members of their family. Richard Hokkyng, the elder of Whitstable, for example, left 40s and bedding to his servant Alice Hokkyng, provided she continued with his daughter Johane until the time of her marriage. If not, she was to receive only 6s 8d and a black sheet.[53] Similarly, William Consaunt of Chislet stipulated that his kinswoman Alice a See was to have to her marriage £6 13s 4d 'if so be that she dwell with my wife till the time of her marriage and do her service in the mean season', or else she was to have nothing. Another servant was to be given 40s 'so that she be in likewise ordered and ruled by my wife'.[54]

Bequests to non-daughters were clearly an important feature of endow-ment for marriage, with significant implications for kin relationships and influences upon marriage decisions outside the immediate nuclear family. Although marriage portions for kin were relatively small and less frequently bestowed than those for daughters, reflecting in part their ancillary and sometimes reversionary nature, it is essential to remember that a certain number of would-be brides would have received additional money and goods from their relatives, masters and mistresses. Ante-mortem transfer to kin would probably also have augmented their potential prospects. Hence, the dowries for daughters presented below must in some cases have been supplemented by bequests and contributions from their more distant relatives. The figures therefore represent only the *minimum* amount apportioned for marriage. Furthermore, since they are concerned with cash-legacies only, they do not account for portions paid to daughters in kind.

A number of studies have drawn attention to those legacies in kind. Cicely Howell indicated the continued payment of mixed-legacies to children, although she attempted to demonstrate an increase in the proportion of cash-only legacies between 1560 and 1600. Poorer small-holders (as opposed to the more prosperous yeomen and husbandmen) still tended to leave legacies in kind in the course of the seventeenth century.[55] In Lupton and Earls Colne, Macfarlane found that money portions were, by far, the predominant ones, but daughters in Lupton could also expect to receive one calf or cow in the later sixteenth century, and occasionally bedding and chests. In certain circumstances only, houses or land might be an 'optional extra'. Remarking upon the 'emphasis on moveable wealth' – in particular that of ready cash, followed by household furniture, linen, chests and other furnishings – Macfarlane admitted the possibility of English girls embellishing their own trousseaus, but saw little evidence for such practices in early modern England compared to Mediterranean societies.[56]

The Kent wills frequently referred to the instuff of household, the livestock and other moveables brought by testators' wives at the time of marriage. Thomas Pyrkyne of Chislet willed in 1549 that his wife Agnes receive 'all her own household stuff which she brought with her when I married ... all her bedding, brass and pewter, brewing vessell, pair of almayne rivetts, a great cupboard and all her chests'.[57] Alexander Maycote, a parishioner of Sturry, specified that his wife Alice should have 'all such instuff of howsehold horse cattall and corne as I had with her none to be mynysshed'.[58] Occasionally, such tangential references to the goods brought as dowry included among them items of silver. According to Thomas Childmell's will of 1496, Katherine had evidently brought 'the day of our mariage' six silver spoons and a little mazer harnessed with silver, and one of gilt.[59] Finding similar references among even poor testators in Banbury, Richard Vann concluded that 'dowering must have gone on in all social ranks'.[60]

A study of the inventories of unmarried women could surely reveal much about the likely contents of their dowries,[61] but only a few inventories of known single women survive for the five Kent parishes under consideration.

Marie Stephens of Chislet had a 'portion' limited to her of £4 out of her deceased father's goods, and a 'portion' given to her by her mother at the time of her remarriage of which £3 was recovered.[62] The virgin Isabel Fowler, also of Chislet, had moveables valued at £17 3s 8d in 1585, which included money held in her own purse, 58s 4d for her wages held in the hands of her dead master's executors and a further cash sum in another man's keeping, her clothes, chests and three kine worth £5.[63] The kinds of moveable goods belonging to young, unmarried girls may also be deduced from the inventory of Thomas Burr of Whitstable made in 1582, to which is appended an inventory of the goods and cattle given by him to his own daughter Anne Burr, and to his stepdaughter Katherine Winter. Both girls and their 'portions' were committed to the governance of specified persons during their 'nonage'. Anne's goods amounted to £14 2s 10d, while Katherine's was significantly less, £8 2s 4d, of which one cow and ten ewes valued at over £3 was the gift of her own father, John Winter. Anne too had animals worth about £6, and although she was allotted the best christening sheet and had a greater share of the household goods, both girls would probably have also brought to their marriages, feather-beds, chests, all kinds of pewter and brass plates, dishes, kettles, pots, pans, candlesticks, spits, silver or silver-fashioned items, and silver rings as part of their dowry.[64] Neither possessed any cash except for the token penny-halfpenny according to the inventory, but it was not unlikely that they would have invested their portions, received cash sums from other quarters, or earned money in service before marriage. As for the spinster Sibell Alcockes of Wye, she died with goods appraised at £33 7d. Although she owned all kinds of clothes, old sheets, bedding, an old chest, a linen wheel, a psalm book and a testament, over £31 worth of her moveables consisted of money held in the hands of a gentleman and a yeoman.[65]

Despite the variety of moveable goods owned by single women, Erickson has identified a marked preponderance of gifts in cash to immediate female kin. For this reason the 'assets of young women more often consisted principally in bonds or ready cash than their brothers did'. She claimed that single women in particular were 'a significant source of cash in the local lending markets', constituting 'by far the most likely to hold their wealth in credits, although the amounts that they loaned out were relatively small'.[66]

An examination of the Kent wills confirms the strong preference for cash payments. Nevertheless some comments should be made about the provision of other kinds of legacies. Of the 501 wills, cash bequests *alone* were generally the norm to all daughters, although some daughters may also have received household items as part of their dowry from both their parents. In a few instances, testators chose to leave livestock instead to their daughters' marriages. Robert Style of Leysdown, in Sheppey, bequeathed to his daughter one cow and 20 acres, and the two daughters of John Lambe of Sutton Valence could expect to bring to their marriages exceptional flocks of 100 ewes each, two silver spoons, but only 60s in cash.[67] The wills also make it clear that daughters might inherit further cash sums, other goods and land, often as reversions, but sometimes as legacies which were not specifically tied to marriage or to a prescribed age.

In the five Kent parishes studied, with the exception of Sturry, land was mentioned among the types of bequest given towards marriage for 7–11 per cent of daughters. In Tenterden at least, such provision may well have been due to such girls not having any unmarried, under-aged brothers.[68] In 1471 John Godday provided that his daughter Margery might receive his lands upon her marriage, but in the event of a son being born to him, the lands were to descend instead to him, and he was to pay his sister at marriage or at the age of 22, 10 marks.[69]

Rather than such land endowments, testators, male and female, were much more likely to leave household gifts to their daughters' marriages. The proportions for Tenterden, Wye, Whitstable and Chislet were respectively 21 per cent, 16 per cent, 23 per cent and 20 per cent, but rarely did such gifts constitute the sole dowry.[70] All kinds of beds, bedding, furniture, linen and utensils were bequeathed. They included sheets, coverlets, pillows, blankets, table cloths, christening sheets, chests, cupboards, crockery, plates, pots, brass and pewter dishes, and silver spoons, goblets and mazers. Widows often gave their personal clothing and paraphernalia. Joane Penny supplemented her daughter's marriage portion of £10, with her apparel, silver hooks, household goods, pewter, a chest, her best beads, a silk ribbon, a purse and a girdle.[71] Another widow of a Tenterden yeoman, Marie Slade, provided that her daughter receive £33 in cash, the rest of the pewter, brass, household implements and furniture, linen, clothes, a further 40s and a testament.[72] A handful of testators bequeathed clothes which had belonged to their wives.[73] John Swanton, a mariner of Whitstable, left his daughter Alice '40s at her day of marriage, and all apparell that was my wife's, and all my instuff'.[74]

Of the other types of goods bestowed in marriage, a very small number of daughters in Chislet were given portions of corn. In the coastal parish of Whitstable, John Smelte left his daughter Elyn 'my weir and ½ boat, willing that whosoever doth marry her shall allow my wife fish for her own household the first year'. His other two daughters were each given two bullocks, two kine and 40s at their day of marriage.[75] In both those parishes, gifts of livestock comprising cattle and sheep (often more than a single animal) formed an additional part of daughters' marriage portions. Some testators distinguished between the age when the flocks were to be invested, and the time of further payment at marriage.[76] The proportion of 23 per cent was nearly three times that found in Wye (8 per cent) and more than twice that in Tenterden (10 per cent).[77] In Tenterden, testators generally gave just one cow, a heifer or bud,

Table 13 Mean dowries over time, omitting those of 3000 shillings or more

Year	Total no. of dowries	Mean dowry of all daughters	Mean dowry Tenterden	No. in Tenterden	Mean dowry Wye	No. in Wye	Mean dowry Whitstable	No. in Whitstable	Mean dowry Chislet	No. in Chislet	Mean dowry Sturry	No. in Sturry
1449–74	38	94.55	92.21	24	71.11	3	20.00	2	118.67	5	133.34	4
1475–99	71	116.67	114.29	35	135.56	21	17.20	6	148.15	9	–	0
1500–24	76	99.56	90.71	33	113.33	22	69.09	11	155.00	8	40.00	2
1525–49	96	205.8	250.30	54	232.00	10	88.77	19	181.21	11	120.00	2
1550–74	116	346.18	622.27	47	105.31	27	78.46	13	255.56	24	182.67	5
1575–99	77	512.34	517.11	45	269.41	17	333.33	3	633.33	6	1133.30	6
All years	474	250.65	316.13	238	152.97	100	85.37	54	239.58	63	450.88	19

along with small amounts of cash or other goods, suggesting perhaps that poorer persons in that parish were more liable to dispose of their few animals in that way.[78]

Although bequests of moveable goods and occasionally endowments of landed property formed part of the dowry for girls in sixteenth-century Kent, it remains clear that the main feature of dowry payments among the will-making population was its predominantly cash form. Some testators gave the choice for portions to be either in cash or its equivalent value in moveable goods.[79] Others provided for portions in cash and goods up to a specified value,[80] but cash dowries were by far the principal item. In Tenterden, 246 out of 275 daughters were given their portions in cash (89 per cent). The proportions for Wye, Whitstable, Chislet and Sturry, amounted to 93 per cent, 70 per cent, 79 per cent, and 96 per cent. It is therefore to this prime consideration that attention must now be turned.

Examining all five parishes together, of 480 dowries found in the wills for which a cash value was specified, the bulk of given values came from Tenterden (238), and a further quarter of the evidence from Wye (Table 13). The number of daughters receiving cash portions was, of course, somewhat higher, since testators who gave such legacies did not always indicate the precise amount. It must also be remembered that the figures represent the number of dowry values for daughters, rather than the actual number of testators bequeathing them, since any individual testator might provide more than one cash dowry.

Six dowries were omitted from the analysis, and were found in the wills of Sir Thomas Kempe, Kt, of Wye, in 1519; the gentleman William Swanne, also of Wye (will of 1597); and the dowry left by a prosperous Chislet yeoman, Robert Dodd, in 1599.[81] Cecile Kemp was to receive her dowry of 300 marks paid in instalments within four years of her marriage.[82] The four daughters of William Swanne were also to receive their portions in instalments with the payment completed five years after marriage. Ursula and Margaret were each provided with £300, while Elizabeth's and Tabitha's portions amounted to £250 each, and were made conditional upon them marrying with the consent of their mother and sister Ursula.[83] Such a practice of extended payment was perhaps more likely to apply to larger than average cash sums, but in Kent, smaller portions might also be paid over a period of up to 11 years, although three years or less was more common.[84]

The marriage portions provided by Sir Thomas Kempe and William Swanne derive from a social group which is not commonly represented among the will-makers. Together with the £200 portion payable to Sara Dodd at her age of 18 or day of marriage, as bequeathed in the will of her wealthy yeoman father,[85] they are disproportionate in size to the rest of the figures used in the following analysis. Moreover, their inclusion would have significantly raised the mean value of dowries found in wills belonging to the last quarter of the century. Their exclusion, however, does not affect the trend observable in average dowry values.

The results given in Table 13 show that the *mean* dowry of daughters was 250s in cash (£12 10s). This was not, however, consistent across the parishes. In the small parish of Sturry, for example, the average for the whole period was 450s (£22 10s). There may be some distortion due to the relatively small number of dowries for that parish (19) coupled with the higher sums given at the end of the period. By contrast, the lowest average dowry was found in Whitstable, being 85s (£4 5s) for the entire period. Otherwise Tenterden had a mean value of 316s (£15 16s). In Wye it was 153s (£7 13s) and in Chislet, 240s (£12).

Corresponding calculations for the sixteenth century are provided by Cicely Howell's study of Kibworth Harcourt, although the criteria she employed are not strictly comparable.[86] Notwithstanding, from her analysis, 55 per cent of cash legacies in the mid-sixteenth century were worth £1–£4, with under 4 per cent worth more than £20.[87] Compared to those cash portions, the values in the Kent wills are higher. In the period 1525–49, for example, 43 per cent were under £4, and 19.8 per cent were £20 and more, while in 1550–74, the figures were 34.5 per cent and approximately 26 per cent.[88]

Erickson and Macfarlane have both attempted to estimate the value of portions according to broad status categories. It should be remembered, however, that their figures derive from a later period. Of 25 portions bequeathed by husbandmen, yeomen and craftsmen in rural Yorkshire, Erickson found that two-thirds were valued at up to £20 only. In the town of Selby, husbandmen, labourers and poorer craftsmen and yeomen usually left £10, while most yeomen and leather craftsmen gave £20. A few daughters of wealthy Yorkshire men received portions worth more than £100. In Bristol and Sussex, too, most portions came to less than £50. For ordinary people they were generally under £30.[89] Macfarlane's findings suggest likewise that the majority of husbandmen's daughters could expect portions of £10–£50, and labourers' daughters probably £1–£5. In Lupton, of the 39 portions which were mainly bequeathed by husbandmen, 33 were under £20, while in Earls Colne, the mode of just 13 portions was £40–£50.[90]

The social and economic status of fathers was clearly an important factor affecting the size of dowry bequeathed. The labourer Richard Mason of Whitstable in 1546 left his two daughters only 6s 8d each at their 'day of marriage'.[91] In contrast, the Wye tanner Nicholas Coke provided in 1541 for his three daughters to receive £20 each at their age of 18 years or marriage. A similar cash sum was willed to any as yet unborn daughter.[92] The exceptionally large dowries given at the upper levels and omitted from the quantitative analysis have already been observed, showing the degree of disparity which could exist within any one parish. Yeomen generally provided larger cash dowries for their daughters than did husbandmen. In Tenterden, in the mid- to late sixteenth century, husbandmen's daughters received sums from £3 6s 8d to £20, while yeomen often gave portions in the £30–£100 range.[93] Considerable variation in dowry values might occur within occupations. Thomas Barrowe in 1565 left a cash portion of only £5,[94] compared to other yeomen like Edward Phyllypp who, in 1578, bequeathed 200 marks (£133 6s 8d) to his daughter Suzanne at her full age of 18 years or marriage.[95]

Such variation in dowry values is unsurprising given the range of wealth behind bland occupational labels current in the sixteenth century. However, the very existence of such a range of dowries available provides a graphic illustration of the way in which marriage might be the key to both upward and downward social mobility in the early modern period. Clearly, to the extent to which the provision of an acceptable dowry alone determined success in courtship, the daughters of relatively wealthy husbandmen might legitimately aspire to marry the sons of relatively poor yeomen, or vice versa, and the daughters of prosperous yeomen could prove a good catch for gentlemen's sons.[96] In what follows, therefore, any discussion of average dowry values must always be qualified by the knowledge that there was wide variation of values around the mean, within any one parish, and its constituent occupational groups. The size of dowries was itself the object of intense negotiation and speculation, determined by wealth, status and the local marriage market, so that such variation is necessarily to be expected. Nevertheless, despite these qualifications, it should be emphasised that the study of dowry values presented here is based upon the largest ever sample of probate evidence, and moreover includes many dowries found in wills dating from the mid-fifteenth century.

As well as the economic status of their fathers, the number of siblings would have affected the size of portions which daughters could expect. In the Kent wills, there was considerable equality in the cash portions bequeathed by individual testators to their several unmarried daughters. In Tenterden, 52 out of 63 testators providing for more than one daughter, gave each the same amount of cash legacy. With few exceptions, daughters in Wye received equal portions to their sisters, and the same applied to 15 out of 19 testators in Whitstable. For the remaining two parishes, the number of instances are fewer, but they still reflect the predominantly partible inheritance allocation of marriage portions.[97]

For all five Kent parishes, the *modal* dowry over the whole period was only 40s (£2) and the *median* value, 133s (£6 13s), but this simply represents the enormous spread of amounts found throughout the years. Figure 5 charts the distribution of dowry values (omitting those of £150+). Each marking represents one or more occurrence of that particular value, and demonstrates quite clearly the wide distribution. As shown in Figure 6, dowries most

Figure 5 Distribution of dowries, daughters only, all parishes, omitting dowries of 3000s+

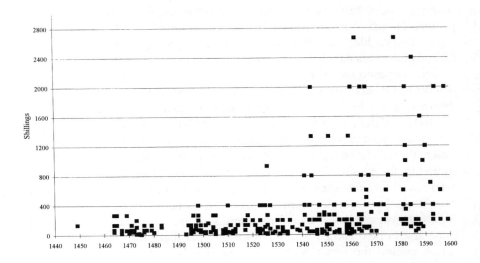

Figure 6 Distribution of dowry values, 1449–1599, all parishes, daughters only

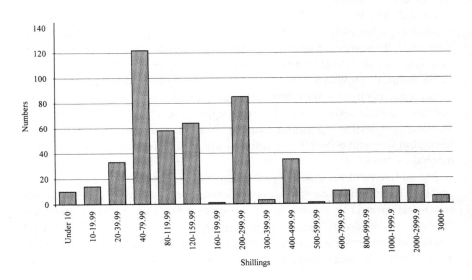

Figure 7 Mean dowries over time, daughters only, omitting 3000s+

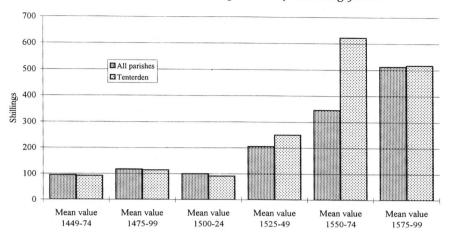

frequently fell into the 40s to 79.99s category over the entire period (£2–£4), but equally significant is the evident range of dowries which is to be expected given the differences in wealth and circumstances among testators.

It is clear from Table 13 that more interesting than the average size of dowry is the change in dowry size over time, and it is to this that we shall now turn. Both Table 13 and Figure 5 show that there was considerable inflation in the value of cash portions bequeathed to unmarried daughters. The mean dowry of all daughters, for all five parishes taken together, remained relatively stable at *c*. 100s (£5) from the mid-fifteenth century to the first quarter of the sixteenth century. Thereafter the dowries display rapid inflation, with the mean for 1525–49 being approximately £10 5s rising to approximately £17 6s in 1550–74, and averaging some £25 12s at the end of the sixteenth century. Over time, therefore, the average dowry increased slightly more than *five-fold* between the mid-fifteenth and late sixteenth centuries.

This inflation is portrayed in Figure 7, where the results for all five parishes combined, and that of Tenterden alone (by far the largest sample), are presented. Such inflation did not mean the elimination of relatively small dowries. Figure 5 illustrates the increasing numbers of large dowries found, but also shows that fairly small payments persisted into the 1580s. In fact, the *modal*, most common, dowry value remained at 40s between 1500 and 1574, and rose to 200s only in 1575–99.[98] One could speculate that there might have been a polarisation of dowries, rather than a general inflation, with only particular social groups able to afford increasingly higher levels of payment. From the results shown, it would be unwise to place too much weight on individual parish variation, or on small movements over time, given the wide

Table 14 Kentish dowries compared to those of the peerage

Date	Mean dowry in shillings	PBH index	Dowry indexed to base 1449–74[a]	Real dowry values[b]
1449–74	94.6	101.5	100.0	98.5
1475–99	116.7	104.6	123.4	118.0
1500–24	99.6	115.5	105.3	91.2
1525–49	205.8	168.8	217.7	129.0
1550–74	346.2	286.4	366.1	127.8
1575–99	512.3	399.2	541.9	135.7

Date	Stone's peerage portions to nearest £100	Stone's aristocratic portion index	Cooper's peerage portions to nearest £50	Cooper's peerage portions where 750 = 100	Cooper's knightly families, average portion in £s	Cooper's knightly families, average portion indexed to 1475–1500
1449–74					282.0	100.0
1475–99	500.0	100.0	750.0	100.0	282.0	100.0
1500–24	500.0	100.0	750.0	100.0	286.0	101.4
1525–49	700.0	140.0	750.0	100.0	286.0	101.4
1550–74	1300.0	260.0	850.0	113.3	859.0	304.6
1575–99	2000.0	400.0	2250.0	300.0	859.0	304.6
1600–24	3800.0	760.0	3550.0	473.3		
1625–49	5400.0	1080.0	5050.0	673.3		
1650–74	7800.0	1560.0	6250.0	833.3		
1675–1724	9700.0	1940.0	9350.0	1246.7		

Source: Cooper, 'Patterns of inheritance', pp. 307–11. PBH index figures represent the average composite price index for each 25-year period, taken from Phelps Brown and Hopkins, *A Perspective of Wages and Prices*, pp. 48–52
[a] Where mean dowry/94.6 x 100
[b] Where indexed dowry/PBH index x 100

range of dowries encountered, and the way in which the size of dowries was affected so markedly by the social, economic and demographic circumstances of testators. Future research could employ an even larger sample of wills to delineate more carefully the parameters of this dowry inflation. The reality behind it, however, of a five-fold increase across the period, seems to be incontestable.

Figure 8 Indexed portions, Kentish dowries compared to those of peerage, where 1475–1500 = 100

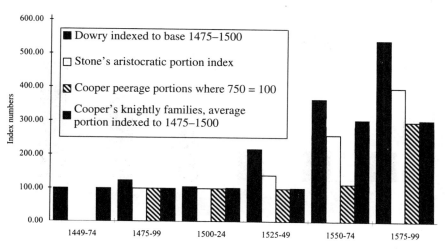

Discussing the inflation of marriage portions among the upper ranks, Outhwaite was convinced of the need for future research into the marriage settlements of lesser folk, professing the 'need to know how far down the social scale such tendencies were revealed'.[99] Although no recent study has really looked at dowry inflation among the humble before 1550, Howell's analysis of the movement in the value of cash legacies at Kibworth compared with that of prices in Leicestershire, suggests that there was also inflation in that parish. She showed a steady rise in the value of cash portions from the 48 per cent of cash-only legacies in 1551–1600 usually worth less than £5 each, to the 52 per cent in 1681–1700 worth about £20 each.[100] Erickson, on the other hand, claimed that such inflation was 'irrelevant to ordinary women', although important to the upper ranks of early modern England. According to her, 'There is no observable rise over time either in parental bequests to unmarried daughters, or in probate accounts with a settlement for payment to the wife in widowhood. Complaints from the well-to-do about the rising costs of their daughters' portions were never echoed at an ordinary level.' For ordinary brides, she asserted, the inflation of portions in the late sixteenth to early eighteenth centuries as experienced foremost by the aristocracy, and to a lesser extent by the gentry, 'would have been simply impossible', given the level of wages.[101] Her remarks may be more applicable to the seventeenth than to the sixteenth century. As the Kent evidence shows, the increase in portions among the will-making population was a clearly discernible phenomenon. The inflation of marriage portions, then, was not restricted solely to the nation's elite.

Figure 9 Dowry indexed to base 1449–74 and PBH

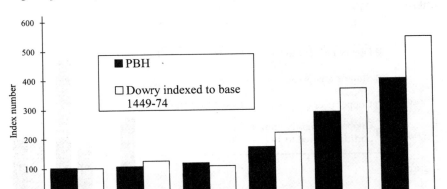

Table 14 and Figure 8 compare the indexed portions of Kentish dowries as shown in the wills, to those of the peerage presented by J. P. Cooper.[102] Figure 8 illustrates the differing *rates* of growth of average dowries by using index numbers. For the actual *values* of the dowries readers should consult Table 14.

The figures for the average marriage portions among the peerage indicate an upward trend, as in Kent, although the rate of increase seems in fact to be *slower* among the peerage in the sixteenth century. Between 1475 and 1549, the average size of portions proposed by peers of the realm was £750, increasing to £850 in 1550–74 and, in the period of greatest inflation in the last quarter of the sixteenth century, reaching £2250. This suggests that the peerage portion inflation multiplied by a factor of three over the whole period; although for peers below the rank of earl, the rise in portions appears to have been rather more rapid. Taking Stone's figures for the aristocracy, portion inflation showed a four-fold increase between 1475 and 1599 to match the inflation of prices. Lower down the social scale, among Cooper's knightly families, portions averaged £282 in 1451–1500. They displayed only minimal inflation over the next 50 years, but then jumped three-fold to £859 in 1551–1600.

Whichever figures are used for comparison, they clearly show the enormous differences between the size of portions at the upper reaches of society and among the majority of ordinary folk. This emphasises the virtual impossibility of couples crossing such financial divides. In the late fifteenth century, for example, there was clearly a huge and unbridgeable gulf between the average dowry offered by knightly families of £282, and the £5 given with humble Kentish brides. The same sort of portion inflation can be seen to have occurred among villagers as among the aristocracy in the sixteenth century. Indeed, it

Figure 10 Average dowry provision for non-daughters

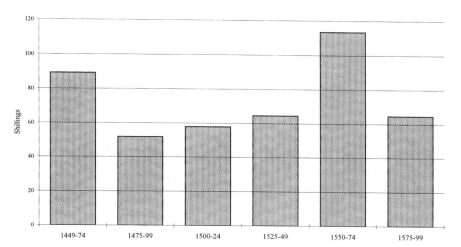

was apparently more rapid. In the sixteenth century, aristocratic bridal inflation did no more than keep pace with price inflation according to Stone, and would it seems have fallen behind, if Cooper's less inflationary figures are correct. The fact that cash dowries underwent considerable inflation in the last quarter of the sixteenth century is not surprising given the sharp price rises of that period. It only remains therefore to measure the extent to which, if at all, there was a *real* increase in dowry inflation in Kent during our period.

Figure 9 and Table 14 show that, if anything, dowries in the five parishes seem to have increased in *real* terms from the mid-sixteenth century by about 30 per cent, essentially outstripping the four-fold increase in the price of a basket full of consumables between 1450 and 1600, with a comparative factor of five.[103] At the same time, while the average cash portions for daughters increased in nominal and real terms, there was no identifiable inflationary trend in the average value of dowry provision for non-daughters over time in money terms, but a dramatic decline in their value in real terms. Perhaps a larger study is needed though, one capable of making finer distinctions between the dowry values and various types of relationship involved, before this decline in real dowries for non-daughters can be understood fully (Figure 10).

The inflation of dowries in the sixteenth century in these Kent parishes may presumably serve as some sort of surrogate index of the income of rural testators. This would assume that there was a constant relationship between income and the size of marriage portions. According to Macfarlane, at the husbandman level, dowry sums were probably equal to one or two years' annual income, and equivalent to three years' income among the middling strata of prosperous yeomen and traders.[104] Along with the rise in the price of consumables, the value of land was also increasing throughout the sixteenth century. Between 1510 and 1600, Wealden land prices increased 4.3 times, nearly tracking that of food prices.[105] Given that money wages did not keep pace with prices,[106] and that dowry inflation apparently exceeded any wage inflation, this must imply that those who relied solely on wages as income in the sixteenth century found themselves increasingly disadvantaged in the provision of dowries. Polarisation in wealth and status extended into the marriage market too.

The dowry sample used in this analysis is by no means a perfect one. It does not concern a controlled group of people comprising the same number of yeomen, husbandmen, craftsmen or any other occupational-status category in all the years surveyed. Hence, we do not yet know whether the inflation of portions was driven by a particular social strata. However, if it is possible to assume that dowry inflation applied to all social levels represented in wills, this may arguably have some bearing on the level of nuptiality. With the inflation of portions the threshold cost of setting up a household would surely have also risen. Some fathers might have required more time to amass sufficient marketable portions for their daughters' marriages. For those saving part of their earnings for marriage, the process of accumulation would likewise have taken a longer time. Ann Kussmaul estimated the possible pooled savings of servants, based on average wages recorded at hiring sessions in Spalding, 1767–85. She showed quite clearly that women earned far less than men and that adult wages were not given till the late teens or early twenties. Although 'it is conceivable that a male and female servant could have pooled their savings and stocked a small farm on their combined savings alone, if they both served at least ten years' the viability of such an enterprise is questionable.[107] With an average annual female wage of just over £2 (in a period when wages would have been far higher than in the sixteenth century) and assuming that at least a third of the earnings were not saved, it would have taken a girl serving in husbandry several years indeed to accumulate the kind of market dowries required in the sixteenth century. This would have been so given that the average portions among the will-making population of Kent in 1575–99 was about £25 (see Table 14). For single women in London in the seventeenth century annual earnings were seldom in excess of £3,[108] and Erickson has suggested that women engaged in husbandry or household service usually received between £1 and £2 per annum in the early modern period.[109] Earnings in service may have provided the opportunity for young girls to finance their own marriage. However, without other means of inherited or transferred wealth from parents, and without other sources of dowry provision from relatives, friends and benefactors, any prospect of entering into marriage would have been certainly delayed or even undermined.[110]

The ability to enter into the married state depended *not* just on the time needed to accumulate sufficient wealth through independent earnings. It also depended upon the critical and expected provision of dowries. The vast literature on the determinants of age of marriage rarely make direct reference to such provision. Instead it is usually assumed that the current or past state of real wages was more important than inherited wealth or ante-mortem property transfer in governing the level of nuptiality in a population.[111] There is little evidence that the dowry of most servants was derived solely from their savings of wages. Although a proportion of servants would have been orphans, without a surviving father to continue to provide for them, the evidence of wills clearly shows that orphanage did not necessarily mean the absence of dowry provision. For those whose parents were still alive at the time of their marriage, entitlement to some provision would have been a universal expectation. Even the poorest members of the population would have considered the provision of a dowry an important part of the making of marriage.

While dowries may have been of somewhat less significance among the very poor sectors of society, the social structure of a typical village would suggest that this strata rarely formed a majority of the population.[112] For most of the ordinary population, even for labourers for whom portions were small, for husbandmen and certainly for yeomen, for the middling sort and for those in the higher social levels, the institutional and economic importance of the dowry was crucial. Although marriage choices inevitably included love and personal preferences among their criteria, historians who have written about those choices have so far, it seems, taken insufficient account of perhaps *the* foremost factor in contemporary marriage mentality, where decisions were constrained by material considerations and expectations.

Until now, this chapter has relied on examining wills to illustrate the extensive provision of dowries at all social levels represented by testators. In providing comparative analysis of five Kent parishes, it has been shown that there were differences in the average size of dowries between the localities. The analysis of wills has also demonstrated the inflation of dowries over time, with implications for the state of the marriage market, and the ease or lack of it, with which couples could embark on marriage. This chapter has used a large number of wills made by ordinary people from the mid-fifteenth century, with some attempt at regional comparisons and long-term overview. It has thus sought so far to rectify the overemphasis on the marriage bargains of the upper classes, the statistical imprecision of single community analysis, and the hitherto neglect of an important subject and source for its study in the sixteenth century.

In what remains of this chapter, the evidence provided once again by the church court depositions will be further examined to illustrate the negotiation of dowries in courtship, and the general significance of material matters in the making of marriage. The wills after all may be regarded in part as retrospective statements, or practical outcomes of transactions and negotiations at the time of courtship, referring as they sometimes do to previous financial agreements.[113]

If little has hitherto been known about dowry levels and trends among the *ordinary* classes of early modern England, still less is known about the actual process of negotiating marriage settlements. It is generally agreed that contemporaries were concerned to establish a financial basis for marriage. Pecuniary matters were considered important in assessing the eligibility of prospective partners, particularly for the upper classes, and to some extent for the courtships of those lower down the social scale. Contemporary literature too, illustrates the practical fiscal issues embedded in courtship and marriage, both reflecting and probing the marriage bargains which might be made.[114] Of the middle classes, Peter Earle has pointed out that 'whatever one may say about the relative significance of love and money in choice of partners, there is absolutely no doubt that money played a very important, if not predominant, part in the process'.[115] Even where the amount endowed was not great, it was, says Erickson, 'as important to the idea of marriage at middling social levels as it was among wealthy families'.[116]

Historians have thus recognised the real and ideological significance of money in marriage and the pervasiveness of marriage settlements at various social levels. However, not enough attention has yet been paid to those *ordinary* folk who comprised the vast majority of the population, and to the process of marriage bargaining among them. There is certainly much that escapes recovery, but although it may be impossible to quantify those pre-marital contracts, be they verbally agreed with a handshake, or concluded in writing,[117] perhaps the closest we can hope to get to their recovery is through an examination of the church court depositions. They provide glimpses of some of the kinds of financial negotiations undertaken, and the motivations, economic pressures and considerations at work during courtship.

Martin Ingram has made it clear that 'property' suits in marriage were commonly heard in the Wiltshire courts at least in the late sixteenth century, demonstrating the prime association between property and marriage.[118] Financial contributions from *both* sides needed to be settled, for settlement depended not just on the bride's portion, but also on the provision reciprocated by the groom.[119] Historians have assumed that the marriage settlements made among the lower social levels were much more varied than the business transactions of the upper ranks.[120] By studying the church court depositions, it is possible to look a little more closely at some of that variety. The manner and circumstances in which marriage bargains were conducted, and the significance of both sets of contributions in the economics of marriage may be observed. One deponent made the comment, 'Now the yong folk be come together for love, but the paren*tes* must cast how they shall live."[121] The reality behind the workings of courtship, however, was more complex than a simple polarity between youth and love on the one hand, and family, authority and materialism on the other.

The misery and anxieties suffered by clients of the astrologer Richard Napier, reveal that the cardinal cause of conflict between parents and children was over choice of marriage partner. Their complaints and disappointments affirm the force of love and passion, as did those of thwarted lovers in the court cases. Also significant, however, was the value they attached to appropriate 'economic and social qualifications'. According to Michael MacDonald, whatever freedom young people were permitted in their courtships was limited by parental influence and rights of veto. Moreover, 'their choices were also restricted in more subtle ways. They themselves were encouraged to internalise the social values and economic realities parents had traditionally been concerned about.'[122] Indeed, it will be argued here, that in choosing a marriage partner, it was not simply a matter of young people submitting to, or resisting, the obvious external pressures imposed by parents, kin and community. No less important was the imperceptible but very real internalisation of values which imposed a set of conventional, moral, and economic and social prescriptions which limited the range of available choices. Such conditioning ensured that, in the end, the majority of marriages were generally based upon a norm of 'essential parity',[123] and a realistic evaluation of economic sense either with or without love. A reading of the church court depositions will confirm that while contemporaries demon-strated the strength of their feelings, they usually exercised discretion in their scrutiny of prospective partners and in their appraisal of their financial resources. As for the details of marital finance, they were often managed under the auspices of attendant family and kin.

Of all the depositions studied for the period 1542–1600, at least a third sufficiently illustrates the weighting of financial considerations in the making of marriages. Either material expectations in the form of dowry or jointure were specified, or promises of marriage were made conditional upon such assurances. In some cases, statements were made which directly or indirectly relayed the cost of living and the setting up of a household. Others exposed the attitudes and frustrations of couples and their kin regarding economic suitability. The very language of bargaining, the consciousness of material worth, and the expressed tenet of social and economic parity are evident. Even, as we shall see, in those individual, anti-materialistic statements, the very self-professed negation of economic motive uses property as a yardstick by which to measure love. The wealth of this evidence alone emphasises the importance and pervasiveness of money matters. Despite the very real existence of love in courtship, it is suggested that, even among ordinary folk, a partner's financial and social standing may have been the most crucial and pivotal consideration in the final choice of marriage partner. It was the one to which all other considerations of love and physical attraction were ultimately subordinated.

It is striking that the matrimony cases rarely mention an individual's *personal* attributes. Although the law sought to establish whether or not the mutual exchange of consent had been given by couples in each case, legal strictures may not have rated individual attributes very highly. Contrary to our modern-day preoccupation with appearance and personality, the rhetoric in the depositions does not abound with romanticised stereotypes. It implies instead, a society whose own ideals depended principally upon more mundane and practical criteria. In some instances where choice of partner was apparently made on account of certain desirable qualities, the qualities which were specified may be regarded as less than individualistic. They were associated rather with conventional requirements underlying concepts of parity and sufficiency, and the concern with family and reputation. Suitability in age and experience appears, as we have seen, to have informed the widow Joan Whiter's choice. William Rolfe, in return, found her to be 'a naturall lyving woman'.[124] A particular 'fancy', when expressed at all, was not necessarily couched in romantic terms. Christine Marshe, also a widow, was reported to have said that she was willing to marry George Gaunt, 'that he was the man that she could be content best to fansy syns her husband dyed/ for that alwaies he did most cherist and make of her child syns her husband departed'.[125] Although contemporary advice literature might promote a range of favourable qualities which included, among wealth and family, considerations of personal virtues, looks, religious persuasion and intellect,[126] the range of qualities commended by deponents themselves was limited, but largely consistent. Elizabeth Godfrey was one deponent who praised John Smith for his intelligence, but although she esteemed it highly, it was still not her sole criterion. She was heard to say that she would 'marry him as one that she loved best above all men for his lernyng witt *and* [my emphasis] honesty; and that she and all she had shuld be at his comm*ande*ment'.[127] In a separate case, the honesty of one William Synger was also advocated, but interpreted as a measure of his economic self-sufficiency and his ability to procure a living.[128]

The association between an individual's honesty and economic verity is, in the context of this argument, hardly surprising. Personal attributes, when mentioned, may be less straightforward than they appear, for they themselves were not value-free. They need to be understood in relation to social attitudes and the expectations of material well-being in an economically hostile environment. Like the implicit equation between personal honesty and economic reliability, the virtue of 'gentleness' too may not have been without derivative connotations of upbringing, background and status. Even the concept and experience of love was not without social reference, for any qualities which might appear to provide economic security could be framed in terms of the language of love. Courting couples might be disposed to love for precisely those qualities which were considered conventionally desirable and sound. Occasionally certain parties themselves were said to have disregarded suitors who were evidently 'pretty' or 'merry', waiting instead upon further family opinion and approval. George Chapman, upon executing a citation, asked Alice Kenwood 'why she had cast of the yong man, saying he was a prety young man. And she therapon said that she could fynd in her hart to love hym as well as ever she did/ but it was her frends doing.'[129] Although in this case she may inwardly have mourned the loss of her 'prety' suitor, the choice of sobriety and safety may have been the guarded, long-term option for all who were nevertheless vulnerable to other personal charms. Marion Wright, being asked whether she loved Henry Davye or John Davye best, allegedly chose the latter at that time, replying, 'Henry Davye is a wilde boye I will none of hime'.[130] Indeed, excess merriment was probably associated more with illicit liaisons than with approvable courtships. Unsurprisingly, therefore, it is cases of defamation which leave more record of deponents who were said to have spoken of physical, personal features as opposed to considered, socially desirable ones. Joan Robynson, for example, reported that one Bigges wife of Sturry had said to her maid while lying in bed, 'I woulde William the myllars servante were here with me for he is a lighte fellowe a cleane legged fellowe and a swete brethed fellowe, and would make us to laughe'.[131] In matrimony cases, where such individual characteristics were rarely commented upon, an implied tension which existed between personal inclination and more prudential foresight was likely to be expressed in emotional outbursts, and within an evidently self-conscious and exaggerated anti-materialist context.

Contravening the conventional requirements of parity and material welfare, some deponents declared their praise of steadfast love even though their chosen partners should possess nothing. The widow Joanne Symnyng was supposed to have promised Edmond Stedall, 'Now my love is set, yf thow wert not worth a peny I wold be torne *with* wild horses rather than I will forsake the.'[132] In the case between Margaret Smith, a servant in Dover, and Robert Richardson, a ship-owner who was thought to be wealthy and worth far more than her, the circumstance of an unequal match may have prompted an overtly generous statement from him. When cautioned to speak carefully, he maintained that he was well aware of his words, saying 'I meane to make her a woman for I have enowgh for her and me, for I had maryed one afore that has a little as she, and god hath blessed me'. Nevertheless, the match was regarded in hindsight as 'a drunken bargayn'.[133] A few deponents seemed to claim that matters of dowry and goods were not an issue. Alice Berry reported that Serafyn Marketman had promised to make her a jointure of £60 if she betrothed herself to him, 'though as he said she was not worth a grote to him'.[134] Joseph Pelham affirmed that he would welcome and receive the widow Christine Warrey if she came to him in bare attire, 'for it is not thy goods but for the that I looke for', said he, yet a matter of £14 divided them.[135] As for the marriage proposed between the servants Edmund Franckling and Amy Turner, of whom there were rumours of incontinency, Franckling vouched that 'it was not for her goods that he would marry her for he had borne her goodwill a great while'. However he expected her friends to 'give her somewhat', even 'make her worth £20'.[136]

In some cases, young couples evidently entered into, and defended, privy contracts despite the apparent displeasure incurred by friends who sought to promote alternative, richer partnerships. The 18-year-old Thomas Cockes, a scholar at the free school in Canterbury, may well have disregarded his family's wishes by matching himself with the daughter of a shoemaker. They 'looked that he the said Cockes should be matched with a better, rytcher and more substantiall mans daughter'.[137] Anti-materialist sentiments might also be expressed in circumstances where individuals were more concerned about other obstacles to their happiness. Jane Mussered, for one, subordinated financial cares to the greater issue of freedom from other contracts. Provided Laurance Claringboll could prove there was no other marriage matter, she said that then 'I will have you, if I goo a begging with you'.[138] In the case of *Filpott* v. *Baull alias Cruttall*, William Filpot sought to demonstrate his disinclination to marry *despite* possible financial advantage. He denied any promise made between him and Barbara Baull. While it was commonly reported that she was 'of more habilyty and worth', he was heard to swear, 'I do not know whether my wif be borne or no, nor I wold have Barbara Baull though she had a thousand thousand pound'.[139] Upon hearing his declaration, Jasper Whitredge immediately went away and noted it in a paper, impressed perhaps by the extremity of the statement.

Such expressions of anti-materialistic sentiment as those cited above might seem to suggest that the motivation for marriage was by no means grounded on considerations of financial security and parity, yet such statements were relatively few in number, and themselves ambiguous. Although economic concerns were clearly not always the *sole* issue, the provision of an adequate dowry and jointure was essential to the marriage plans of most couples. Partners, their families and friends, sought to protect their long-term interests and made practical plans for their future. Even when they made declarations to the contrary, by using monetary considerations in a negative way to gauge their professed love, they demonstrated in so doing, that genuine and paramount consciousness of money which dominated contemporary attitudes.

Far more common in the deposition cases is that bulk of evidence which illustrates directly the fundamental concern over the economics of marriage. Such concern is expressed in a language which is itself one of bargaining, transaction and negotiation, and which reveals the general awareness of each individual's financial standing and prospects. James Philpot declared to Elizabeth Savye's parents 'that he was com to make a bargine for mariage',[140] and Joanne Symnyng referred to her marriage promise as an agreement 'upon a bargayn'.[141] Assessing the 'worth' and 'ability' of parties, whether or not one was generally deemed 'in substance, honesty and good condicions worthy and sufficient to marry',[142] was crucial. It was reported that Mary Galle stayed the asking of the banns in Whitstable because her mother wouldn't consent to her marrying Richard Savor who 'was not of wealthe'.[143] As for Anne Philpott, she cried bitterly when she discovered the state of her lover's indebtedness.[144] For some, the realisation of inadequate financial resources would have frustrated romantic hopes, or caused the breakdown of further negotiation. In the case of *Divers* v. *Williams*, Elizabeth's mother Agnes also apparently stayed the banns upon hearing that her daughter's suitor 'was nothing worth', 'for sayd mother Williams yt was said he was worth £40 but now it is sayd he can scarce keepe and maynteyne himselfe'.[145] Common report judged there to be 'greate odds and difference between John Spayne's wealth and Judith Symons' wealth'. While she may have been 'reputed a very poor maid and of no ability' in that particular match, her master had been firmly opposed to her earlier affair with Thomas Kennet, on the grounds 'that he could not away with such beggerly maryadges'.[146] Yet it was not just masters and family who rejected 'beggerly marriages'. Couples themselves weighed up each other's possibilities, and were intrinsically involved in the economic practicalities of maintenance and sufficient living. The prospects of each partner were at issue, as was the expectation of some financial return. Percival Denbye was alleged to have said that he was content to marry Agnes Jhonson of Thanington, 'if her frends would gyve anythinge with her'.[147] Although the actual amount required was not specified in this case, the deposition evidence makes it clear that the question of 'how much' was vital to proceedings. For Moses Balden, it seems that ultimate choice depended upon adequate and best provision. Joanne Brokwell claimed that she was willing to marry him, but a week later he told her that 'except her father wold geve with her as largely as he Balden may have in an other place, he wold not have her', and thereupon they broke off.[148]

As well as relying on their inheritance and marriage gifts, young couples embarking on marriage were advised to accumulate sufficient means for setting up a household. According to William Gibbes of Sturry, when Richard Bonnam requested his goodwill to marry with his covenant servant Prudence Bramelo, he, Gibbes, 'advised hym for that he was but poore and litill worthe that he wold tarry so long tyme and gather somewhat togither in the meane time wherewith they might then better stay themselfs and be able to lyve when they shuld marry'.[149] Courting couples were all too acutely conscious of the veracity of such counsel. John Beeching admitted the realistic need to acquire the appropriate 'wherewithall to maynteyn a wif' before making any promises of marriage. He confessed that he had told Alice Pynnocke several times that 'yf god would prosper him with any lyvinge wherbye he might be able to keepe her, he could fynde in his harte to bestow himself upon her'.[150] Partners were aware, too, of the cost of living, not just the intitial outlay incurred in forming a household, but the permanent drain on resources, as they complained of financial responsibility. After two years, John Yonge continued to deliberate in his suit for marriage despite having obtained parental goodwill. Finally, in making further material demands, he complained to Joane Marshe, 'what I shall doe to marrye you saythe he with 10[li] what is that to kepe a woman withall all her tyme, and therupon she byd him to make no further accompt of her and lykwyse he byd her does as she lyst or wold'.[151]

Even given the relatively modest amount, the matter of financial provision remained important. For those in the lower reaches of society, the pooling of resources might represent the bare minimum necessary for household sub- sistence. At more respectable social levels, it was also a question of main- taining one's social status. In her letter to William Alcock, Jane Hardres, 'gentlewoman', wrote that she would 'dissolve her love' because she could not procure her father's goodwill, 'neyther was his ability sufficient to maynteyne her'. She claimed that she could not live and keep house under the expenses of £300 per annum, and that what he promised her 'wouldn't be sufficient for their maintenance'.[152]

The combination of economic necessity and social position was the concern of the parties themselves, their family and kin, and that of the general community. The making of a financial settlement was also a universal expectation. The widow Christine Burret said that *'for the speche of the world* she wold loke to be assured first of a ioyntur of foure nobles by the yere, in consideration that he [Mark Austen] shuld have a good substaunce by her'.[153] As settlement was also a collective priority, so the failure to negotiate it might be regarded as a matter of some shame which could 'make the cuntry to talk'.[154] It was vital too that there should be no great disparity in the match. Girls contemplating marriage sought to secure for themselves jointures which were worthy of their dowries.[155] More generally, great importance was placed upon the pairing of like with like. Assessing the match between Mary Oldfield and Thomas Colly, two deponents gave the following opinions. One said that 'he thinketh there is noe disparidgment between the parties for the fathers of both are accounted honest yomenlyke men'. The other likewise said, 'he thinks no great disparidgment ... for fathers of both are accounted honest men and such as their children may match together without disparidgment yf please them'.[156]

Such comments as those recorded in the preceding paragraphs serve to illustrate the conscious evaluation of each partner's economic and social position and material credibility within marriage. They suggest that a large part of the rationale behind particular marriage choices did rest upon pecuniary matters. Looking further at the deposition evidence, the process of matrimonial negotiation and bargaining may be considered somewhat more closely. A little more may be said about the familial situation of the parties involved in the court cases, about the complex business of negotiation, those who took part, the settlements which were expected from both sides, and the role of family and friends in conducting the affairs and contributing to the marriage.

About a quarter of the sample involved widows, at times also widowers or those described as elderly. While negotiations could, it seems, be conducted by the widow alone, widows were not independent of other people's influence or advice. In Elizabeth Chamber's case, her father was evidently instrumental in procuring a jointure of Mathew Rayner's lands and possessions worth 20s per annum in lands, £100 in moveable goods, and a lease of his farm of Boughton court. He promised that in return Mathew would 'have a good substance of her'. Cyriak Petit described him as a 'beneficiall father in her preferment', who had once again done for her what he regarded to be 'a sufficient advancement with the honesty of the person'.[157] Where fathers were less prominent, other relatives could remain conspicuous when it came to details of the marriage 'bargayne'. Promising to redeem the widow Joan Whiter's lands with his own goods, William Rolf agreed to 'lett her and her counsaile make it and deyvysse it as well as they could', referring to her counsel of friends and cousins.[158] Further deliberations in this case likewise involved cousins, brothers and other of the widow's kin.[159]

Widows might have been generally more experienced and financially advantaged than women entering marriage for the first time, but considered within the framework of a predominantly patriarchal and male-oriented society, their independence and effectiveness as bargainers should not be overestimated. It is quite possible that most widows felt insecure in the process of negotiation, aware of their educational shortcomings compared to their prospective partners, and the latter's surely heavier participation in economic and legal activity. Where men were involved in conducting property negotiations, the very fact of their involvement could have ensured a more advantageous settlement.

If widows were indeed by no means exceptionally independent when it came to such negotiations, what was, however, special about their circumstances and settlements was the often crucial issue of children surviving from previous marriages. Returning to William Rolf's agreement to fetch in the widow's lands with a payment of £21, he promised furthermore that her children should come to the lands at 21 years of age. Another widow, Thomasine Adams, made her promise of marriage to John Holbein conditional upon him making her a jointure of all his father's lands, and giving to

her children £6 13s 4d 'at such convenient time as she require'.[160] One
Margaret Smith told Nicholas Nicholls 'that she'd marry with none but such a
one as wolde be bounde with sufficient suerties with him to pay her childrens
portion'.[161] It was not uncommon for widows to reject their suitors for their
failure to safeguard their children's interests, or make payments over and
above the legacies due to them. Most were concerned with the protection of
their own children, but some also sought assurances for their kin. Besides
requesting a jointure from Mark Austen, Christine Burret intended to see her
granddaughter 'a little wenche also bestowed in marriage', saying that
'bicause she was an old woman ~~and shulde be riche unto hym~~ she wold loke to
have a ioynter acording to his promise and the money to be delivered by Marke
which her daughter's daughter should have at her marriage'.[162] In certain
cases the intention to acquire the maximum financial benefit may have been a
necessary precaution for widows calculating their self-interest and those of
their children. Elizabeth Overie, the widow of Simon Overie of Littlebourne,
contemplated marriage with one John Terry. She asked an elderly fellow
parishioner to speak to John's father, in order to get the best possible settlement 'for her and her children viz. £80 for her children, and as much as
possible for her', her own friends requiring a bond of £100 for her.[163]
Nevertheless, even relatively modest sums demanded for the widow's children
could present a real stumbling-block in negotiations, and hinder the making
of an amicable settlement. With the aged couple Joseph Pellam and Christine
Warrey, the so-called trifling matter of him entering into a bond to pay her
children £14 provoked disagreement and delay, so much so that others began
to feel ashamed.[164]

Although a sizeable proportion of the deposition cases demonstrate the
importance of property negotiations in remarriages and the special nature of
their settlements, the majority of cases dealt with people entering marriage for
the first time. Some of them were clearly in their late teens. Either partner
might have one or both parents still alive, living probably under familial or
kin-based auspices, within home or service. Presumably therefore they were
somewhat more dependent upon the expressed consent and pleasure of their
parents, 'friends' and masters, than those fully orphaned by circumstances.
Since the involvement of both sets of parents of both parties is rarely
mentioned in the cases, it is likely that at least one parent out of the four was
already deceased. This would accord with the demographic finding that in the
early modern period, a third of all children were at least partially orphaned
before reaching the age of 21.[165] In a few cases, the parties were said to be the
children of yeomen stock,[166] very occasionally of 'gentle status',[167] but most
commonly they were the ordinary folk in husbandry and in domestic service.

While some parents denied any interference in their children's marriage
plans, where matters of property and finance were concerned, surviving

parents were in fact principally involved in the marriage negotiations. An all-male agreement was made between the party John Spyrer of Lyminge, his yeoman father, and Bartholomew Watts of Folkestone, father to Alice. It was settled that Watts should give with his daughter £40 worth, if Spyrer and his son would be bound to leave her so much land during her life worth £80, or alternatively £4 worth of land by the year.[168] Negotiations in another case involving Katherine Jhonson's stepfather and Robert Jacobb's father resulted in a dowry worth £30 in money matched by a jointure provided by old Jacobb and his son.[169] At times, the suitor alone apparently assumed responsibility for conducting negotiations. Helen Cocke, for example, reported how Edward Laurence required from her father £30 or £40 in marriage with her, but because her father couldn't pay that sum, he no longer persisted in his suit.[170] Mothers too participated in the marriage bargaining, especially as the sole surviving parent. According to Pleasance Redwood's deposition, her mother did indeed grant her goodwill to Robert Sloden, but only on condition that he find sufficient surety to leave Pleasance in her widowhood 'double so much as her mother should give with her'.[171] Erickson has emphasised the role of widowed mothers, of mothers generally, and even of daughters themselves in negotiating settlements.[172] The Kent depositions, however, would seem to suggest the continued and perhaps greater importance of the male figure, that of the father, the possible role of the stepfather, brother,[173] master,[174] and of friends, cousins and kin, in meeting together to agree upon the goods to be given in marriage.[175]

The depositions reveal that contentment to marry was often couched in terms of a successful financial conclusion being reached. They make it evident that property bargains were not just an important part of marriage proceedings, but frequently a specified condition in promises of marriage. Such communications provoked conflict, resentment, 'brablyng' and 'controversi' among the participants, and the failure to perform financial agreements could result in the breakdown of negotiations, as partners broke off even at the point of a fixed wedding day. Elizabeth Overie, for example, claimed that a day had been appointed for the wedding, but that it took no effect because the conditions were not performed.[176] What is also apparent is that the making of settlements involved the thorough viewing of all property, whether land, houses, household stuff or cattle. In the case where Juliane Barnes, her stepfather, master and dame went to Steven Bridgeman's house, she 'with her frends did peruse his house, lands, cattall and goods', about a week before financial agreements were reached and promises of marriage exchanged.[177] Often, the settlements required written agreements, bonds and sufficient sureties.[178] In the marriage between Robert Lawe and Alice Harris, Richard Maicot of Faversham was sent for to draw up a writing wherein Alice would give Robert all the goods she had or might have. Upon the writing being made, she put her seal to it, subscribed her mark, and delivered it together with a groat 'in token of possession of her goods' as her act and deed to Robert Lawe.[179]

The deposition evidence illustrates clearly the expectation and necessity for endowment to come from *both* sides. The question of a girl's marriage portion and the amount she would be worth, was matched with the question of jointure, sometimes described as a 'joynter or dowrye', provided in the event of her widowhood. Richard Tusten, for example, was said to have offered Godline Allen a 'joynter or dowrye of XX[tie] nobles a yere' during her lifetime.[180] Unfortunately the evidence of individual cases does not usually allow for the relative values of the contributions or 'worth' to be compared, as they tend to provide either only the value of the girl's portion, or the value of the jointure, but not both. Where the combined information does exist, the cases considered might arise precisely because of the 'greate odds and difference' between their wealth.[181] Although the actual financial contribution is sometimes specified, more generally, the 'worth' of particular parties is given a monetary assessment. Furthermore, the alternative forms of a lump sum, and a value in the form of an annuity which was common for jointures, make comparisons problematic.

Where lump sums for dowry were specified the amount negotiated among the church court litigants and their 'friends' usually ranged between £10 and £40, entirely compatible with the average size of dowries revealed in wills from this period.[182] However, the assessment of moveables *combined* with land in certain cases, contributions from outside the nuclear family, and the inclusion of a few more prosperous, higher-status families, meant that some prospective brides were inevitably worth more. While at the husbandman level, a girl might be worth £20 in marriage,[183] the daughter of an 'honest yomenlyke man' in the mid- to late sixteenth century might be given £40 to her marriage,[184] and a gentlewoman a dowry worth several hundred pounds.[185] Brides-to-be were frequently promised an assured annuity as jointure; £1–£5 per annum was common, but amounts varied, and annuities were at times combined with a lump sum in moveable goods. The detailed case of *Hannyng* v. *Knowler* (1577) illustrates the possible complexities. The comparative worth of the parties, and the size of the promised jointure and dowry, were evidently a matter of some dispute. Hannyng was said to have promised her a jointure of all his lands, assuring her £6, £7, £8 or £9 per annum out of his lands plus, at the insistence of her grandfather, £40 in moveables. Godlina Knowler could expect to receive a portion worth about £80, and £6 per annum in lands. According to one estimate, she was in fact worth £120 in money and moveables and £8 a year in lands.[186] The will of her grandmother, Alice Oven of Chislet (will 19 June 1573), made it clear that Godlina would inherit her great cauldron, the cupboard, the table and a half share of her remaining moveables at 18 years old, as well as money invested for her, and her grand-mother's dwelling-place.[187]

In their evaluations, the parties involved were careful to calculate future prospects and income upon the death of parents and kin, but as well as anticipating their inheritance, they were also aware of the possible limitations. It was said that John Spayne, as the only son of Simon, was worth £30 in lands, and £200 in money and stock at the time of the marriage allegation, but that after the death of his father and grandmother, his lands would be worth £66 13s 4d by the year.[188] Compared to Katherine Wyborn, worth £140 or £160 in goods and land, Mark Giles was accounted 'a husbandman, serves his father, and is little worth as long as his father lives'.[189] Negotiations made by the deponents reveal too that just as jointures might come in the form of a lump sum or an annuity incorporating house, lands and moveable goods, the dowries might also include landed possessions and moveables. However, as established earlier in this chapter, cash values were most common. Some prospective grooms evidently demanded other forms of provision or assistance, such as a marriage dinner,[190] or a rented house to dwell in for a time,[191] and further contributions from masters and 'friends' were also forthcoming. Suspicious circumstances presumably prompted William Gibbes's liberality to his servants Prudence Bramelo and Richard Bonnam. He promised 20 nobles to her marriage, in addition to timber provisions and a place to live.[192] Other masters assisted couples with accommodation, or agreed to bear part of the wedding dinner charges.[193] Henry Thompson of Lenham promised John Bradley the lease of his farm because, as he said, 'Bradley had been a good and faithful servant ... these 3 years, and in regard of furtherance of marriage'.[194] 'Friends' offered small gifts, in one case two bushels of wheat and a half seam of malt.[195] In another case, a former suitor, James Lambart, gave Agnes Wills 3s 4d to her marriage with Richard Benet, in order to show her that he was contented.[196]

The provision of dowries, then, was very far from being an activity restricted to the more wealthy social groups in early modern England. Having used the biggest ever sample of wills to examine such provision, this chapter has established that even those of relatively low social status – labourers and husbandmen, as well as yeomen and craftsmen – sought to provide portions or dowries to their daughters after their deaths. Assuming that the activities of will-makers reflect the experience of the living population, then it seems legitimate to conclude that few of those marrying in fifteenth- and sixteenth-century Kent would have done so without at least some resources. These would have been mainly cash, but also moveable goods and occasionally immovable property, inherited or transferred from parents or from other members of the extended, real and 'fictive' family. Indeed, for many brides, dowries or portions from the wider family group could have been a valuable supplement to their total dowry. The evidence we have does suggest that the value of dowries provided by relatives may have been declining in real terms over the sixteenth century, perhaps as the extent of dowry inflation forced relatives to concentrate their resources on their immediate family. Nevertheless, kin did not merely give material assistance to those relatives intending marriage, they were also clearly instrumental in influencing marriage decisions and acting as negotiators during courtship.

Marriage prospects must have been bleaker for more couples at the end of our period than at the beginning, given the inflation of dowries that appears to have occurred in the later sixteenth century. As we have seen, the portions specified in Kent wills increased about five-fold, apparently outstripping the general price inflation and the rate of dowry inflation among the aristocratic elite. This suggests strongly that for those partly or wholly dependent on wages, the provision of an adequate dowry would have become increasingly difficult. If we can assume that dowry inflation implies a more competitive marriage market, fewer wage-earners could have competed with the increasing incomes of those earning greater profits from rising food prices after the mid-sixteenth century. In the Kent parishes studied, there appeared to be substantial local variation both in the timing of the increase and in the average size of dowry found. More research is required before the actual parameters of the dowry inflation of the sixteenth century are visible clearly, but the existence of such inflation cannot be doubted. It must have placed further obstacles in the path to the altar for the poorest members of the community in the sixteenth century.

The importance of dowry inflation goes beyond possible demographic consequences. The evidence from depositions emphasises the ways in which the size of dowry reflected contemporary concerns with social position, status and future prospects. The very process of courtship was a matter of financial bargaining, even for what might be regarded as relatively small sums of money, involving estimations of worth, credit[97] and property on both sides. While the range of dowries identified here illustrates the degree of marital endogamy within social groups prevalent in the sixteenth century, the dowry inflation is suggestive, too, of the way in which increases in income might bring newly prosperous social groups within financial reach of those higher in the status hierarchy. There they would have been able to compete with their social betters in the provision of adequate dowries. Dowry inflation, then, might provide an opportunity for upward social mobility for those families who prospered, but enforced 'celibacy' for individuals who did not, in the harsh later years of the sixteenth century.

NOTES

1 Kaplan ed., *The Marriage Bargain*, pp. 1–11. Anthropologists, by contrast, have paid due recognition to the importance of dowry in certain societies, seeing it as a measurement and expression of status, of family relations and conjugal roles, and as a way of regulating co-operation between social groups. See, e.g., J. Goody and S. J. Tambiah, *Bridewealth and Dowry* (Cambridge, 1973); J. Goody, *The Development of the Family and Marriage in Europe* (Cambridge, 1983), pp. 240–61; Mair, *Marriage*, ch. 4, 'The cost of getting married'; A. Barnard and A. Good, *Research Practices in the Study of Kinship: Research Methods in Social Anthropology* (London, 1984, repr. 1987), pp. 114–17; J. K. Campbell, *Honour, Family and Patronage: a Study of Institutions and Moral Values in a Greek Mountain Community* (New York and Oxford, 1964, repr. 1979), pp. 44–6; Davis, *People of the Mediterranean*, pp. 181–2, 188–94.

2 Erickson, *Women and Property*, p. 91; Macfarlane, *Marriage and Love*, pp. 277–8.

3 See also, A. L. Erickson, 'Common law versus common practice: the use of marriage settlements in early modern England', *Economic History Review*, 2nd ser. 43:1 (1990), 21–39.

4 For definitions of jointure, and for a description of the common law governing women's property in marriage, see Erickson, *Women and Property*, pp. 24–8; Erickson, 'Common law versus common practice', pp. 24–5; Macfarlane, *Marriage and Love*, pp. 272–6, 281–5; Houlbrooke, *The English Family*, pp. 83, 209.

5 Erickson, *Women and Property*, p. 81.

6 *Ibid.*, pp. 86–9, 119–28; Erickson, 'Common law versus common practice', pp. 28–31; R. B. Outhwaite, 'Marriage as business: opinions on the rise in aristocratic bridal portions in early modern England', in N. McKendrick and R. B. Outhwaite eds, *Business Life and Public Policy: Essays in Honour of D. C. Coleman* (Cambridge, 1986), pp. 21–37; J. P. Cooper, 'Patterns of inheritance and settlement by great landowners from the fifteenth to the eighteenth centuries', in Goody, Thirsk and Thompson eds, *Family and Inheritance*, pp. 192–327; Macfarlane, *Marriage and Love*, pp. 264, 281.

7 Stone, *The Crisis of the Aristocracy*, pp. 290–3; Outhwaite, 'Marriage as business', p. 25.

8 Cooper, 'Patterns of inheritance', pp. 221, 307, 310; Stone, *The Crisis of the Aristocracy*, p. 290; Outhwaite, 'Marriage as business', pp. 23–5, 29; Erickson, 'Common law versus common practice', pp. 30–1; Erickson, *Women and Property*, pp. 120–2.

9 Macfarlane, *Marriage and Love*, p. 264. Cf. Stone, *The Crisis of the Aristocracy*, p. 291, who suggests that by the early seventeenth century few fathers would have given portions worth less than one year's income. Some examples of aristocratic portions are also cited in Erickson, *Women and Property*, p. 86; L. Stone, *Road to Divorce: England, 1530–1987* (Oxford, 1990), p. 309, for the portion of £10,000 brought by Anne Pierrepont in 1658 to John Lord Roos; Cooper, 'Patterns of inheritance', pp. 306–27.

10 Outhwaite, 'Marriage as business', p. 23; Stone, *The Crisis of the Aristocracy*, pp. 291–2; Erickson, *Women and Property*, pp. 119–20; Erickson, 'Common law versus common practice', p. 30; Macfarlane, *Marriage and Love*, p. 281.

11 Outhwaite, 'Marriage as business', pp. 26–36; Stone, *The Crisis of the Aristocracy*, pp. 292–3; Erickson, *Women and Property*, pp. 121–2.

12 D. O. Hughes, 'From brideprice to dowry in Mediterranean Europe', *Journal of Family History* 3:3 (1978), 262–96 (pp. 288–90).

13 Erickson, *Women and Property*, p. 122.

14 Outhwaite, 'Marriage as business', p. 35; Cooper, 'Patterns of inheritance', pp. 221–2, 311, using evidence compiled from 49 wills and 27 settlements for 1501–1600. For dowry inflation in the early sixteenth century among the noble and knightly class, see also, B. J. Harris, 'A new look at the Reformation: aristocratic women and nunneries', *Journal of British Studies* 32:2 (1993), 89–113 (esp. p. 97). Some indication of the size of gentry portions at the end of the fifteenth and early sixteenth centuries can be found in Oestmann, *Lordship and Community*, pp. 14–15.

15 Erickson, 'Common law versus common practice', pp. 30–1; Erickson, *Women and Property*, pp. 86–9, 120–2. See also Macfarlane, *Marriage and Love*, p. 264.

16 Earle, *Making of the English Middle Class*, pp. 196–7.

17 Erickson, *Women and Property*, pp. 129–51; Erickson, 'Common law versus common practice', pp. 31–6.

18 Erickson, *Women and Property*, pp. 87–8.

19 Macfarlane, *Marriage and Love*, p. 264.

20 Howell, 'Peasant inheritance customs', pp. 149–52.

21 Hughes, 'From brideprice to dowry', p. 281; Howell, 'Peasant inheritance customs', p. 144; Erickson, *Women and Property*, p. 96; Macfarlane, *Marriage and Love*, pp. 263, 265; Goody, *Development of the Family and Marriage*, pp. 243–5. Also, Harris, 'Women and nunneries', pp. 94–5, uses wills to show how often men left money to their daughters with the intention that it should be used as portions to marry.

22 See above, chapter 5, pp. 171–5.

23 PRC 17/25/16.

24 PRC 17/25/47.

25 For a complete list of wills examined in this chapter, see, O'Hara, 'Sixteenth-century courtship', pp. 285–322.

26 Vann, 'Wills and the family', pp. 361–3.

27 Earle, *The Making of the English Middle Class*, pp. 187–8.

28 Erickson, *Women and Property*, p. 94.

29 Stone, *The Crisis of the Aristocracy*, pp. 273–4.

30 Other instances of restrictions can be found in Ingram, *Church Courts*, pp. 140–1; Coppel, 'Will-making on the deathbed', p. 41; J. A. Johnston, 'Family, kin and community in eight Lincolnshire parishes, 1567–1800', *Rural History* 6:2 (1995), 179–92 (pp. 182–3).

31 PRC 17/7/133v.

32 PRC 17/7/62.

33 PRC 17/21/110v.–12.

34 PRC 32/38/208.

35 The exclusion of the P.C.C. wills excludes those few disproportionately large dowries from the social elite, who frequently possessed property in more than one location. This study thus allows for better examination of those social groups below the rich, who were genuinely resident in the parishes chosen.

36 See also Erickson, *Women and Property*, p. 84. Spufford, *Contrasting Communities*, pp. 112, 143, 159, uses the terms 'dowry' and 'dower' interchangeably.

37 For examples, see O'Hara, 'Sixteenth-century courtship', p. 212.

38 Cooper, 'Patterns of inheritance', p. 309.

39 PRC 17/6/177v.

40 See also, Erickson, *Women and Property*, p. 73.

41 PRC 17/26/200.

42 Hughes, 'From brideprice to dowry', pp. 284–5; Erickson, *Women and Property*, pp. 95–6; P. H. Cullum, '"And hir name was Charitie": charitable giving by and for women in late medieval Yorkshire', in P. J. P. Goldberg ed., *Woman is a Worthy Wight: Women in English Society, c. 1200–1500* (Stroud, 1992), pp. 182–211 (see pp. 198–9). See, e.g., W. J. K. Jordan, *The Charities of London, 1480–1660: the Aspirations and the Achievements of the Urban Society* (London, 1960), pp. 184–5.

43 E.g. Macfarlane, *Marriage and Love*, pp. 267–8, 276. Legacies, gifts and financial benefits from masters and fellow servants among the wealthier mercantile class are cited in Ben-Amos, *Adolescence and Youth*, pp. 172–5, 179–80. Also, Harris, 'Women and nunneries', p. 95, found that nearly 10 per cent of her 393 male testators left dowries to other female kin who included sisters, nieces and stepdaughters, but particularly granddaughters.

44 Erickson, *Women and Property*, pp. 85–6, 215–17.

45 In Tenterden, the total number of non-daughters was 83. For Wye, of 27 mentioned, 8 were granddaughters, 5 god-daughters, 6 nieces, 6 servants and the remaining were unspecified kin.

46 PRC 17/39/276–7v. (1566).

47 PRC 17/48/7–8v. (1589).

48 PRC 32/13/97.

49 PRC 17/3/208 (1477).

50 PRC 17/39/225 (1566), Tenterden.

51 PRC 17/16/301 (1525), Tenterden.

52 PRC 17/19/391 (1533).

53 PRC 17/17/188 (1527).

54 PRC 17/17/254 (1527).

55 Howell, 'Peasant inheritance customs', pp. 150–2. The general shift from legacies in kind to legacies in cash is not, however, an obvious one. Fig. 4, p. 150, is not easy to interpret in her work since we do not know what constitutes 'portions in kind', nor do we know the different proportions of kind-cash in the category of mixed legacies to make such comparisons intelligible.

56 Macfarlane, *Marriage and Love*, pp. 265–6. For the embroidery of linen, and the significance of a bride's trousseau of beds, sheets and whitewear in southern Europe, see e.g., Davis, *People of the Mediterranean*, pp. 181–2, and J. Schneider, 'Trousseau as treasure: some contradictions of late nineteenth-century change in Sicily', in Kaplan ed., *The Marriage Bargain*, pp. 81–120. J. Goody, 'Introduction', in Goody, Thirsk and

Thompson eds, *Family and Inheritance*, p. 2, wrote 'that an endowment at marriage is more likely to be of moveables than of land itself'.

57 PRC 17/29/265.

58 PRC 17/8/33 (1499).

59 PRC 17/6/192 (Sturry).

60 Vann, 'Wills and the family', p. 362. See also, Elliott, 'Single women', p. 95; Houlbrooke, *The English Family*, pp. 84–5; Spufford, *Contrasting Communities*, p. 112.

61 Erickson, *Women and Property*, p. 85, used the inventories of six Lincolnshire servants.

62 PRC 10/24/287.

63 PRC 10/14/218.

64 PRC 10/13/319–27.

65 PRC 10/19/239v.–40 (16 Sept. 1591).

66 Erickson, *Women and Property*, p. 81. Two-thirds of 113 will-makers who left cash to immediate kin, preferred female legatees. For a general division of property, see also pp. 61–8, 215–16.

67 PRC 17/9/325–v.

68 For circumstances behind land bequests, see also, Erickson, *Women and Property*, pp. 61–2; Macfarlane, *Marriage and Love*, pp. 265–6.

69 PRC 17/2/66v.–7 (Tenterden).

70 Once again, Sturry is the exception, since few daughters in that parish received anything other than cash. The total number of daughters for which dowry is mentioned in some form or another is as follows: Tenterden 275; Wye 115; Whitstable 65; Chislet 82; Sturry 23. Percentages for each parish do not, of course, amount to 100 per cent if the separate categories are added together, since any daughter could receive more than one type of legacy.

71 PRC 17/35/194–5 (Chislet, 1561).

72 PRC 17/48/417–18 (1592).

73 See also, Erickson, *Women and Property*, pp. 215–16, for a comparison of goods distributed by women and men. She found that women bequeathed clothing more frequently than men.

74 PRC 17/23/38 (1544).

75 E.g., see, PRC 17/29/265–6 (Thomas Pyrkyne, Chislet, 1549); PRC 17/40/349 (1570).

76 E.g. PRC 17/22/29v.–30 (John Cotenar, Chislet, 1539); PRC 17/19/2 (John Hokken, elder, Whitstable, 1529).

77 For Sturry, the numbers are too small for calculating percentages, but an exceptional bequest of 100 sheep and 10 marks was made by Thomas Gylbert of Sturry in 1465 to his daughter Johane at 16 years, PRC 17/1/151v.

78 E.g., see, PRC 17/20/111–v. (Nicholas Geffrey, Tenterden, 1534); PRC 17/20/235–v. (Agnes Broke, widow, Tenterden, 1536); PRC 17/40/195v.–6v. (John Lomas, whitesmith, Tenterden, 1568).

79 E.g., see, PRC 17/16/181–v. (William Ketyng, Tenterden, 1524); PRC 17/37/139–41 (John

Bryckenden, Tenterden, 1563). In Sturry, testators often bequeathed portions in money or its money worth.

80 See, e.g., PRC 17/16/233v.–4v. (John Adam, Wye, 1525).

81 PRC 17/14/216–18; PRC 17/51/295v.–6v.; PRC 17/51/323–4.

82 PRC 17/14/216–18.

83 PRC 17/51/295v.–6v.

84 E.g., see, PRC 17/10/30v.–1v. (Richard Elgor, Wye, 1504); PRC 17/9/28–9 (John Beverley, elder, Wye, 1505); PRC 17/18/87–8 (William Dod, husbandman, Wye, 1523); PRC 17/12/566v.–8 (John Donett, Tenterden, 1517). Macfarlane, *Marriage and Love*, p. 269, claims that ordinarily compared to large aristocratic portions, portions were usually paid very quickly. See also Earle, *Making of the English Middle Class*, pp. 197–8; Houlbrooke, *The English Family*, p. 83, especially in the first half of his period; Stone, *The Crisis of the Aristocracy*, pp. 288–9

85 PRC 17/51/323–4.

86 See above, pp. 193, 199.

87 Howell, 'Peasant inheritance customs', p. 150.

88 O'Hara, 'Sixteenth-century courtship', p. 231, Figs 6.6d–e.

89 Erickson, *Women and Property*, pp. 88–9.

90 Macfarlane, *Marriage and Love*, p. 264.

91 PRC 17/26/43.

92 PRC 17/23/71–3.

93 E.g., see, PRC 17/26/66v.–7v. (William Pyers, 1548); PRC 17/49/35v.–6v. (Walter Morlen, 1593).

94 PRC 17/39/131–2.

95 PRC 17/43/216v.–17v.

96 Erickson, too, *Women and Property*, p. 87, notes the 'extensive overlap' in dowries among wealthy classes and the lower ranks of the gentry. See Elliott, 'Mobility and marriage', for social mobility at marriage.

97 See also, Howell, 'Peasant inheritance customs', p. 144, on the equality of marriage portions at Kibworth, and Erickson, *Women and Property*, pp. 68–78, for a discussion of 'the egalitarian approach of most will-makers', whether in areas practising partible inheritance or primogeniture. Cf. Cooper, 'Patterns of inheritance', p. 312, where eldest daughters usually received more.

98 O'Hara, 'Sixteenth-century courtship', pp. 230–1, Figs 6a–f chart the distributions by 25-year periods.

99 Outhwaite, 'Marriage as business', p. 35.

100 Howell, 'Peasant inheritance customs', pp. 149–51.

101 Erickson, *Women and Property*, p. 138.

102 Cooper, 'Patterns of inheritance', pp. 307–11.

103 E. H. Phelps Brown and S. V. Hopkins, *A Perspective of Wages and Prices* (London and

New York, 1981), ch. 2, 'Seven centuries of the prices of consumables, compared with builders' wage rates', pp. 13–59.

104 Macfarlane, *Marriage and Love*, p. 264.

105 Zell, *Industry in the Countryside*, pp. 44–50.

106 The agricultural labourer's wage in southern England increased just over two times between 1450 and 1600 compared to a 4.5-fold increase in the cost of living, see, C. G. A. Clay, *Economic Expansion and Social Change: England 1500–1700*, vol. 1: *People, Land and Towns* (Cambridge, 1984), p. 50.

107 Kussmaul, *Servants in Husbandry*, pp. 38–9, 81–2.

108 Elliott, 'Single women', p. 95.

109 Erickson, *Women and Property*, p. 85.

110 Cf. Macfarlane, *Marriage and Love*, p. 267. He estimates a period of 10 years' service, and a portion of £10 needed at that social level, and argues that a girl would have been able to accumulate this herself. For estimates of annual earnings of a regularly employed labourer in southern England (£10 8s in the early seventeenth century), see P. Bowden's figures in Thirsk ed., *The Agrarian History of England and Wales*, IV, p. 657. A virgate holder's income would have been 60–70 per cent higher than the fullest employed agricultural wage-earner, with an estimated annual net profit of £14 9s 3d.

111 Wrigley and Schofield, *Population History*, pp. 402–53, esp. pp. 421–2.

112 Tronrud, 'Dispelling the gloom', p. 12.

113 E.g., PRC 17/39/18v. (William Besfilde, yeoman, Tenterden, 1565). In his will he referred to the gifts made to his daughter's sons as being 'in full discharge of my promise to the father to my son [in-law] William Bereworth to make my daughter Sibell or her heirs worth £30 after my death'.

114 Cook, *Making a Match*, pp. 124–7, 133–50.

115 Earle, *Making of the English Middle Class*, p. 199.

116 Erickson, *Women and Property*, pp. 89–90.

117 See Kaplan ed., *The Marriage Bargain*, p. 2; Erickson, 'Common law versus common practice', p. 35.

118 Ingram, *Church Courts*, pp. 196, 205.

119 Erickson, *Women and Property*, p. 91.

120 Houlbrooke, *The English Family*, p. 84; Erickson, *Women and Property*, pp. 102–13.

121 C.C.A.L., MS. X/10/18, f. 54v., *Giles v. Wyborn* (1577).

122 MacDonald, *Mystical Bedlam*, pp. 88–98 (p. 97).

123 Cook, *Making a Match*, p. 47.

124 See above, chapter 3, p. 99.

125 C.C.A.L., MS. X/10/ 8., f. 195, *Gaunt v. Marshe* (?1560/2).

126 Cook, *Making a Match*, p. 39.

127 C.C.A.L., MS. X/10/12, f. 46, *Smith v. Godfrey* (1564).

128 C.C.A.L., MS. X/10/3, f. 25, *Synger v. Smyth* (1546).

129 C.C.A.L., MS. X/10/6, f. 187v., *Buckner v. Kenwood* (1557–58).

130 C.C.A.L., MS. X/10/6, f. 39, *Davye v. Wrighte* (1554).

131 C.C.A.L., MS. X/10/3, fos 41v.–4, *Bigge v. Robynson* (1548).

132 C.C.A.L., MS. X/10/8, fos 152–3, *Stedall v. Symnyng* (1562).

133 C.C.A.L., MS. X/10/12, f. 95, *Smith v. Richardson* (1564).

134 C.C.A.L., MS. X/10/21, fos 80–2, *Marketman v. Berry* (1581).

135 C.C.A.L., MS. X/11/2, fos 321v.–3, 317–18v., *Pelham v. Warrey* (1591).

136 C.C.A.L., MS. X/11/1, fos 116–v., *Turner v. Franckling* (1586–87).

137 C.C.A.L., MS. X/10/11, fos 213–14v., *Richards v. Cockes* (1570).

138 C.C.A.L., MS. X/11/6, f. 192v., *Claringboll v. Mussered* (1593).

139 C.C.A.L., MS. X/10/16, fos 138, 139v., 143–4v., *Filpott v. Baull alias Cruttall* (1575).

140 C.C.A.L., MS. X/10/2, fos 32v.–3, *Savye v. Philpott* (1542).

141 C.C.A.L., MS. X/10/8, fos 156v.–7v., *Hamond v. Symnyng* (1562).

142 C.C.A.L., MS. X/10/19, fos 36v.–7v., *Vydyan v. Pym* (1583–84).

143 C.C.A.L., MS. X/11/1, f. 251–v., *Savor v. Galle* (1589).

144 See above, chapter 3, p. 114.

145 See above, chapter 2, p. 58.

146 C.C.A.L., MS. X/11/5, fos 251v., 260v.–1, 269v., *Symons v. Spayne* (1598).

147 C.C.A.L., MS. X/10/3, fos 91v.–2, *Jhonson v. Denbye* (1548).

148 C.C.A.L., MS. X/10/18, fos 213v.–14v., *Balden v. Brokwell* (1580).

149 C.C.A.L., MS. X/10/11, fos 41v.–2v., *Bramelo v. Bonnam* (1568).

150 C.C.A.L., MS. X/10/14, fos 98–9v., *Pynnocke v. Beeching* (1572).

151 C.C.A.L., MS. X/10/18, f. 236–v., *Marshe v. Yonge?* (1580).

152 C.C.A.L., MS. X/11/3, fos 1–3, 5v.–7v., 56v.–7, *Alcocke v. Hardres* (1598).

153 C.C.A.L., MS. X/10/6., f. 127–v., *Austen v. Burrett* (1556).

154 C.C.A.L., MS. X/11/2, fos 317–18v., *Pelham v. Warrey* (1591–92).

155 C.C.A.L., MS. X/10/11, fos 273v.–4, *Cheese v. Chub* (?1569).

156 C.C.A.L., MS. X/11/3, fos 138–9, *Oldfield v. Colly* (1599).

157 C.C.A.L., MS. X/10/8, fos 115v.–17, 118–21v., 124–5v., 126–8, *Rayner v. Chamber* (1561). See also above, chapter 1, pp. 36–7.

158 C.C.A.L., MS. X/10/4, fos 50–1, 52–3, 58v., 60–v., 80v.–3v., 89, 94v., *Rolf v. Whiter* (1549).

159 E.g., see, *ibid.*, MS. X/10/7, fos 296v.–7, 299–300, *Tusten v. Allen* (1567).

160 C.C.A.L., MS. X/10/6, fos 76–7, 81v.–2, *Holbein v. Adam* (1554–55).

161 C.C.A.L., MS. X/10/7, fos 166v.–7, *Nicholls v. Smith* (?1567).

162 C.C.A.L., MS. X/10/6, fos 127–30v., 132–3, *Austen v. Burrett* (1556).

163 See above, chapter 3, p. 114.

164 See above, p. 218.

165 Erickson, *Women and Property*, p. 93.

166 C.C.A.L., MSS. X/10/4, fos 117–20, *Spyrer v. Watts* (1550); X/11/3, fos 130–2, 137, 138, 139, *Oldfield v. Colly* (1599).

167 C.C.A.L., MSS. X/11/3, fos 1–3, 5v.–7v., 43–4, 56v.–7, 58–9; Y/3/2, f. 66, *Alcocke v. Hardres* (1598).

168 C.C.A.L., MS. X/10/4, fos 117–20, *Spyrer v. Watts* (1550).

169 C.C.A.L., MS. X/10/4, fos 114v.–18, 124, *Jacobb v. Jhonson* (1550). It is not clear whether the jointure was to be worth £60 or £30.

170 C.C.A.L., MS. X/10/12, f. 92, *Cocke, ex parte Edward Laurence* (1564).

171 C.C.A.L., MS. X/10/10, fos 49v.–50, *Sloden v. Redwood* (1563).

172 Erickson, *Women and Property*, pp. 93–4.

173 E.g., see, C.C.A.L., MS. X/10/10, f. 18–v., *Aunsell v. Court* (1563); MSS. X/11/1, fos 208–9; X.11.2, f. 70 and v., *Fookes v. Lowes* (1588).

174 E.g., see, C.C.A.L., MSS. X/10/8, fos 115v.–17, 118–21v., 124–8, *Rayner v. Chamber* (1561); X/10/12, fos 210v.–14, *Whetnall v. Holman* (1566).

175 See, e.g., C.C.A.L., MS. X/10/4, fos 17, 20v.–1, 34, *Clement v. Weldishe* (1549); *ibid.*, f. 124v., *Bonnekar v. Lowe + Boreman* (1550).

176 C.C.A.L., MS. X/11/1, f. 336–v., *Terrie v. Overie* (1585). Also MS. X/10/19, f. 264, *King v. Otway + Wood* (1583).

177 C.C.A.L., MS. X/10/7, fos 319–23v., *Bridgeman v. Cole v. Barnes* (1560s). Also, MSS. X/10/4, fos 117–20, *Spyrer v. Watts* (1550); X/10/8, fos 118–20, *Rayner v. Chamber* (1561); X/10/9, fos 56v.–7v.; *Hannyng v. Cockman* (1563); X.10.9, fos 27v.–8, 32–v., *Rolf v. Fryer* (1563).

178 E.g., see, C.C.A.L., MSS. X/10/5, fos 51v.–2, *Lucket v. Webbe* (1552); X/10/7, fos 294v., 296v.–7, 299–300, 302v., *Tusten v. Allen* (1567); X/10/7, fos 77v., 81, 104, *Lyon v. Cole* (1560).

179 C.C.A.L., MS. X/11/1, fos 185–7, *Lawe v. Harris* (1588).

180 C.C.A.L., MSS. X/10/7, fos 299–300, *Tusten v. Allen* (1567). Also, X/10/7, fos 77v., 81, 104, *Lyon v. Cole* (1560); X/10/15, fos 1–2, *Joyce + Marchaunt* (1560s).

181 See, e.g., C.C.A.L., MS. X/11/5, f. 261, *Symons v. Spayne* (1598).

182 See above, Table 13.

183 C.C.A.L., MS. X/11/1, f. 116–v., *Turner v. Franckling* (1586–87).

184 C.C.A.L., MS. X/11/3, fos 130–1, 138, *Oldfield v. Colly* (1599); MS. X/10/4, fos 117–20, *Spyrer v. Watts* (1550).

185 C.C.A.L., MS. X/11/3, fos 1–3; MS.Y/3/2, f. 66, *Alcocke v. Hardres* (1598).

186 For full references to this case, C.C.A.L., MSS. X/10/16, fos 284–90, 292–3, 295–303v., 308–11, 312v.–16, 326v.–9, 336v.–7; X.10.18, fos 1–11v.; Y/3/16, f. 15.

187 PRC 32/32/178, fos 178v.–81v.

188 C.C.A.L., MSS. X/11/5, fos 242v., 251v., 269v., *Symons v. Spayne* (1598).

189 C.C.A.L., MS. X/10/18, fos 49v.–52, 53, *Giles* v. *Wyborn* (1577).

190 C.C.A.L., MS. X/10/18, f. 236–v., *Marshe* v. *Yonge* (1580).

191 C.C.A.L., MS. X/11/3, fos 131v.–2, 137, *Oldfield* v. *Colly* (1599).

192 C.C.A.L., MS. X/10/11, fos 33–5, 41v.–2v., *Bramelo* v. *Bonnam* (1568). It is likely in this case that Prudence was already pregnant with her master's child.

193 E.g., see, C.C.A.L., MSS. X/11/1, f. 116–v., *Turner* v. *Franckling* (1587); X/11/5, f. 253, *Symons* v. *Spayne* (1598).

194 C.C.A.L., MS. X/11/5, f. 135, *Bradley* v. *Shurt* (1596).

195 C.C.A.L., MS. X/10/3, fos 91v.–2, *Jhonson* v. *Denbye* (1548).

196 See above, chapter 3, p. 113.

197 For the general importance of credit-worthiness in the marketplace, see, Muldrew, 'Interpreting the market', *passim*.

Epilogue

This book is avowedly experimental. It is the first to have concentrated solely on courtship and on the sixteenth century as a distinct whole. It has also sought to open up new perspectives on the making of marriages among ordinary people. By subjecting church court records to close textual analysis the processes and practices of courtship have been examined. Analysing a very large sample of wills has uncovered the material provisions made for marriage by ordinary folk and revealed some of their accompanying expectations. Even at the level of the most humble Kentish villager, there was far more to the making of marriage than the legally recognised verbal exchanges. Indeed, the subject of courtship deserves much more attention than it has usually received, and should not be treated purely as an aspect of marriage and the family and of studies of households and their formation. Sixteenth-century folk knew that courtship involved many economic and social calculations and negotiations made by couples, their relatives and their neighbours. A special language of gifts and tokens was incorporated, go-betweens were often deployed, and courtships progressed through stages often recognised by ritual drinking and feasting, frequently taking place in particular social arenas or spaces. Ordinary people made pragmatic calculations as to the worth and value of potential partners and made careful financial provision for sons and daughters. It was commonly perceived that marriage in the sixteenth century was not an individual matter, but one which had ramifications affecting family, kin and the wider community. Courtship practices, customs and rituals reflected this reality. This book was written in the belief that it is only by understanding such processes, that we can truly appreciate how marriages were made among the ordinary English population.

This book began by discussing the historiography of courtship in early modern England. In particular it drew attention to the centrally debated issue of freedom versus constraint in the choice of marriage partner and in the conduct of courtship. It now concludes by arguing that much of the recent work has placed unwarranted stress on the extent to which individuals followed their romantic inclinations. The reaction to Lawrence Stone's interpretation of the English family has similarly placed too much emphasis upon the relative freedoms from parental, family or community interference which individuals are often said to have possessed. The evidence from Kent suggests that such descriptions are misleading and inappropriate, at least for the sixteenth century. Any dichotomy drawn between love and individual auto-nomy, as opposed to parental and community control, is oversimplistic. Such a perspective does scant justice to the more subtle reality, for courtship took place within a matrix of relationships, and courting couples themselves operated according to a set of internalised expectations.

This has to be said because, at first sight, many of the empirical findings of this study might be thought to lend themselves to supporting Stone's view of sixteenth-century courtship, a view that is largely left implicit in his family schema. The emphasis placed here on the influence and involvement of relatives, friends and community during courtship, the use of go-betweens, the planning and ritual strategies involved, and the importance contem-poraries gave to issues of property and money in the conduct of courtship, might all seem to conform to certain aspects of Stone's 'open-lineage family' model. Even his second model, the 'restricted patriarchal family', contains some recognisable characteristics, notably in its emphasis on the continuing, even increasing, role of parents or masters in family life and decision-making, and the level of public interference in upholding moral values.

Stone's schematic model of family development is, however, just the sort of extreme, simplistic modelling that should be avoided. If his earlier model bears some resemblances to some of what has been discussed in this book, it is because it happens to imply more emphasis on formal structures in court-ship than has become fashionable recently. In reality, the search for individual as opposed to family or community choice is fundamentally misconceived and probably unhelpful. Although this study has detected some changes over time in measurable things like dowry sizes, courtship horizons or marriage age thresholds, there is little indication of any change in what may be described as the 'culture of courtship' found in the sixteenth century. That culture endured throughout the course of the sixteenth century.

Rather than erecting schematic models of family change, a more fruitful approach to understanding the making of marriage in the past, would be to achieve a better appreciation of those constraints imposed on courting couples by that very 'culture of courtship'. The influences exercised from within and outside the family, and more impersonal social and economic forces, may have been of a positive or negative kind, but the decision to marry involved too many social, cultural and economic calculations to be left to the couple themselves. Individual marriage choices were made within a complex range of normative, community, kinship and practical constraints.

The first chapter of this book indicated that many individuals, parents, kin, fictive kin and neighbours might counsel and impose pressures on marriage decisions. Such constraints were felt widely in obvious as well as subtle ways and they were difficult to ignore or oppose. It has been argued, in fact, that the making of marriage took place within what may be described as the 'social-moral' community, in which a variety of groups, networks and kindred could use both formal and informal means to influence couples embarking on marriage. Economic leverage, moral sanctioning or even physical intimidation might facilitate or impede intended matches. The wide range of interests involved manifested itself in the ritual procedures which marked the structured process of courtship. Many interested parties would participate in symbolic acts of ritual that could include witnessing and mediating. Such participation demonstrated the ways in which a marriage might affect the reputation, social structure or patterns of kinship of a collectivity. Extensive participation by outsiders in the courtships of others shows that kin and community still mattered in the sixteenth century.

The importance of outsiders in courtship is also suggested by the evidence highlighting the previously underestimated part of 'go-betweens'. Those persons, acting out their varying roles for a range of motives, appeared with great frequency in the church court cases examined here. They were, indeed, a commonplace in the literature of the period. The structure and hints of formality implied by the use of intermediaries in courtships well below the rank of the elite is again highly suggestive. It reveals how pervasive was society's involvement in the courtships of its individual members.

The gifts and tokens which were exchanged frequently during courtship, also serve to emphasise the structured nature of that process in the sixteenth century. They were used and given at different stages in courtship, their precise meaning being related to the nature, timing and circumstances of the gift. The rich 'language' of tokens deployed indicates the care and caution required to negotiate a marriage in the sixteenth century. It illustrates too, perhaps, how the importance of the courtship process had generated a rich cultural tradition among the populace. This cultural context of courtship is one which historians have largely overlooked.

The restrictions imposed by distance and suitable meeting-places also require more attention. Although historians have studied the marriage horizons of those couples who married in church, less has been discovered about the geographical situation of partners during courtship. Evidence derived from Act books, however, confirmed the essentially restricted horizons of courting couples and revealed other constraints on courtship imposed by the physical environment. The patterns found varied by region and settlement type, and courtship distances tended to differ according to marketing connections and trade routes. It was suggested that towards the end of the sixteenth century those horizons may have expanded a little. The majority of courtships, however, were always conducted between partners in reasonably close proximity. Such behaviour, in addition to being constrained by the level and pace of economic activity, also seems to have occurred very much in particular places and on specific days. Couples were especially likely to meet in 'liminal spaces' such as fairs, alehouses, marketplaces and less formal arenas like stiles and gates. The 'structured courtship' in sixteenth-century Kent therefore allowed transgression, licence and experimentation but tended to occur most often in prescribed arenas and locally defined spaces and at special times.

The timing of courtship might also be affected in less tangible ways. That there existed notional ages at which individuals became eligible for marriage is another aspect of early modern courtship which has been relatively unconsidered. This book has argued that couples, their families and friends brought to the courtship process a further set of internalised assumptions regarding the appropriate minimum ages at which marriage might take place. The evidence drawn from wills suggested that testators recognised certain numerical ages as significant milestones in the achievement of maturity and marriageability. Over time, increasingly, this was seen as 21 for men and in the late teens for women. The sixteenth century emerges as a period when fewer and fewer testators sought to endow children in their early teens and also seems to be a time when particular numerical ages emerged as especially significant thresholds. Courting couples and those wider groups involved in the making of their marriages, as deposition evidence revealed, also possessed notions of appropriate age which limited, informed and restricted choices.

These structures and constraints of sixteenth-century courtship, however, cannot be readily understood unless the importance of dowry is appreciated fully. The giving of portions was by no means restricted to the social elite. Provision of dowries by parents, even those of relatively humble rank, seems to have been widespread. For some brides, dowries from the *wider* kin group also proved a valuable, although declining in real terms over the century, supplement to their marital prospects. Deposition evidence illustrates above all the fundamental concern on the part of most courting couples to get the economics of their marriage right. It was material considerations, rather than personal attributes, which were often paramount. The evidence from a large sample of wills showed that the sixteenth century was one of significant dowry inflation for the relatively humble villager as well as for the social elite, although more studies are needed to confirm the exact chronological and regional variations of this phenomenon. Whether or not the increasingly polarised nature of the marriage market forced individuals and their families to look further afield for partners of appropriate standing, drawing even more upon intermediaries to negotiate matches over wider distances, can only be surmised. Certainly, the language of bargaining, estimates of worth and reputation, the participation of parents, family and friends, the use of go-betweens and other cultural expectations and traditions associated with entry into the married state, have to be considered in the context of the importance attached by all participants to the transfer of even relatively modest amounts of property at marriage. They reveal the crucial material element in the making of marriage in the sixteenth century.

The interpretation of courtship offered has sought to engage more closely with the popular perception of marriage formation, and with contemporaries' experience of the several constraints imposed upon their marriage choices and decisions. The approach has tried to stretch our understanding and provide a more nuanced account of courtship in the relatively neglected sixteenth century. In its focus on the continued importance of family, kin, fictive kin and community in this period, it points the way for further reappraisals of the family and other collectivities. Recent anthropological discussion has suggested more complex and subtle definitions of the concept of kindred which may enrich our understanding of sixteenth-century English society. Historians could benefit from this wider and more flexible definition, to recognise the importance of the metaphorical use of the idiom of kinship by contemporaries, those whom they embraced or treated as kin, and to whom they felt morally obligated. In this way, the extensive participation by outsiders in the courtships of others might be properly appreciated.

In sum, then, this book has argued that courtship and the making of marriage should be understood in the context of the restructuring of relationships, of property transmission, and those questions of family, status, reputation and community self-definition that marriage plans entailed. Unsurprisingly, given its importance, its making involved social and ritual processes where the exchange of symbolic gifts, various forms of transactions, and the widespread involvement of members of family and community occurred. Whatever the legal definition of marriage, the negotiation and communication of marriage in practice possessed far greater cultural and social signifiance to those participating in its formation.

Appendix: map of Kent parishes

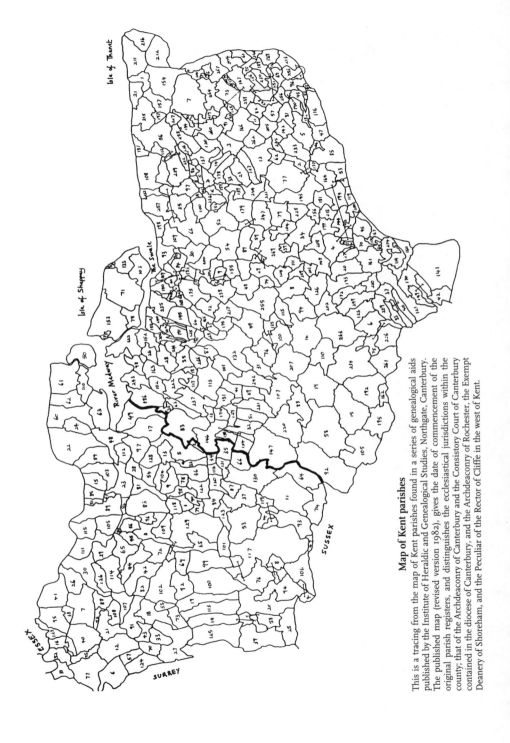

Map of Kent parishes

This is a tracing from the map of Kent parishes found in a series of genealogical aids published by the Institute of Heraldic and Genealogical Studies, Northgate, Canterbury. The published map (revised version 1982), gives the date of commencement of the original parish registers, and distinguishes the ecclesiastical jurisdictions within the county; that of the Archdeaconry of Canterbury and the Consistory Court of Canterbury contained in the diocese of Canterbury, and the Archdeaconry of Rochester, the Exempt Deanery of Shoreham, and the Peculiar of the Rector of Cliffe in the west of Kent.

KEY: PARISH NUMBERS

1	Acol		St Alphege	81	Ewell	
2	Acrise		St Andrew	82	Eythorn	
3	Adisham		St George	83	Fairfield	
4	Aldington		St Margaret	84	Faversham	
5	Alkham		St Mary Bredman	85	Folkestone	
6	Appledore		St Mary Magdalen	86	Fordwich	
7	Ash		St Mildred	87	Frinsted	
8	Ashford		St Peter	88	Frittenden	
9	Badlesmere	A	St Dunstan	89	Godmersham	
10	Bapchild	B	St Mary, Northgate	90	Goodnestone iux	
11	Barfrestone	C	St Martin		Faversham	
12	Barham	D	St Paul	91	Goodnestone iux	
13	Bearsted	E	St Mary Bredin		Wingham	
14	Bekesbourne	47	Capel le Ferne	92	Goudhurst	
15	Benenden	48	Challock	93	Graveney	
16	Bethersden	49	Charing	94	Great Chart	
17	Betteshanger	50	Charlton	95	Great Mongeham	
18	Bicknor	51	Chart Sutton	96	Guston	
19	Biddenden	52	Chartham	97	Hackington	
20	Bilsington	53	Cheriton	98	Halstow	
21	Birchington	54	Chilham	99	Ham	
22	Bircholt	55	Chillenden	100	Harbledown	
23	Bishopsbourne	56	Chislet	101	Harrietsham	
24	Blackmanstone	57	Coldred	102	Hartlip	
25	Blean	58	Cranbrook	103	Harty	
26	Bobbing	59	Crundale	104	Hastingleigh	
27	Bonnington	60	Davington	105	Hawkhurst	
28	Borden	61	Deal	106	Hawkinge	
29	Boughton Aluph	62	Denton	107	Headcorn	
30	Boughton under Blean	63	Detling	108	Herne	
31	Boughton Malherbe	64	Doddington	109	Hernehill	
32	Boughton Monchelsea	65	Dover	110	High Halden	
33	Boxley		St Mary in the Castle	111	Hinxhill	
34	Brabourne		St James	112	Hoath	
35	Bredgar		St Mary	113	Hollingbourne	
36	Bredhurst	66	Dunkirk, extra parochial	114	Hope	
37	Brenzett	67	Dymchurch	115	Hothfield	
38	Bridge	68	East Langdon	116	Hougham	
39	Brook	69	East Sutton	117	Hucking	
40	Brookland	70	Eastbridge	118	Hurst	
41	Broomfield	71	Eastchurch	119	Hythe	
42	Broomhill	72	Eastling	120	Ickham	
43	Buckland (near Dover)	73	Eastry	121	Ivychurch	
44	Buckland (near	74	Eastwell	122	Iwade	
	Faversham)	75	Ebony	123	Kenardington	
45	Burmarsh	76	Egerton	124	Kennington	
46	Canterbury	77	Elham	125	Kingsdown	
	All Saints	78	Elmley	126	Kingsnorth	
	Cathedral	79	Elmstead	127	Kingston	
	Holy Cross	80	Elmstone	128	Knowlton	

129 Langley
130 Leaveland
131 Leeds
132 Lenham
133 Leysdown
134 Linton
135 Little Chart
136 Little Mongeham
137 Littlebourne
138 Loose
139 Lower Hardres
140 Luddenham
141 Lydd
142 Lydden
143 Lyminge
144 Lympne
145 Lynsted
146 Maidstone
147 Marden
148 Mersham
149 Midley
150 Milsted
151 Milton (near Canterbury)
152 Milton iux Sittingbourne
153 Minster, Sheppey
154 Minster, Thanet
155 Molash
156 Monks Horton
157 Monkton
158 Murston
159 Nackington
160 New Romney
161 Newchurch
162 Newenden
163 Newington iux Sittingbourne
164 Newington iux Hythe
165 Newnham
166 Nonington
167 Northbourne
168 Norton
169 Oare
170 Old Romney
171 Orgarswick
172 Orlestone
173 Ospringe
174 Otham
175 Otterden
Oxenden (incl. with Wingham)
176 Oxney
Oxney, Isle of

177 Paddlesworth
178 Patrixbourne
179 Petham
180 Pluckley
181 Postling
182 Poulton
183 Preston iux Faversham
184 Preston iux Wingham
185 Queenborough
186 Rainham
187 Reculver
188 Ringwould
189 Ripple
190 River
191 Rodmersham
192 Rolvenden
193 Ruckinge
194 Saltwood
195 Sandhurst
196 Sandwich
St Mary
St Peter
St Clement
197 Sarre
198 Seasalter
199 Sellindge
200 Selling
201 Sevington
202 Shadoxhurst
203 Sheldwich
204 Sholden
205 Sibertswold
206 Sittingbourne
207 Smarden
208 Smeeth
209 Snargate
210 Snave
211 St John the Baptist, Thanet (Margate)
212 St Lawrence, Thanet (Ramsgate)
213 St Margaret at Cliffe
214 St Mary in the Marsh
215 St Nicholas at Wade, Thanet
216 St Peter, Thanet
217 Stalisfield
218 Stanford
219 Staple
220 Staplehurst
221 Stelling
222 Stockbury
223 Stodmarsh

224 Stonar
225 Stone iux Faversham
226 Stone in Oxney
227 Stourmouth
228 Stowting
229 Sturry
230 Sutton
231 Sutton Valence
232 Swalecliffe
233 Swingfield
234 Tenterden
235 Teynham
236 Thanington
237 Thornham
238 Throwley
239 Tilmanstone
240 Tonge
241 Tunstall
242 Ulcombe
243 Upchurch
244 Upper Hardres
245 Waldershare
246 Walmer
247 Waltham
248 Warden
249 Warehorne
250 West Hythe
251 West Langdon
252 Westbere
253 Westcliffe
254 Westenhanger
255 Westwell
256 Whitfield
257 Whitstable
258 Wickhambreux
259 Willesborough
260 Wingham
261 Wittersham
262 Womenswold
263 Woodchurch
264 Woodnesborough
265 Wootton
266 Wormeshill
267 Worth
268 Wychling
269 Wye

West Kent (Diocese of Rochester, etc.)

1 Addington
2 Allington
3 Ash
4 Ashurst
5 Aylesford
6 Beckenham
7 Bexley
8 Bidborough
9 Birling
10 Brasted
11 Brenchley
12 Bromley
13 Burham
14 Capel
15 Chalk
16 Charlton
17 Chatham
18 Chelsfield
19 Chevening
20 Chiddingstone
21 Chislehurst
22 Cliffe
23 Cobham
24 Cooling
25 Cowden
26 Crayford
27 Cudham
28 Cuxton
29 Darenth
30 Dartford
31 Deptford
St Nicholas
St Paul
32 Ditton
33 Downe
34 East Barming
35 East Farleigh
36 East Malling
37 East Peckham
38 East Wickham
39 Edenbridge
40 Eltham
41 Erith
42 Eynsford
43 Farnborough
44 Farningham
45 Fawkham
46 Footscray
47 Frant
48 Frindsbury
49 Gillingham

50 Graine
51 Gravesend
52 Greenwich
53 Hadlow
54 Halling
55 Halsted
56 Hartley
57 Hayes
58 Hever
59 Higham
60 High Halstow
61 Hoo, All Hallows
62 Hoo, St Mary
63 Hoo, St Werbergh
64 Horsmonden
65 Horton Kirkby
66 Hunton
67 Ifield
68 Ightham
69 Kemsing
70 Keston
71 Kidbrook, extra parochial
72 Kingsdown
73 Knockholt
74 Lamberhurst
75 Lee
76 Leigh
77 Lewisham
78 Leybourne
79 Leybourne, detached
80 Longfield
81 Luddesdown
82 Lullingstone
83 Meopham
84 Mereworth
85 Milton
86 Mursted
87 Nettlested
88 Northcray
89 Northfleet
90 Offham
91 Orpington
92 Otford
93 Pembury
94 Penshurst
95 Plumstead
96 Ridley
97 Rochester
St Margaret
St Nicholas
Cathedral
98 Ryarsh
99 Seal

100 Sevenoaks
101 Shipbourne
102 Shoreham
103 Shorne
104 Snodland
105 Southfleet
106 Speldhurst (Groombridge)
107 St Mary, Cray
108 St Paul's, Cray
109 Stansted
110 Stoke
111 Stone
112 Strood
113 Sundridge (Ide Hill)
114 Sutton at Hone
115 Swanscombe
116 Teston
117 Tonbridge (Southborough, Tunbridge Wells)
118 Trotterscliffe
119 Tudley
120 Wateringbury
121 West Farleigh
122 West Malling
123 West Peckham
124 West Wickham
125 Westerham
126 Wilmington
127 Woolwich
128 Wouldham
129 Wrotham (Plaxtol)
130 Yalding

Bibliography

PRIMARY SOURCES

CANTERBURY CATHEDRAL ARCHIVES AND LIBRARY

Canterbury Diocesan Records

Consistory Court Deposition Volumes

    X/10/2 – X/10/21 (1541–1584)

    X/11/1 – X/11/6 (1585–1601)

Archdeaconry Court Deposition Volumes

    PRC 39/1 – PRC 39/24 (1555–1602)

Miscellaneous Consistory Court Papers

    J/J1 – J/J3 (1595–97)

Act Books

The Consistory Court Act Books contain Instance business mostly relating to the court's sessions in Canterbury, but also to sessions held when the court went on circuit through Hythe, Romney and Dover. The volumes are not in any consistent chronological order but cover the years 1474–1602.

    Y.1.10

    Y.1.12–Y.1.18

    Y.2.1–Y.2.3

    Y.2.5–Y.2.6

    Y.2.8–Y.2.22

    Y.2.25–Y.2.30

    Y.3.1–Y.3.3

    Y.3.10–Y.3.16

    Y.3.18–Y.3.22

    Y.4.1

Parish Records

Parish register of Chislet

    U3/55/1/A1   1538–1562

    U3/55/1/A2   from 1562

Parish register of Whitstable

U3/131/1/1   1549–1746

Parish register of Sturry

U3/48/1/i   from 1538

Parish register of Wye

U3/174/1/A1   1538–1602

U3/174/1/A2   1603–1726

CENTRE FOR KENTISH STUDIES (FORMERLY KENT ARCHIVES OFFICE)

Parish Records

Parish register of Tenterden

P 364/1/1   from 1544

Probate Records

Wills Archdeaconry and Consistory

For a complete list of wills used see O'Hara, 'Sixteenth-century courtship', pp. 285–323. The following volumes of wills cover the years 1449–1603.

PRC 17/1–PRC 17/52

PRC 32/2–PRC 32/5

PRC 32/7

PRC 32/9–PRC 32/16

PRC 32/20

PRC 32/24

PRC 32/30–PRC 32/32

PRC 32/34–PRC 32/36

PRC 32/38

Inventories Archdeaconry and Consistory

For a detailed list of inventories used see O'Hara, 'Sixteenth-century courtship', pp. 324–8. The following volumes of inventories cover the years 1565–1603.

PRC 10/1–PRC 10/30

PRC 21/2

PRC 21/5–PRC 21/7

PRC 21/14

PRC 22/1

PRINTED SOURCES

Brand, J., *Observations on Popular Antiquities: Chiefly Illustrating the Origin of Our Vulgar Customs, Ceremonies, and Superstitions* (2 vols, London, 1813)

Bullen, A. H. ed., *Some Shorter Elizabethan Poems: an English Garner* (Westminster, 1903)

Burn, R., *The Ecclesiastical Law* (8th edn, London, 1824)

Census of Great Britain, 1851, Population Tables 1: Numbers of Inhabitants (vol. 1, 1852)

Conset, H., *The Practice of the Spiritual or Ecclesiastical Courts* (1st edn, 1681; 3rd edn, London, 1708)

Cowper, J. M. ed., *Canterbury Marriage Licences, 1568–1618* (Canterbury, 1892)

Evans, J., *English Posies and Posy Rings* (London, 1931)

Furley, R., *A History of the Weald of Kent* (vol. 2, pt ii, Ashford, 1874)

Furnivall, F. J. ed., *Child Marriages, Divorces and Ratifications etc. in the Diocese of Chester, A.D. 1561–6*, Early English Text Society, original series 108 (London, 1897)

Hasted, E., *The History and Topographical Survey of the County of Kent* (2nd edn, Canterbury, 1797–1801, facsimile edn, 1972)

Hovenden, R. ed., *The Parish Register of Chislet, Kent, 1538–1707* (London, 1887)

Love and Courtship in Renaissance Prints, Temporary Exhibition at the Fitzwilliam Museum (Cambridge, March–June 1989)

Plomer, H. R. ed., *Index of Wills and Administrations in the Probate Registry at Canterbury, 1396–1558 and 1640–1650*, Kent Records VI (London, 1920)

St Clare Byrne, M. ed., *The Lisle Letters* (London, 1983)

Strutt, J., *A Compleat View of the Manners, Customs, Arms, Habits and of the Inhabitants of England from the Arrival of the Saxons Till the Reign of Henry VIII* (3 vols, London, 1775)

Swinburne, H., *Treatise of Spousals or Matrimonial Contracts* (London, 1686, reprinted New York and London, 1978)

Thompson, R. ed., *Samuel Pepys' Penny Merriments* (London, 1976)

Victorian Valentine Cards, Temporary Exhibition at the Heritage Centre (Canterbury, February 1988)

Woodward, D. ed., *The Farming and Memorandum Books of Henry Best of Elmswell: 1642*, Records of Social and Economic History, new series 8 (London, 1984)

SECONDARY TEXTS

Unless otherwise stated the place of publication is London.

ABBREVIATIONS

C&C   *Continuity and Change*

EcHR   *Economic History Review*

JFH   *Journal of Family History*

LPS   *Local Population Studies*

P&P   *Past and Present*

SH   *Social History*

Addy, J., *Sin and Society in the Seventeenth Century* (London and New York, 1989)

Addy, J., *Death, Money and the Vultures: Inheritance and Avarice, 1660–1750* (1992)

Amussen, S. D., '"Being stirred to much unquietness": violence and domestic violence in early modern England', *Journal of Women's History* 6:2 (1994), 70–89

Amussen, S. D., 'Punishment, discipline and power: the social meanings of violence in early modern England', *Journal of British Studies* 34 (1995), 1–34

Anderson, M., *Approaches to the History of the Western Family, 1500–1914* (London and Basingstoke, 1980)

Andrewes, E. J., 'Land, family and community in Wingham and its environs: an economic and social history of rural society in east Kent from *c.* 1450–1640' (Ph.D. thesis, University of Kent, 1991)

Aspects of Folk Life in Europe: Love and Marriage, International European Exhibition organised by the Ministry of French Culture and the Ministry of Flemish Culture (Musée de la Vie Wallonne, Liège, 4 July –5 October 1975)

Bailey, F. G. ed., *Gifts and Poison: the Politics of Reputation* (Oxford, 1971)

Baker, M., *Discovering the Folklore and Customs of Love and Marriage* (Aylesbury, 1974)

Bakhtin, M., *Rabelais and His World*, trans. H. Iswolsky (Cambridge, Massachusetts, 1968, 1984 edn)

Barnard, A. and A. Good, *Research Practices in the Study of Kinship: Research Methods in Social Anthropology* (1984, reprinted 1987)

Ben-Amos, I. K., 'Service and the coming of age of young men in seventeenth-century England', *C&C* 3:1 (1988), 41–64

Ben-Amos, I. K., *Adolescence and Youth in Early Modern England* (New Haven and London, 1994)

Bercovitch, E., 'The agent in the gift: hidden exchange in Inner New Guinea', *Cultural Anthropology* 9:4 (1994), 498–536

Bloch, M., 'The long-term and the short-term: the economic and political significance of the morality of kinship', in J. Goody ed., *The Character of Kinship* (Cambridge, 1973), pp. 75–89

Bloxham, C. and M. Picken, *Love and Marriage* (Devon, 1990)

Bonfield, L., 'Normative rules and property transmission: reflections on the link between marriage and inheritance in early modern England', in L. Bonfield, R. Smith and K. Wrightson eds, *The World We Have Gained: Histories of Population and Social Structure* (Oxford, 1986), pp. 155–76

Bossy, J., 'Blood and baptism: kinship, community and Christianity in Western Europe from the fourteenth to the seventeenth centuries', in D. Baker ed., *Sanctity and Secularity: the Church and the World* (Oxford, 1973), pp. 129–43

Boulton, J., *Neighbourhood and Society: a London Suburb in the Seventeenth Century* (Cambridge, 1987)

Bibliography

Boulton, J., 'Neighbourhood migration in early modern London', in Clark and Souden eds, *Migration and Society* (1987), pp. 107–49

Boulton, J., '"Economy of time"? Wedding days and the working week in the past', *LPS* 43 (1989), 28–46

Boulton, J., 'Itching after private marryings? marriage customs in seventeenth-century London', *London Journal* 16:1 (1991), 15–34

Bourdieu, P., *Outline of a Theory of Practice*, trans. R. Nice (Switzerland, 1972; 1st English trans. Cambridge, 1977)

Bradford, E. ed., *Roses are Red: Love and Scorn in Victorian Valentines* (1986)

Brennan, E. R., A. V. James and W. T. Morrill, 'Inheritance, demographic structure and marriage: a cross-cultural perspective', *JFH* 7:3 (1982), 289–98

Brodsky, V., 'Widows in late Elizabethan London: remarriage, economic opportunity and family orientation', in L. Bonfield, R. Smith and K. Wrightson eds, *The World We Have Gained: Histories of Population and Social Structure* (Oxford, 1986), pp. 122–54

Brundage, J. A., 'Concubinage and marriage in medieval canon law', *Journal of Medieval History* 1 (1975), 1–17

Brundage, J. A., *Law, Sex, and Christian Society in Medieval Europe* (Chicago and London, 1987)

Brundage, J. A., 'The bar of the Ely Consistory Court in the fourteenth century: advocates, proctors, and others', *Journal of Ecclesiastical History* 43:4 (1992), 541–60

Brundage, J. A., 'Proof in canonical criminal law', *C&C* 11:3 (1996), 329–39

Burnett, M. T., 'Giving and receiving: *Love's Labour's Lost* and the politics of exchange', *English Literary Renaissance* 23:2 (1993), 287–313

Bury, S., *An Introduction to Rings* (1984)

Bury, S., *An Introduction to Sentimental Jewellery* (1985)

Butcher, A. F., 'The origins of Romney freemen, 1433–1523', *EcHR*, 2nd series 27 (1974), 16–27

Butcher, A. F., 'The honest and the lewd in sixteenth-century Canterbury: the case of Mrs. Butterwick', unpublished paper delivered at the graduate research seminar, department of history, University of Kent (19 October 1983)

Calhoun, J. C., 'History, anthropology and the study of communities: some problems in Macfarlane's proposal', *SH* 3 (1978), 363–73

Calhoun, J. C., 'Community: toward a variable conceptualization for comparative research', *SH* 5 (1980), 105–29

Campbell, J. K., *Honour, Family and Patronage: a Study of Institutions and Moral Values in a Greek Mountain Community* (New York and Oxford, 1964, reprinted 1979)

Capp, B., 'Will formularies', *LPS* 14 (Spring 1975), 49–50

Carlson, E. J., 'Courtship in Tudor England', *History Today* 43 (August 1993), 23–9

Carlson, E. J., *Marriage and the English Reformation* (Oxford, 1994)

Carter, M., 'Town or urban society? St Ives in Huntingdonshire, 1630–1740', in C. Phythian-Adams ed., *Societies, Cultures and Kinship, 1580–1850: Cultural Provinces and English Local History* (Leicester, 1993), pp. 77–130

Chalklin, C. W., *Seventeenth-Century Kent: a Social and Economic History* (1965)

Chalklin, C. W., 'A seventeenth-century market town: Tonbridge', in M. Roake and J. Whyman eds, *Essays in Kentish History* (1973), pp. 89–99

Chambers, J. D., *Population, Economy and Society in Pre-Industrial England*, ed. W. A. Armstrong (Oxford, 1972)

Chartier, R. ed., *Passions of the Renaissance*, trans. A. Goldhammer (Massachusetts, 1989)

Chaytor, M., 'Household and kinship: Ryton in the late sixteenth and early seventeenth centuries', *History Workshop Journal* 10 (1980), 25–60

Cherry, J. and M. Redknap, 'Medieval and Tudor finger rings found in Wales', *Archaeologia Cambrensis* 140 (1991), 120–9

Clark, P., 'The migrant in Kentish towns, 1580–1640', in P. Clark and P. Slack eds, *Crisis and Order in English Towns, 1500–1700: Essays in Urban History* (1972), pp. 117–63

Clark, P., 'The ownership of books in England, 1560–1640: the example of some Kentish townsfolk', in L. Stone ed., *Schooling and Society* (Baltimore, 1976), pp. 95–111

Clark, P., 'Popular protest and disturbance in Kent, 1558–1640', *EcHR*, 2nd series 29:3 (1976), 365–82

Clark, P., *English Provincial Society from the Reformation to the Revolution: Religion, Politics and Society in Kent, 1500–1640* (Hassocks, 1977)

Clark, P., 'The alehouse and the alternative society', in D. Pennington and K. Thomas eds, *Puritans and Revolutionaries: Essays in Seventeenth-Century History Presented to Christopher Hill* (Oxford, 1978), pp. 47–72

Clark, P., *The English Alehouse: a Social History, 1200–1830* (1983)

Clark, P., 'Migrants in the city: the process of social adaptation in English towns, 1500–1800', in Clark and Souden eds, *Migration and Society* (1987), pp. 267–91

Clark, P., 'Migration in England during the late 17th and early 18th centuries', in Clark and Souden eds, *Migration and Society* (1987), pp. 213–52

Clark, P. and D. Souden eds, *Migration and Society in Early Modern England* (1987)

Clark, P. and D. Souden, 'Introduction', in Clark and Souden eds, *Migration and Society* (1987), pp. 11–48

Clay, C. G. A., *Economic Expansion and Social Change: England 1500–1700*, vol. 1: *People, Land and Towns* (Cambridge, 1984)

Cockburn, J. S., 'Patterns of violence in English society: homicide in Kent, 1560–1985', *P&P* 130 (1991), 70–106

Collinson, P., 'Cranbrook and the Fletchers: popular and unpopular religion in the Kentish Weald', in P. N. Brooks ed., *Reformation Principle and Practice: Essays in Honour of A. G. Dickens* (1980), pp. 171–202

Comaroff, J. L. ed., *The Meaning of Marriage Payments* (1980)

Cook, A. J., *Making a Match: Courtship in Shakespeare and His Society* (Princeton, 1991)

Cooper, J. P., 'Patterns of inheritance and settlement by great landowners from the fifteenth to the eighteenth centuries', in Goody, Thirsk and Thompson eds, *Family and Inheritance*, pp. 192–327

Bibliography

Coppel, S., 'Wills and the community: a case study of Tudor Grantham', in P. Riden ed., *Probate Records and the Local Community* (Gloucester, 1985), pp. 71–90

Coppel, S., 'Will-making on the deathbed', *LPS* 40 (Spring 1988), 37–45

Crawford, P., 'The construction and experience of maternity in seventeenth-century England', in V. Fildes ed., *Women as Mothers in Pre-Industrial England* (1990), pp. 3–38

Cressy, D., 'Kinship and kin interaction in early modern England', *P&P* 113 (1986), 38–69

Cressy, D., *Birth, Marriage and Death: Ritual, Religion and the Life-Cycle in Tudor and Stuart England* (Oxford, 1997)

Croft, P., 'Libels, popular literacy and public opinion in early modern England', *Historical Research* 68 (1995), 266–85

Cullum, P. H., '"And hir name was Charite": charitable giving by and for women in late medieval Yorkshire', in P. J. P. Goldberg ed., *Woman is a Worthy Wight: Women in English Society, c. 1200–1500* (Stroud, 1992), pp. 182–211

Daunton, M., 'Introduction', in M. Daunton ed., *Charity, Self-Interest and Welfare in the English Past* (1996), pp. 1–22

Davis, J., *People of the Mediterranean: an Essay in Comparative Social Anthropology* (1977)

Davis, N. Z., 'Beyond the market: books as gifts in sixteenth-century France', *Transactions of the Royal Historical Society*, 5th series, 33 (1983), 69–88

Derrett, J. D. M., 'Henry Swinburne (?1551–1624) civil lawyer of York', *Borthwick Papers* 44 (1973)

Dixon, M., 'Economy and society in Dover, 1509–1640' (Ph.D. thesis, University of Kent, 1992)

Dobson, M., '"Marsh fever" – the geography of malaria in England', *Journal of Historical Geography* 6:4 (1980), 357–89

Donahue Jr, C., 'The policy of Alexander the Third's consent theory of marriage', in S. Kuttner ed., *Proceedings of the Fourth International Congress of Medieval Canon Law* (Rome, 1976), pp. 251–81

Donahue Jr, C., 'Proof by witnesses in the church courts of medieval England: an imperfect reception of the learned law', in M. S. Arnold, T. A. Green, S. A. Scully and S. D. White eds, *On the Laws and Customs of England* (North Carolina, 1981), pp. 127–58

Donahue Jr, C., 'The canon law on the formation of marriage and social practice in the later middle ages', *JFH* 8 (1983), 144–58

Douglas, M., *Purity and Danger* (1966, 1984 edn)

Drake, M., 'Age at marriage in the pre-industrial West', in F. Bechhofer ed., *Population Growth and the Brain Drain* (Edinburgh, 1969), pp. 196–207

Dulley, A. J. F., 'Four Kent towns at the end of the middle ages', *Archaeologia Cantiana* 81 (1966)

Earle, P., *The Making of the English Middle Class: Business, Society and Family Life in London, 1660–1730* (1989)

Eddison, J. and C. Green eds, *Romney Marsh Evolution, Occupation, Reclamation*, Monograph 24 (Oxford University Committee for Archaeology, 1988)

Elliott, V. B., 'Mobility and marriage in pre-industrial England: a demographic and social structural analysis of geographical and social mobility and aspects of marriage, 1570–1690, with particular reference to London and general reference to Middlesex, Kent, Essex and Hertfordshire' (Ph.D. thesis, University of Cambridge, 1979)

Elliott, V. B., 'Single women in the London marriage market: age, status and mobility, 1598–1619', in R. B. Outhwaite ed., *Marriage and Society: Studies in the Social History of Marriage* (1981), pp. 81–100

Emmison, F. G., *Elizabethan Life: Morals and the Church Courts* (Chelmsford, 1973)

Erickson, A. L., 'Common law versus common practice: the use of marriage settlements in early modern England', *EcHR*, 2nd series 43:1 (1990), 21–39

Erickson, A. L., *Women and Property in Early Modern England* (London and New York, 1993)

Everitt, A., 'The community of Kent in 1640', in A. Everitt, *The Community of Kent and the Great Rebellion, 1640–60* (Leicester, 1966, 1973 edn), pp. 20–55

Everitt, A., 'The market towns', in P. Clark ed., *The Early Modern Town* (1976), pp. 168–204

Fletcher, A., 'Men's dilemma: the future of patriarchy in England, 1560–1660', *Transactions of the Royal Historical Society*, 6th series 4 (1994), 61–81

Flinn, M. W., *The European Demographic System, 1500–1820* (Brighton, 1981)

Fox, A., 'Ballads, libels and popular ridicule in Jacobean England', *P&P* 145 (1994), 47–83

Foyster, E., 'A laughing matter? Marital discord and gender control in seventeenth-century England', *Rural History* 4:1 (1993), 5–21

Gillis, J. R., 'Peasant, plebeian, and proletarian marriage in Britain, 1600–1900', in D. Levine ed., *Proletarianization and Family History* (Orlando, 1984), pp. 129–62

Gillis, J. R., *For Better, For Worse: British Marriages, 1600 to the Present* (Oxford and New York, 1985)

Gluckman, M., 'Les rites of passage', in M. Gluckman ed., *Essays on the Ritual of Social Relations* (Manchester, 1975), pp. 1–52

Goldberg, P. J. P., 'Female labour, service and marriage in the late medieval urban North', *Northern History* 22 (1986), 18–38

Goldberg, P. J. P., 'Marriage, migration, servanthood and life-cycle in Yorkshire towns of the later Middle Ages: some York cause paper evidence', *C&C* 1 (1986), 141–69

Goldberg, P. J. P., *Women, Work and Life-Cycle in a Medieval Economy: Women in York and Yorkshire, c. 1300–1520* (Oxford, 1992)

Goody, J., 'Introduction', in Goody, Thirsk and Thompson eds, *Family and Inheritance*, pp. 1–9

Goody, J., *The Development of the Family and Marriage in Europe* (Cambridge, 1983)

Goody, J., and S. J. Tambiah, *Bridewealth and Dowry* (Cambridge, 1973)

Goody, J., J. Thirsk and E. P. Thompson eds, *Family and Inheritance: Rural Society in Western Europe, 1200–1800* (Cambridge, 1976, paperback edn, 1978)

Gottlieb, B., 'The meaning of clandestine marriage', in R. Wheaton and T. K. Hareven eds, *Family and Sexuality in French History* (Philadelphia, 1980), pp. 49–83

Gottlieb, B., *The Family in the Western World: From the Black Death to the Industrial Age* (Oxford, 1993)

Bibliography

Gowing, L., 'Gender and the language of insult in early modern London', *History Workshop Journal* 35 (1993), 1–21

Gowing, L., *Domestic Dangers: Women, Words and Sex in Early Modern London* (Oxford, 1996)

Haigh, C. A., 'Slander and the church courts in the sixteenth century', *Transactions of the Lancashire and Cheshire Antiquarian Society* 78 (1975), 1–13

Hair, P. E. H., 'Bridal pregnancy in rural England in earlier centuries', *Population Studies* 20 (1966), 233–43

Hajnal, J., 'European marriage patterns in perspective', in D. V. Glass and D. E. C. Eversley eds, *Population in History* (1965), pp. 101–43

Hanley, H., 'Population mobility in Buckinghamshire, 1578–1583', *LPS* 15 (1975), 33–9

Harley, D., 'Historians as demonologists: the myth of the midwife-witch', *Social History of Medicine* 3 (1990), 1–26

Harris, B. J., 'A new look at the Reformation: aristocratic women and nunneries', *Journal of British Studies* 32:2 (1993), 89–113

Harris, O., 'Households and their boundaries', *History Workshop Journal* 13 (1982), 143–52

Helmholz, R. H., *Marriage Litigation in Medieval England* (Cambridge, 1974)

Herlihy, D., 'Origins of English individualism', *JFH* 5 (1980), 235–6

Hill, B., 'Household and kinship', *P&P* 88 (1980), 142

Hindle, S., 'The shaming of Margaret Knowsley: gossip, gender and the experience of authority in early modern England', *C&C* 9:3 (1994), 391–419

Hindle, S., 'Custom, festival and protest in early modern England: the Little Budworth wakes, St Peter's Day, 1596', *Rural History* 6:2 (1995), 155–78

Hollingsworth, T. H., 'The demography of the British peerage', *Population Studies*, supplement to 18:2 (November 1964), i–iv, 3–108

Homans, G. C., *English Villagers of the Thirteenth Century* (New York, 1970)

Hoskins, W. G., 'English provincial towns in the early sixteenth century', in P. Clark ed., *The Early Modern Town* (1976), pp. 91–105

Houlbrooke, R. A., *Church Courts and the People During the English Reformation, 1520–1570* (Oxford, 1979)

Houlbrooke, R. A., *The English Family, 1450–1700* (London and New York, 1984)

Houlbrooke, R. A., 'The making of marriage in mid-Tudor England: evidence from the records of matrimonial contract litigation', *JFH* 10 (1985), 339–52

Houlbrooke, R. A., 'Reading history: the pre-industrial family', *History Today* 36 (1986), 49–52

Houlbrooke, R. A. ed., *English Family Life, 1576–1716* (Oxford, 1988)

Houston, R. and R. Smith, 'A new approach to family history?', *History Workshop Journal* 14 (1982), 120–31

Howell, C., 'Peasant inheritance customs in the Midlands, 1280–1700', in Goody, Thirsk and Thompson eds, *Family and Inheritance*, pp. 112–55

Hughes, D. O., 'From brideprice to dowry in Mediterranean Europe', *JFH* 3:3 (1978), 262–96. Reprinted in Kaplan ed., *The Marriage Bargain*, pp. 13–58

Hutson, L., 'The displacement of the market in Jacobean city comedy', *London Journal* 14:1 (1989), 3–16

Ingram, M., 'Ecclesiastical justice in Wiltshire, 1600–1640, with special reference to cases concerning sex and marriage' (D.Phil. thesis, University of Oxford, 1976)

Ingram, M., 'Communities and courts: law and disorder in early seventeenth-century Wiltshire', in J. S. Cockburn ed., *Crime in England, 1550–1800* (1977), pp. 110–34

Ingram, M., 'Spousals litigation in the English ecclesiastical courts, *c*. 1350–1640', in R. B. Outhwaite ed., *Marriage and Society: Studies in the Social History of Marriage* (1981), pp. 35–57

Ingram, M., 'Ridings, rough music and the "reform of popular culture" in early modern England', *P&P* 105 (1984), 79–113

Ingram, M., 'The reform of popular culture? Sex and marriage in early modern England', in B. Reay ed., *Popular Culture in Seventeenth-Century England* (1985), pp. 129–65

Ingram, M., 'Ridings, rough music and mocking rhymes in early modern England', in B. Reay ed., *Popular Culture in Seventeenth-Century England* (1985), pp. 166–98

Ingram, M., *Church Courts, Sex and Marriage in England, 1570–1640* (Cambridge, 1987)

Ingram, M., 'Juridical folklore in England illustrated by rough music', in C. W. Brooks and M. Lobban eds, *Communities and Courts in Britain, 1150–1900* (1997), pp. 61–82

Jessup, F. W., *Kent History Illustrated* (Maidstone, 1973 edn)

Johnston, J. A., 'Family, kin and community in eight Lincolnshire parishes, 1567–1800', *Rural History* 6:2 (1995), 179–92

Jones, J. and K. Ames, *Love Tokens* (Devon, 1992)

Jordan, W. J. K., *The Charities of London, 1480–1660: the Aspirations and the Achievements of the Urban Society* (1960)

Kaplan, M. A., 'For love or money: the marriage strategies of Jews in imperial Germany', in Kaplan ed., *The Marriage Bargain*, pp, 121–63

Kaplan, M. A., 'Introduction', in Kaplan ed., *The Marriage Bargain*, pp. 1–11

Kaplan, M. A. ed., *The Marriage Bargain: Women and Dowries in European History* (New York and London, 1985)

Kemp, J., 'Kinship and the management of personal relations: kin terminologies and the "axiom of amity"', *Bijdragen Tot De Taal-Land-en Volkenkunde* 139 (1983), 81–99

Kemp, J., 'Processes of kinship and community in north central Thailand', *Seminar on Cognitive Forms of Social Organisation in South-east Asia* (Amsterdam, 6–8 January 1983), pp. 352–72

Kemp, J., 'The manipulation of personal relations: from kinship to patron clientage', in H. T. Brummelhuis and J. Kemp eds, *Strategies and Structures in Thai Society* (Amsterdam, 1984), pp. 55–71

Kertzer, D. I., 'Anthropology and family history', *JFH* 9 (1984), 201–16

Klapisch-Zuber, C., *Women, Family, and Ritual in Renaissance Italy*, trans. L. G. Cochrane (Chicago and London, 1985)

Klein, L. M., 'Your humble handmaid: Elizabethan gifts of needlework', *Renaissance Quarterly* 50:2 (1997), 459–93

Bibliography

Kunz, G. F., *Rings for the Finger* (Philadelphia, 1917, reprinted New York, 1973)

Kussmaul, A. S., 'The ambiguous mobility of farm servants', *EcHR*, 2nd series 34 (1981), 222–35

Kussmaul, A. S., *Servants in Husbandry in Early Modern England* (Cambridge, 1981)

Lambiri-Dimaki, J., 'Dowry in modern Greece: an institution at the crossroads between persistence and decline', in Kaplan ed., *The Marriage Bargain*, pp. 165–78

Laslett, P., 'Mean household size in England since the sixteenth century', in P. Laslett and R. Wall eds, *Household and Family in Past Time: Comparative Studies in the Size and Structure of the Domestic Group Over the Last Three Centuries* (Cambridge, 1972), pp. 125–58

Laslett, P., 'Characteristics of the Western family considered over time', *JFH* 2 (1977), 89–114

Laslett, P., *Family Life and Illicit Love in Earlier Generations: Essays in Historical Sociology* (Cambridge, 1977)

Laslett, P., *The World We Have Lost* (1965, 1979 edn)

Laslett, P., *The World We Have Lost: Further Explored* (1983)

Laslett, P., 'Notes and queries: the institution of service', *LPS* 40 (Spring 1988), 55–60

Laurence, A., *Women in England, 1500–1760: a Social History* (1994)

Levine, D., '"For their own reasons": individual marriage decisions and family life', *JFH* 7:3 (Fall 1982), 255–64

Levine, D. and K. Wrightson, 'The social context of illegitimacy in early modern England', in P. Laslett, K. Oosterveen and R. M. Smith eds, *Bastardy and its Comparative History* (1980), pp. 158–75

Lord, E., 'Fairs, festivals and fertility in Alkmaar, North Holland, 1650–1810', *LPS* 42 (Spring 1989), 43–53

Love Spoons from Wales (Cardiff, 1973)

MacCormack, G., 'Reciprocity', *Man* 11 (1976), 89–103

MacCormack, G., 'Mauss and the "spirit of the gift"', *Oceania* 52:4 (1982), 286–93

McCracken, G., 'The exchange of children in Tudor England: an anthropological phenomenon in historical context', *JFH* 8 (1983), 303–13

MacDonald, M., 'Review of L. Stone, *Family, Sex and Marriage*', *Sixteenth-Century Journal* 10:2 (1979), 122–3

MacDonald, M., *Mystical Bedlam: Madness, Anxiety and Healing in Seventeenth-Century England* (Cambridge, 1981, paperback edn, 1983)

Macfarlane, A., 'The regulation of marital and sexual relationships in seventeenth-century England, with special reference to the County of Essex' (M.Phil. thesis, University of London, 1968)

Macfarlane, A., *The Family Life of Ralph Josselin: a Seventeenth-Century Clergyman: an Essay in Historical Anthropology* (Cambridge, 1970, New York, 1977 edn)

Macfarlane, A., 'History, anthropology and the study of communities', *SH* 2 (1977), 631–52

Macfarlane, A., 'Modes of reproduction', *Journal of Development Studies* 14 (1978), 100–20

Macfarlane, A., *The Origins of English Individualism: the Family, Property and Social Transition* (Oxford, 1978)

Macfarlane, A., 'The informal social control of marriage in seventeenth-century England: some preliminary notes', in V. Fox and M. Quitt eds, *Loving, Parenting and Dying: the Family Cycle in England and America* (New York, 1980), pp. 110–21

Macfarlane, A., 'The myth of the peasantry: family and economy in a northern parish', in R. M. Smith ed., *Land, Kinship and Life-Cycle* (Cambridge, 1984), pp. 333–49

Macfarlane, A., *Marriage and Love in England: Modes of Reproduction, 1300–1840* (Oxford, 1986)

Macfarlane, A., S. Harrison and C. Jardine, *Reconstructing Historical Communities* (Cambridge, 1977)

McIntosh, K. H. ed., *Sturry: the Changing Scene* (Ramsgate, 1972)

McIntosh, M. K., 'Servants and the household unit in an Elizabethan English community', *JFH* 9:1 (1984), 3–23

McIntosh, M. K., *A Community Transformed: the Manor and Liberty of Havering, 1500–1620* (Cambridge, 1991)

Mair, L., *Marriage* (1977)

Maltby, B., 'Easingwold marriage horizons', *LPS* 2 (Spring 1969), 36–9

Marchant, R. A., *The Church Under the Law: Justice, Administration and Discipline in the Diocese of York, 1560–1640* (Cambridge, 1969)

Matlock Population Studies Group, 'Wills and their scribes', *LPS* 8 (Spring 1972), 55–7

Mauss, M., *The Gift: Forms and Functions of Exchange in Archaic Societies*, trans. I. Cunnison, (1954, 1980 edn)

Meyjes, N. P., *Character and Beauty of Dutch Painting in the Seventeenth Century* (Netherlands, 1957, English–Dutch edn)

Millard, J., 'A new approach to the study of marriage horizons', *LPS* 28 (Spring 1982), 10–31

Mitterauer, M., *A History of Youth*, trans. G. Dunphy (Germany, 1986, English trans., Oxford, 1992)

Moore, E. W., 'Medieval English fairs: evidence from Winchester and St Ives', in J. A. Raftis ed., *Pathway to Medieval Peasants* Papers in Medieval Studies 2 (Pontifical Institute of Medieval Studies, Toronto, 1981), pp. 283–99

Muldrew, C., 'Interpreting the market: the ethics of credit and community relations in early modern England', *SH* 18:2 (1993), 163–83

Muldrew, C., 'Rural credit, market areas and legal institutions in the countryside in England, 1550–1700', in C. W. Brooks and M. Lobban eds, *Communities and Courts in Britain, 1150–1900* (1997), pp. 155–77

Newman, H., *An Illustrated Dictionary of Jewellery* (1981)

Newman, K., 'Portia's ring: unruly women and structures of exchange in *The Merchant of Venice*', *Shakespeare Quarterly* 38 (1987), 19–33

Noonan Jr, J. T., 'Power to choose', *Viator: Medieval and Renaissance Studies* 4 (1973), 419–34

Noonan Jr, J. T., *Bribes* (New York, 1984)

Bibliography

Oestmann, C., *Lordship and Community: The Lestrange Family and the Village of Hunstanton, Norfolk, in the First Half of the Sixteenth Century* (Woodbridge, 1994)

Ogilvie, S. C., 'Coming of age in a corporate society: capitalism, pietism and family authority in rural Wurttemberg, 1590–1740', *C&C* 1:3 (1986), 279–331

O'Hara, D., 'Review of A. Macfarlane, *Marriage and Love in England*', *EcHR*, 2nd series 40:1 (1987), 113–14

O'Hara, D., '"Ruled by my friends": aspects of marriage in the diocese of Canterbury, c. 1540–1570', *C&C* 6 (1991), 9–41

O'Hara, D., 'The language of tokens and the making of marriage', *Rural History* 3:1 (1992), 1–40

O'Hara, D., 'Sixteenth-century courtship in the diocese of Canterbury' (Ph.D. thesis, University of Kent, 1995)

Outhwaite, R. B., 'Introduction: problems and perspectives in the history of marriage', in Outhwaite ed., *Marriage and Society*, pp. 1–16

Outhwaite, R. B. ed., *Marriage and Society: Studies in the Social History of Marriage* (1981)

Outhwaite, R. B., 'Marriage as business: opinions on the rise in aristocratic bridal portions in early modern England', in N. McKendrick and R. B. Outhwaite eds, *Business Life and Public Policy: Essays in Honour of D. C. Coleman* (Cambridge, 1986), pp. 21–37

Outhwaite, R. B., *Clandestine Marriage in England, 1500–1850* (London and Rio Grande, 1995)

Patten, J., 'Patterns of migration and movement of labour to three pre-industrial East Anglian towns', in Clark and Souden eds, *Migration and Society*, pp. 77–106

Pelling, M., 'Child health as a social value in early modern England', *Social History of Medicine* 1 (1988), 135–64

Phelps Brown, E. H. and S. V. Hopkins, 'Seven centuries of the prices of consumables, compared with builders' wage rates', in E. H. Phelps Brown and S. V. Hopkins, *A Perspective of Wages and Prices* (London and New York, 1981), pp. 13–59

Phillips, R., *Putting Asunder: a History of Divorce in Western Society* (Cambridge, 1988)

Phythian-Adams, C., *Re-thinking English Local History*, Department of English Local History Occasional Papers, 4th series 1 (Leicester, 1987)

Pitt-Rivers, J. A., 'Honour and social status', in J. G. Peristiany ed., *Honour and Shame: the Values of Mediterranean Society* (1965), pp. 19–77

Pollock, L. A., 'Embarking on a rough passage: the experience of pregnancy in early modern society', in V. Fildes ed., *Women as Mothers in Pre-Industrial England* (1990), pp. 39–67

Poole, E., 'Will formularies', *LPS* 17 (Autumn 1976), 42–3

Poos, L. R., 'Population turnover in medieval Essex: the evidence of some early-fourteenth-century tithing lists', in L. Bonfield, R. Smith and K. Wrightson eds, *The World We Have Gained: Histories of Population and Social Structure* (Oxford, 1986), pp. 1–22

Poos, L. R., *A Rural Society After the Black Death: Essex, 1350–1525* (Cambridge, 1991)

Poos, L. R., 'Sex, lies, and the church courts of pre-Reformation England', *Journal of Interdisciplinary History* 25:4 (1995), 585–607

Porter, E., *Cambridgeshire Customs and Folklore* (1969)

Pound, J. F., 'The social and trade structure of Norwich, 1525–1575', in P. Clark ed., *The Early Modern Town* (1976), pp. 129–47

Quaife, G. R., *Wanton Wenches and Wayward Wives: Peasants and Illicit Sex in Early Seventeenth-Century England* (1979)

Radcliffe-Brown, A. R., 'Introduction', in A. R. Radcliffe-Brown and C. D. Forde eds, *African Systems of Kinship and Marriage* (Oxford, 1975), pp. 43–60

Richardson, R., 'Wills and will-makers in the sixteenth and seventeenth centuries: some Lancashire evidence', *LPS* 9 (Autumn 1972), 33–42

Roper, L. J., ' "Going to church and street": weddings in Reformation Augsburg', *P&P* 106 (1985), 62–101

Rushton, P., 'The testament of gifts: marriage tokens and disputed contracts in north-east England, 1560–1630', *Folk Life* 24 (1985–86), 25–31

Rushton, P., 'Property, power and family networks: the problem of disputed marriages in early modern England', *JFH* 11 (1986), 205–19

Schneider, J., 'Trousseau as treasure: some contradictions of late nineteenth-century change in Sicily', in Kaplan ed., *The Marriage Bargain* (1985), pp. 81–120

Schofield, R., 'English marriage patterns revisited', *JFH* 10:1 (Spring 1985), 2–20

Segalen, M., *Love and Power in the Peasant Family: Rural France in the Nineteenth Century*, trans. S. Matthews (Paris, 1980, Oxford, 1983)

Segalen, M., *Historical Anthropology of the Family*, trans. J. C. Whitehouse and S. Matthews (Cambridge, 1986)

Sharpe, J. A., 'Defamation and sexual slander in early modern England: the church courts at York', *Borthwick Papers* 58 (1980), 1–36

Sharpe, J. A., 'Litigation and human relations in early modern England: ecclesiastical defamation suits at York', Past & Present Society conference (1980), pp. 6–17

Sharpe, J. A., 'Plebeian marriage in Stuart England: some evidence from popular literature', *Transactions of the Royal Historical Society*, 5th series 36 (1986), 69–90

Sharpe, P., 'The total reconstitution method: a tool for class-specific study?', *LPS* 44 (Spring 1990), 41–51

Sheehan, M. M., 'The influence of canon law on the property rights of married women in England', *Medieval Studies* 25 (1963), 109–24

Sheehan, M. M., *The Will in Medieval England from the Conversion of the Anglo-Saxons to the End of the Thirteenth Century* (Toronto, 1963)

Sheehan, M. M., 'The formation and stability of marriage in fourteenth-century England: evidence from an Ely register', *Medieval Studies* 33 (1971), 228–63

Sheehan, M. M., 'Choice of marriage partner in the middle ages: the development and mode of application of a theory of practice', *Studies in Medieval and Renaissance History*, new series 1 (1978), 3–33

Sheehan, M. M., 'Marriage theory and practice in the conciliar legislation and diocesan statutes of medieval England', *Medieval Studies* 40 (1978), 408–60

Sheehan, M. M., 'The European family and canon law', *C&C* 6:3 (1991), 347–60

Siraut, M., 'Physical mobility in Elizabethan Cambridge', *LPS* 27 (Autumn 1981), 65–70

Smith, R. M., 'Kin and neighbours in a thirteenth-century Suffolk community', *JFH* 4 (1979), 219–56

Smith, R. M., 'Human resources', in G. Astill and A. Grant eds, *The Countryside in Medieval England* (Oxford, 1988), pp. 188–212

Spouse, N. H., 'Attitudes and expectations: families in sixteenth-century Sandwich, 1500–1558' (M.A. thesis, University of Kent, 1993)

Spufford, M., 'The scribes of villagers' wills in sixteenth- and seventeenth-century Cambridgeshire and their influence', *LPS* 7 (Autumn 1971), 28–43

Spufford, M., *Contrasting Communities: English Villagers in the Sixteenth and Seventeenth Centuries* (Cambridge, 1974, paperback edn, 1979)

Spufford, M., 'Peasant inheritance customs and land distribution in Cambridgeshire from the sixteenth to the eighteenth centuries', in Goody, Thirsk and Thompson eds, *Family and Inheritance*, pp. 156–76

Spufford, M., 'Will formularies', *LPS* 19 (Autumn 1977), 35–6

Spufford, M., *Small Books and Pleasant Histories* (1981)

Spufford, M., 'The pedlar, the historian and the folklorist: seventeenth-century communications', *Folklore* 105 (1994), 13–24

Stallybrass, P. and A. White, 'The fair, the pig, authorship', in P. Stallybrass and A. White, *The Politics and Poetics of Transgression* (1986), pp. 27–43

Stone, L., *The Crisis of the Aristocracy, 1558–1641* (Oxford, 1965, abridged edn 1967, reprinted 1977)

Stone, L., *The Family, Sex and Marriage in England, 1500–1800* (New York, 1977, abridged paperback edn, Harmondsworth, 1979)

Stone, L., 'Illusions of a changeless family', *The Times Literary Supplement* (16 May 1986)

Stone, L., *Road to Divorce: England, 1530–1987* (Oxford, 1990)

The Story of the Love Spoon (Cardiff, 1973)

Strathern, M., *The Gender of the Gift: Problems with Women and Problems with Society in Melanesia* (Oxford, 1988, paperback edn, 1990)

Strathern, M., 'Partners and consumers: making relations visible', *New Literary History* 22:3 (1991), 581–601

Tadmor, N., 'The concept of the household-family in eighteenth-century England', *P&P* 151 (1996), 111–40

Takahashi, M., 'The number of wills proved in the sixteenth and seventeenth centuries: graphs, with tables and commentaries', in G. H. Martin and P. Spufford eds, *The Records of the Nation* (Woodbridge, 1990), pp. 187–213

Thirsk, J. ed., *The Agrarian History of England and Wales, 1500–1640* (vol. 4, Cambridge, 1967)

Thirsk, J., 'The farming regions of England', in Thirsk ed., *The Agrarian History of England and Wales, 1500–1640* (vol. 4, Cambridge, 1967), pp. 1–112

Thirsk, J. ed., *The Agrarian History of England and Wales, 1640–1750* (vol. 5, pt ii, Cambridge, 1985)

Thomas, K., 'History and anthropology', *P&P* 24 (1963), 3–24

Thomas, K., *Religion and the Decline of Magic: Studies in Popular Beliefs in Sixteenth- and Seventeenth-Century England* (1971, paperback edn, Harmondsworth, 1973, reprinted 1980)

Thomas, K., 'Age and authority in early modern England', *Proceedings of the British Academy* 62 (1976), 1–46

Thompson, E. P., 'Anthropology and the discipline of historical context', *Midland History* 3 (1972), 41–55

Thompson, E. P., 'Rough music reconsidered', *Folklore* 103:1 (1992), 3–26

Titow, J. Z., 'Some differences between manors and their effects on the conditions of the peasant in the thirteenth century', *Agricultural History Review* 10 (1962), 1–13

Tittler, R., 'Money-lending in the West Midlands: the activities of Joyce Jefferies, 1638–49', *Historical Research* 67 (1994), 249–63

Tribe, K., 'Origins of English individualism', *SH* 4 (1979), 520–2

Tronrud, T. J., 'Dispelling the gloom: the extent of poverty in Tudor and early Stuart towns: some Kentish evidence', *Canadian Journal of History* 20 (1985), 1–21

Tronrud, T. J., 'The response to poverty in three English towns, 1560–1640: a comparative approach', *Histoire Sociale* 18:35 (1985), 9–27

Urry, W., *Christopher Marlowe and Canterbury*, ed. A. F. Butcher (1988)

Van Gennep, A., *The Rites of Passage*, trans. M. B. Vizedom and G. L. Caffee (1960, paperback edn 1977)

Vann, R. T., 'Review essay of L. Stone, *Family, Sex and Marriage*', *JFH* 4:3 (1979), 308–15

Vann, R. T., 'Wills and the family in an English town: Banbury, 1550–1800', *JFH* 4 (1979), 346–67

Victoria County History of Kent, vol. 3 (1932)

Vovelle, M., 'Cultural intermediaries', in M. Vovelle, *Ideologies and Mentalities*, trans. E. O'Flaherty (Oxford, 1990), pp. 114–25

Wall, A., 'For love, money or politics? A clandestine marriage and the Elizabethan Court of Arches', *Historical Journal* 38 (1995), 511–33

Wallenberg, J. K., *Kentish Place-Names* (Uppsala, 1931)

Wallenberg, J. K., *The Place-Names of Kent* (Uppsala, 1934)

White, S. D. and R. T. Vann, 'The invention of English individualism: Alan Macfarlane and the modernization of pre-modern England', *SH* 8 (1983), 345–63

Wilson, A., 'The ceremony of childbirth and its interpretation', in V. Fildes ed., *Women as Mothers in Pre-Industrial England* (1990), pp. 68–107

Witney, K. P., *The Jutish Forest: a Study of the Weald of Kent from 450 to 1380 AD* (1976)

Woodcock, B. L., *Medieval Ecclesiastical Courts in the Diocese of Canterbury* (London and Oxford, 1952)

Wrightson, K., 'Alehouses, order and reformation in rural England, 1590–1660', in E. Yeo and S. Yeo eds, *Popular Culture and Class Conflict, 1590–1914* (Hassocks, 1981), pp. 1–27

Bibliography

Wrightson, K., 'Household and kinship in sixteenth-century England', *History Workshop Journal* 12 (1981), 151–8

Wrightson, K., *English Society, 1580–1680* (1982)

Wrightson, K., 'Kinship in an English village: Terling, Essex, 1550–1700', in R. M. Smith ed., *Land, Kinship and Life-Cycle* (Cambridge, 1984), pp. 313–32

Wrightson, K. and D. Levine, *Poverty and Piety in an English Village: Terling, 1525–1700* (New York and London, 1979)

Wrigley, E. A., 'Age at marriage in early modern England', *Family History* 12 (1982), 219–34

Wrigley, E. A. and R. S. Schofield, *The Population History of England, 1541–1871: a Reconstruction* (1981, paperback edn, 1989)

Wrigley, E. A. and R. S. Schofield, 'English population history from family reconstitution: summary results, 1600–1799', *Population Studies* 37 (1983), 157–84

Zell, M., 'Suicide in pre-industrial England', *SH* 11:3 (1986), 303–17

Zell, M., *Industry in the Countryside: Wealden Society in the Sixteenth Century* (Cambridge, 1994)

Index

Page references in *italics* refer to tables and maps; *n* before a page reference indicates a note on that page.

Index

Barrowe, Thomas, 205
Barrowe v. *Thomlyns*, 66
Battle, 130
Baull, Barbara, 147, 218
Baxter, Henry and Elizabeth, 147
Baxter, Thomas, 76, 147
Baxter v. *Cotton*, 76, n96, 147, n157
Beale, William, 112, 116, 143, 160
Beane, Anne, 145–6
'bedfellows,' 38, 107, 163
Bedford, Jane, 77, 114
Beeching, John, 70, 219–20
Beere, John, 117
Bell, George, 84
Bellingham, Peter, 103, 114, 150
Ben-Amos, I. K., 173
Benenden, 32–3, 131, 144–5
Benet, Richard, 113, 225
Benet v. *Lambart*, 113, n120
Bennet, Peter, 105–6
Bennet, Thomas, 143
Bennet v. *Smyth*, 143, n156
Berry, Alice, 66, 217–18
Berry, Sibill, 66
betrothals, formal, 10, 37–9, 64, 75, 80, 80, 103
Bett, Alice, 34
Bett, George, 65
Bewman, Alice, 196
Bigge v. *Robynson*, 217, n233
Blean, 17, 57
Blechinden, Thomas, 111
Bodell, William, 198
Bonar, Bernard, 36
Bonfield, L., 167–8
Bonham, John, 116, 145
Bonham v. *Ellet*, 116, n121,
Bonnam, Richard, 125, 133, 219, 225
Bonnekar v. *Lowe & Boreman*, n234
books, 70–1, 75, 89, 201
    see also Act books; conduct books; literature
Bouche v. *Cadman*, 42, n53
Boughton Aluph, 148
Boughton Maleherbe, 111
Boughton under Blean, 36, 104
Bourdieu, P., 60
Boykett, James, 114
Bradley, John, 225
Bradley v. *Shurt*, 225, n235

Bramelo, Prudence, 133, 147, 219, 225
Bramelo v. *Bonnam*, 125, 133, nn153, 219, 225, n233, n235
Brenchley, 144
Brent, Mr, 150
brewers, 21, 41
bridales, 43
brideprice payments, 60, 190
    see also dowries
bridewealth *see* brideprice payments
Bridge, Christopher, 115
Bridgeman, Stephen, 104, 223
Bridgeman v. *Cole & Barnes*, 223, n234
Bridger, Joan, 84
Bridges, John, 160
Bristol, 130, 134, 204
Brodnex, Mr Thomas, 145–6
'brokers', 100, 104
    see also intermediaries
Brokwell, Joanne, 219
Brooke, Mr, 161
Brooke, Thomas, 130
Brooke v. *Browne*, 130, n153
Browne, Dorothy, 130
Browne, Elizabeth, 44
Browning, Elizabeth, 47
Bryant, Thomas, 130, 143–4, 147–8
Buckland, 110
Buckner v. *Kenwood*, 217, n233
builders and building trade, 19–20, 103, 110
Burche, Martha, 140–1
Burleigh, Lord, 100
Burmarsh, 47
Burr, Anne, 200
Burr, Thomas, 200
Burret, Christine, 40, 220, 222
butchers, 20–1, 110
Butler, Suzanne, 148
Butterwick, Agnes, 38, 107–8, 111–12, 117, 139, 144, 149

Cadman, William, 42
Calais, 131
Cambridgeshire, 16
Canterbury church courts, 21, 35, 64, 71–2, 72, 77, 103, 105–6, 217
    Archdeaconry Court, 8, 169
    Consistory Court, 8, 57, 101, 108, 169
    coverage and population, 16–21, 17–18, 131